A Synthesis of Time

Konstantinos Retsikas

A Synthesis of Time

Zakat, Islamic Micro-finance and the Question of the Future in 21st-Century Indonesia

palgrave
macmillan

Konstantinos Retsikas
Department of Anthropology & Sociology
SOAS University of London
London, UK

ISBN 978-3-030-34935-6 ISBN 978-3-030-34933-2 (eBook)
https://doi.org/10.1007/978-3-030-34933-2

This Palgrave Macmillan imprint is published by the registered company Springer Nature Switzerland AG.
The registered company address is: Gewerbestrasse 11, 6330 Cham, Switzerland

Acknowledgements

Research for this book has been supported by a variety of institutions and individuals both in Indonesia and in the UK. I would like to begin by thanking the Economic and Social Research Council (ESRC) for a three-year grant (RES- 062-23-2639) that provided the initial opportunity to carry out fieldwork in Indonesia for twelve months, from September 2011 to September 2012. The writing of this book was further supported by a British Academy Mid-Career Fellowship (2018–2019). I would like to extend my gratitude to the British Academy for assisting the delivery of such an unconventional project, especially at a time when EU citizens' place such as myself in the UK remains uncertain.

In Indonesia, I have had the privilege of collaborating with an array of individuals and organisations both scholarly and active in the field of Islamic welfare provision, in the cities of Surabaya and Jakarta. I am deeply indebted to them for their generosity, hospitality and assistance in seeing this project through. In Surabaya, I relied heavily on support by *Universitas Airlangga*. Tri Joko Sri Haryono and I. Basis Susilo of the Faculty of Social and Political Studies facilitated the acquisition of necessary research permits, while Dr Nur Welan of the Faculty of Humanities was instrumental in introducing me to key people. At the same time, Dr Muhamad Nafik Hadi Ryandono and Dr Imron Mawardi of the Faculty of Economy and Business shared with me on multiple occasions their knowledge and insights into Islamic economics and the potential for *zakat* to alleviate poverty. In Jakarta, *Universitas Islam Negeri* (UIN) *Syarif Hidayatullah Jakarta* kindly sponsored my research, providing facilities and concrete assistance to that effect. Dr Amelia Fauzia has been a source of enduring assistance and a long-term interlocutor. The same goes for Prof Arskal Salim, Prof Irfan Abubakar of the Centre for the Study of Religion and Culture, Prof Amin Summa and Dr Asep Saepudin Jahar of the Faculty of Syariah and Law. In 2018, during a short-term visit, I was able to briefly rejoin the intellectual atmosphere at UIN and update myself on developments that had taken place during my absence.

The greatest generosity, assistance and encouragement have however come from people involved in some capacity or another with the three specific zakat management bodies I came to be most deeply involved with in the course of my research. Since in this book I refer to these organisations and to specific individuals indirectly only, through the use of pseudonyms to avoid bringing unwanted attention and unwelcomed scrutiny to their activities and programmes, I take the liberty here to mention them with their real names. It is a tremendous sense of obligation I owe to Abdul Kadir Baraja, Jauhari Sani, Khoirul Anam, M. Machsun, Kamil Muchtar, Guritno, Menik Soejitno, Atik Ramadhan, M. Adb. Kohar, KH Muammal Hamidy, Dr Muhammad Usman, Ismail Said, Arifin Purwakananta, Erie Sudewo, Muhammad Shufyan Bahri, Ali Yasin, Ulul Awalia, Suprapti, Herdiansah, Nina Mintarti, Arif Rahmadi, Nur Efendi, Ronio Romantika, Rizki Hidayat, Pras Purworo, Rio Ferdian Hudiyanto, Rusdi Saleh Koto and Eko Setiaji. May this book prove of value to your undertaking! The most significant input however has come from Shohib Essir and Muhtar Tajuddin, especially as our relationship quickly developed from research assistantship to mutual respect and long-term friendship.

I would also like to extend my thanks to Prof Didin Hafidhuddin, Achmad Subianto, Mohammad Siddik and Tito Kurniawan for the interest they took in my research and for sharing with me critical aspects of Indonesia's future direction in zakat affairs. I am also grateful to KH Ali Mustofa Ya'qub, KH Adburrahman Nafis, KH Abdusshomad Buchori, Ismail Nachu, Wildatul Akmala and Siti Aisah for enriching my research with their example and practice, both intellectual and hands-on.

Thanks are due to the publishers and editors of the following journals for allowing me to use parts of already published materials. Sections of Chap. 2 have previously appeared in an article entitled 'Reconceptualising zakat in Indonesia: Worship, Philanthropy and Rights' (***Indonesia and the Malay World*** 42 (124): 337–357). Chapter 3 puts a further spin on arguments first made in 'Introduction' and 'The Gift of Future Time: Islamic Welfare and Entrepreneurship in 21st Century Indonesia' (in K. Retsikas (ed.) ***Value Transfers in Southeast Asia: Religion, Charity, and Subjectivity*** *in an Era of Neoliberal Reform*. South East Asia Research (Special Volume) 25 (3): 134–151). The materials discussed in Chap. 4 have been previously considered in 'The Promise: Islamic Micro-finance and the Synthesis of Time' (*Deleuze Studies* 9 (4): 475–502), while Chap. 7 is based on reworkings of 'The Other Side of the Gift: Soliciting in Java' (*Heidelberg Ethnology*, Occasional Paper No. 4). I would like to thank Taylor & Francis, Edinburgh University Press and SOAS University of London for their assistance with the necessary permits.

Contents

1 Dis-closing Intervals 1

2 Dividing the Present 37

3 Justifying Law 67

4 Anticipating Life 105

5 Promising Deliverance 141

6 Contracting the Future 177

7 Soliciting Time 213

8 Rewinding the Reel 249

Bibliography 255

Index 271

List of Tables

Table 3.1	*Pondok Infak Mulia*, breakdown of funds collected between 1993 and 2011 in Indonesian rupiah	77
Table 3.2	*Surabaya Peduli Ummat*, breakdown of funds collected between and 1990 and 2010 in Indonesian rupiah	89
Table 3.3	*Surabaya Peduli Ummat*, breakdown of donor numbers between 1990 and 2010	90
Table 4.1	*Dana Keadilan Indonesia*, funds in billion rupiah	117
Table 4.2	*Dana Keadilan Indonesia*, number of donors	117

CHAPTER 1

Dis-closing Intervals

I had arrived at *Pondok Infak Mulia*'s headquarters early on that day, on my way to join other volunteers and staff at *Plaza Senayan*, a most exclusive, high-class mall situated at the thumping centre of Jakarta's business and administrative district. The aim was to promote the organisation's work in poverty alleviation and solicit public support. It was mid-August, at the height of the dry season, during the second half of *Ramadan*, the ninth in succession month in the Islamic calendar dedicated to fasting. Even though I never underestimated the challenges my Muslim interlocutors are in the habit of overcoming regularly, that is year-in and year-out, in terms of having to go without food and water from dawn to dusk, the summer of A.D. 2012/A.H. 1433 was quite instructive: for alongside the disciplines of the fast which I always found myself unable to withstand, they also had to endure the tests and tribulations of an everyday life otherwise expected to carry on with as little disturbance as possible. Sharing the same metropolitan area with more than 30 million people, packed in densely populated neighbourhoods, themselves sided by modern, sky-high towers, all busy with making ends meet, forming long traffic jams in the unending pursuit of greater returns for inputs expended, is already a big ask. To add to this blend of conditions, the demand to perform good deeds (*amal*) was a test of faith bound to increase the rhythms the city lived on, intensifying its connections, swelling its contours. I should clarify myself: amongst Muslims in Indonesia as well as elsewhere in the Islamic world, subjecting oneself to privation that causes to experience hunger

K. Retsikas, *A Synthesis of Time*,
https://doi.org/10.1007/978-3-030-34933-2_1

immediately and first-hand is understood as requisite for the cultivation of feelings of empathy and compassion, especially with the difficult situations facing others less fortunate. And thus, during Ramadan, the well-off are tested with raising money for the poor, donating clothes and food, engaging in commensality with them, breaking the fast together. My presence at *Pondok Infak Mulia*'s headquarters that day was meant for similar purposes: studying the social overflowing with itself, observing its grids undergoing rejuvenation, while participating, body and soul, in this very process, was my end of the story.

Because all the sofas available at the reception were taken by young volunteers waiting to be interviewed, I took a chair and set it next to the receptionist. The latter was engaged in conversation with a bespectacled, well-dressed man, probably in his mid-fifties and carrying an expensive-looking black leather handbag. As it turned out, he was visiting *Pondok Infak Mulia* (PIM henceforth) in his capacity as *muzakki*, his intention being to conduct *zakat* worship. Zakat which derives from the Arabic verb *zakā* carries the meaning of increase and growth as well as purification, stands for the third pillar of the Islamic faith, second only in importance to the five daily prayers and the confession of the faith. Its performance is a major religious ritual and an obligation that befalls all adult Muslims of adequate financial means, involving the transfer of value from those under such obligation (*muzakki*) to those with a valid entitlement to it. Amongst the latter the most important are the needy and poor (*fakir miskin*). Picking up his leather handbag, the well-dressed man clarified that the zakat he was 'outing' (*mengeluarkan*) that day belonged to the category of *zakat profesi*, that is, it was related to income generated from practising a profession such as medical doctor, architect or office manager. The receptionist posed a series of questions the purpose of which was to make sure the visitor's calculations as to the amount of zakat due were accurate. Without the slightest hesitation, the receptionist asked about the visitor's annual salary, the relevant percentage applicable and whether the payment was to be made on an annual or monthly basis. The middle-aged man replied straightforwardly that his annual salary for the past year totalled 452 million rupiah, equivalent roughly to $45,000, an amount easily placing him amongst an expanding number of elite professionals and managers in the city, normally employed at multinational corporations. He also added that he wished to pay his zakat on an annual basis, informing the receptionist that he had already checked with PIM's website: thus, his calculations were based on PIM's suggestion of a 2.5% levy on the proceeds of *profesi*. Next, the receptionist asked whether the man's calculations were made on the basis of net or gross income: the bespectacled visitor replied that that it was his gross income that he wished to zakat, an answer which should have delighted his interlocutor. At that point, the well-dressed man took a plastic freezer bag out of his black leather handbag, and placing it on the receptionist's desk, removed a couple of bundles containing cash in fresh and crispy notes of 100,000 rupiah, passing them to the receptionist. The receptionist started counting the money silently, flexing his fingers with considerable dexterity and speed, skills more often found amongst bank cashiers. After the first count gave him a total of 11.3 million rupiahs, the receptionist started filling an electronic receipt on the computer. The receipt in question, called *formulir setoran donasi*, records the personal details of the *muzakki*, the kind of transfer involved, that is whether it relates to zakat, alms (*infak/sedekah*) or endowment (*wakaf*), the amount transferred to the organisation and the *muzakki*'s tax number and total annual income. The form comes in three different coloured copies: the white is stored at the counter, the rose is sent to the organisation's accounting department and the green is handed to the *muzakki*. This copy the *muzakki* can present to Indonesian tax officials, requesting that the amount of zakat paid is deducted from his annual taxable income.

While a hard copy of the receipt was printed, the receptionist counted the money once more. Having satisfied himself that he held the correct amount, he turned his face to the visitor, offering his right hand. With the two men locked in a soft handshake, their heads cast down, eyes closed, the receptionist went to recite the opening chapter of the Quran, *al-Fatihah*. He then offered the following prayer for the benefit of his partner: *semoga Allah memberikan pahala atas apa yang telah anda berikan, menjadikannya suci dan mensucikan, serta Allah memberikan keberkahan atas harta anda yang tersisa*, which can be translated as 'may Allah give you merit for what you have yourself given and make it pure and purifying as well as bless the remaining of your property.' To this, the well-dressed man uttered *amin* as declaration of his affirmation. The receptionist then inserted the green copy of the receipt to a branded envelop and passed it with both his hands in a gesture of respect, thanking the visitor once more for the trust he placed in the organisation. At this point the man made his excuses and quickly exited the premises, bringing thus the ritual to its conclusion.

In twenty-first century Indonesia, performing zakat can also take place through bank transfers, off- and online. PIM has been on the forefront of making such services available to the public, asking *muzakki* to confirm the transfer of funds by telephoning or emailing its offices, along with providing further information. The latter is required for the receipt's safe delivery at the *muzakki*'s address, usually accompanied by a copy of PIM's monthly magazine, inclusive of its financial report, containing details of programmes currently carried out and listing the precise amounts invested. I asked Pak Budi, the receptionist, about any issues arising in face-to-face encounters. He replied that sometimes zakat payers protest for having *zakat profesi* calculated on the basis of gross income, asking for it to be reduced first in accordance with expenses incurred for basic needs such as food, school fees and credit card repayments. In the ensuing negotiations, Pak Budi uses as his guide a set of instructions issued by PIM's board of *syariah* (Islamic law) experts. The latter clarify that loan servicing payments for house and car purchases are indeed deductible; however, food expenses, school fees and other credit card payments are excluded from the list of deductions. Pak Budi admitted that having to deal with personal financial circumstances sometimes brings him in an awkward position: on the one hand, he wants to avoid getting into anything resembling an argument with would-be zakat payers who might after -all decide against transferring their zakat to PIM, taking their business elsewhere. On the other hand, the more steadfast, he said, he is with bringing relevant jurisprudential provisos to bear, the greater the value of financial resources available to PIM stands to be; as a result, he added, '*Insya Allah* (God willing), it won't be long before PIM is truly successful in making poverty in Indonesia a thing of the past.'

Reducing, if not totally eradicating, poverty is an earnest mission undertaken and a passionate promise publicly made by a series of new institutional actors in Indonesia, amongst which PIM counts as one of the most prominent. Such actors are also keen to demonstrate the potential inherent in Islam for bringing about significant improvements in the life conditions for the entire community of the faithful, safeguarding the delivery of prosperity and well-being to each and every one of its members, especially the needy and the poor, both in this life and in the next. Since 1999, such institutional actors are known as *Lembaga Amil Zakat* (LAZ) or Zakat Management Bodies: they have been tasked by both state and civil society with the purpose of assisting the overcoming of the mounting challenges and difficulties characterising the present situation as far as the economic predicament[1] and the general level of religious awareness and piety of millions of Indonesians is concerned. For Zakat

Management Bodies bringing about the required improvements in the economic and religious life of the nation is an interchangeable, mutually supportive exercise: for them, putting Islam to work in everyday life is a move that encompasses in a single pounce the ceremonial and the commercial, joining inexorably the liturgical to the pecuniary. In this context, the pursuit of a better livelihood in a strictly economic sense is indubitably conceived contra the 'purificatory' operations of Western modernity (Latour 1993), and understood as attainable only through the enhancement of an array of religious disciplines, and vice versa.

The principal methods LAZ deploy in implementing the promise of making a brighter, more prosperous and pious future arrive is the subject matter of this book. In the following pages I show that one of the most significant interventions LAZ perform in the social life of the nation has been a comprehensive re-positioning of zakat from an annual ritual of worship to a significant financial asset and a fundamental instrument of achieving socio-economic justice.[2] In parallel with other parts of the Islamic world, LAZ in Indonesia have highlighted zakat as a much required supplement to ongoing efforts towards the creation of an Islamic economy (*ekonomi Islam*) in the country: such Islamic economy, they collectively note, should not be solely based on the avoidance of *riba* (commonly understood as interest) in the banking and financial arrangements of the *ummat*. Instead it should be grounded in a redistributive sense of justice as envisioned in the Quranic injunction to zakat and strengthened by the development of value transfer mechanisms appropriate to the contemporary context. The search for divine-inspired justice (*keadilan*) has been an indispensable part of the recent reconceptualisation of zakat: in this regard, LAZ have been at the forefront of the introduction of a series of jurisprudential innovations as to the kinds of livelihood activities subject to zakat levy. *Zakat profesi*, for example, is one such recent invention (see Chap. 2) for it was unknown in the country before the 1980s for wealth generated from the practising of professions to be part of the conduct of financial worship, as zakat applied mainly to the proceeds of agriculture and commerce.

Institutional actors such as LAZ have been part and parcel of a more general resurgence of the faith in the post-1998 Indonesia when demands for an Islamic revival have been voiced from a multiplicity of quarters. Such calls have ranged from the fighting of *jihadi* wars, advocating for an Islamic revolution and the adoption of *syariah* as the foundation of the state, to the propagation of broad Islamic values as the basis of a democratic culture and a re-invigoration of Sufi spirituality (Azra 2004; Bruinessen 2013). Ricklefs (2012) who sees the Islamisation of contemporary Indonesia as part of a longer historical process stretching back to the late nineteenth century, notes that Islam has come to play an increasingly influential role in the public sphere, infusing politics, administration and economics with normative content. In the past four decades or so, debates on Islam and its pertinence to contemporary challenges have spread out from mosques and *madrasah* to markets, offices and universities, and are carried out in newspapers and magazines, mainstream television channels and online sites. As Hasan observes, Islam's movement to the centre of Indonesian public life has been accompanied by the faith's strong association with an expanding and highly assertive middle class, whereby piety serves as an index of high social status (2009: 229). It is precisely because the assertion of middle-class identity has been couched in moral terms, that participation in middle class is mainly sought through the public engagement with religious signs: the further the latter are from the reach of the many—a taste for designer Islamic clothing, the acquisition of a house in an elite Islamic complex, the undertaking of the pilgrimage to Mecca in the company of renowned Islamic scholars, the establishing of an Islamic endowment—the more solid one's claim to social distinction is supposed to be.

Under the sign of actualising a zakat-grounded justice, LAZ situate themselves at the very space of a 'separation-connection' internal to the class divide: it is their mission to collect and manage zakat and other resources such as voluntary alms, endowments, corporate social responsibility (CSR) funds and so on from the expanding middle and upper classes, so as to subsequently transfer them to those deemed worthy of assistance and support amongst the needy and poor populating the Indonesian nation, and sometimes the international arena too. LAZ's systematic, thoroughly planned and well-executed interventions in the spheres of disaster relief, education, health and exceedingly in the livelihood activities of the poor through the development and deployment of Islamic micro-finance, forms a major dimension of the manner in which LAZ endeavour to deliver on their promises of making present challenges and difficulties pass, hastening the coming of a thriving future. This is the second story the current book tells: the pursuit of a *syariah*-compliant mode of community development that aims to convert poor recipients of zakat into affluent enough entrepreneurs so that they are liable to pay zakat, a transformation anticipated to occur in the not-so-distant future through the particular application of the disciplines of Islamic micro-finance, is instrumental in synthesising time in a specific manner, channelling its flow in specific directions, making it serve specific ends. Key in the design and delivery of such temporality is the instigation and subsequent supervision of an interval: LAZ situate themselves amidst a temporal break, itself marked by the transfer of value from the affluent to the poor, via a form of intermediation deemed essential for achieving community empowerment and collective advances in piety. No longer either immediate or direct, the distribution of zakat and other *syariah*-compliant and humanitarian financial resources is punctuated by stages and phases making up a distinct temporal process. Such process is duly created and organised by Islamic welfare organisations that portray themselves as indispensable in delivering positive economic and pietistic developments.[3] The study of the temporal caesura in question serves as the *raison d'être* of this book: highlighting the complexity of its carving, stressing the performativity of its implementation, explicating the techniques of its governance along with the ingenuity of the struggles established to counter its effects, is the subject matter of the second half of the book.

Staging Encounters

In order to contend theoretically with the temporal interval instituted by contemporary practices of Islamic welfare bodies engaged in zakat management and the delivery of Islamic micro-finance programmes, the study relies on staging a series of encounters amongst the disciplines of anthropology, philosophy and Islamic studies. This is an endeavour that intentionally duplicates the very methods LAZ rely upon: in seeking to overcome the present and open up a path to an-other future, LAZ engage critically and selectively with contemporary processes of value creation present as much in global modes of capitalist production, inclusive of financial capitalism, as in the procedures of classical and modern Islamic jurisprudence and expert bodies of knowledge such as the disciplines of Islamic economics, Islamic finance and development studies. The experiments LAZ are running consist in contingent, unstable and discerning combinations of instruments and apparatuses that originate in highly differentiated domains of practice: any innovation involved is largely the effect of putting to work such assemblages. Taking inspiration from such method, the current study pursues the theorisation of the temporality LAZ institute and administer, through putting in place an eclectic blend of perspectives that promise to de-compartmentalise knowledge production and undiscipline the conceptual process, creating a clearing for thinking otherwise.

The encounter amongst anthropology, philosophy and Islamic studies conducted here involves the re-invigoration of an ethics of friendship. Echoing Nietzsche, Deleuze defines philosophy in terms that exceed narrow disciplinary boundaries, writing that '*philosophos* does not mean "wise man" but "friend of wisdom." But "friend" must be interpreted in a strange way: the friend, says Zarathustra, is always a third person between the "I" and "me" who pushes me to overcome myself and to be overcome in order to live' (2012: 5). The encounters I therefore stage are based as much on philosophy acting as anthropology's friend, and vice versa, as on Islamic studies providing a close partner to anthropological endeavours, and the other way around. Such encounters entail that anthropological commonplaces in the shape of central presuppositions and key conceptual schemata are subjected as much to philosophical critique as to scrutiny from perspectives internal to Islamic studies to attain new conceptual rigour and theoretical fullness. Putting anthropology in peril, especially as far as the question of the purported equivalence of the categories of zakat and the gift are concerned, is a strategy that is meant to renew anthropology's capacity to think the unthought (see Foucault 2002: 413): rather than announcing its premature death, returning anthropology to a thought-provoking exercise and an undertaking in wonder necessitates the mounting of a well-calibrated challenge. In this book, the challenge is articulated partly from the direction of a disciplinary exterior and is sustained by the combined effect of productive engagements with philosophy and Islamic studies. Additionally, the challenge in question is intrinsically related to the act of placing at the uncompromising centre of anthropological attention a mode of sociality founded on a one-way transfer of value (zakat). As I show throughout this study, zakat escapes capture by the conceptual apparatus of reciprocity primarily because it contains no stipulation of returns due, generating no future obligations on behalf of its 'recipients.' The outcome of challenging the signs of the 'gift' and 'reciprocity' in the name of zakat is laid out clearly and fully in Chap. 7 and, as a thought experiment, it goes hand in hand with its reverse, that is, the test Islamic studies are subjected to by anthropological modes of attention.

Cross-disciplinary encounters are asymmetrical events, requiring for their accomplishment the incessant reversibility of positions. It is highly demanded that philosophical propositions and premises fundamental to

Islamic studies are in turn exposed to and endangered by ethnographic description so to as to achieve vigour, palpability and immediacy. Consequently, what this book offers to Islamic studies is a situated ethnography of a practice fundamental to the faith—the transfer of zakat—that is also critical and evaluative of the way in which such transfer is increasingly conducted in contemporary Indonesia. At the centre of ethnographic attention are both the jurisprudential and legal frameworks in which the practice of zakat has been cast recently and the micro-financial arrangements newly put in place for assumedly enhancing its potential impact in alleviating poverty. The ethnography is offered in the true spirit of friendship: situated at the third person gap between the 'I' and the 'me,' it means to cut both ways. It does so by bringing into sharp focus what remains largely unelaborated and/or intentionally suppressed by dominant framings of zakat in Indonesia. As I show in Chap. 2, the latter by means of construing zakat either as an obligation or as a philanthropic gift, push to the margins of intelligibility alternative understandings of it as a right, neutralising their effects and deactivating their implications. The reversibility of positions returns similar results in the case of Islamic micro-finance. In Chap. 5, I endeavour to show how the dispensation of promises, the supply of credit and the cultivation of indebtedness as techniques assumed necessary for *syariah*-compliant community empowerment actually work so as to severely compromise the entire undertaking: instead of working towards the overcoming of the present, Islamic micro-finance is at serious risk of ensuring that the present is incessantly repeated, albeit with minor modifications, reinstating it in an improved register.

The encounters with philosophy are an equally complicated affair. The study draws its entire *problematique* regarding the question of time from three key figures of the poststructuralist movement who were also contemporaries making their mark in the intellectual circumstances of France in the 1960s and 1970s. Deleuze's (2004, 2008) transcendental empiricism, Derrida's (1997, 2011) method of deconstruction and Foucault's (2002) genealogical mode of critique provide a most solid and fertile ground in reference to which anthropology could begin to move beyond its conventional treatment of time as an object amongst other objects. Such reduction is effected in large measure by time's subordination to either the principle of labour, after the Marxist paradigm (see Bear 2014, 2016), or to the study of collective representations set against a backdrop of an assumedly objective reality, following Durkheim's school of thought (see Gell 1992; Munn 1992; Guyer 2007; Hamann 2016). In a manner reminiscent of the Kantian revolution which uncoupled time from movement, dissociating its measurement from the observation of the successive positions occupied by celestial bodies in the sky as previously posited by Aristotle, the challenge for anthropology is to break with the habit of deriving the notion of time from the exclusively human activity of producing commodities and mental representations. Anthropology should instead seek to situate production along with everything else that exists in time, that is, inside the very stream of becoming.[4] What is required of us anthropologists is in other words an immense reconfiguration of our thinking according to which time is no longer defined by wage-labour and positivist distinctions posited as first principles that give time its value, significance and relevance. Instead time is to be posited as the transcendental condition *par excellence*, the only dimension adequate to and coterminous with life, the social inclusive, giving the latter the determinate shapes and multiple forms it takes in every instance. For this switch to be accomplished, the point of ethnographic departure must change and accordingly become the following confession of an unwavering faith:

> Everything which moves and changes is in time, but time itself does not change, does not move any more than it is eternal. It is the form of everything that changes and moves, but it is an immutable Form which does not change. It is not an eternal form, but in fact the form of that which is *not* eternal, the immutable form of change and movement. (Deleuze 1985: viii)

The act of raising the power of thinking to time, itself configured as the constancy of the inconstant, is the hallmark of the anti-foundationalism siting at the heart of poststructuralist thought. This attitude is perhaps best exemplified by Foucault (2002) who carries out of philosophy's critical project in an entirely new, temporal register. While traditionally philosophers have been looking into establishing the primacy of this or the other substance, essence or principle as the universal and permanent ground of existence, reducing in effect life into one and the self-same norm, be it the Good, Reason, Spirit or simply God, Foucault's genealogical inquiries, taking after Nietzsche's own (2003), were dedicated to inverting such direction of travel, subjecting all forms of transcendence to the test of time's passing. Foucault's histories of systems of thought, inclusive of the modern invention of the domain of economy (2007, 2008) that I discuss in detail in Chap. 4, are paradigmatic attempts at showing that nothing stands outside of time: all forms of living, thinking and acting are temporally given. Because of that they are unnatural and arbitrary, contingent and conditional. In this regard, Foucault's practice of critique as the historical problematisation of the present, is a deeply political act: as it is undertaken with an eye towards unsettling the presumed and the connoted, it always carries the most vital 'Promise-Threat' (*la Promesse-Menace*) (2002: 351) of unburdening thought from the weight of values past and present, opening things up once again, while releasing the under-determined and the unthought, themselves features of the future as the empty form of time.[5]

What the current study offers to the demand for analysing social life in a temporal manner, that is as a discontinuous, always already fluctuating occurrence, takes the shape of a supplement in the contemporaneity of diverse forms of living economically and ethically. Part of my argument is that zakat and Islamic micro-finance practises in today's Indonesia are instrumental in setting up and organising a discrete mode of temporality that is itself built on top of *a non-economistic concept of the economy* propounded as essential. As is well known, Foucault's genealogical readings (2007, 2008) of the rise of neoliberalism in Euro-America from the 1970s onwards have highlighted the ongoing carving of an expansive domain of the economy as totally separate from what remains of the ensemble of social relations, endowing it with an own rationality and *sui generis* norms and standards. His works have moreover emphasised the parallel positing of *homo economicus* as the figure necessary to carry this task forward by means of an endless pursuit of maximisation of use-value as consumer and an unrelenting amplification of returns on investments as entrepreneur. Implicit in Foucault's account of times past is the parallel rise in Western Europe of a secular conception of (wo)man: such conception ascribes to (wo)man a finite status, itself the result of discourses portraying him/her as subject to an infinite array of needs and a new consciousness that construes him/her as destined to an inescapable *telos*. As an organism amongst other organisms, (wo)man has been increasingly taken, by Western secular moderns at least, to share the same destiny as other species, marked by an unstoppable movement towards gradual demise and eventual decease. However, this specific view of death as life's terminus, encasing the otherwise optimistic and wealth pregnant future of a Western entrepreneurial temporality within the bounds of a bleak biological *telos*, is totally absent from the Muslim milieu I encountered in Indonesia. It is precisely because Muslims in Indonesia and elsewhere posit death as the gateway to an after-life and the very cause of such transition, akin in the words of Al-Ghazali, a most prominent twelfth-century Islamic scholar, to 'a change of state' (in Bedir and Aksoy 2011: 290) that the future summoned by experiments with zakat and Islamic micro-finance is embedded within a temporal horizon of profound salvific connotations. Such horizon extends indefinitely to the end-of-times and the coming of the Day of Judgment, when the counting of sins and good deeds is expected to commence by the Creator. The coinage of a non-economistic concept of the economy that I develop in Chap. 4 is meant to take account of the differential metaphysics of death at play, especially as the latter embeds the futurity of promises of plenty made by Islamic welfare organisations within a wider and undecided salvific prospect. The fact that such prospect is taken to involve aporetic processes of converting values attained in this life to posthumous credits/debts and to necessitate procedures of deferred accounting reinforces the argument for unbounding the concept of the economy from any particular constrains, be that secular and neoliberal (see also Retsikas and Marsden 2018), casting it adrift, keeping it open.

In the same way death divides the lives of the faithful into a 'before' and 'after,' signifying an event of singular consequences that manages to effect a separation and, at the same time, to foster a connection between two dissimilar halves, so too the performance of *zakat fitrah* (a levy placed on all believers) which takes place before the month of Ramadan concludes, incurs a parting between times past and times yet-to-come. This is so for the practice of *zakat fitrah* gives the chance to all the faithful to emerge from such a period of intense discipline and devotion with their sins and misdemeanours remitted, effectively constituting their persons anew as if born again. The pertinence of the practice of inserting cuts that interrupt and differentiate the flow of time is also manifested with regards to *zakat maal*, the zakat levied on wealth on condition it reaches a certain threshold. For Muslims, the conduct of *zakat maal* effectively splits wealth (*maal*) into two distinct and asymmetrical shares, one that is the zakat payer's own to keep and enjoy and an-other portion that rightfully belongs to others to use and appreciate. The transfer of the second share to professional bodies such as LAZ so that it is managed appropriately, that is for purposes of *syariah*-inspired empowerment regimes, sets up the time of a meanwhile. It is in this manner that a certain, yet imprecise interval is repeatedly initiated, organised and administered. And it is during such interval that zakat as the share-due-to-others slowly and gradually makes its way from Zakat Management Bodies towards eventual claimants, principally the poor and the needy. The very theorisation of contemporary zakat and Islamic micro-finance practices in Indonesia in terms of the performance of cuts or caesuras that effect a synthesis of time by means of generating partings and establishing connections is a credit extended to this study by Gilles Deleuze, the French philosopher who more than anyone else sought to radically reconfigure the entire discipline of Western philosophy so as to make it equal to the immanence of time.

In very simple terms, Deleuze performs this reconfiguration by means of positing time as a 'form of interiority' (1985: ix): contra to common sense this maxim does not mean that 'time is the interior in us' and thus a matter of human consciousness and representation, but rather the opposite, 'it is the very interiority in which we are, in which we move, live, and change' (Deleuze 1997: 80). As such time corresponds to the very world-in-flux we occupy, being coextensive with the real we inhabit. However Deleuze observes that time is also difficult for us to perceive, the reason being that the relation we enjoy with the real is one of tacit acquiescence whereby we assume that what we normally encounter in everyday life has always already been given and is thus essential and necessary for the continuation of life-as-we-know-it. Time and its foregrounding of change and difference would ordinarily escape our attention were it not for specific techniques and intercessions (such as the genealogical mode of critique, see above) that render its constant passing evident and visible. In his later work, Deleuze grants the invention of cinema, especially the cinema after the Second World War, with making time perceptible, and devises the concept of the crystal-image so as to convey that what this new cinema allows audiences to experience is the very constitution of time, that is *its endless splitting in two directions at once.* In respect of this splitting, Deleuze writes,

> What constitutes the crystal-image is the most fundamental operation of time: since the past is constituted not after the present that it was but at the same time, time has to split itself in two at each moment as present and past, which differ from each other in nature, or, what amounts to the same thing, it has to split the present in two heterogeneous directions, one of which is launched towards the future while the other falls into the past. Time has to split at the same time as it sets itself out or unrolls itself: it splits in two dissymmetrical jets, one of which makes all the present pass on, while the other preserves all the past. Time consists of this split, and it is this, it is time that we *see in the crystal.* The crystal-image was not time, but we see time in the crystal. (1997: 81, emphasis in the original)

A cinematic crystal is a patterned composite of audio-visual images themselves arranged in such manner that they manifest the temporal relations pertaining amongst events as the latter unfold on the screen, preceding and succeeding one another. In this regard, what the crystal-image[6] accomplishes is the replication in a visual-aesthetic register of the very constitution of time: if time is another name for succession, signifying the passage from a 'before' to an 'after,' the sole condition under which succession is possible is for the present to be endlessly divisible, subject to a fissuring from within. For change to occur, every moment, cinematic or otherwise, must be dividing itself in its very unfolding, splitting itself internally into a passing away and a waiting to come. Without such caesura occurring, there would be no time, no change would ever take place, only the repetition of an indistinguishable, self-same present. And because the latter is a logical and empirical impossibility,[7] foreign as much to life as to death, the very interval the splitting of time creates in the non-coincidence of its infinite flow corresponds to the transcendental condition of time itself.

For Deleuze, time's infinite schism necessitates as its complement the undertaking of a highly synthetic exercise, itself involving the assembly and arrangement of the effects the caesura is endlessly creating: the differential dimensions of time the internal fissure has separated into a constant passing away, an elusive being-present and a deferred yet-to-come must be brought together in diverse yet determinate ways, lest chaos and the world's descent into an undifferentiated abyss take hold. In his monumental study entitled *Difference and Repetition* (2008), Deleuze undertakes the task of critically revisiting the history of Western philosophy with an eye towards elucidating the way a synthesis of time has been performed by some of its key practitioners. Having as his guide the ascription of priority to one or another of the temporal dimensions, Deleuze identifies three syntheses of time. In the first synthesis of habit, inspired by Hume, the interruptions brought about by the caesura are carefully wrapped inside the dominant role played by the living present which repeats itself almost identically due to the habitual patterns of stimulus-response organising the relations between things past and things to come. In the second synthesis of time, Deleuze elaborates Bergson's notion of a virtual or 'pure' past that has never actually been lived as equal to the caesura for it allows for time to be foregrounded as divisible, providing the condition of the present forever lapsing. In this case, involuntary memory synthesises the living present and the future into its subordinate dimensions, slowly absorbing both into folds overcrowded with the contents of times past. In the third synthesis of time, inspired by Nietzsche's eternal return, the caesura no longer looks backwards; instead it marches towards the yet-to-come, endlessly affirming the new. Here, time is irretrievably released from the dominance of the living present and the pure past: both dimensions are now made to act in the service of a future full of un-actualised potential and empty of contents, inclusive of determinate subjects and a priori conditions (see also Deleuze 2012).

In Chaps. 5 and 6, I discuss in great detail the Deleuzian treatment of time in terms of the differential syntheses of the 'break-flows' (Deleuze and Guattari 1983: 38) the internal fissure releases, and elaborate at length on the 'separation-connections' prescribed by the intervals instituted by Islamic welfare organisations in the course of micro-financial dispensations of zakat and other forms of aid. Close, meticulous ethnographic examination of the processes at play points out that LAZ perform a most compelling synthesis of time that accords the future a pre-eminent role. The pre-eminence of the future is contingent on the excitement and the intensity with which LAZ undertake to make extensive promises regarding the delivery of well-being-to-come to an audience of underprivileged citizens. Committed and resolute acts of promising prosperity in this world and salvation in the next constitute the very grounds on which Islamic micro-finance tailors and deploys its own array of specialist techniques and instruments, enabling the insertion of *syariah*-compliant intervals in the conduct of financial experiments with the poor. Practitioners and institutions regard such intervals as both necessary and essential for the cultivation of skills and the building of capacities deemed conducive for bringing about incremental improvements to the levels of entrepreneurship and piety available to lower strata of the population. In as much my conceptual exploration of the caesuras and the futurity underpinning said micro-finance practices is mediated by (my reading of) Deleuze's reading of Nietzsche's synthesis of time, it also comprises a supplement that at once reworks and refines, repeats and distils further the Deleuzian/Nietzschean thesis. The supplement in question relates to the argument I put forward in Chap. 5 that *promising* is a highly differentiated practice for its activity can be orientated to the temporal in decidedly dissimilar ways. In a nutshell, the distinction I draw is as follows: whereas Nietzsche's promise of eternal return inserts cuts in the flow of time that make the new, the different and the unexpected arrive, blocking all and every determination from returning, the caesuras micro-financial interventions put in place make the same and the known return, albeit with significant alterations.

Such alterations are cast in the language of progress and development as improvements that are themselves waiting to be assessed on a quantitative scale. In other words, whilst both classes of promise, and their agents, are committed to the overcoming of the present, especially in terms of its deficiencies and hardships, their positioning in relation to the yet-to-come as the ultimate source of value is evidently and dynamically divergent. While the Deleuzian/Nietzschean synthesis embraces all that the future has to offer, welcoming it as the gateway to the open-ended and the radically new, the synthesis LAZ perform is exclusively interested in times-to-come as the improved and enhanced versions of the self-same present. In other words, whereas the eternal return finds in the future the resolve to and the prospect for unsettling the present, the promises of Islamic microfinance encounter in the yet-to-come a resource useful for achieving the present's promotion and development. In a way, the incommensurability of the two manners of promising can be restated as follows: to the always untimely question the eternal return raises, that asks 'how can the "now" forever come to be other than it presently is?,' (self-)improvement responds with a conditional clause, wishing 'If only there could be more of the present to cherish.'[8]

Yet another source of thinking about the constitutive role of time and difference relates to Derrida's (1997, 2011) efforts at deconstructing the 'metaphysics of presence,' which form the third foundation for the present study. As is well known, the 'metaphysics of presence' is a concept Derrida borrows from Heidegger to denote the privilege the Western philosophical tradition has accorded to that which is, or that which appears. For Derrida, the privileging of presence, essence and identity as the ground for the conduct of such inquiry has involved as its corollary the suppression of questions into that which allows presence, essence and identity to come to be (or appear) the way it does. In the 'Afterword' to *Limited Inc.* (1988), Derrida defines metaphysics as

> The enterprise of returning "strategically," ideally, to an origin or to a "priority" thought to be simple, intact, normal, pure, standard, self-identical, in order *then* to think in terms of derivation, complication, deterioration, accident, etc. All metaphysicians, from Plato to Rousseau, Descartes to Husserl, have proceeded in this way, conceiving good to be before evil, the positive before the negative, the pure before the impure, the simple before the complex, the essential before the accidental, the imitated before the imitation, etc. And this is not just *one* metaphysical gesture among others, it is *the*

> metaphysical exigency, that which has been the most constant, the most profound and most potent. (1988: 93; emphasis in the original)

Derrida's early oeuvre (1997, 2011) is a powerful demonstration that ever since Plato's *Theaetetus*, Western philosophy has equated presence with thinking, the latter taken as an engagement in interior monologue, that is, a singular event relating to auto-affection and occurring 'naturally' in the process of hearing-oneself-speak silently. The valorisation of interior monologue, Derrida's argument continues, has allowed for the subject to be construed as self-identical: in the event of hearing-oneself-speak, one's thoughts are assumed to be present at the very instant of their silent utterance. In this regard, auto-affection has been granted the status of corresponding to meaning's most profound origin; during its occurrence, meaning is taken to achieve its highest degree of transparency and immediacy, hearing one's voice, even in silence, makes one's being both immediately manifest and directly available to understanding. It is precisely this set of associations, equivalences and hierarchies that Derrida unpacks ever so decidedly and incisively in *Of Grammatology* (1997) and *Voice and Phenomenon* (2011), with both texts appearing in French in the same year (1967).

In *Voice and Phenomenon*, Derrida's deconstructive method of thinking with Husserl against Husserl demonstrates that while, on the one hand, Husserl's phenomenology conforms to the Western canon that ascribes 'a unity of thought and voice' (2011: 41) in the determination of being, on the other, it offers some of the conceptual means necessary for questioning its assumptions, interrupting its authorising of what passes as knowledge (see also Hodge 2007).[9] It is on account of Husserl's emphasis in the *Logical Investigations* on internal speech acts generating sense with unsurpassed clarity of intent and immediacy of meaning, writing that 'for the acts in question are themselves lived by us at that very instant [*im selben Augenclick*, literally "in the blink of an eye"]' (Husserl in Derrida 2011: 41), that Derrida claims that Husserl's phenomenology ultimately depends on a mode of temporality whereby the significance of the present derives from the now being entirely coincidental with itself, and thus internally indivisible and absolutely undifferentiated. And yet, such conclusion is at odds, Derrida shrewdly observes, with the arguments Husserl advances in his other major work, *The Phenomenology of Internal Time Consciousness*. There Husserl describes the 'living present' as in constant tension with itself for it splits and divides itself up ad infinitum between the immediate memory (Husserl calls retention) of the now that has just passed and the anticipation (Husserl calls pretension) of the now that is about to appear. In this regard, Derrida credits Husserl with foregrounding a philosophical counter-movement that conceives of presence as thoroughly inhabited by non-presence: because the present is constantly haunted by traces of what has been and is permanently undone by indications of what might arrive, it is repetitively opened up by an alterity internal to itself. In this manner, presence is completely and conclusively fissured in its very possibility by time, especially by time's unstoppable, irrepressible passing. As Derrida writes,

> Since sense, as Husserl has recognised, has a temporal nature, it is never simply present. It is always already engaged in the "movement" of the trace, that is, in the order of "signification." Sense has always already exited from itself into the "expressive stratum" of lived-experience. Since the trace is the relation of intimacy of the living present to its outside, the openness to exteriority in general, to the non-proper, etc. *the temporalisation of sense is from the very beginning "spacing."* As soon as we admit space at once as "interval" or difference and as openness to the outside there is no absolute interiority. [...] [Presence] is "in" time. It is the pure exiting of time to the outside of itself. It is outside-of-itself as the self-relation of time. (2011: 72, emphasis in the original)

Derrida's neologism '*différance*' (2011: 58–59) captures two senses of difference *as deferral* and *différance* as difference. As such, it conveys his critical insight on the primacy of time: presence rather than being formally opposed to process is temporal through and through. For this very reason, presence amounts to a dynamic and unstable phenomenon that is entirely derivative of its enmeshment in an infinite unfolding, a becoming equal to time's constant splitting itself apart. *Différance* is nothing less and nothing more than the poststructuralist demand for placing meaning, the good, the true and the self within a temporal framework, the rendering of all values secondary to temporal contingency. Elaborating further on this very demand, Derrida has subjected to deconstructive critique two conceptual paradigms that are of immediate importance to the purposes of this study. In Chap. 3, I recount the vital significance of Derrida's (1990) insistence on uncoupling the concept of justice from the institution of the law, showing how his incisive commentary of Benjamin's 1921 treatise on violence accomplishes to release the search for justice from finding completion within the enclosures created for it by state law. The critical purchase offered by Derrida's move of making justice foreign to law, excessive of the present and the very trait of a future-to-come has profound consequences for productively interrogating a series of legal measures undertaken in Indonesia in the post-1998 era that have made zakat a direct concern of the state, legislating in effect as to its rationale, objectives and permissible or preferred mode of conduct, all in the name of popular sovereignty and public welfare. Such deconstructive reading of Indonesian zakat laws and juridical procedures is explicitly aimed at opening them to critique, revealing their tacit assumptions and blind spots, while also delivering zakat and its potential from their unwarranted domestication by state power.

In Chap. 7 it is deconstruction itself that forms the subject of a critique articulated from an ethnographic perspective, itself arising from a consideration of non-normative transfers of zakat as encountered in urban Java. The occasion for this exercise is provided by Derrida's intercession on the literature on the 'gift' as undertaken in *Given Time* (1992), a work aiming to drive a further wedge between philosophical deconstruction and anthropological versions of structuralism. While I am in entire agreement with Derrida's critique of the Maussian and Lévi-Straussian enclosure of the 'gift' within an economy of exchange and a symbolic economy of language that effectively reduces it to a by-word for substitution, reciprocity and credit/debt, I do claim that Derrida's own rethinking of the excessive dimensions of the 'gift' on the grounds of a temporality conditioned by a double forgetting (the forgetting of the passing of the gift and the forgetting of this forgetting (see 1992: 15–18)) is insufficiently robust for effecting a break in thought and for providing the grounds of practicing an otherwise. My effort nevertheless is to affirm and renew deconstruction and in this vein, I propose the concept of ***soliciting***: emerging from an ethnographic description of involuntary transfers of zakat conducted by means of anonymity and stealth, soliciting presents a more radical challenge to the common-sense equation of the good, the true and the reasonable with generous and beneficent gift-giving. Soliciting manages to break both with contractual exchange and Derridean versions of the 'gift' for its practice is entirely untimely, and thus always already unanticipated, unexpected and surprising. Moreover, because its activity originates not from the intentions of a subject a priori cast as donor but from the direction of an unfathomable, unidentifiable and enigmatic other, it presents the best chance *we* have of conducting a trans-valuation of our values in the service of a unburdening the future from the return of self-presence. In this sense, soliciting amounts to a mode of promising that more than any other instance of value transfer discussed in this ethnographic study, performs a future synthesis of time appropriate and commensurate to the Deleuzian/Nietzschean eternal return of the different and the new.

Micro-financing Alternatives

In a recent appraisal of the global arena of Islamic micro-finance institutions, Malcolm Harper (2017), a distinguished expert, keenly notes the novelty of the practices at hand. Islamic micro-finance, he writes, is a relatively new phenomenon, having grown alongside the practise of mainstream micro-finance that has itself been operating on a globally significant and commercially successful scale since the 1990s. Out of a total of 15 Islamic micro-finance institutions from across the globe included in the survey conducted by Harper and Khan (2017), the vast majority (13) begun their operations after the year 2000. In Indonesia, the first Islamic micro-finance institutions, the Islamic Savings and Credit Cooperatives, commonly known as *Baitul Maal wat Tamwil*, date from the early 1990s: their establishment has been part of the creation of a dual banking and finance system in the country—conventional and Islamic (or *syariah*-based), a process that witnessed the foundation of large Islamic commercial banking institutions such as *Bank Mualamat Indonesia* and several Islamic rural banks (*Bank Perkreditan Rakyat Syariah*) (Antonio Muhammad 2008, Lindsey 2012, Sakai 2014). Despite Indonesia being a latecomer in Islamic banking when compared with Egypt or Malaysia, for example, it does count amongst the earliest cases to experiment with Islamic micro-finance. This has to do with Indonesia being home to one of the most successful conventional micro-finance models worldwide, that is the reformed village units developed by *Bank Rakyat Indonesia* in the 1980s which furnished 'the largest financially self-sufficient micro banking system in the world' (Henley 2010: 173). Despite such promising beginnings, Islamic cooperatives found hard to replicate the successes of their conventional counterparts. After a period of rapid expansion around the time of the Asian financial crisis (1997), BMT faced an array of challenges that eventually led to their significance in providing religiously approved financial services to the enterprising poor, mainly small-scale traders in urban areas, declining steeply. Such was the rate of waning influence that according to Seibel (2012) the majority of 3000 registered BMT in 2012 were assumed to be dormant or technically bankrupt.

Parallel to the establishment of Islamic cooperatives, the Islamic reform movement in Indonesia also proceeded with the foundation of a series of zakat management agencies—LAZ or *Lembaga Amil* Zakat. The latter are significantly less well known in scholarly circles for their engagements with *syariah*-compliant micro-finance: though dating from the same period as other Islamic finance providers, LAZ are, as I have already noted, Islamic welfare foundations the purpose of which is to alleviate poverty through promoting and delivering what are perceived as philanthropic activities. Such activities conform to a model inspired and sanctioned by the practice of zakat, the third pillar of the faith and an obligatory ritual involving a wealth transfer all well-to-do Muslims are required to complete once a year as a testament of their faith, for the benefit of others, the poor and the needy being the most prevalent. Within this remit, LAZ have sought to mediate relations between haves and have-nots, managing increasingly fraught class tensions in the country. By expanding into the dispensing of Islamic micro-financial services to the country's enterprising poor and providing much-needed support for the small-scale businesses, LAZ have engaged in running community empowerment programmes on an explicitly non-commercial, not-for-profit basis. The manner in which leading LAZ have proceeded to do so, the complexities involved in the delivery of services, the innovations implemented, the challenges faced and the controversies given rise to, as well as the multi-stranded, multi-level set of relationships promoted and cultivated with those construed as recipients of financial and other aid, are the subject matter of this book.

Micro-finance refers to the provision of financial services to the poor, especially those who are traditionally excluded from financial services, on a scale appropriate to their capacity to service the obligations involved. The term includes facilities for savings, insurance and money transfers (remittances); however, the micro-financial activity that has attracted the most attention—commercial, governmental and scholarly—is micro-credit. Micro-credit refers to the provision of small loans, usually on a short-term basis and with the requirement for collateral having been replaced by group guarantees, for the purpose of investment in productive activities (Goenka and Henley 2010; Elyachar 2005; Hospes and Lont 2004). The United Nations designation of 2005 as the 'International Year of Microcredit,' meant that micro-finance had within a short period of time been widely acknowledged by reputed international organisations such as the International Monetary Fund and the World Bank, as a fundamental instrument for breaking the vicious cycle of poverty in which many people are trapped on a global scale. Such recognition inaugurated a new epoch in governmentality according to which the repeat advancement of credit on the basis of ever larger in value interest-bearing loans, is deployed as a fundamental tool for creating adequate levels of investment and opportunity for self-employment amongst the poor so that the latter are able to realise their full entrepreneurial potential. In this context, Islamic micro-finance was conceived as a response to the perceived shortcomings the propagation of financial capitalism was positing for Muslims, especially as far as their reliance on the charging of interest for the generation of profit was concerned. Islamic micro-finance initiatives also meant to demonstrate Islam's provision of an all-encompassing alternative for the pursuit of human social, political and economic welfare: this claim had been a central component of the discipline of Islamic economics ever since calls for its creation were first voiced in the 1960s and 1970s (see Azhar 2010). What the invention and implementation of Islamic micro-finance made apparent at the turn of the millennium was that most of the poor living in Muslims countries had yet to be successfully brought into the fold of Islamic financial alternatives. As Islamic banks and other financial institutions had focused their activities for the most part, on the upper echelons of Muslim entrepreneurship, it was a matter of some urgency that Islamic finance expanded so as to encompass the lower social strata, spreading in this way the message of the faith and making sure that ethical reform and salvation was at hand not only for the select few at the top but also for those at the bottom.

To Islamic economists and activists alike, an Islamic alternative has been conceived as the contemporary pursuit of a divinely ordained model of justice in the intermediate space between capitalism and communism (Chapra 1992, 2014; Kuran 2004). As Hefner notes, 'Islamic economics presents itself as a salutary third way: avoiding the inegalitarian excesses of modern capitalism but unleashing the energies of entrepreneurs and merchants' (2006: 17). The distinction from communism has been easy to assert, given the insistence of the faith on private property, un-coerced exchange and the sanctity of contracts. At the same time, the claim that Islam supports an advanced welfare system for the prevention of exploitation, ensuring interventions on behalf of public interest, has found a most solid ground in the practice of zakat. Zakat has been widely proposed by

Islamic economists and campaigners as a key component of building an Islamic 'moral economy': in their eyes, it exemplifies the notion that precisely because a Muslim person holds property as a trustee for God, property must serve ends higher than the mere satisfaction of one's needs. In this regard, the transfer of zakat is extensively cited as a means for purifying the wealth the faithful can subsequently enjoy ***and*** an instrument for building mutuality with others (Tripp 2006: 124). In nutshell, zakat is extorted for the promotion of social justice and the sanctioning of the redistribution of wealth, while its resource allocation efficiencies are also credited with the strengthening of economic stability and the stimulation of growth. According to the Pakistani philosopher and founder of Islamic economics, Maulana Maududi (2011), zakat is a most necessary instrument for effectively reigning over the worst excesses of the unfettered pursuit of profit in favour of a divinely approved and socially conscious mode of livelihood. According to Maududi, the significance of zakat to an Islamic economy is so great that it requires government's intervention in the collection and distribution of dues for the benefit of the disadvantaged. In the same vein, Sayyid Qutb, a most prominent intellectual and leading member of the Egyptian Muslim Brotherhood, argues that the transfer of zakat from the rich to the poor has major effects: increasing the spending power of the poor leads to increases in production and a general upturn in employment rates which, in turn, means that more work is available for the poor who can proceed to make a living on an independent basis (see Philipp 1990: 130).

Along with the injunction to zakat, an Islamic economy is widely conceived as founded on the prohibition of *riba*, which most jurists understand as the charging of interest on capital in all forms. However when compared to zakat, it is the prohibition of *riba* that has become the most recognisable sign of a distinctive approach to economic well-being, operating as a hugely emotive emblem of the claim that there exists a whole, coherent Islamic system for the structuring of human livelihood pursuits, equipped with its own laws and mechanisms.[10] While there is still considerable debate amongst Muslim jurists and intellectuals as to whether the Quranic term *riba* equates with modern practices of interest,[11] the majority of scholars are of the opinion that such equivalence is clear and unmistakable: for these scholars any contract involving a fixed, predetermined return on a loan or investment constitutes *riba* and is thus forbidden. The Pakistani economist and one of the most widely cited Islamic economists in the world, who helped establish the International Centre for Research in Islamic Economics in Jeddah, Saudi Arabia, Muhammad Nejatullah Siddiqi, states flatly that 'Muslim society never legitimised interest throughout the thirteen centuries prior to domination by imperialist powers. It managed its economy and carried out domestic and international trade without the institution of interest' (1983: 9). The ban on any form of interest in contemporary Islamic banking and (micro-)finance is grounded partly on revivalist accounts and partly on the core tenet that money in Islam is not meant to act as an earning asset in and of itself (Warde 2010); if profit is to ensue, it can only originate in activities that require individual exertion and promote relative equality amongst partners. In this regard, making money out of money is charged as morally reprehensible because it involves no effort on the part of the creditor whose sees his/her idleness rewarded. Earning interest is also seen as inherently unjust because the creditor is kept insulated from bearing any of the risk of the investment involved: in counter-distinction, it is the debtor who is left exposed to the possibility of business failure and default as he/she has to compensate the creditor beyond the cost of the initial loan even if the venture hits trouble though at no fault of his/her own (Mills and Presley 1999; Visser 2009). Amongst Islamic economists, interest as *riba* is additionally abhorred for allowing or leading to the exploitation of the poor from institutional and non-institutional moneylenders who are guaranteed a return at the expenses of the vulnerable who assume all the risk. Extrapolating from such ethical and legal positions, an Islamic alternative economy is put in practice on the basis of the provision of financial services, both macro- and micro-, according to what Siddiqi identifies as the 'principles of *mudaraba* (profit sharing) and *shirkah* (partnership)' (1983: 11). Such principles apply to contractual agreements that exclude any *haram* or sinful commercial or productive ventures such as the sale of pork and alcohol, and are further characterised by 'material finality,' that is they are tied, directly or indirectly, to a real, tangible asset as opposed to speculation. While in the early days of the development of Islamic finance and banking, it was 'profit and loss sharing' forms of partnership such as those of *musharaka* and *mudaraba* that were taken to represent the ideal from an Islamic point of view, the list of permissible financing methods has expanded exponentially over the ensuing decades. Key in this development has been the invention and dissemination of ever new classes of Islamic finance products to cover a huge variety of circumstances and situations, sometimes at the expense of considerable debate and internal disagreement. Such expansion has been motivated by pressures to make Islamic finance instruments compete commercially and in a sustainable manner with conventional, interest-based methods that, over the same period witnessed an explosion due to the neoliberal 'democratisation' of credit/debt devices (Graeber 2011). The expansion has moreover been aided by the exercise of new jurisprudential reasoning, capable of introducing innovations by means of cultivating analogies with contracts already approved by classic jurists. As a result, relatively new kinds of financing vehicles involving leasing (*ijarah*), prepaid forward sales (*salam*) and asset-backed securities (*sukuk*) have joined the ranks of cost-plus sale (*murabaha*) and insurance (*takaful*) instruments.

Ethnographic studies of the processes of creativity and experimentation at play in the Islamic reinvention of economic living have been regrettably few. Save for a couple of exceptions, we know very little of the institutional challenges encountered, the legal impasses overcome, the commercial innovations introduced in the Middle East, London, New York and Singapore by professional experts and clients/consumers of Islamic finance contracts. For one, Rudnyckyj's (2019) has recently charted the ways in which the Malaysian state has spearheaded a tremendous effort to make Kuala Lumpur, the nation's capital, a central node in a global network of Islamic finance with the aim of rivalling other more established conventional banking centres. Such project has been conducted on the premise of moving the overall framework of contractual obligations away from debt-based instruments as promoted by financial capitalism, in favour of equity-based models involving ethical partnerships as guaranteed by the faith. At the same time, a sustained effort to reform the subjectivities of the respective population has taken place as the latter is systematically re-trained to embrace the values of risk and entrepreneurship on the basis that risk taking is a pious and collective endeavour (2019: 243). Rudnyckyj's study complements nicely Maurer's (2006) earlier work on the designing and circulation of Islamic mortgages in the US. Though a lot more attentive to the legal disciplines and regulatory procedures that underpin the marketing of such products, Maurer stresses too the wider politics involved. This is especially true in the post-September 11 era where Islamic mortgages are 'particularly important as Muslim Americans come to experience themselves as a collectivity that is less marked by ethnic, factional or sectarian differences and more by their demand for full political inclusion and cultural citizenship' (2006: 100). In other words, though taking an Islamic route, Muslim Americans' stake to national belonging passes equally through the very same dream of home ownership.

Ethnographic studies such as the above make clear that Islamic finance's claims to providing an alternative to financial capitalism can't be taken for granted as they are constantly haunted by accusations to the contrary, by insiders and outsiders alike. Such evaluative path is perhaps more pronounced in Maurer's (2005) study entitled *Mutual Life, Ltd* which puts claims to difference to the test by looking at experiments in Islamic finance in Indonesia alongside alternative monetary values such as the Ithaca Hour, the oldest and largest local currency system operating in the US independently of the state-backed US dollar. While both undertakings recognise 'the inseparability of the moral and the technical' (2005: 152), there is enough interface between the way the Islamic finance and Ithaca Hour conduct exchange, on the one hand, and that of conventional economic behaviour, on the other, so as to raise serious doubts as to whether what is on offer corresponds to a comprehensive alternative. While in the case of Ithaca Hour, it is the fact that labour time counts as the standard of value that compromises the experiment, in Islamic finance what is at primarily at issue is the perceived sidestepping of the prohibition of *riba* through accounting tricks or reverse engineering as in the case of cost-plus sale (*murabaha*) where the value of the mark-up is fixed in advance and is partly calculated in relation to prevailing interest rates to enable the product to achieve market efficiencies. Doubts as to the intentional or otherwise replication of undesirable capitalist norms have generated acute anxieties amongst Islamic finance practitioners who like Siddiqi (2006) argue for constant vigilance to be exercised so that the industry is periodically purified of illegitimate imitations and duly returned to the distinctive basics of equity-based partnerships.

Partly due to *murabaha* being also predominant in Islamic micro-finance (Harper 2017: 192), similar criticisms are voiced against Islamic variants of finance inclusivity from the side of practitioners and other insider experts. In this context, the paucity of critical ethnographic engagements with the practice in question is near total. With the exception of Kustin's (2017) doctoral work which focuses on one of the world's largest commercial Islamic micro-finance providers, the Islami Bank Bangladesh Limited (see also Kustin 2015), the current book is the first anthropological account of the development and deployment of the instruments of Islamic micro-finance, especially in a non-commercial context that is immediately tied to the alleviation of poverty amongst the enterprising poor and the advancement of a *syariah*-inspired economy. As such, the present study intervenes productively in a newly emerging field in which interest has so far been limited to Islamic legal and economic experts, long-term practitioners and activists (see Ali 2011; Khan 2008; Obaidullah and Khan 2008). By engaging closely with such works and deeds, the aim is to problematise key concerns, interrogate central assumptions and offer new and unanticipated perspectives on a phenomenon currently in process. The perspective I advance is based as much on ethnographic observations of events as unfolded in Java, Indonesia in 2011–2012 (the period of my fieldwork) as on creative encounters with the poststructuralist philosophy of time of Deleuze, Foucault and Derrida. I should make clear that I am not setting out to evaluate the degree to which Islamic micro-finance departs, or not, from conventional products and contractual arrangements. Neither do I seek to evaluate whether Islamic micro-finance eventually delivers on its promises such as lifting the poor out of poverty and empowering women as it is mostly women who are primary target for its services both in Indonesia and worldwide (see Beik 2013; Sakai and Fauzia 2016). My concerns are different and have to do with the operationalisation of the practise of making promises itself; what I highlight is the temporal effects the deployment of Islamic micro-financial contractual agreements have on time, its fissure and synthesis. The question I begin from is how, by what means and to what effects does Islamic micro-financial techniques and instruments make time pass, bringing about future redemption, itself conceived both in economic and religious terms as well-being in this world and salvation in the hereafter. Indonesia, the world's most populous Muslim country and home to approximately 60% of all Islamic micro-finance loans in terms of amount dispersed worldwide (Sandi and Khan 2017), is one of the most apposite contexts for pursuing the question of the legal, organisational, financial and technical assemblages created for the purpose of synthesising time in favour of making a pious future of plenty to come. The fact that according to a recent report by the Asia Foundation (2013: 10; see also Parinduri 2014; Vial 2011), small and medium enterprises generate 56% the country's GDP and absorb more than 96% of the workforce, makes the question of time and the elaboration of its cutting and organisation, at once highly pertinent and incredibly urgent.

Notes

1. According to the Indonesian Central Statistics Agency (BPS, *Badan Pusat Statistik*), there has been a clear downward trend in poverty in Indonesia ever since data first became available in 1976: on the basis of BPS's own poverty line definition, itself based on the expenditure required to obtain 2100 calories of food per capita per day, plus an allowance of essential non-food items, between 1976 and 2010, the poverty rate fell from 40.1% to 13.3% of the population. Notwithstanding such remarkable achievement, partly a result of the pursuit of economic growth policies by the 'developmental state' of the New Order (1966–1998), it remains the case that the data conveys an overly optimistic picture: first because the poverty line is drawn too low of what is required for safeguarding adequate standards of living and second because it excludes from view a large share of the population hovering just above the poverty line adopted. This share corresponds to millions who because of their sensitivity to slight changes in their mode of livelihood and the overall economy can find themselves living below the official standard quite easily and abruptly. The vulnerable and uncertain status of large sections of the population is best exemplified in two occasions when official poverty rates went sharply up: between 1996 and 1999, that is during the Asian financial crisis, when the rupiah lost 85% of its value against the US dollar, food prices escalated, igniting protests and riots, and leading to a major political crisis, the poverty rate rose from 17.3% to 23.4%. Again, between 2005 and 2006, when an upsurge in domestic fuel prices by an average of 125% and an increase in the price of rice, Indonesia's staple food, brought about a hike in official poverty rates from 15.9% to 17.8% (Suryahadi et al. 2012; see also Miranti 2017; Leeuwen 2016).
2. An increasing number of studies of zakat have recently appeared, mostly undertaken by historians such as Singer (2008), geographers (Atia 2013) and anthropologists. The latter focus on the politics of international Islamic aid organisations (Benthall and Bellion-Jourdan 2003) and of recent changes in their orientation to philanthropy (Ibrahim and Sherif 2008) as well as on the middle-class networks that Islamic aid supports and sustains in Middle-Eastern societies (Clark 2004) and the subjectivities it helps to engender in South India (Osella and Osella 2009; Osella and Widger 2018). The current study adds a new dimension, exploring the ways in which the contemporary management of zakat organises the passing of time: as key to alternative, Islamic imaginings of economic prosperity, I show how zakat is related to the practice of Islamic micro-finance and the achievement of justice in the future.

3. Islamic welfare organisations are not alone in what is otherwise a global phenomenon that includes secular institutions. Amongst a myriad of studies, Li's (2006, 2007) critical work on the range of development actors active in Indonesia, the stakes involved in the process and the strategies available has been most insightful.
4. Two previous studies have set us on the right direction. Fabian's devastating critique (2014) springs from examining anthropological knowledge practices within a temporal horizon: it highlights the 'coevalness' early anthropologists denied to the very peoples they were studying by means of (mis-)construing the latter's contemporaneity as literally living in a primitive past, a move that enabled in turn projects of colonial domination. More recently, Ssorin-Chaikov's (2017) experiment of setting side by side two figures both named Lenin, one from the 1920s and the other from the 1990s, astutely explores time as a composition: his book's key proposition that 'time is relational' (2017: 6) allows him to highlight temporality as an arrangement of interrupted sequences and an assortment of separate components, all linked together in a thick network of co-implication by means of relations of succession and substitution. On his way to accomplishing this, he also offers a valuable critique of Gell's (1992) work on time.
5. In *Thus Spoke Zarathustra*, Nietzsche outlines the scholar's task at hand in the parable of the three metamorphoses, sequencing how it is that 'the spirit becomes a camel, and the camel a lion, and finally the lion a child' (2006: 16), the child being equal to 'innocence and forgetting, a new beginning, [...] a sacred yes-saying' (17).
6. Deleuze (1997) clarifies that crystal-images are of different kinds: depending on the way they assemble visual signs, he differentiates them into 'perfect crystals,' 'flawed crystals,' 'crystal of seeds' and 'decaying crystals' (see also Oliver 2016).
7. It is simply impossible to think of temporal succession in terms of indivisible presents. As Bryant (2019) notes, if the now *first* existed as an indivisible moment and *then* was constituted as past, effected by its own demise, it would require that the now begins to elapse after it has ceased to be. Because this is infeasible, and yet time does pass, the present must lapse in its very occurrence. As a consequence, the now must be internally fissured between a passing away and a yet-to-come, such that the now is always already divided into two virtual dimensions (one extending to the past and the other to the future) that are never present in their actuality (see Deleuze 1997: 81–82, 2004: 151; also Zourabichvili 2012: 102–110).
8. In Chaps. 5 and 6, I elaborate further on this dissonance, linking it to the concept of the 'will to power' and developing its counterpart, the 'will to improve'. The conceptual pair is meant to indicate the future affirmative and future neutralising potential entailed in promising as an internally differenti-

ated practice. To avoid any misunderstanding, I must distance myself from a common error: as Deleuze notes, 'every time we interpret will to power as "wanting or seeking power," we encounter platitudes which have nothing to do with Nietzsche's thought. If it is true that all things reflect a state of forces then power designates the element, or rather differential relationship, of forces which directly confront one another. [...] Power is therefore not what the will wants, but on the contrary, the one that wants in the will. [...] The one that ... does not refer to an individual, to a person, but rather to an event, that is to the forces in their various relationships [...], and to the genetic relationship which determines these forces' (2012: ix–x).

9. *Of Grammatology* (1997) is also set in motion in large measure by Derrida reading de Saussure against de Saussure, often with remarkable astuteness, noting that while de Saussure is true heir to a tradition that downplays writing in favour of speech, he nevertheless makes an intervention of critical importance: in describing the relation between the signified and the signifier as arbitrary and eschewing any foundational reference to a reality out-there, de Saussure makes possible to think of certain types of sign (e.g., the spoken word) as equally conventional and thus no more natural than other types of signs, inclusive of the written. While I cannot get into further details here, it is essential to note that what Derrida means by writing, especially '*arche-writing*' in *Of Grammatology* (1997), is closely related to his critique of auto-affection and the temporalisation of sense as discussed in *Voice and Phenomenon* (2011). The often different emphases and various concepts Derrida deploys in his works are wholly congruent with his effort at creating a philosophy singularly dedicated to upsetting and reversing hierarchies, while releasing the different and the other from everything holding it down.
10. Additionally, there is the prohibition of the sale of *gharar* or an excessive level of risk and uncertainty regarding future events and qualities of goods which, if present, invalidates the contract. More particularly, *gharar* refers to the sale of improbable items whose existence is uncertain and indeterminable on the basis that transactions of this kind are akin to gambling (El-Gamal 2006: 58–60). The prohibition of *gharar* underscores the importance of mutually agreed upon contracts whereby one-sided or two-sided incompleteness of information, however intentional or unintentional it might be, must be kept to a minimum.
11. In Indonesia, two major organisations accept that any form of interest is prohibited: the Indonesian Council of Islamic Scholars (*Majelis Ulama Indonesia*) and *Muhammadiyah* have issued *fatwa* to that effect with MUI's edict in particular, defining *riba* as any 'additional charges levied on the postponement of agreed payments' (Soemitra 2016; Lindsey 2012: 109). In contrast, a third organisation, *Nahdlatul Ulama*, which operated three conventional banks in the 1950s and 1960s, sees the matter as subject to different opinions or unresolved.

Bibliography

Ali, Nazim S. 2011. *Shari'a-Compliant Microfinance*. London: Routledge.

Antonio Muhammad, Syafii. 2008. Islamic Microfinance Initiatives to Enhance Small and Medium Enterprises. In *Expressing Islam: Religious Life and Politics in Indonesia*, ed. Greg Fealy and Sally White, 253–266. Singapore: ISEAS.

Asia Foundation. 2013. *Access to Trade and Growth of Women's SMEs in APEC Developing Economies: Evaluating the Business Environment in Indonesia*. Jakarta: Asia Foundation.

Atia, Mona. 2013. *Building a House in Heaven: Pious Neoliberalism and Islamic Charity in Egypt*. Minneapolis: University of Minnesota Press.

Azhar, Rauf. 2010. *Economics of an Islamic Economy*. Leiden: Brill.

Azra, Azyumardi. 2004. Political Islam in Post-Soeharto Indonesia. In *Islamic Perspectives in the New Millennium*, ed. Virginia Hooker and Amin Saikal, 133–149. Singapore: ISEAS.

Bear, Laura. 2014. Doubt, Conflict, Mediation: The Anthropology of Modern Time. *Journal of the Royal Anthropological Institute* 20 (S1): 3–30.

———. 2016. Time as Technique. *Annual Review of Anthropology* 45: 487–502.

Bedir, Ahmet, and Şahin Aksoy. 2011. Brain Death Revisited: It Is Not 'Complete Death' According to Islamic Sources. *Journal of Medical Ethics* 37: 290–294.

Beik, Irfan Syauqi. 2013. *Economic Role of Zakat in Reducing Poverty and Income Inequality. A Case Study in the Province of DKI Jakarta, Indonesia*. Saarbrücken: Lambert Academic Publishing.

Benthall, Jonathan, and J. Bellion-Jourdan. 2003. *The Charitable Crescent: Politics of Aid in the Muslim World*. London: I.B. Tauris.

Bruinessen, Martin van, ed. 2013. *Contemporary Developments in Indonesian Islam and the "Conservative Turn" of the Early Twenty-First Century*. Singapore: Institute of Southeast Asian Studies.

Bryant, Levi. 2019. The Time of the Object: Towards the Ontological Grounds of Withdrawal, online document. https://larvalsubjects.files.wordpress.com/2011/02/timeofobject-10-tex.pdf. Accessed 20 Aug 2019.

Chapra, Muhammad Umer. 1992. *Islam and the Economic Challenge*. Leicester: The Islamic Foundation.

———. 2014. *Morality and Justice in Islamic Economics and Finance*. Cheltenham: Edward Elgar.

Clark, Janine. 2004. *Islam, Charity and Activism: Middle-Class Networks and Social Welfare in Egypt, Jordan and Yemen*. Bloomington: Indiana University Press.

Deleuze, Gilles. 1985. *Kant's Critical Philosophy*. Trans. Hugh Tomlinson and Barbara Habberjam. Minnesota: Minnesota University Press.

———. 1997. *Cinema 2. The Time-Image*. Trans. Hugh Tomlinson and Robert Galeta. Minneapolis: University of Minnesota Press.

———. 2004. *The Logic of Sense*. Trans. Mark Lester. London: Continuum Press.

———. 2008. *Difference and Repetition*. Trans. Paul Patton. London: Continuum Press.

———. 2012. *Nietzsche and Philosophy*. Trans. Hugh Tomlinson. London: Continuum Press.

Deleuze, Gilles, and Félix Guattari. 1983. *Anti-Oedipus. Capitalism and Schizophrenia Vol. 1*. Minneapolis: University of Minnesota Press.

Derrida, Jacques. 1988. *Limited Inc*. Evanston: Northwestern University Press.

———. 1990. Force of Law: The "Mystical Foundation of Authority". *Cardozo Law Review* 11 (5–6): 919–1045.

———. 1992. *Given Time: I. Counterfeit Money*. Trans. Peggy Kamuf. Chicago: University of Chicago Press.

———. 1997. *Of Grammatology*. Trans. Gayatri Chakravorty Spivak. Baltimore: John Hopkins University Press.

———. 2011. *Voice and Phenomenon. Introduction to the Problem of the Sign in Husserl's Phenomenology*. Trans. Leonard Lawlor. Evanston: Northwestern University Press.

El-Gamal, Mahmood. 2006. *Islamic Finance: Law, Economics, and Practice*. Cambridge: Cambridge University Press.

Elyachar, Julia. 2005. *Markets of Dispossession*. Durham: Duke University Press.

Fabian, Johannes. 2014. *Time and the Other: How Anthropology Makes Its Object*. New York: University of Columbia Press.

Foucault, Michel. 2002. *The Order of Things*. Oxon: Routledge.

———. 2007. *Security, Territory, Population*. Hampshire: Palgrave Macmillan.

———. 2008. *The Birth of Biopolitics*. Hampshire: Palgrave Macmillan.

Gell, Alfred. 1992. *The Anthropology of Time: Cultural Constructions of Temporal Maps and Images*. Oxford: Berg.

Goenka, Aditya, and David Henley. 2010. *Southeast Asia's Credit Revolution: From Moneylenders to Microfinance*. London: Routledge Studies in the Growth Economies of Asia.

Graeber, David. 2011. *Debt. The First 5,000 Years*. Brooklyn: Melville House.

Guyer, Jane. 2007. Prophecy and the Near Future: Thoughts on Macroeconomic, Evangelical, and Punctuated Time. *American Ethnologist* 34 (3): 409–421.

Hamann, Byron. 2016. How to Chronologize with a Hammer, Or, the Myth of Homogenous, Empty Time. *HAU: Journal of Ethnographic Theory* 6 (1): 261–292.

Harper, Malcolm. 2017. What Do the Cases Tell Us? In *Islamic Microfinance: Shari'ah Compliant and Sustainable?* ed. Malcolm Harper and Ajaz Ahmed Khan. London: The Schumacher Centre, Practical Action Publishing.

Harper, Malcolm, and Ajaz Ahmed Khan. 2017. *Islamic Microfinance: Shari'ah Compliant and Sustainable?* London: The Schumacher Centre, Practical Action Publishing.

Hasan, Noorhaidi. 2009. The Making of Public Islam: Piety, Agency, and Commodification on the Landscape of the Indonesian Public Sphere. *Contemporary Islam* 3: 229–250.

Hefner, Robert. 2006. Islamic Economics and Global Capitalism. *Society* 44 (1): 16–22.

Henley, David. 2010. Microfinance in Indonesia: Evolution and Revolution, 1900–2000. In *Southeast Asia's Credit Revolution: From Moneylenders to Microfinance*, ed. Aditya Goenka and David Henley. London: Routledge.

Hodge, Joanna. 2007. *Derrida on Time*. Abingdon: Routledge.

Hospes, Otto, and Hotze Lont. 2004. *Livelihood and Microfinance: Anthropological and Sociological Perspectives on Savings and Debt*. Chicago: University of Chicago Press.

Ibrahim, Barbara, and Dina Sherif. 2008. *From Charity to Social Change: Trends in Arab Philanthropy*. Cairo: The American University of Cairo Press.

Khan, Ajaz Ahmed. 2008. Islamic Microfinance: Theory. In *Policy and Practice*. Islamic Relief: Birmingham.

Kuran, Timur. 2004. *Islam and the Mammon: The Economic Predicaments of Islamism*. Princeton: Princeton University Press.

Kustin, Bridget. 2015. *Islamic (Micro)Finance: Culture, Context, Promise, Challenges*. Seattle: Bill & Melinda Gates Foundation.

———. 2017. *Islamic (Micro)Finance and the Possibility of Justice*. PhD Thesis, John Hopkins University.

Latour, B. 1993. *We Have Never Been Modern*. Cambridge, MA: Harvard University Press.

Leeuwen, van Bas. 2016. The Development of Inequality and Poverty in Indonesia. *Bulletin of Indonesian Economic Studies* 52 (3): 379–402.

Li, Tania Murray. 2006. *Neo-liberal Strategies of Government through Community: The Social Development Program of the World Bank in Indonesia*. International Law and Justice Working Papers No. 2.

———. 2007. *The Will to Improve: Governmentality, Development, and the Practice of Politics*. Durham: Duke University Press.

Lindsey, Tim. 2012. Between Piety and Prudence: State Syariah and the Regulation of Islamic Banking in Indonesia. *Sydney Law Review* 34: 106–127.

Maududi, Maulana Sayyid Abul Ala. 2011. *First Principles of Islamic Economics*. Leicester: Islamic Foundation.

Maurer, Bill. 2005. *Mutual Life, Limited: Islamic Banking, Alternative Currencies, Lateral Reason*. Princeton: Princeton University Press.

———. 2006. *Pious Property: Islamic Mortgages in the United States*. New York: Russell Sage Foundation.

Mills, Paul, and John Presley. 1999. *Islamic Finance: Theory and Practice*. Basingstoke: Macmillan.

Miranti, Riyana. 2017. Understanding the Relationships between Development Factors and Regional Poverty: What Have We Learned from Indonesia. *Journal of Poverty* 21 (6): 483–507.

Munn, Nancy. 1992. The Cultural Anthropology of Time: A Critical Essay. *Annual Review of Anthropology* 21: 93–123.

Nietzsche, Friedrich. 2003. *The Genealogy of Morals*. New York: Dover Publications.

———. 2006. *Thus Spoke Zarathustra*. Cambridge: Cambridge University Press.

Obaidullah, Mohammed, and Tariqullah Khan. 2008. *Islamic Microfinance Development: Challenges and Initiatives*. Jeddah: Islamic Research and Training Institute, The Islamic Development Bank.

Oliver, Bert. 2016. Deleuze's "Crystals of Time", Human Subjectivity and Social History. *Phronimon* 17 (1): 1–32.

Osella, Filippo, and Caroline Osella. 2009. Muslim Entrepreneurs in Public Life between India and the Gulf: Making Good and Doing Good. *Journal of the Royal Anthropological Institute* 15 (S1): S202–S221.

Osella, Filippo, and Tom Widger. 2018. 'You Can Give Even If You Have Only Ten Rupees': Muslim Charity in a Colombo Housing Scheme. *Modern Asian Studies* 52 (1): 297–324.

Parinduri, Rasyad. 2014. Family Hardship and the Growth of Micro and Small Firms in Indonesia. *Bulletin of Indonesian Economic Studies* 50 (1): 53–73.

Philipp, Thomas. 1990. The Idea of Islamic Economics. *Die Welt des Islams* XXX: 117–139.

Retsikas, Konstantinos, and Magnus Marsden 2018. Alternate Modes of Prosperity. In *Invisible Hands of Life: Alternate Modes of Prosperity*, ed. K. Retsikas and M. Marsden. HAU: Journal of Ethnographic Theory (Special Section) 8 (3): 596–609.

Ricklefs, Merle. 2012. *Islamisation and Its Opponents in Java: A Political, Social, Cultural and Religious History, c. 1930 to Present*. Singapore: National University of Singapore Press.

Rudnyckyj, Daromir. 2019. *Beyond Debt: Islamic Experiments in Global Finance*. Chicago: University of Chicago Press.

Sakai, Minako. 2014. Establishing Social Justice Through Financial Inclusivity: Islamic Propagation by Islamic Savings and Credit Cooperatives in Indonesia. *TRaNS: Trans-Regional and -National Studies of Southeast Asia* 2 (2): 201–222.

Sakai, Minako, and Amelia Fauzia. 2016. Performing Muslim Womanhood: Muslim Business Women Moderating Islamic Practices in Contemporary Indonesia. *Islam and Christian-Muslim Relations* 27 (3): 229–249.

Sandi, Rio, and Ajaz Ahmed Khan. 2017. Co-Operative Islamic Microfinance: Daarl Qu'ran BMT from Jakarta, Indonesia. In *Islamic Microfinance: Shari'ah Compliant and Sustainable?* ed. M. Harper and A.A. Khan. London: The Schumacher Centre, Political Action Publishing.

Seibel, Hans Dieter. 2012. Islamic Microfinance in Indonesia: The Challenge of Institutional Diversity, Regulation and Supervision. In *Shari'a-Compliant Microfinance*, ed. S. Nazim Ali. London: Routledge.

Siddiqi, Muhammad Nejatullah. 1983. *Issues in Islamic Banking*. Leicester: Islamic Foundation.

———. 2006. Islamic Banking and Finance in Theory and Practice: A Survey of State of the Art. *Islamic Economic Studies* 13 (2): 1–48.

Singer, Amy. 2008. *Charity in Islamic Societies*. Cambridge: Cambridge University Press.

Soemitra, Andri. 2016. Higher Objectives of Islamic Investment Products: Islamizing Indonesian Capital Markets. *Studia Islamika* 23 (2): 237–269.

Ssorin-Chaikov, Nikolai. 2017. *The Lenins: A Brief Anthropology of Time*. Chicago: Hau Books.

Suryahadi, Asep, Gracia Hadiwidjaja, and Sudarno Sumarto. 2012. Economic Growth and Poverty Reduction in Indonesia Before and After the Asian Financial Crisis. *Bulletin of Indonesian Economic Studies* 48 (2): 209–227.

Tripp, Charles. 2006. *Islam and the Moral Economy. The Challenge of Capitalism*. Cambridge: Cambridge University Press.

Vial, Virginie. 2011. Micro-Entrepreneurship in a Hostile Environment: Evidence from Indonesia. *Bulletin of Indonesian Economic Studies* 47 (2): 233–262.

Visser, Hans. 2009. *Islamic Finance: Principles and Practice*. Cheltenham: Edward Elgar.

Warde, Ibrahim. 2010. *Islamic Finance in the Global Economy*. Edinburgh: Edinburgh University Press.

Zourabichvili, François. 2012. *Deleuze: A Philosophy of the Event Together with the Vocabulary of Deleuze*. Trans. Kieran Aarons. Edinburgh: Edinburgh University Press.

CHAPTER 2

Dividing the Present

At the last third of every Ramadan, a brief and fairly unmarked event takes place in Java and across the entire Muslim world. The event which takes place annually and is usually conducted in private, unaccompanied by the elaboration and fanfare that marks most public ritual occasions on the calendar, bears the name of *zakat*. Zakat comes from the Arabic verb—*zakā*- and carries the meaning of 'that which increases' and 'that which grows' as well as 'that which purifies'. The ritual involves the transfer of value, either in kind or money, and its conduct is a religious obligation, standing for the third pillar of the faith, second only in importance to the five daily prayers and the confession of the faith. There are two types of zakat, zakat on persons (*zakat fitrah*) and zakat on wealth (*zakat maal*). While the first must be conducted by every Muslim, before the month of Ramadan is over, so as to ensure that every member of the community of the faithful has enough food to partake in the celebrations following the end of the fasting month, the second involves a wealth transfer that must be completed once a year by better-off Muslims only. The conduct of *zakat maal* entails the considered deduction of a determinate portion of specified categories of the lawful wealth well-off persons command, and its allocation for the benefit of persons of other classes as enumerated in the Quran, the most important of which are the destitute and the poor (*fakir miskin*). The transfer's successful completion is held to have a purificatory and multiplicative effect: as well as purifying the faithful from the sins they have accumulated over the year, testifying to their

K. Retsikas, *A Synthesis of Time*,
https://doi.org/10.1007/978-3-030-34933-2_2

victory over unwelcomed desires such as greediness and self-indulgence, *zakat maal* has a cathartic effect on the residual wealth which is henceforth deemed clean (*bersih*) enough for one to enjoy and dispose to his/her liking. Failure to subtract and transfer zakat as well as amounting to apostasy and thus eternal damnation, brings about punishments in this life too: zakat 'is never left commingled with other property without bringing about its ruin' (Zysow 2012), precipitating droughts, loss of livestock and other forms of misfortune. In contrast, its careful calculation, repeated subtraction and judicious allocation opens the door to divine rewards for Allah is held to recompense handsomely those who obey his commandments with due sincerity and modesty.

Jonathan Benthall (1999) has coined the term 'financial worship' as zakat's equivalent; the term successfully conveys some of the challenges the practice of zakat poses, especially as it forces us to acknowledge that the manner in which the economic and the religious, rather than corresponding to axiomatically given domains of human praxis that are inherently separate, in traditions other than ours, come to reciprocally presuppose and implicate one another instead. In this book, I set out to take things further and show that in addition to defining a field of everyday practice that makes no necessary or prior assumptions about the lines that supposedly demarcate the ceremonial from the monetary, zakat practice in Indonesia corresponds to a plateau that seeks to organise everything it contains within it under the single sign of submission to divine will. This includes temporality, itself understood as the organisation of time's passing by means of instating intervals of differential, asymmetrical value. For the faithful, zakat counts amongst the mechanisms that set the temporal rhythms of salvation, prosperity and well-being: it is periodicity itself, or more accurately it participates in a divine mode of making time pass. Both *zakat fitrah* and *zakat maal* are conducted once a year based on the Islamic lunar calendar (*hijriah*), itself starting from the Prophet Mohammad's migration from Mecca to Medina set on the 19 July 622 in the Julian calendar. Due to their periodic nature, both forms of zakat are events repeated over time, corresponding to regular happenings which incidence is as much stipulated as anticipated. In this regard, they contribute to the creation and maintenance of a normative order of time in an image ordained by Allah. While *zakat fitrah* always take place before the fasting month of Ramadan is over, *zakat maal* applies to certain categories of wealth the value of which exceeds a certain threshold (*nisab*), whereby such wealth has been in one's possession for a full one-year holding period (*haul*). In Java, *haul* is sometimes calculated based on Ramadan's return, with the transfer of *zakat maal* often accomplished during the fasting month. Part of the reason for this is that Ramadan enjoys an intimate connection with the performance of the other key purification ritual, itself involving fasting from food, water and sex from dawn to dusk. In addition, Ramadan is the time when other optional forms of supplication such as the *tarawih* prayers and Quranic recitation sessions, are customarily held. Such intense combinations of piety are geared towards achieving an overall increase in the likelihood of bountiful reward by Allah, at a most opportune moment—Ramadan being the holy month when the Quran was bestowed to mankind. Where however *zakat maal* is levied on land produce rather than other forms of wealth such as livestock, the proceeds of commerce or gold and silver, the *zakat maal*'s transfer follows the agricultural cycle, with the allocation normally taking place immediately upon harvest.

As well as dividing the passing present into two halves—with one half taking charge of an immediate past tainted by sins, moral failings and misdemeanours, while the other opens to a future that is in turn bright, light and full of optimism of attaining salvation—*zakat maal* involves the division of wealth into two distinct shares, one for oneself and another for others. Such division is an act favourable in the eyes of Allah. The conduct of zakat inserts cuts in the flow of time, making time pass by means of differentiating wealth into distinct, unequal portions, forcing their separation. The activity of cutting time depends on and involves the apportioning of wealth as its necessary condition. This cutting entails several distinct undertakings: arranged in succession, it involves identifying the wealth subject to zakat and calculating the respective rates applying and distributing the zakat in question to diverse recipients according to judgements already made as to their appropriateness, via the foundational act of apportioning the wealth itself into shares, one that is one's to keep and one that is due to others as a rightful claim. Though the Al-Quran does stipulate the categories of persons endowed with such right in *Surat At-Taubah*, verse 60—they are the destitute, the poor, the zakat collectors, new converts, slaves, debtors, those advancing God's cause and the wayfarers—it does not define the types of wealth subject to zakat nor does it state the rates to be applied. It is normally left to the *hadith* literature, concerning the words and deeds of the Prophet, to provide directives as to these and other questions, such as the minimum value/threshold over which zakat pertains (*nisab*) and the rule of the one-year holding period (*haul*).

Al-Qardawi, the foremost authority on matters of zakat jurisprudence, notes that the Prophet 'did not impose zakat except on growing and producing assets of which the Arabs at this time had several kinds,' such as livestock (camels, cows and sheep), money, gold and silver used as business assets and in the form of savings, crops and fruits such as wheat, barley and dates, and hidden treasure (2000: 60). The Quranic clarity of claimants and the Prophetic example of how-to-zakat notwithstanding, it is most significant to stress that both the categories of persons entitled to zakat and the kinds of property subject to it, along with a myriad of additional matters, have been the explicit concern of Islamic scholars for their definition, explanation and elaboration, sparking important debates and leading to divergences in the practice of zakat across the spatial and temporal terrain of the Muslim world, with the consequence that the practice differs from one country to another, and from one era to the other.

The present study focuses on contemporary Indonesia, and most particularly on Java, with the opening chapter charting the manner in which the practice of zakat has been changing over the past five decades or so. This has been the result of major restructurings in the political economy of the country and the consequent re-articulation of relations of inequality, as well as, deep and recurring reforms taking place in the way key tenets of the faith are understood, propagated and enacted, especially amongst a leading segment of Javanese society. Central in the unfolding of my argument is the contention that at the same time that zakat repeatedly makes time pass by dividing wealth up and transferring it to its rightful claimants, zakat is subject to time's passing: as such it is exposed to other forces which power and influence shape its performance. It is precisely because zakat participates in time as a force amongst other forces that it performs time by cutting into it, reorganising its contours and synthesising anew its breaks. In order to show the ways in which zakat practice has been participating in time, I set out to discuss specific works of Islamic jurisprudence composed by Indonesian Islamic scholars, placing such works within the context of changing relations of inequality. In line with other authors, I am highlighting the role the emergence of a middle class of urban educated professionals has played and the difference the spread of 'modernist' or 'neo-modernist' discourses regarding the faith has made, especially as the later have been propagated by these very same professionals from the 1970s to the present (see Abubakar and Bamualim 2006; Fauzia 2013; Latief 2012; Salim 2008; Jahar 2006;

Hefner 2000; Effendy 2003; Liddle 1996). The argument I put forward is that over the past fifty years or so a most definite reconceptualisation of zakat has taken place in Indonesia, whereby zakat has changed from a largely unmarked and little elaborated upon ritual of annual worship to a fundamental concern and instrument of socio-economic justice. In what follows, I concentrate on explicating the traditional understanding of zakat, followed by the analysis of the jurisprudential discourses that precipitated its reconfiguration. My reading of such discourses is critical in the sense that I bring attention to the fact that the repositioning of zakat both as an obligation equivalent to tax and a gift comparable to a philanthropic intervention, by leading Muslim intellectuals and faith-based organisations alike downplays other, alternative understandings of zakat as right. I content that such reconceptualisation ultimately rests on a perspective which privileges the practising of Islam as a religion of transcendence, and sides with the positions of zakat payers, often at the expense of recognising the immanent presence of the divine and those human others to whom zakat is owed as a right.

Carving out such critical position means neither siding blindly with *emic* understandings, nor with subjecting them to judgments informed by values liberal reasoning is turning universal. The route I have chosen is distinct and owes its existence as much to Nietzsche's perspectivism (2003) as to Derrida's deconstruction (1997). To the extent that all knowing (this book included) emanates from particular positions,[1] being conditional on the assumption of perspectives always and already specific, the critical task is none other than the unsettling of the very givenness and finality with which knowledge literally embalms itself. For this to happen, it is essential to bring back to the analytic fold the uncommon and the residual: the latter correspond to positions left orphaned and un-occupied, springing from perspectives which, if not outrightly suppressed, are actively marginalised and excluded from recognition within the limits set by dominant discourses. In this regard, a brave dissection of any system of knowledge entails an exercise in reverse engineering, a painstaking demonstration of the very methods that have gone into its construction and maintenance as a closed, circular system. If perspectivism/deconstruction carries a promise, it is equivalent to undertaking a risk: bringing attention to the elements excluded, marginalised and suppressed, means opening a door for them to trace a line of flight, so that they start exercising an influence once again!

Purifying Growth

From September 2011 to September 2012, I conducted ethnographic fieldwork on zakat practices and activities, dividing my time between the East Java provincial capital, Surabaya, and Indonesia's national capital, Jakarta, and focusing my energies on three institutions of zakat collection, management and distribution: to preserve their anonymity I have renamed them as *Surabaya Peduli Ummat*, *Pondok Infak Mulia* and *Dana Keadilan Indonesia*. All three are well known nationally and have taken part in relief operations internationally. In 2011, their combined number of donors was almost 350,000, while a significantly larger number of people having received support from them. Their collective income for the same year was close to £20 million, and their joint workforce was close to 1400 employees, not including volunteers. The three institutions run a vast number of programmes comprising of educational and health provision for the poor, small business training and micro-finance, *dakwah* (Islamic propagation), mosque construction, disaster relief and humanitarian missions in rural and urban locations. In Chaps. 3 and 4 I discuss their history, organisational structures and outlook. In the present chapter, I focus on discursive emphases, shifts and blind spots in the Indonesian landscape of zakat. The discourses in question emanate from a multiplicity of institutional settings, including yet not limited to the ones I have had the chance of working closely with. The important thing to remember about such institutions which in Indonesia are known as *Lembaga Amil Zakat*, commonly abbreviated as *LAZ*, are two: first, they were formed in the last few years of New Order rule (1966–1998), or immediately after, and became truly active during the *reformasi* period, that is, from 1998 to the present. Second, LAZ are aligned with 'modernist' and 'neo-modernist' interpretations of Islam which are popular amongst the urban milieu of educated, middle-class Muslims including bureaucrats, professionals and businessmen (Latief 2013). Within this overarching context, their practices depart from 'traditionalist' understandings of zakat in the sense that LAZ have sought to redraw the relevant jurisprudential map through the exercise *ijtihad*. *Ijtihad* refers to arriving to a decision in Islamic law by means of personal effort and independently of any school of Islamic jurisprudence. As such, it is opposed to *taqlid* which stands for conforming to the stipulations of religious experts without examining the basis of their reasoning. This practice modernist Muslims see as the hallmark of 'traditionalist' Islam found mostly in rural villages and poor urban neighbourhoods. In order to appreciate these jurisprudential efforts and their social effects more fully, it is necessary to discuss the relevant terminology.

The *Encyclopedia of Islam* defines *sedekah* as 'voluntary alms in distinction to obligatory alms, frequently also termed sedekah but more commonly known as *zakat*' (Weir and Zysow 2012). It also notes that zakat is the 'obligatory payment by Muslims of a determinate portion of their lawful property for the benefit of the poor and other enumerated classes' (Zysow 2012). Because zakat rarely refers to voluntary giving in the Quran, it mostly expresses the portion of one's wealth 'paid out' (*keluarkan*) as a duty. The transfer of this share amounts to worship—*ibadah*—for zakat is the third pillar of Islam. The understanding of zakat as key component of Islamic ritual life forms the basis of Muslim practice across the world. For Muslims in Java as well as elsewhere, zakat is intrinsically related to safeguarding, multiplying and purifying one's soul and wealth: conducting zakat worship brings not only the faithful closer to Allah but also serves to purify the hearts of believers from hedonism and decadence. It also renders the remainder of wealth clean (*bersih*) for one to enjoy. Rather than reducing the amount of wealth at one's disposal, zakat increases it for handing over zakat to its rightful owners, that is the eight categories of people as enumerated in the Quran,[2] opens the door to more rewards, material and otherwise, being received from Allah. In addition, zakat protects the wealth that remains from being stolen, going missing, getting lost or simply being scattered around. When zakat is not handed over, it is said to bring about misfortune, potentially causing the person who failed to observe the practice to fall ill. Those who refuse to carry out zakat are held to have become *kafir* (unbelievers) and on Judgment Day, it is said they will come face to face with the wealth they withheld for not transferring the zakat due is a major sin. It is said that such people will be pursued by their 'gold and silver treasure' in the shape of a large fearsome bold serpent featuring twin horns and long teeth which will bite hard at their stingy hands for 50,000 years.

Zakat has received very little sustained attention by ethnographers of Java and Southeast Asia more generally. Though it is often mentioned in many ethnographic accounts, this is mostly done in passing and with reference to *zakat fitrah*, that is, zakat every Muslim must carry out. With few exceptions, most notably Scott's (1987) article on Malaysia, zakat on wealth (*zakat maal*), the main pre-occupation of this book, is rarely deliberated or theorised in works of Islamic practice in the region in an extensive and sustained manner. While this is trend might be slowly changing, much of what we know comes from the work of historians such as Amelia Fauzia (2013). Fauzia emphasises that traditionally the conduct of zakat, both *fitrah* and *maal*, has involved either the direct allocation of zakat by the payer (*muzakki*) him/herself to persons entitled to it of his/her own choosing, or has proceeded by its transfer to an informal, temporary committee of local purview. Such committees are customarily organised by mosques, Quranic boarding schools and neighbourhoods, their objective being to collect and distribute zakat within a delimited time period, mainly during and immediately after Ramadan—after which they disband, only to appear again the following year. Such grass-root committees, which sometimes coalesce around locally known Islamic scholars (*kyai*), commonly distribute the proceeds in the vicinity of their operation, following a *hadith* to that effect, and they do so immediately, without delay, keeping the interval involved between zakat assembly and dispersal to a minimum. Amongst the usual beneficiaries of either method are orphans and widows as they are held to be the neediest of the 'destitute' (*fakir*), as well as, students and scholars of Islam as the most representative of 'those advancing God's cause' (*fi sabilillah*). At the same time, amongst contemporary zakat activists there is the widespread assumption that, as Salim puts it, 'zakat is perhaps the religious duty least complied with by Muslims' (2008: 12). And despite survey results such as that conducted by PIRAC in 2004 (Kurniawati 2005), which found that only a small percentage (7.5%) of people who self-declared as eligible for zakat did not proceed with its transfer, there is the persistent sense in metropolitan circles that the majority of Indonesian Muslims fail to conduct zakat because of lack of adequate understanding of the procedures regarding how to calculate it (especially *zakat maal*) and when, where and how to transfer it. In this respect, urban-based zakat activists often argue that this lamentable situation is partly because rural religious teachers rarely supply relevant instructions, and partly because Islamic jurisprudence on the issue is full with unresolved debates that make things difficult for those without the required expertise.

There is no doubt that zakat jurisprudence is too intricate and elaborate a subject to delve into at length here. And yet there is reason enough to note briefly that classical Islamic jurists have often wondered why zakat applies to certain kinds of wealth (*maal*) only and the main theory they have articulated rests on the notion of growth. As Al-Qardawi's summary makes clear (2000: 53–80), this theory emphasises that zakat is due on wealth provided that the latter is capable of increase, both actually and virtually. Thus, livestock is subject to zakat for animals bear young and multiply; agricultural produce is subject to zakat for it is growth itself; gold and silver as far as they are used as storage of value and media of exchange are also subject to zakat. At the same time, agricultural fields are not subject to zakat, and the same goes for one's own home and for gold and silver jewellery. In this regard, it is said that assets that are in use and circulation are exempt from zakat: for example, Abdusshomad Buchori, the head of the Indonesian Council of Islamic Scholars branch in Surabaya, has written a small book (2011) in which he argues that a second house is not subject to zakat, but income derived from rent on this house is subject to it. However, Muhammad Nafik, head of *Ekonomi Syariah* department at *Universitas Airlangga* in Surabaya, pushing things further, argues that a second house should also be subject to zakat for it indexes hoarded wealth. According to this Islamic economist, zakat is intended to encourage Muslims to constantly utilise their assets for productive use because through such utilisation and circulation, prosperity is achieved.

Another interesting aspect relates to the fact that zakat shares its association with growth with *riba*, a term that denotes ways of achieving increase which are explicitly forbidden to Muslims (*haram*). While the prohibition of *riba* is clear, there are intense disagreements amongst scholars about which practices fall under it (see El-Gamal 2006; Kuran 2004; Warde 2010). Some commentators understand *riba* as referring to exploitative, excessive usury, while most jurists take it to indicate any kind of monetary increase for a loan provided and thus as equivalent to interest. The prohibition of *riba* and the obligation of zakat is instructive for it relates to the unmediated versus mediated distinction. In *riba*, growth results directly from human-to-human interaction, while by bringing the human in contact with the divine, zakat triangulates these interactions, acknowledging the divine as immanently present in the unfolding of the social, and as the ultimate source of prosperity. In other words, zakat presents the event of the social as a triadic rather than a dyadic affair. According to this conception, there is no prior differentiation of the social into distinct domains, such as the sphere of the religious and the province of the economic. Rather what is emphasised is that prosperity and good fortune are contingent on triadic relations. These relations are based on a double affirmation of alterity: engaging with the otherness of the divine and the otherness of other humans through zakat is what ensures well-being, material and otherwise.

Re-framing Zakat

Understandings of zakat started changing in Indonesia most clearly and profoundly from the late 1970s and most definitely from the 1980s onwards, partly as a result of the wider movement for the 'renewal' of Muslim faith, and partly in response to the political economic changes that New Order policies brought about (see Salim 2008; Fauzia 2013; Jahar 2006). The 1980s was perhaps the apex of the New Order as the regime had secured the consent of large parts of the population, governing the country on top of a wave of prosperity, itself generated through opening the economy to foreign investment and attendant export-oriented industrialisation. Long gone was of the violence of the 1960s that saw the massacre of close to 1 million people for their alleged ties to the Indonesian Communist Party as well as many regional rebellions that threatened the newly founded nation-state with disintegration. However, the fruits of economic development were unevenly distributed as large parts of the country especially in rural areas were steeped in poverty. This was a situation a new generation of Muslim intellectuals found deplorable and worked hard to rectify through various interventions.

The movement for 'Islamic renewal' (*gerakan pebaharuan Islam*) that Muslim intellectuals such as Nurcholish Madjid and Munawir Sjadzali advocated laid emphasis on the contextual rather than the literal understanding of the scriptures and called upon the faithful to undertake the effort of distinguishing between the eternal truths of the faith and the historically contingent nature of many institutions and interpretations that had developed from the time of the Prophet to the present day (Hefner 2000).[3] In order for the distinction between the divine and the human to be achieved, and thus, for Islam to acquire contemporary relevance, the movement seized on the practice of *ijtihad*, the continuous interpretation of the revelation through individual effort and the application of reason. Such re-interpretation was to be carried out within the context of achieving the primary 'intentions' or 'goals' of *syariah* (*maqasid syariah*) and Muslim intellectuals in Indonesia as well as elsewhere often took this 'intention' to be *maslaha*, itself equivalent to common good, public benefit or human welfare broadly conceived.[4] Social welfare framed in terms of *maslaha* came therefore to serve as the foundation of a series of discussions, debates and arguments advanced in Indonesia, and often came to be presented as adequate basis for issuing particular rulings or opinions even independently of specific scriptural references. Along with other Quranic concepts, zakat came to be seen in the light of *maslaha*.

In 1986, Amien Rais, a political scientist with a doctorate from the University of Chicago on the Egyptian Muslim Brotherhood, and future leader of Muhammadiyah, Indonesia's largest modernist organisation, delivered a controversial speech. The speech advocated re-interpreting zakat in the contemporary context of Indonesia's persistent problems with poverty and sought to redefine its purpose as to securing people's welfare. In the spirit of Islam as a religion of justice, Rais proposed the notion of *zakat profesi* or zakat on regular income (salary and wages) (1987, 1998; see also Latief 2012, 2014). This notion had a lasting impact on the discursive landscape of zakat in Indonesia for it contained several salient features. First, it was an innovation in Islamic jurisprudence as salary and wages had not previously been considered wealth subject to zakat, according to classically trained scholars. Second, the notion reflected changes in the political economy of Indonesia; in particular, the broad shift from an economy based on agriculture to a modern one in which people practised professions in a fast-industrialising setting, and for which they received regular income as wages. Third, the ratio of zakat to wealth Rais proposed was significantly higher than that applied to other categories of wealth by classically trained scholars. To Rais, 2.5% (or 1/40th) of one's wealth was not enough for the achievement of social justice. As the occupations *zakat profesi* was applied to were relatively high paying including law, medicine and architecture, Rais proposed that for zakat to be fair, it had to be proportional, and thus should correspond to 1/10th (10%) or 1/5th (20%) levy on regular earnings. He argued that it would not be fair if peasants paid 10% of the crops grown on irrigated fields and wealthy urban professionals were subject to no zakat at all or to zakat equivalent to 2.5% of their income.

Rais' proposal meant to bridge the widening gap between rich, powerful pious Muslims and their poor and marginalised counterparts in rural and urban settings. The three decades of economic growth, industrialisation and urbanisation New Order policies brought about, witnessed an unprecedented rise of Muslims into the ranks of the urban middle class and into positions of managerial, financial and political control both in the private and the state sector (see Hefner 2000; Ricklefs 2012). This development opened up an unprecedented gap between rich and poor Muslims even as it closed the gap between rich, powerful pious Muslims and their non-pious Muslim and non-Muslim counterparts, thus calling into question the authority of emerging Muslim elites to speak in the name of Islam and of their fellow Muslims. Rais' re-interpretation of the Quranic injunction to zakat must be understood as an effort to reconnect

Indonesian Muslims across different strata, assuage any lingering anxieties and concerns over legitimate leadership, while recasting the newly found wealth of urban, educated elites as compliant with the dictates of religion.

Notwithstanding its pragmatism, Rais' jurisprudential innovation came from a certain theological background. It entailed a reimagining of the space of worship from a two-dimensional to a three-dimensional one. Modernists and neo-modernists have long emphasised that zakat is as much about the vertical relations humans enjoy with God as about the horizontal relations pertaining amongst humans themselves. On the whole they have conveyed this double aspect through dividing worship (*ibadah*) into two major categories: the *hablu minallah* that involves acts that foreground one's relation to Allah and background relations with other (wo) men, and the *hablu minannaas* that underscores the relations worshippers entertain with other people, back-staging relations with God. In this context, concerns over public welfare and social justice did not originate in a secular ethos: in addition to promoting the broad goals of Islamic law, such concerns are a direct part of Islamic worship. Such worship however is not just about '*ritual*,' an English loan word that zakat activists often associate with 'traditionalist' understandings of zakat. According to them, 'traditionalist' zakat practices are wanting for they are limited to addressing the verticality of *hablu minallah*. In contrast, zakat activists and others proceed to expand the field of worship to encompass relations with other humans, the good conduct of which serves (wo)man as much as God. As such, caring for the welfare of others and taking concrete action for its promotion is an act that ultimately brings one closer to God.

Initially Rais' proposal was met with dismay as many scholars pointed out that it was an unlawful innovation (*bidah*). In 2003, almost twenty years after it was first proposed, it was finally accepted by the Indonesian Council of Islamic Scholars—*Majelis Ulama Indonesia*—that issued an edict (*fatwa*) to that effect. However, a different rate was applied. Whereas Rais' proposal was based on analogising *zakat profesi* to zakat for agriculture produce of irrigated fields (10%) and to zakat for natural resources like oil and precious metals (20%), MUI's edict sanctioned a 2.5% rate as applicable, effectively making *zakat profesi* analogous to zakat on commerce.[5] This meant that, at least for some, the goal of social justice had yet to be achieved.

A few years after Rais' controversial speech, another Islamic scholar, Masdar Farid Mas'udi reignited the issue of the social relevance of zakat with the publication of a book titled *The Religion of Justice* (*Agama*

Keadilan 1991). In contrast to Rais, Mas'udi is trained in the classical Islamic sciences and in his youth was involved with faith-based NGOs advocating pluralism, human rights and democracy. His approach to Islamic jurisprudence emphasised *ijtihad*; yet in contrast to Rais, Mas'udi started from the recognition of the internal diversity and flexibility of traditional jurisprudential sources and of close engagement with them (Feener 2007: 174–181). Mas'udi insisted that justice is the ultimate goal of *syariah* and that *ijtihad* is required for making such divinely inspired justice applicable to the variety of socio-economic contexts and circumstances Muslims find themselves in.

Like Rais, Mas'udi highlighted the social dimensions of zakat, emphasising its redistributive purpose; this he achieved through bringing attention to what he saw as the fundamental similarity of zakat and state taxation, thus creating a new ground for the articulation of government policies, the personal responsibilities of Indonesian Muslims and the pursuit of justice. His interpretation was based on an excursion into Islamic history. He noted that while the examples set by the Prophet Muhammad and the four caliphs were based on the state administration of zakat in the form of taxation, subsequent developments in Islamic history led to the uncoupling of state finances from zakat. This uncoupling Mas'udi found lamentable arguing that the diminishment of zakat's importance in governance had brought about both economic injustice and increased levels of corruption in the disbursement of public funds. Such a situation should and could be rectified, Mas'udi continued, only if contemporary Indonesian Muslims started considering taxes paid to the state as zakat. Mas'udi's point was that as long as Muslim citizens were meant to pay their taxes as zakat, that is with the requisite religious intention (*niat*),[6] this would not only spare them from a double burden but would also bring about a major change in the country's political culture, making the government more responsible, transparent and accountable in the utilisation of public funds. The state would not only have to distribute such funds in accordance to religious stipulations but it would also be compelled to promote social justice.

It is instructive at this point to note that both Rais and Mas'udi became major public figures in the 1990s and 2000s. Rais emerged as a key figure of the *reformasi* movement that brought Suharto down in May 1998. Subsequently, he went to found and lead a new political party, becoming chairman of the People's Consultative Assembly (1999–2004). In 2004, Mas'udi ran a failed campaign for the leadership of *Nahdlatul Ulama*,

Indonesia's largest Muslims organisation representing 'traditionalist' Islam. His popularity had already suffered a major blow in 2002 when he took a second wife, a highly controversial practise in Indonesia. It goes without saying that Mas'udi proposal for the equation of tax and zakat was criticised not only by economists, technocrats and politicians but also by other Islamic scholars who pointed out the differences between one's duties to Caesar and to God, lest the former acquires the attributes of the latter. In a 2005 book rejoinder to the debate, Mas'udi hardened his position, taking a distinctly conservative line. In particular he argued that zakat fits into the right to levy tax that the state holds exclusively, writing that 'the primary task of the state, as the executor of Allah's decrees, is to eradicate the hunger of the hungry, and to make those who feel insecure, secure' (2005: 157). While in the past the argument about the equivalence of tax and zakat was made with the intention of equipping a pious citizenry with the means of holding a state (New Order) widely acknowledged to be corrupt to account, in the new book the argument shifts, and the equivalence of zakat and tax is put to the service of furthering the interests of the (post-New Order) state. Here zakat occupies the role of a fiscal instrument and a source of public finance that is wholly subordinated to state power, especially as Mas'udi's proposal is unambiguously framed in the language of Islamism. In this respect, the scholar claims that religion and the state are indissolubly joined in Islam, with religion 'providing the direction, while the state giving the requisite form' (2005: 166), noting that 'the vision religion provides will be of no consequence without the state as the container of its actualisation' (2005: 167).

In Mas'udi's latest work (2005), zakat equals an obligation the faithful owe to Allah on an annual basis, and it is precisely because religion and the state can't be separated that zakat corresponds to a duty, like tax, they owe to the state. In this situation, the compulsory nature of zakat as worship is directly translated into an state enforceable liability: while the Quran remains silent as to the way the obligation of conducting zakat is to be conducted, Mas'udi suggests that it imperative that the state utilises the full force of the law to compel compliance, making sure that all Muslim citizens enact the dictates of religion, which are also the laws of the land (2005: 158). Because Mas'udi approaches religion through the prism of transcendence, he conceives zakat as an obligation, first and foremost to a distant and arbitrary God, and secondarily and by implication, to an equally faceless and demanding state: both figures, God and the state, are united in their power over the faithful with the authority of the latter understood as emanating from the absoluteness of the former. It goes without saying that in this scheme the only realistic option is, as the author makes clear, for zakat is to be managed exclusively by the state, with its collection, management and distribution been closely regulated and monopolised by state institutions.[7]

Another scholar whose jurisprudential work exercised a seminal influence in Indonesia is Didin Hafidhuddin, a classically trained Islamic scholar with links to the Agricultural University Bogor and the State Islamic University Syarif Hidayatullah Jakarta. Hafidhuddin has the unique characteristic of combining expert scholarship with a long history of engagement with the practice of zakat, first as a chairman of the Syariah Supervisory Board of *Dompet Duafa*, one of Indonesia's most respected Islamic charitable organisations, and subsequently as chairman (2005–2015) of BAZNAS—*Badan Amil Zakat Nasional*—the central government institution of zakat management. His study titled *Zakat in the Modern Economy* (2002) is important for a number of reasons: following the work of Al-Qardawi (2000), it made the case that new categories of legal persons (such as companies) and new kinds of wealth associated with the modern context should not be excluded from zakat. By means of analogic reasoning, Hafidhuddin demonstrated that company revenues, income from currency trading and savings in the form of investments in housing and the stock market, for example, should be included in zakatable wealth, therefore expanding significantly the overall value that zakat as a financial asset might have for a country like Indonesia, a member of the 'G20' most advanced economies in the world. His intervention additionally sanctioned putting zakat assets into new uses: zakat, Hafidhuddin argued, should not be distributed exclusively for 'consumptive' (*konsumtif*) purposes, that is, for meeting the immediate needs of its rightful claimants (*mustahik*) in terms of food, shelter and so on. Instead it could be spent on 'productive' (*produktif*) undertakings the objective of which is to improve over the longer term the conditions the recipients find themselves in, by providing, for example, some of the necessary funds for education and healthcare services as well as entrepreneurship training and capital for micro-enterprises (2002: 10–12, see Chapter 5).

In 1999, the Prosperous Justice Party, the key vehicle of political Islam in the country, set to make religion the basis of both society and the state, after a model championed by the Muslim Brotherhood of Egypt, nominated Hafidhuddin as its presidential candidate. His candidacy though, didn't progress to the second round for lack of adequate votes. As to the relation of zakat and the state, Hafidhuddin accords the latter a prominent, though not exclusive, role departing in significant ways from Mas'udi. Even though both scholars agree that zakat is a most important instrument for furthering the goal of justice as envisioned in Islam, alleviating both extreme and relative poverty, they differ as to the way they want to see this obligation implemented and enforced. In other words, while both start from the position that zakat is too important a matter to be left up to individual believers to conduct (or not), Hafidhuddin's proposal involves entrusting institutions of both civil society and the state with the authority of implementing the divine directive to zakat. In this regard, he references *Surat At-Taubah*, verse 103 from the Quran which calls for 'zakat to be taken (*ambil*) from a portion of their wealth,' explaining that only those institutions formally recognised by the state with such a task, have the sole and undisputed authority to forcefully remove zakat (2002: 124–125). In the post-New Order Indonesia, such institutions include both faith-based organisations that have been set up by concerned members of the society, and non-structural arms of the government found at various levels of administration (see Chap. 3): Hafidhuddin is keen to acknowledge the contributions both types of institutions have made in spreading the message of zakat, raising people's awareness, improving its management. However, as Indonesian law has never turned zakat into a matter of compulsion, Hafidhuddin explicitly advocates for this situation to change: his position is for the obligation to zakat to be enshrined into the national statute book, whereby all institutions involved in zakat management are granted the authority to forcefully deduct zakat from the faithful, in their capacity as representatives of the state (*penguasa yang diwakili oleh para petugas zakat, wajib memaksanya* (2002: 52)).

Filantropi and *Cariti*

During my fieldwork in the early 2010s, a very noticeable trend amongst LAZ or Zakat Management Bodies was that staff would consistently seek to convey zakat to me and others using English loan words, through the distinction between *cariti* and *filantropi*. The concepts' introduction to Indonesia is related to a research project: between 2001 and 2004, the Centre for the Study of Religion and Culture at the State Islamic University Syarif Hidayatullah Jakarta with support from the Ford Foundation carried out a most ambitious research project into zakat and *sedekah* practices across the archipelagic state, the aim being the evaluation of the untapped potential of the Islamic civil society sector for development purposes. Significantly, the project framed its problem using a conceptual framework based on the concepts of *cariti* and *filantropi* (see Bamualim et al. 2006; Abubakar and Bamualim 2006). Pointedly, the discourse the project helped give rise to, with *filantropi* as its preferred foundation, is at variance with the jurisprudential interventions of Mas'udi and Hafidhuddin, especially as it sought to reposition the practice of zakat away from its propagation as an obligation enforceable by the state, towards its recognition as a sacred value in need of being upheld by socially responsible Muslims as individual believers and concerned citizens. The onus to conduct zakat was therefore placed by such discourse squarely on the better-off and the wealthy, the *muzakki*: they were invited to conceptualise and implement the divinely ordained duty to zakat as an ultimate duty of care towards others less fortunate. Key in cultivating the corresponding motivations was not only the promotion of objectives limited to worship, such as pleasing Allah and gaining his rewards, but the additional opportunity for *muzakki* to make a difference via the bestowal of a gift. In the post-New Order era, zakat came to be alternatively conceived as the transfer of financial assistance to the poor and the destitute, especially at a time when their lives were crippled by the economic and political crisis facing the country in the late 1990s and early 2000s. The discourse of *filantropi* privileged the promotion of social justice not through making zakat comparable to a duty levied by the state, but by means of making zakat equivalent to gift-giving.

For the researchers involved in the project and the zakat agencies I worked with, the two terms, *cariti* and *filantropi*, have radically different meanings. Charity denotes immediate relief; it is seen as focused on short-term projects and is generally thought of as having limited impact on poverty alleviation. Quite understandably, this is a practice that the agencies in question seek to dissociate themselves from. On the other hand, *filantropi* is viewed as much more beneficial to the poor, indexing engagements that are longer term and designed to have a lasting impact on poverty reduction. It is no coincidence then that several zakat organisations have been seeking to develop new areas of intervention and, without abandoning their previous programmes of poverty relief, they have been more readily orientating themselves to community development and empowerment. Community empowerment is carried out though running well-equipped schools and hospitals, dispensing loans for small businesses, establishing cooperatives and micro-enterprises, providing business training and in some cases even advocating on behalf of the poor for policy changes such as maintaining fuel subsidies and for better legal protections for Indonesian migrant workers abroad. Here we are certainly a long way from classical jurisprudence for innovative programmes such as these have been scrutinised by the agencies' own *syariah*-compliance boards and evince new kinds of jurisprudential reasoning.

The deployment of English loan words has far-reaching consequences, some of which I want to highlight here. One of the implications of using the term *filantropi* is that of aligning Islamic zakat practice with standards and values that are assumed to be universal and transcendent, shared by all humanity and thus, independent of historical, theological and cultural contingencies. In this way, the differences between zakat and Christian ελεημοσύνη (Greek, alms, mercy, pity) or Buddhist *dāna* (Sanskrit, selfless giving, un-attachment, letting go) are taken to be differences of degree rather than kind. Any such practice is understood to correspond to the empirical manifestation of a transcendent moral imperative, with such imperatives assumed to be both common and widespread in all religions. Diverse enactments are therefore related to one another in the same manner the specific is tied to the general, with important differences across the spectrum relegated to matters of appearance, being merely incidental of values supposed to be pan-human and pan-religious. Despite its obvert comparative shortcomings, there are undeniable reasons for being sympathetic to such perspective: I read the resort to a universal moral code as an effort to counter stereotypes of Islam in the era of the 'war on terror' that portray it as the antithesis, if not the mortal enemy of the West. The appropriation of the term *filantropi* and the re-orientation of programmes towards community development and empowerment actively realign Islam with contemporary discourses on poverty reduction emanating from international development bodies and non-governmental organisations as respected as the World Bank, the Asia Development Bank, the United Nations, Save the Children, Oxfam and so on. According to its advocates, the term philanthropy/*filantropi* refers to a specific project of empowering the poor and the underprivileged by cultivating the skills and capacities that would enable them to reach their full potential as human beings and global citizens. Leaving aside for the moment the fact that this project amounts to an effort to govern the poor according to neoliberal tenets (see Chaps. 4, 5 and 6), a new phase in the social life of zakat in Indonesia started in the early 2000s, one in which Islamic appeals to justice have been inflected by empowerment-oriented discourses that promote democracy, good governance and a strong civil society.

Relocating zakat in what are assumed to be the universal human values has certain unintended consequences. Notwithstanding the issue that the Greek term philanthropy did originally encompass human relations with God (Constantelos 1968), in the post-Enlightenment era, it has acquired strong secular tones, referring mainly to the care men show to each other out of feelings of fellowship. In addition, in Eastern Christianity, philanthropy is embedded in a theological tradition free of legalistic coercions: as such the term implies that givers are free to choose whether (and what) to give or not, with such transfers understood as free gifts, that is the generous giving away of one's own property for the benefit of others. While the history of charity, especially the tithe, has been both long and complex in Western Christianity in medieval times (see Grell and Cunningham 1997; Borsay and Shapely 2007), the advent of the industrial revolution and the rise of capitalism have seen a return of the emphasis on volition: in the modern context the concept of philanthropy indexes the benevolence of the rich in an era of free will and extreme inequality. Such understanding is perhaps best exemplified by a section published in the *Economist* in January 2011, evocatively titled 'The Few: A Special Report on Global Leaders.' The report was published after the collapse of Lehman Brothers and during an unravelling global crisis, detailing the demographic and geographical spread as well as the makings and lifestyles of the new superrich. Significantly, the report concluded with a reminder of the responsibilities of the few, asserting that 'in democracies the elites serve the masses' both through the jobs they create and through philanthropy. It moreover encouraged the superrich to follow the examples of well-known philanthropists such as John D. Rockefeller, Andrew Carnegie and Bill Gates who, having set up their own foundations, could 'measure their success not by how much they disburse but by the return they earn on their charitable investment, measured in lives saved or improved' (2011: 20).

Such responsibilities however differ in significant ways from those entailed by zakat, something the discourse on *filantropi* obviates, obstructing differences from coming into view. Concealed is not only the voluntarist character of liberal and neoliberal practices of giving which contrast sharply with the obligatory nature of zakat, but even more the differences regarding the sets of relations people can form with objects, that is 'property.' In other words, liberal and neoliberal practices regarding generosity are permeated by conceptions of private, individual property rights which entail the forfeit of the object given. In contrast, zakat is conducted on the basis of conceptions of property and rights to it, which are significantly distinct and extremely complex to unravel. In this respect, it is important to note that zakat as seen from an alternative perspective to those privileged by current discourses in Indonesia, corresponds to a break, a cut or caesura that forms a legal requirement for the establishment of rights of possessing wealth. With respect to zakat, Sayyid Qutb, the leading member of the Egyptian Muslim Brotherhood in the 1950s and 1960s, notes that it effects the 'purification of property itself, because it means paying what is due on the property, after which its possession is legal' (2000: 162). Another important authority, Yusuf al-Qardawi concurs, writing that zakat 'is not mere charity left to the righteousness of individuals as part of their good deeds. [This is so for it] is a right of the poor in the wealth of the rich, a right decided by the true Owner of wealth, God, and imposed on those who have been given control of that wealth by Him. Zakah thus does not humble or humiliate the receiver nor it make the rich get a higher rank, ethically or socially' (2000: 23). The status of zakat as right (*hak*, from *haqq* which in Arabic also means truth, correctness, reality) indicates that a person in Islam can proceed to enjoin rights of possession and disposal of wealth in a legitimate manner only after a set portion of it has been duly transferred to its rightful owners. Such people are none other than the eight categories named in the Quran as zakat claimants, the *mustahiq*, literally those entitled to zakat. The primary category of those entitled to zakat is the destitute and the poor.

Zakat differs from philanthropic giving in that the wealth transferred is not one's own to offer (or keep) as it properly belongs to others. Adjusting our language for requisite precision demands that we speak of wealth transferred (or handed over) rather than bestowed: a *mustahiq* is not a recipient but a person entitled to that wealth. Recognition of the rights of *mustahiq* requires therefore the 'removal' (*keluarkan*) of zakat, with such act being necessary for legality to take effect: calculating the exact portion of wealth due to others and transferring it promptly provides the foundation on which all else is erected. According to this perspective, it is only the remainder one can claim to possess and dispose; it is only what remains after this process of calculation, division, partition and apportion has taken place that is legally one's to take hold of. In other words, the kinds of 'private, individual property rights' envisioned are not absolute but contingent on the performance of zakat; as such, they do not accrue automatically from the labour process, whether intellectual or manual, as political economists from Locke to Marx would have it, but follow upon zakat's division and partition, founded upon the transfer of other people's dues

(Powell 2009). Moreover, such 'property rights' are better understood within a theological context that fully acknowledges Allah as the creator of everything and of humankind as His steward.[8]

The alternative, 'counter-hegemonic' understanding of zakat as right (*hak*) however marginalised and side-lined it might be, is not totally absent from the Indonesian context: occasional reference to a particular Quranic verse attests to this.[9] The verse in question is no. 19 from *Surah Adh-Dhariyat* (the Winds); it sometimes features in conversations on the issue and in print and electronic materials promoting zakat. In 2012 it appeared in a leaflet produced by *Dompet Dhuafa*, one of Indonesia's most respected and innovative Islamic welfare bodies, with a view of promoting *zakat profesi*. The leaflet presents a visualisation of the purifying effects of zakat on zakat payers (*muzakki*), featuring the photo of a well-off nuclear family having gathered over a kitchen sink. All three members smile widely, and while looking at each other in a congratulatory manner, they wash their hands carefully. On the left side of the photo some newly rinsed vegetables are posed with humans and produce waiting, one assumes, for dinner time to come. On the other side of leaflet, verse 19 is cited in Indonesian, framing the overall message: '*Dan dalam harta-harta mereka ada hak untuk orang-orang yang memerlukan, baik yang meminta maupun yang tidak.*'[10] The English translation runs either as, 'And in their properties there was the right of the beggar [sic] who asks and the poor who does not ask others' (see The Noble Qur'an), or as, 'And in their wealth was what was due to him who asked, and him who was kept back from asking.'[11] In this highly modern portrayal of domestic harmony, zakat as the right of other people is explicitly acknowledged along with the conception that the legitimate possession and consumption of wealth is predicated on the prior deduction of zakat.

Otherwise it is simply stealing: the non-deduction and non-transfer of zakat tallies with the illegal and unlawful taking away of the property of another. In this respect we are reminded of something I noted above: if a Muslim hands over zakat, it is expected that one's wealth, business and so on will be protected and possibly multiplied by Allah; if not, they will be destroyed, get lost or vanish into thin air. Punishment for the non-deduction of zakat is not only met in the afterlife with the wealth withheld assuming the shape of a monstrous snake but has consequences in this life too with many a misfortune befalling, the decrease of wealth one enjoys been amongst them. Seen from the perspective of *hablu minallah*, the non-transfer of zakat is an affront to Allah for it amounts to avoiding submission in worship and is thus considered akin to unbelief. Yet seen from the perspective of *hablu minannaas*, it is basically a crime against the eight categories of people entitled to zakat. While the first perspective pertaining to sin is readily repeated time and again in innumerable number of occasions that range from televised sermons to small study groups, all privileging the transcendent nature of human obligations to the divine, the second perspective that conceives zakat as relating to immanence—'And in their properties there was the right of'- and construes the failure to conduct it as stealing enjoys relatively little currency amongst both Islamic scholars and zakat activists. The latter are overall keen to construe the pursuit of socio-economic justice through zakat either as a matter of philanthropic giving or advocate for state enforcement of Islamic law, effectively insisting on the a priori separation of haves from have-nots and of rulers from ruled. The strength of both discourses, their proliferation across the social body of the nation, and their elaboration in numerous vistas in recent years has been accomplished at the expense of the immanence thesis of zakat as right which remains relatively unappreciated and undervalued.

Putting immanence at the centre of our understanding demands the articulation of a new ground for enacting and conceptualising sociality. Here are some notes towards this task: normally zakat is owed when a certain threshold of value (*nisab*) is reached, with *nisab* currently calculated to correspond to 85 grammes of 24 carat gold. Zakat is to be transferred either immediately as in the case of agriculture produce, following upon the harvest and before the crop reaches one's barn, or within the time period marked by the passing of a full lunar year (*haul*) as in the case of the proceeds of commerce. In both occasions two distinct categories of persons, the *mustahiq* and the *muzakki*, have rights to the new wealth ('growth') generated with each category entitled to a portion of it by divine decree. In the case of immediate division, the crop is instantly cut into two parts. This act differentiates wealth into an inside and an outside, producing a fixed share, which is one's own, and a share belonging to others. In the case of the division pertaining to the full year rule (*haul*), the parting is postponed for a considerable length time. During this interval, it is difficult and indeed impossible to differentiate between what is one's own and what belongs to others; this is a time when the boundaries between the self and other have been displaced in favour of a zone of amorphous inter-involvement and fluid co-implication. According to this reading of zakat practice, the distinction between the self and the other is set to emerge subsequently and consequently to wealth's division and the conduct of zakat.

Along with the under-appreciation of conceptual difficulty and complexity, what is also missing from due recognition in contemporary Indonesian discourses is the dependency of those owing zakat to those to whom zakat is owed. For the *muzakki*'s salvation in the hereafter and their fate in this world depends to a certain extent upon the readiness and willingness of the *mustahiq* to accept and receive the wealth transfer. It is only on condition of such acceptance that the wealthy can safely take possession of the remaining wealth generated, enjoy and pass it to their kin in a way that is legitimate and, equally importantly, see it multiply. Construing zakat as debt owed rather than as gift donated or an obligation in need of state enforcement has important implications for it reverses the positionalities the discourse on *filantropi* generates: the *muzakki* can no longer assume the position of the 'giver' or 'donor,' the social distinctions involved are duly reconstituted and imagined anew, the *mustahiq* are understood to render a service by accepting zakat and as such they come to occupy a position of distinction vis-à-vis zakat payers. While zakat activists in Indonesia are careful to stress that transferring zakat to the destitute and the poor has to be done in such a way that their pride is not injured and their feelings are not hurt, not deriding them for their condition or in any way blaming them for their poverty, they nevertheless shy away from going as far as al-Ghazali. A prominent twelfth-century Islamic scholar, al-Ghazali in his magisterial study titled 'Revival of the Religious Sciences,' explicitly commends at length on the significance of such reversals, writing

> Actually the [*muzakki*] should deem himself a beneficiary and the poverty-stricken, by virtue of accepting his [zakat] which is due to God, his benefactor. For in this lie man's justification and his salvation from Hell-fire. Had the poverty-stricken declined to accept his [zakat], man would have remained under the obligation to zakat. It is his duty therefore to acknowledge that he is under the obligation to the poverty stricken who has made his hand substitute of God in receiving the dues [which man owes to] God. (1966: 37)[12]

Exclusive Views

In New Order Indonesia, widespread considerations regarding poverty and acute anxieties regarding the poor surfaced at a time when the state-led development programmes initiated in the 1970s, improved the overall economy, creating new sources of wealth. The latter contributed in turn to the formation of a new middle class comprising of educated urban professionals, most of who were *pribumi* ('native') Muslims. In this context, a new discourse on zakat was articulated: this discourse was as much as the outcome of concerns over new forms of inequality taking hold in the country, as a by-product of a new wave of Islamic consciousness coming to fruition and serving both to underpin claims to distinction and to reinforce the legitimacy of the new wealth the new middle class commanded. In the first instance, zakat came to be re-conceptualised not only as part of an annual ritual performed so as to bring the faithful closer to Allah, but also as a social duty necessary for the maintenance of social peace, essential for the promotion of socio-economic justice and a means for bringing a corrupt state to account. From the late-1990s onwards, as a result of the fall of the New Order, amidst calls for *reformasi* and the creation of a democratic polity, a vibrant civil society and the empowerment of the poor, zakat came to be seen in new light, reconstituted as a gift generously bestowed by the well-off to those less fortunate. The discourse on zakat as philanthropy tied zakat's conduct to the personal circumstances of individual believers, making personal piety the single-most important reason propelling its performance. During the same period however, a distinct orientation to matters of the faith highlighted that for zakat to meet its potential regarding the alleviation of poverty, its practice had to be promoted, protected and enforced by a reformed Indonesian state. Such state, the Islamist discourse claimed, had to be actively created on the basis of a concerted effort (political, economic and civic) of embedding *syariah*—'Islamic law'-in the national statute, with the transition to a post-New Order Indonesia providing the best opportunity possible for this to occur. In this regard, certain activists and intellectuals advocated for the state-in-the-making to be officially and legally responsible for the collection, management and disbursement of zakat, calling for penalties to be imposed on *muzakki* who failed to honour their obligation (see Chap. 3).

The periodisation of zakat practice I have offered in this chapter serves to emphasise important shifts in its social life in Indonesia in the past fifty years. Despite its divine origination, zakat does not form a timeless constant. Rather its practice is subject to historical breaks and discontinuities with important points of transition in-between. Taking such periodisation with its shifts and thresholds into account has allowed me to bring into sharper focus a route to justice that is yet to be traversed. Such route is intimately bound up with issues and concerns which if not altogether suppressed from public discourses, endure mostly at the margins and are difficult to grasp, articulate and raise from within the limits set by dominant discourses. In contrast to the prominence afforded to zakat as a matter of personal piety, itself tied to individual consciousness, or a duty to Allah that requires the intervention of the state to be implemented, the deconstructive account I offered here has highlighted that which remains unelaborated and un-distinguished in contemporary discourses: the view of zakat as the right of ***mustahiq*** and a debt owed by the ***muzakki*** occupies the place of the element actively repressed. The discursive inattention to and political obviation of claiming zakat as right is partly related to understandings of Islam as a religion of transcendence: both sides of the debate, that is, both philanthropists and statists, conceive of relations between Allah and (wo)man as bound up with a series of obligations and promises. In this regard, the promise of salvation in exchange for strict compliance with the divine commandments is the most important. Statists and philanthropists differ only in relation to the agents each side entrusts with ensuring obedience: while statists call upon the legal apparatus of the state to deliver submission to divine will, philanthropists rely mostly on guilt, bad conscience and remorse. What is sacrificed on the altar of promise and obligation is the potential offered by a view of zakat as right: the unqualified, a priori immanence of alterity along with the ultimate dependency of the dominant on the dominated are studiously excluded from coming into view, becoming blocked from turning actual.

I return to such potentiality, figuring out what it entails, in the penultimate section of the book (Chap. 7). In the next chapter, I proceed to delve deeper into the clash between proponents of zakat as gift and those who wish to see greater state involvement in zakat administration through a discussion of the profound changes in the regulatory landscape of zakat undertaken in the immediate aftermath of the New Order's collapse and as part of the rising Islamisation of Indonesian society. I focus on a series of disputes surrounding the passing of the current zakat law (Zakat Management Law 2011, no. 23) which culminated in a judicial review at the constitutional court, itself supported by several LAZ. In the next chapter, I also go on to discuss two specific LAZ with the requisite amount of detail and level of depth. My endeavour is not related to taking sides: it should be already apparent that I am utterly cold to either 'option'. What I am primarily concerned with is to chart the consequences legal, technical and organisational instruments and arraignments have on time, its synthesis and passing. What is always at stake in such disputes is the future direction of affairs: legal, technical and organisational mechanisms and procedures are deployed with the explicit aim of intervening in the flow of time, shaping its outlines in highly determinate ways.

Notes

1. As Nietzsche puts it, 'there is only a seeing from a perspective, only a "knowing" from a perspective' (2003: 86).
2. These are mentioned in *Surat At-Taubah*, verse 60. For contemporary understandings of the categories concerned see Fauzia (2013: 234), commonly they are the destitute, the poor, the zakat collectors, new converts, slaves, debtors, those advancing God's cause and the wayfarers.
3. N. Madjid explicitly critiqued the idea of an Islamic state which he found to correspond to the sacralisation of a human institution and advocated for the 'compatibility' of Islamic and democratic values, see Madjid (2001).
4. On *maslaha* as a principle of Islamic jurisprudence and its relevance for the reformist movement, see Hallaq (2001).
5. See *fatwa* Number 3, Year 2003, on *Zakat Penghasilan* in *Himpunan* 2003: 87. The edict contains no guidance as to whether *zakat profesi* follows upon completion of *haul*, the customary one-year period that applies to commercial activities, and/or whether it is acceptable for it to proceed on the basis of automatically deducted monthly payments, as is commonly practiced by many institutions and professionals in Indonesia.
6. Zakat's validity as an act of worship depends on the requisite intention, with the person liable having to name the transfer as such. Some jurists prefer the intention to be declared silently, rather than openly, so as to spare the recipient from embarrassment. When zakat is transferred to a collector (*amil*) the *niat* is stated openly and accompanied by a bilateral declaration of offer and acceptance (*ijab kabul*) that marks all *syariah*-approved contracts, inclusive of marriage, as valid.
7. Mas'udi currently serves as commissioner (2015–2020) at BAZNAS—*Badan Amil Zakat Nasional*—the central government institution of zakat management. BAZNAS' powers were significantly augmented as the result of Law on Zakat Management No. 23, 2011. See Chap. 2.
8. Islam, Abdul-Rauf writes, 'protects and endorses the personal right to own what one may freely gain, through legitimate means. It is a sacred right. Yet human ownership is tempered by the understanding that everything, in the last analysis, belongs to God. What appears to be ownership is in fact a matter of trusteeship' (1984: 19). In this regard, it is important to add that wealth in Islam is 'posited as a component of man's trial on earth' (Turner 2006: 63), amounting to a temptation and test of faith: whether it leads to salvation or ruin depends on how one uses the wealth in one's possession.
9. On the side-lines of their treatises, both Rais (1987) and Hafidhuddin (2002) recognise zakat as right, with Rais cautioning his audience to 'remember that what we have so far paid as zakat belongs entirely to the poor. It is totally their right whether they use the moneys to buy nutritious

food, pay fees for study, buy clothing, or fulfil other urgent needs' (1987: 61). Similarly, for Hafidhuddin (2002: 9) zakat as *hak* enjoys the status of 'clear determination' (*ketetapan yang bersifat pasti*) in the Quran, but curiously he refrains from exploring the full implications of such observation.

10. Go to http://ahadees.com/arabic-surah-51-60.html for the Arabic text and expert recitation.
11. See http://www.theonlyquran.com/quran/Az-Zariyat/English_EH_Palmer/?ayat=1&pagesize=0
12. The quote is from *Kitab Asrar al-Zakah* which is the fifth book of the first quarter of the larger study entitled, *Ihya' 'Ulum Al-Din. Kitab Asrar al-Zakah* has been translated by Nabih Amin Faris as The Mysteries of Almsgiving [sic] (1966).

Bibliography

Abdul-Rauf, Mohammad. 1984. *A Muslim's Reflections on Democratic Capitalism*. Washington, DC: American Enterprise Institute for Public Policy Research.

Abubakar, Irfan, and Chaider S. Bamualim. 2006. *Filantropi Islam and Keadilan Sosial*. Ciputat: Centre for the Study of Religion and Culture.

Al-Ghazali, Abu Hamid Mohammad ibn Mohammad. 1966. *The Mysteries of Almsgiving*. Lahore: Sh. Muhammad Ashraf.

Al-Qardawi, Yusuf. 2000. *Fiqh Al-Zakat: A Comparative Study of Zakat Regulations and Philosophy in the Light of the Qu'ran and the Sunna*. Vol. 1 & 2. Jeddah: Scientific Publishing Centre King Abdulaziz University.

Bamualim, Chaider, et al., eds. 2006. *Islamic Philanthropy and Social Development in Contemporary Indonesia*. Ciputat: Centre for the Study of Religion and Culture.

Benthall, Jonathan. 1999. Financial Worship: The Quranic Injunction to Almsgiving. *Journal of the Royal Anthropological Institute (N.S.)* 5 (1): 27–42.

Borsay, Anne, and Peter Shapely, eds. 2007. *Medicine, Charity, and Mutual Aid: The Consumption of Health and Welfare in Britain, c. 1550–1950*. Aldershot: Ashgate.

Buchori, Abdusshomad. 2011. *Zakat: Sebuah Potensi yang Terlupakan*. Surabaya: BAZ Jatim.

Constantelos, Demetrios. 1968. *Byzantine Philanthropy and Social Welfare*. Rutgers: Rutgers University Press.

Derrida, Jacques. 1997. *Of Grammatology*. Trans. Gayatri Chakravorty Spivak. Baltimore: John Hopkins University Press.

Economist. 2011. The Few: A Special Report on Global Leaders. January 22.

Effendy, Bahtiar. 2003. *Islam and the State in Indonesia*. Singapore: Institute of Southeast Asian Studies.

El-Gamal, Mahmood. 2006. *Islamic Finance: Law, Economics, and Practice*. Cambridge: Cambridge University Press.

Fauzia, Amelia. 2013. *Faith and the State: A History of Islamic Philanthropy in Indonesia*. Leiden: Brill.

Feener, Michael. 2007. *Muslim Legal Thought in Modern Indonesia*. Cambridge: Cambridge University Press.

Grell, Ole Peter, and Andrew Cunningham, eds. 1997. *Healthcare and Poor Relief in Protestant Europe: 1500–1600*. London: Routledge.

Hafidhuddin, Didin. 2002. *Zakat dalam Perekonomian Modern*. Jakarta: Gema Insani.

Hallaq, Wael. 2001. *Authority, Continuity, and Change in Islamic Law*. Cambridge: Cambridge University Press.

Hefner, Robert. 2000. *Civil Islam: Muslims and Democratization Indonesia*. Princeton: Princeton University Press.

Jahar, Asep Saepudin. 2006. The Clash of Muslims and the State: Waqf and Zakat in Post-Independence Indonesia. *Studia Islamika* 13 (3): 353–395.

Kuran, Timur. 2004. *Islam and the Mammon: The Economic Predicaments of Islamism*. Princeton: Princeton University Press.

Kurniawati, H., ed. 2005. *Muslim Philanthropy. Potential and Reality of Zakat in Indonesia. Survey Results in Ten Cities*. Depok: PIRAC/Ford Foundation.

Latief, Hilman. 2012. *Islamic Charities and Social Activism: Welfare, Dakwah and Politics in Indonesia*. PhD Thesis, Utrecht University.

———. 2013. Islam and Humanitarian Affairs: The Middle Class and New Patterns of Islamic Activism. In *Islam in Indonesia: Contrasting Images and Interpretations*, ed. J. Burhanudin and Kees van Dijk. Amsterdam: Amsterdam University Press.

———. 2014. Contesting Almsgiving in Post-New Order Indonesia. *American Journal of Islamic Social Sciences* 31 (1): 16–50.

Liddle, William. 1996. The Islamic Turn in Indonesia: A Political Explanation. *Journal of Asian Studies* 55 (3): 613–634.

Madjid, Nurcholish. 2001. Potential Islamic Doctrinal Resources for the Establishment and Appreciation of the Modern Concept of Civil Society. In *Islam and Civil Society in Southeast Asia*, ed. M. Nakamura, S. Siddique, and B. Omar Farouk. Singapore: Institute of Southeast Asian Studies.

Mas'udi, Masdar Farid. 1991. *Agama Keadilan: Risalah Zakat (Pajak) dalam Islam*. Jakarta: P3M.

———. 2005. *Pajak itu Zakat: Uang Allah untuk Kemaslahatan Rakyat*. Bandung: Mizan.

Nietzsche, Friedrich. 2003. *The Genealogy of Morals*. New York: Dover Publications.

Powell, Russell. 2009. Zakat: Drawing Insights for Legal Theory and Economic Policy from Islamic Jurisprudence. *University of Pittsburgh Tax Review* 7 (43): 43–101.

Qutb, Sayyid. 2000. *Social Justice in Islam*. Kuala Lumpur: Islamic Book Trust.

Rais, Amien Muhammad. 1987. *Cakrawala Islam antara Cita dan Fakta*. Bandung: Mizan.

———. 1998. *Tauhid Sosial: Formula Menggempur Kesenjangan*. Bandung: Mizan.

Ricklefs, Merle. 2012. *Islamisation and Its Opponents in Java: A Political, Social, Cultural and Religious History, c. 1930 to Present*. Singapore: National University of Singapore Press.

Salim, Arskal. 2008. *The Shift in Zakat Practice in Indonesia: From Piety to an Islamic Socio-Political- Economic System*. Chiang Mai: Silkworm Books.

Scott, James. 1987. Resistance without Protest and without Organisation: Peasant Opposition to Zakat in Malaysia and the Christian Tithe. *Comparative Studies in Society and History* 29 (3): 417–452.

Turner, Colin. 2006. Wealth as an Immortality Symbol in the Qur'an: A Reconsideration of the māl/amwāl Verses. *Journal of Quranic Studies* 8 (3): 58–83.

Warde, Ibrahim. 2010. *Islamic Finance in the Global Economy*. Edinburgh: Edinburgh University Press.

Weir, T.H., and A. Zysow. 2012. Sadaka. In *Encyclopaedia of Islam, Second Edition*, ed. P. Bearman, Th. Bianquis, C.E. Bosworth, E. van Donzel and W.P. Heinrichs. Consulted online on 10 November 2018. https://doi.org/10.1163/1573-3912_islam_COM_0956

Zysow, Aaron. 2012. Zakāt. In *Encyclopaedia of Islam, Second Edition*, ed. P. Bearman, Th. Bianquis, C.E. Bosworth, E. van Donzel and W.P. Heinrichs. Consulted online on 10 November 2018. https://doi.org/10.1163/1573-3912_islam_COM_0282

CHAPTER 3

Justifying Law

In Indonesia, the tensions inherent in the '*zakat* movement' (*gerakan zakat*) between proponents of deep state involvement and direct enforcement and those activists propagating the achievement of socio-economic justice (*keadilan*) through the cultivation of social mindedness, especially amongst the country's economically better-off Muslims, came to a head in the early to mid-2010s. After several years of deliberation, in late 2011, a new zakat law was passed in the House of People's Representatives (Law No. 23/2011). In the name of justice and progress, the new law sanctioned a radical revamping of the organisational structures already in place for administering zakat in the country, institutionalising a hierarchy amongst zakat management bodies, through awarding key coordinating and regulatory functions to state bodies, making BAZNAS (*Badan Amil Zakat Nasional*, National Zakat Management Agency), a 'non-structural' arm of the government, the centrepiece around which the new zakat architecture would revolve. The new law caused profound distress to many civil society–based zakat management organisations (Fauzia 2013; Susetyo 2018): the latter felt that their roles in turning zakat into a public concern and their successes with community empowerment and justice through promoting the faith and implementing pro-poor interventions were actively jeopardised and severely undermined by the new law.

The majority of civil society–based zakat organisations had come to existence in the later years of the New Order—and/or immediately following its downfall in 1998–at a time when a rising Islamic consciousness

K. Retsikas, *A Synthesis of Time*,
https://doi.org/10.1007/978-3-030-34933-2_3

amongst the urban, educated elites and an acute crisis at the level of the governing oligarchy had brought about a significant rapprochement between the state and Muslim interests (Effendy 2003; Hefner 2000; Bruinessen 2013). This realignment was subsequently strengthened, especially during the Habibie government (1998–1999), when the reformation of the Indonesian polity and the instituting of new standards of democracy, accountability and transparency went hand in hand with various efforts at creating a vibrant civil society, most often than not, through the implementation of Islamic values broadly conceived. As several commentators have shown, in the course of the 1990s, the movement for 'Islamic renewal' (*gerakan pebaharuan Islam*) that figures such as Nurcholish Madjid and Munawir Sjadzali initiated back in the 1970s in an effort to revitalise both the faith and the nation (see Chap. 2), achieved considerable political prominence: the foundation of the Indonesian Association of Muslim Intellectuals (ICMI) in 1990, the compilation of Islamic law in 1991 and the establishment of the first Islamic bank in 1991 were amongst the early signs of the ascendancy of Islamic legal and economic solutions to the challenges faced by a developing nation. Such ascendancy was given further impetus by the Asian financial crisis of 1997: the crisis marked a sudden downturn in the economic fortunes of the country, with the rupiah losing much of its value against the US dollar, factories laying off staff, prices of basic goods rocketing sky high and Indonesia's population of poor increasing dramatically in a short period of time. Due to the pressures the Asian financial crisis generated, the New Order collapsed: the spur towards *reformasi* and the increased assertion of Islamic identity meant that zakat as a *syariah*-compliant instrument for delivering assistance to the masses came at that particular historical juncture to be appreciated with a new found urgency.

The introduction of Law No. 38/1999 on Zakat Administration by the Habibie government marked the very first time a comprehensive bill regulating zakat had been inserted in the statute book of the country. Up to that point, state intervention in the administration of zakat had been kept to a minimum, leaving zakat largely a matter for religious figures to advise and admonish, and individual Muslims free to heed or ignore. Whether to pay zakat or not, and whether to pay it directly to beneficiaries of their choice or channel it through socio-religious institutions was mostly an individual matter. Despite the fact that since achieving independence in 1949, there had been several attempts to impose on Muslims the obligation to implement *syariah*, the Indonesian state of both the Soekarno and

Suharto periods had positioned itself staunchly against such outcome, identifying itself as neither a secular nor a theocratic state—its ideological principles of *Pancasila* included 'belief in one and only God,' without however specifying Him by name. While this characterisation remains still valid today, a series of legal reforms instituted especially in the 1990s, the 1999 zakat statute included, marked a significant break in the sense that the Indonesian state increasingly assumed for itself the responsibility of legislating Islam. Creating and enshrining in positive law a national system for administering zakat was a manifestation of a new dynamism in the relation between the state and Islam, the fall of the New Order precipitated. As Lindsey puts it, from the 1990s onwards, a new pattern began emerging in Indonesia, whereby 'the state is responding to pressure from Muslim groups to revise and expand the scope of shari'a but usually doing so in a way that keeps Islamic legal traditions within the formal legal and administrative framework of the state' (2012: 3).

According to law makers and members of the national 'zakat movement,' the 1999 and 2011 zakat statutes correspond to legal instruments for making time pass, delivering justice (***keadilan***): it is by means of instituting a break away from patterns of the past deemed problematic, detrimental or simply undesirable that an alternative future is made to come about as a more prosperous and just version of the present. Both statutes sit alongside a variety of associated tools such as presidential decisions, governmental regulations, guidelines and so on.[1] They are all explicitly deployed as a special set of apparatus geared to splitting time open, making the present pass, bringing about a brighter, fairer future. The present the 1999 zakat law endeavoured to make pass was steeped in a multidimensional crisis engulfing Indonesia: the crisis was equally political, economic and moral. Overcoming this crisis, its uncertainties, trauma and violence, was an objective shared by both representatives of the state, especially the Ministry of Religion that initiated proceedings, and existing zakat organisations. The time-making capacities of the law, which channels the direction the future takes through approving, recognising, and encouraging certain types of conduct while prohibiting, repressing or simply discouraging others, was readily apparent to the zakat activists that sought and welcomed the application of state regulation. State intervention justified itself on the grounds of furthering the religiosity (Islam) of the populace and assisting in the delivery of socio-economic justice: the statute opens with stating its purpose as enhancing the state's ability in assisting Muslim citizens perform their religious duties, that is conducting zakat worship, while at the same time promoting social justice through putting in place a system for collecting, managing and distributing zakat that will be of direct benefit to the poor and the needy (see also Jahar 2006: 368). The statute, in other words, constituted zakat as much as a personal, religious issue as a matter of national importance; concurrently, it promised the enactment of justice as hinging on successfully lifting people out of poverty, linking such endeavour back to the dimension of zakat as a financial asset of considerable, untapped value.

The necessity for regulating the administration of zakat was understood to stem from realising zakat's full potential as a source of funds to improve the social security of disadvantaged citizens. In this regard, the statute envisioned access to and management of such a national asset to require an exercise in institution building: the 1999 law established two new categories of institutions, the state's own ***Badan Amil Zakat*** or BAZ and private ***Lembaga Amil Zakat*** or LAZ, and recognised them as best qualified for administering zakat. The law did not prohibit in any shape or form systems of zakat collection and distribution prevalent so far in Indonesia, that is the 'traditional' system that relied on informal, temporary mosque committees and on personal, direct distribution to zakat claimants. However, the new statute did provide the required state recognition, legal support and regulatory encouragement for zakat to become the concern of formal, modern, specialist institutions, either government-sponsored or private/civil society–based, directing them to administer their resources in a professional, transparent manner and in full accord with modern managerial standards and techniques (Alfitri 2006; Fauzia 2013; Salim 2008). At the same time, it enshrined in positive law the compulsory status zakat enjoys for Muslims of required means in Islamic law; yet it rendered such recognition largely inoperative as the law shied away from imposing any sanctions on those who failed to comply, something that advocates for the state enforcement of zakat found disappointing.[2]

While the 1999 zakat law was the product of a certain convergence, articulated at a critical time of the nation, between the interests of the state, especially the Ministry of Religion, and the interests of those representing zakat amongst civil organisations, the Zakat Administration Law of 2011 marked a significant disagreement, with a very public fallout taking place between key institutional actors. Both the law's drafting process and its introduction in late 2011 was accompanied by uncharacteristically heated debates between those pro and against the content of the new regulations, leading eventually to a request for a judicial review at the Constitutional Court by many prominent LAZ (Fauzia 2013; Susetyo 2018). The latter felt that the new law not only diminished their role significantly but also 'put their very existence in peril' (*ingin mematikan LAZ*). At the heart of the matter were a series of clauses stipulating greater centralisation of zakat administration at the hands of state organs, BAZ and especially BAZNAS (established in 2001 by Presidential Decision) with the latter acquiring extra-supervisory and coordinating powers. The move towards greater state control was accompanied by the imposition of new, stricter requirements for the operation of LAZ which were required to form Islamic mass organisations (*organisasi masyarakat Islam*) as well as the imposition of stiff penalties on unlicensed zakat collectors such as mosque zakat committees (Salim 2015; Halimatusa'diyah 2015). The decade that separated the introduction of the two statutes saw public awareness of zakat rising, with its increasing institutionalisation effectively turning zakat into a financial resource the size of which could be counted, projected and relied upon. Bamualim (2009: 82), for example, estimates that annual zakat payments were in the region of 19.3 trillion rupiah, or more than 2 billion US dollars, for 2009, while a study undertaken by Islamic economists put the potential of zakat for the entire country significantly higher, at 82.70 trillion rupiah, and 91 trillion rupiah for the years 2009 and 2011, respectively (Firdaus et al. 2012). In the early 2010s, competition for control of this important source of revenue publicly pitted those favouring zakat's greater centralisation at the hands of government against those who conceived it as a community affair, requiring light regulation, and management by trusted civil organisations, both of the formal, professional and informal, temporary variety. Oftentimes, the fault line between the two sides of the debate also concerned the primary meaning each attributed to zakat: while those siding with greater centralisation placed emphasis on zakat as a *syariah*-imposed obligation and sought to actively involve the Indonesian state in its enforcement, the latter insisted on zakat as a philanthropic, voluntary transfer that is a matter of individual piety and care for the plight of others less fortunate to make.[3]

The post-New Order state's regulatory attention to zakat and the latter's enclosure within a bureaucratic framework, itself promoting repeated institution building and advanced managerial expertise was an intervention justified, as I have already noted, on the basis of its promotion of socio-economic justice (*keadilan*) and popular welfare (*kemaslahatan rakyat*). From a scholarly perspective, such rhetorical claims however well-intentioned might be, can't and should not be taken for granted; instead they should be scrutinised and problematised for the effects they have on precisely the very terms they assume as principal and presuppose as fundamental. In this particular instance, at stake is the state's equation of law with justice, the means–ends equivalence the state and its allies construct between the necessity for statutory regulation and the persistent, diffuse demand for *keadilan*. Scholarly problematisation, it is very important to point out, is not only about evaluating the contents of specific statute, the substance of this or the other law; it does not simply concern whether this or that law is fair, impartial, disinterested. Rather it is about law with capital L, and concerns the very kernel of its making, arrangement and deployment. The fact that LAZ conceived the 2011 zakat law to be 'unjust' (*tidak adil*), and actively resisted its application, is of secondary importance. The matter at hand has to do with the tautological nature of law, its circularity and reiterative attitude. One way to demonstrate this is by calling attention to the inevitability of LAZ seeking protection from the 2011 law only by means of appealing to law. The unavoidability of pursuing justice through petitioning yet another law-making body—the Constitutional Court, the highest judicial authority in Indonesia and an integral part of the state—effectively embeds justice, any sense and conception of it, firmly within law-making. The absence of an external point of view to law guarantees such outcome. At the same time, the inevitability in question turns law, that is, the very process of law's ongoing fabrication, into a perpetually self-fulfilling and ceaselessly self-perpetuating exercise. Governing by means of the liberal art of the rule-of-law, as Indonesia resembles no longer anything close to an authoritarian regime, entails encasing justice in the very self-making of the law.

In his magisterial '*Force of Law*' (1990), and subsequently in his '*Specters of Marx*' (1994), Derrida performs a very significant uncoupling of justice from its entanglements with law (*droit*).[4] This destructive exercise is conducted on the basis of the disparate, opposing even, methods through which law and justice synthesise time, each proceeding to organise the temporal in its own, distinct manner. To put it as simply as possible, while justice for Derrida corresponds to the figure of the ghost whose appearance is always already untimely, eluding thus the present and exceeding any form of presence/identity/certainty, law is grounded on the incessant reiteration in the living present of an event that has already taken place in a remote, almost inaccessible past whence its happening involved, quite significantly, the outpouring of a foundational violence. This very original act of violence is both reiterated in the living present by the law's ongoing application—law amounts to little if not enforced after all—and, at the same time, is obviated, 'mystified,' prevented from surfacing in all its naked glory by means of law's constant appeal to justice. However, according to Derrida, justice as a pure concept, unencumbered by law, belongs neither to the living present nor to the past: it comes from the future, a future forever deferred, remaining endlessly to-come (*á venir*). Writes, Derrida

> Law (*droit*) is not justice. Law is the element of calculation, and it is just there be law, but justice is incalculable, it requires us to calculate the incalculable; and aporetic experiences are the experiences, as improbable as they are necessary, of justice, that is to say of moments in which the decision between just and unjust is never insured by a rule. (1990: 947)

The aporetic experience of justice for Derrida is guaranteed not by law, either of the human or divine variety, but by figures such as ghosts which exist in the gap between something and nothing, actuality and non-actuality, life and death. Their appearance is always untimely as it can't be foretold, sanctioned or regulated by any code. Ghosts such as that faced by Shakespeare's Hamlet, the Prince of a rotten State, are 'the tangible intangibility of a proper body without flesh, but still the body of some*one* as some*one* other' (1994: 6). And yet they communicate through speaking, placing urgent demands on the living, not stopping from appearing till those selected to be their addressees prove themselves equal to circumstance, raising up to meet the call for justice. The appearance of apparitions marks justice as incumbent on both a first time and its eternal repetition as forever new: 'a spectre is always a revenant. One cannot control their comings and goings because it begins *by coming back*' (1994: 11, emphasis in the original). The return of the ghost involves it tracing a curve which folds back time: it is precisely on the line of this curve that justice is articulated. The apparition has 'its provenance in what by essence has not yet come-from [*provenu*], still less come about, and which therefore remains to come. The passage of this time to the present comes from the future to go toward the past, toward the going of the gone' (1994: 28).

If justice is therefore contingent on the performance of a time synthesis that effects the overcoming of the past and the present by welcoming the future, foregrounding an openness the unknown, by contrast, law repeats a violent past in the living present while blocking all routes that might lead to the new and the other. Despite law's claims to exercise itself in the name of justice, justice is betrayed by law for law knows only of codification: whereas justice speaks to the singularity of circumstances, law addresses the universal; whereas justice is commensurate to the posing of a question that could elicit a response, law recognises only the absoluteness of a false dilemma—something is either legal or illegal, one is either guilty or innocent—and is always ready geared to passing a sentence; whereas justice is a subject-less force that comes from an-other, law stems from the self-authorised monopoly of the exercise of force. Derrida talks of a performative tautology 'structuring any foundation of law, one which performatively produces the conventions that guarantee the validity of the performative, thanks to which one gives oneself the means to decide between legal and illegal violence' (1990: 987). At the heart of such performative duplication is the repetition of a founding violence on the basis of which any claims to the monopoly of the use of force and the very authority to make the distinction between legal and illegal, draw their designation as habitual and reasonable, customary and common sense. For Derrida, past violence is at once at the origin of law—it is a violence that founds law since it cannot be justified by any a priori, pre-existing legality—and is endlessly repeated in the living present, with the latter being organised around the law's ongoing reign as arbiter of values. The very violence of an exceptional past event envelops the present as much as the future, encasing them to its tight embrace: unable to break with it, the present and the future are destined to conserve the past to infinity: 'It belongs to the structure of fundamental violence that it calls for the repetition of itself and founds what out to be conserved, conservable, promised to heritage and tradition, to be shared. [....] Conservation in its turn refounds, so that it can conserve what it claims to found' (1990: 997).

A Growing Network

If for Derrida justice is impossible to name, define, pronounce for it is situated beyond the horizon of knowledge, coming from the direction of a future which content is as much unanticipated as is continually renewed, for Nasim Setiawan, the communication and resources director of *Pondok Infak Mulia*, one of Indonesia's most prominent and innovative LAZ, the contours of justice and the apparatus necessary for its pursuit are to a large degree already given, specified in the letter and spirit of the law, secular as well as religious. The astonishingly rich variety of programmes *Pondok*

Infak Mulia has put in place, along with the internal structures the organisation has itself developed over the years so as to invent, implement, support and revise, in equal measure, its intervention in Indonesian society, aim towards a single objective: the transformation of ***mustahik*** into ***muzakki***, that is, the conversion of zakat claimants, primarily the poor and the needy, into people affluent enough so as to qualify for the payment of zakat, is a political project which anticipates a future full of promise. Nasim explained that

> In Islam what matters is that there is balance (*keseimbangan*) between rich and poor, so zakat is about the distribution of funds from the rich to the poor, about justice (*keadilian*). One is free to pursue riches as long as one also commits to the principle of zakat. The contemporary understanding of the economy places less emphasis on production and more on balanced distribution, which is what zakat is about. The obligation placed on companies to pay corporate social responsibility is proof of a new direction in economic thinking. However there is no place in the world today which uses zakat as an alternative to conventional economics. This has yet to emerge and we have to support its coming into being.

Pondok Infak Mulia (PIM) came into being in Jakarta in July 1993 and its founding is inseparable from the establishment in the early 1990s of the Association of Indonesian Muslim Intellectuals (ICMI), *Bank Muamalat*, the first Islamic bank in Indonesia, and *Republika*, a daily newspaper functioning as the mouthpiece of ICMI and closely allied with New Order authorities in its last years in power (see Rahardjo 2003). For Nasim, all four institutions were part of a single *gerakan Islam moderen*, a movement for a modern Islam, itself representing urban Muslims equipped with 'a new consciousness' (*kesadaran baru*). Despite the fact that its members had not been educated in traditional Islamic subjects—in their majority, they were graduates of non-faith-based institutions, having studied secular disciplines such as engineering, law and accountancy—they were nevertheless, Nasim continued, 'committed to Islam as an alternative for providing a guide to the challenges of modern life,' political as much as economic. With ICMI and *Republika* providing the required intellectual leadership in associational life, and *Bank Muamalat* furnishing the financial grounds for the pursuit of *syariah*-compliant profit, that is a profit free from interest and unwarranted speculation,[5] *Pondok Infak Mulia* (PIM)'s mission was to showcase the potential of zakat, with the latter reformed and re-interpreted in such a way so as it is capable of delivering Indonesians from present dearth and poverty into a future of plenty.

Originally PIM was legally constituted as a *yayasan* (foundation): its philanthropic mission involving the collection, management and distribution of *syariah* funds for public benefit.[6] Along with zakat of both *fitrah* and *maal* varieties (see Chap. 2), PIM did engage in collecting, managing and distributing *infak*, *sedekah* and *wakaf*, something that continues to this day.[7] Jurisprudentially speaking, *sedekah* is the voluntary alms Muslims are 'strongly recommended' (*sunna mu'akkada*) to give: it is normally conceived in counter-distinction to zakat, the obligatory wealth transfer the affluent are required to perform annually as the third pillar of faith. Despite the fact that in the Quran *sedekah* entertains a wider meaning than zakat, denoting interchangeably mandatory and voluntary transfers (Weir and Zysow 2012), canonical interpretations have given rise to historical practices in which zakat is fixed by law as to the nature and value of property it applies to and the categories of people designated as its rightful recipients. Because no such legal stipulations apply to *sedekah*, the giver is free to decide who s/he will give what, how much and when. As such, *sedekah* is often couched as excess, with zakat indexing the bare minimum of requirements.[8] When *sedekah* transfers are meant to have enduring benefits for the donor as much as for the recipients, they take the legal form of *wakaf* which is often comparable to the Western institution of a charitable trust. *Wakaf* which means 'to hold' in Arabic, implies the preservation of an asset to infinity, with its deployment expected to meet a public benefit objective as stipulated by the donor in the original act of making such grant.[9] Meanwhile, *infak* which etymologically means 'to spend' is yet another form good deeds take in Islam, designating a gift given without any expectation of reward or return except for the glory of Allah. Despite the diverse nature of funds managed, it is zakat first and foremost that stood out in the PIM discourse about achieving justice as zakat corresponds to the third pillar the faith, being a fundamental part of worship individual Muslims of means are expected to perform in evidence of their faith. As can be seen in Table 3.1,[10] zakat was originally the only type of Islamic moneys the organisation collected and distributed: while its financial significance has over the years been somewhat diminished—zakat accounts for between 40% and 50% of total funds collected in recent years—it has continued to furnish the sign under which an alternative, more prosperous and pious future is actively been sought.

Table 3.1 *Pondok Infak Mulia*, breakdown of funds collected between 1993 and 2011 in Indonesian rupiah

Year[a]	*Zakat*	*Sedekah*	*Humanitarian aid*	*Wakaf*	*Project tied sedekah*	*Sacrificial offerings*	*Total exc. Sacrificial offerings*	*Grand total*
1993	87,868,209						87,868,209	87,868,209
1994	506,110,483					117,077,500	506,110,483	623,187,983
1995	291,399,230	205,236,328	690,541,674			153,249,500	1,187,177,232	1,340,426,732
1996	787,851,134	353,948,216	78,036,525			342,573,100	1,219,835,875	1,562,408,975
1997	1,018,933,664	522,783,150	218,582,275			430,357,897	1,760,299,089	2,190,656,986
1998	1,977,504,526	1,361,059,987	579,194,352			935,563,000	3,917,758,865	4,853,321,865
1999	3,442,751,636	1,328,313,124	1,728,296,172	36,358,000		1,140,993,111	6,535,718,932	7,676,712,043
2000	6,845,403,445	1,106,144,193	3,502,339,634			2,201,217,900	11,453,887,272	13,655,105,172
2001	11,773,058,922	1,792,133,856	876,350,375	50,610,000		3,646,628,805	14,492,153,153	18,138,781,958
1423 H (1/1/2002–5/11/2002)	5,931,066,781	1,240,730,747	1,616,937,148	624,364,100			9,413,098,776	9,413,098,776
1423/1424 H (6/11/2002–26/10/2003)	13,855,762,438	1,776,788,960	1,128,205,956	389,300,500		4,562,785,000	17,150,057,854	21,712,842,854
1424/1425 H (27/11/2003–14/11/2004)	15,316,930,269	2,537,865,830	496,870,191	637,983,000		4,382,985,000	18,898,649,290	23,372,634,290
1425/1426 H (15/11/2004–4/11/2005)	18,412,116,845	2,585,580,593	10,046,659,002	517,912,500		7,134,645,000	31,562,268,940	38,696,913,940
1426/1427 H (4/11/2005–22/10/2006)	20,255,341,469	5,119,961,494	13,158,470,857	1,313,559,280		8,034,890,000	39,847,333,100	47,882,223,100
1427/1428 H (23/10/2006–12/10/2007)	29,014,940,822	7,259,975,734	4,113,617,525	1,940,218,271		8,642,467,400	42,328,752,352	50,971,219,752
1428/1429 H (12/10/2007–31/9/2008)	39,126,080,688	8,714,558,350	859,406,920	1,943,495,777	10,056,980,694	10,156,840,000	60,700,522,430	70,857,362,429
1429/1430 H (1/10/2008–21/8/2009)	42,527,115,998	12,557,801,324	2,632,656,262	3,640,545,176	11,819,411,002	12,138,207,000	73,177,529,762	85,315,736,761

(*continued*)

Table 3.1 (continued)

Year[a]	*Zakat*	*Sedekah*	*Humanitarian aid*	*Wakaf*	*Project tied sedekah*	*Sacrificial offerings*	*Total exc. Sacrificial offerings*	*Grand total*
1430–1431 H (22/8/2009–9/8/2010)	57,713,538,291	8,478,578,993	9,933,845,636	9,693,591,636	16,296,236,435	16,997,624,000	102,115,791,021	119,113,415,021
1431/ 1432 H (10/8/2010–31/7/2011)	64,341,482,765	12,228,441,509	7,619,013,332	41,683,548,895	12,195,362,186	19,639,746,000	138,067,848,686	157,707,594,686
1432/1433 H (1/8/2011-ongoing 27/10/2011)	45,302,242,167	6,852,231,090	623,266,765	4,909,382,167	13,126,105,827		70,813,228,016	
TOTAL	333,225,257,616	69,169,902,338	59,279,023,835	62,471,487,135	50,367,990,347	100,657,850,213	574,513,661,321	675,171,511,534

[a]From 2002 till 2011, the organisations' accounting period changed to follow the Islamic calendar

PIM counts amongst the largest and most successful LAZ or zakat managing bodies in Indonesia: its collected funds have grown from almost 88 million rupiah in 1993 to almost 158 billion rupiah, or 17.5 million US dollars, in 2010–2011. A spectacular rate of growth is also noted in the numbers of donors: from a handful of journalists working at *Republika*, together with their friends and family, in 1993, to a total of 6547 in 2003, subsequently rising to 18,464 in 2011. According to PIM's own data, the majority of its donors are from the Greater Jakarta area, also known in Indonesia as *Jabodetabek*, an expansive area of urban sprawl surrounding Indonesia's capital city that stretches from Jakarta city centre outwards to include the regencies of Bogor and Bekasi in West Java and Tangerang in Banten. With a population of over 28 million, this region is the very beating heart of the country's economic, intellectual and administrative life where a very significant portion of the country's wealth, material as well as immaterial, is being produced and consumed. PMI's donors, in addition to being evidently pious Muslims and of a reformist/modernist inclination, are members of a fast expanding middle class. Again, according to PIM's own data, more than 50% of its donors have had university education: in addition, 45.2% are categorised by PIM as 'middle class' (*kelas menengah*) for they declare a monthly income of between 2 and 5 million rupiah per month, and a further 29.8% are considered as 'upper middle class' (*kelas menengah atas*) with monthly income between 5 and 10 million rupiah, in 2011. PIM acts not only as a huge redistributive machine that re-allocates wealth from the better-off to the poor, but also acts to transfer wealth away from the economic and bureaucratic centre to less developed regions located further away, helping thus the nation to achieve balance both in vertical and horizontal terms. Central in this endeavour is PIM's network of offices and branches: while a total of six 'service offices' (*kantor pelayanan*), all located in *Jabodetabek*, attend primarily to donors, a total of eight branches (*kantor cabang*) project PIM's vision and mission to other parts of Indonesia, where they work in collaboration with local partners, implementing appropriately tailored poverty alleviation programmes, and engaging in fund raising, albeit in a limited capacity. To such extensive network, PIM has added nine representative offices (*kantor perwakilan*) across Indonesia, and three international branches—in Hong Kong, Australia and Japan—along with a tenth representative office in Korea. The international arms of the organisation are taking advantage of Indonesian diasporic populations of students and workers, mainly domestic staff, engaging them to act not only exclusively but also interchangeably as activists, donors and recipients of support.

As one of the first organisations to spring from the Islamic movement for the reconceptualisation of zakat from an annual worship ritual to an instrument of socio-economic justice, PIM has reconfigured in a most dramatic manner the organisational apparatus through which zakat as an instrument of redistribution and a financial asset is harvested, managed and deployed. Up to the late twentieth century, the majority of *muzakki* would channel their zakat locally, either directly to recipients they personally knew or through committees, themselves attached to mosques, small prayer houses (*musollah*) and Islamic boarding schools. Such committees were of a temporary nature, effectively operating during the last three days of Ramadan, when the more widely recognised variety of zakat, *zakat fitrah*, was being transferred. Such committees were moreover staffed by senior males such as mosque administrators (*pengurus/takmir masjid/musholla*) and/or local religious figures such as *ustad* (Quranic teachers) and *kyai* (traditional Islamic scholars), on a part-time, non-professional basis. What PIM and the broader movement for zakat reform have done over the past four decades or so, is not only to popularise the notion of *zakat maal*, advocating for it to be performed as necessary supplement to *zakat fitrah*, but also for zakat and other Islamic funds to be handled by permanent institutions, applying modern management principles and equipped with internal and external oversight structures guaranteeing transparency and accountability. Such *moderen* institutions are the preferred option for they are seen as more effective, more efficient organisational vehicles, partly due to employing educated staff of various, specialist skills and partly due to the operations being of national, or even international, scale. Such competencies and scales are deemed necessary for zakat and other Islamic funds to reach their full potential: instead of functioning as short-term charitable relief, religious moneys are to spearhead an alternative, Islamic model for the long-term empowerment of the poor.

PIM has been a key advocate for such a change of paradigm in zakat management. As a leading member of *Forum Zakat* (FOZ), the national association of professional zakat management bodies, it has worked tirelessly to propagate and standardise such a model, including by means of enshrining it in the appropriate regulatory framework: two years after FOZ was established, its efforts borne fruit with the passing of Zakat Administration Law No. 23/1999. As I have already noted, the 1999 law introduced for the first time a national system of zakat collection and distribution in Indonesia by recognising two key forms of specialist, permanent institutions to deal with zakat management: the government's own *Badan Amil Zakat* or BAZ, and private *Lembaga Amil Zakat* or LAZ. Already existing zakat collection institutions affiliated with regional administrations and active in certain parts of the country, though with little success,[11] were given the mandate to fashion themselves to BAZ, while already existing private, philanthropic foundations involved in zakat collection, such as PIM, were to convert themselves into LAZ. In the eyes of the 1999 law, BAZ and LAZ which were to form at various administrative levels starting from the national down to the district, were of equal standing[12]: both BAZ and LAZ were assigned the same functions, namely to collect, distribute and utilise effectively zakat as well as *infak* and *sedekah*, 'according to the stipulations of Islamic tenets' (*sesuai dengan ketentuan agama*).[13] In the national zakat system put in place in post-New Order Indonesia, the principal authority for the direction of state policy was entrusted to the Directorate of Zakat at the Ministry of Religion: it was equipped with the mandate to formulate and implement policies, supervise BAZ and LAZ, issue respective permits and certificates, monitor and evaluate activities. To be recognised by the Directorate, LAZ had to fill an application, have a work plan, income from zakat along with *muzakki* and *mustahik* data, a system of accounting and provide a statement of willingness to be audited. In 2011, a total of 18 LAZ operating at the national level had been granted a licence, and they belonged to one of following three categories: LAZ such as *LAZNU* (*Nahdlatul Ulama*) and LAZ *Muhammadiyah* were the affiliates of large Islamic socio-religious organisations operating in the country since the 1920s, LAZ such as LAZ *BAZMA (Baituz Zakat Pertamina)* and LAZ *Yayasan Baitul Maal BRI (Bank Rakyat Indonesia)* were linked to large corporations such as the national oil company, banks and so on collecting zakat and other funds from employees, retirees and customers (see Latief 2013), and finally, LAZ such as PIM, *Surabaya Peduli Ummat* (SPU, see below) and *Dana Keadilan Indonesia* (DKI, see Chap. 4) that represent civil society organisations promoting general public welfare. According to Nasim Setiawan,

> We wanted to avoid making PIM an NGO. Instead we turned it into a *Lembaga Amil Zakat*. We wanted to stay away from the NGO label as NGOs is a tool of foreign governments, and their funding comes from abroad. In contrast, LAZ are bottom-up institutions and their funding comes from donations, from the people (*rakyat*); their orientation is to protect the people. It was the zakat law of 1999 which allowed us to claim that we are neither an NGO nor a foundation (*yayasan*) but a LAZ.

For Nasim Setiawan, a father of four young children in his mid- to late 40s with fast greying hair and a convivial smile adorning his face, the fostering of a truly reciprocal relation with the *rakyat* was of paramount concern. Amongst the unique characteristics of PIM is its internal architecture, the way PIM has been designed to deliver on its mission: PIM, Nasim continued, has been conceived so that it forms a two-way communicative connection with the *rakyat*; such connection gives it the capacity to proliferate its activities in many new directions at once, always in tune with changing circumstances, and with unparalleled speed. Meeting the challenge of designing a vehicle responsive and capable enough to react to various circumstances with the required sensitivity, promptness and ingenuity, was what the invention of a Multi-Corridor Network (*Jejaring Multi-Koridor* or JMK) has been all about, he added.

> It was one of PIM's founders who came up with the idea of a JMK shape. He did not want PIM to grow fat and big. He wanted it to be slim and consist of several parts with their own mission and vision, acting autonomously. The JMK concept is about PIM's mission and vision being pulled down (*dibetot*, Javanese, brought down) to the people; there it creates something; this something is then lifted up once again (*dipompa lagi*) so as to give birth to a new organisation of its own. JMK's purpose is to create new institutions continuously, to create new centres of virtue endlessly. In other words, PIM has created a network and each nod in this network is supported by PIM to create its own network in turn. PIM is situated at the centre, not precisely as a holding company but similar to that. And we support these other organisations of ours to form yet even more organisations. This is a cheap and winning strategy for creating a vibrant civil society.

Since 2001, PIM has established numerous institutions: each is active in a distinct domain, equipped with own director, provided with separate budget and increased levels of autonomy to plan and deliver its own specialist programmes while being supported, both financially and otherwise, with zakat and other funds, by PIM. The multiplication of organisations the Multi-Corridor Network concept has fostered over the years has been subject to careful regulation so that it keeps true to an unvarying, precise route outlining a triangle: as Nasim explained, each side of 'the triangle of empowerment' the JMK has given rise to corresponds to a specific area of intervention, with social empowerment (*pemberdayaan sosial*), economic empowerment (*pemberdayaan ekonomi*) and advocacy (*advokasi*) relating to discrete areas of an otherwise holistic approach to poverty alleviation.

The social empowerment agenda is implemented by several institutions delivering basic services to the poor and the needy inclusive of health, education and disaster relief. In 2012, the list of institutions in charge of health services included a free health clinic in Ciputat, South Tangerang and a brand new hospital in Parung, Bogor. A separate institution in charge of education provision was running three distinct programmes: a teacher training school that aims to improve teaching skills and competencies, two free-of-charge high schools dedicated to gifted pupils and a scholarship programme for underprivileged students attending state-run universities. At the same time, humanitarian assistance has been delivered to victims of earthquakes and floods throughout the country by a specialist disaster management centre offering relief in major national and local emergencies such as the Aceh tsunami of 2004 and the Merapi volcano eruption in Central Java in 2011. The centre has also delivered food aid to Afghanistan and Iraq. In the sphere of economic empowerment, separate institutions and programmes have been created to assist the poor and the needy with different aspects of securing better livelihoods, especially in the areas of capital provision, the strengthening of production and improvements in the marketing of commodities. For example, PIM is operating an agriculture institute that assists poor farmers in better managing agricultural resources, training them in the cultivation of organic foodstuffs and the tending of the rural environment in a sustainable manner. Concurrently, PIM is running a programme offering support to animal husbandry farmers and breeders in underdeveloped areas of Indonesia that includes direct livestock provision and intensive mentoring. Perhaps the most innovative and far-reaching arm of PIM in matters of economic empowerment is *Indonesia Mandiri*, an institution created to promote Islamic micro-finance as an alternative to conventional micro-finance initiates (see Chap. 5).

In the area of advocacy, PIM conducts policy review exercises, explicitly contesting government policies when it regards that they put the *rakyat* at a disadvantage, employing expert advice and organising seminars and petitions to that effect. It has also established a research institute with the objective of conducting studies into zakat with an eye towards the optimisation of its management, and has built a network with other civil society institutions both in Indonesia and abroad that led to the establishment of World Zakat Forum. Finally, it has created an organisation to offer specialist support to Indonesian migrant workers abroad who often fall victims to unscrupulous agents and forbidding employers, assisting them with legal matters and training them with the acquisition of new skills. In 2011, PIM announced the creation of *PIM Corpora*, a for-profit company modelled on the principles of social enterprise, and consisting of several divisions, including a second-hand store, a consultancy company, an Islamic micro-finance business and a construction firm, with the latter specialising in renovating public facilities such as mosques, schools and clinics, in areas affected by natural disasters. The seed capital for the company which has PIM as its majority shareholder was provided by *hak amil*: as zakat collector and distributor (*amil*) PIM considers itself, and is widely considered by others in Indonesia, as entitled to one-eighth of the zakat funds collected—*amil* is one of the eight *asnaf* or categories of zakat claimants as stipulated in the Quran.[14] The returns on investment will be dedicated for strengthening *Corpora* itself so that its businesses become sustainable in the long-term; a second, not-specified part of the profits is to be returned to PIM so as to be distributed to other categories of *mustahik*.

The treatment of zakat as a finance asset capable of being invested for the generation of future profit is the result of new jurisprudential reasoning performed by, amongst others, PIM's *syariah*-compliance board (*dewan syariah*), itself consisting of three eminent experts in Islamic jurisprudence. Such approach is of direct relevance not only to PIM's for-profit projects but is of considerable consequence to PIM's engagement with a specific category of zakat claimants. PIM understands the Quranic category *fakir*, the first amongst the eight *asnaf*, as relating to a person who possesses no wealth or assets whatsoever. Such people find themselves in absolute, urgent need. PIM helps *fakir* with what it classes as 'consumptive aid,' that is forms of assistance that meet their immediate needs for food, shelter, medicine and so on. At the same time, it understands *miskin*, the second in order of *asnaf*, to refer to a person who though possessing some wealth, assets or skills finds him/herself often in serious difficulty with ensuring that his/her needs, and those of his/her family, are meet regularly and adequately. As a result of contemporary jurisprudential reasoning, PIM assist such persons through the distribution of what is called 'productive aid,' inclusive of 'productive zakat' (*zakat produktif*). The zakat in question is distributed in the form of business capital and training sessions that aim to boost the income of poor households engaged in some form of small-scale production or trade (see Chap. 5). Of particular note is also PIM's efforts at recalibrating the meaning of *fi riqob* which corresponds to the fifth category of *mustahik* as outlined in the Quran. While classic Islamic jurisprudence interprets *fi riqob* to refer to slaves and/or bondsmen with zakat thus earmarked for buying their freedom,

PIM's *syariah* board has proceeded to widen the term's application: by means of analogical reasoning, it has included Indonesian domestic workers abroad, often subjected to exhausting and indeterminate work schedules, arbitrary wage deductions and other forms of harassment as modern instances of enslavement, sanctioning the use of zakat for the provision of support which is mainly dispensed through a specialist institution (see above). The same tendency for a broad re-interpretation of Quranic terms applies to the category of *muallaf*: strictly speaking the term, corresponding to the fourth *asnaf*, covers recent converts to Islam who experience difficulties due to having been repudiated by their families and communities. PIM however finds such understanding restrictive and insists that to qualify as the recipients of zakat, *muallaf* have to be poor (*miskin* and/or *fakir*), powerless or in some way threatened. Moreover, in full compliance with its espousal of global humanitarian standards and in promotion of an ethic of inclusivity, PIM distributes zakat to non-Muslim poor, as long as they do not pose a threat to Islam, even though the organisation fully acknowledges that assisting Indonesia's Muslim poor remains its absolute priority.

Enduring Goodness

Surabaya Peduli Ummat (SPU) is another, older organisation promoting zakat and other Islamic funds for achieving socio-economic justice (*keadilan*): it shares with PIM the mission of transforming *mustahik* into *muzakki*, empowering zakat claimants, primarily the poor and the needy, with the capacities required for turning themselves into people affluent enough so as to be eligible for the payment of zakat. As I have noted above, this is a socio-political endeavour that directs itself towards the future: its undertaking engages with the yet-to-come as a fundamental pre-occupation. The future is deemed integral in the overall exercise of seeking socio-economic justice: such justice is forthcoming, awaiting, pending. What is anticipated as just and prefigured as to-come is closely tied to the making of a promise: the promise is to be found in the programmes LAZ have developed, the mechanisms they have advanced, the tools and instruments they have created for delivering such a future. The yet-to-come is envisioned as full of monetary prosperity, general affluence and widespread piety. These are the contents of justice, its very substance. SPU is working towards making such future happen with vigour, dedication and commitment. Working towards a predetermined objective, found as is in the

Quranic injunction to zakat, means that the future in question is envisioned as already known. In this regard, LAZ provide the high-speed engines, propelling the present to change and improve.

Surabaya Peduli Ummat was established in the provincial capital of East Java, Surabaya, a major commercial and industrial urban centre equipped with a large port and surrounded by fertile agricultural lands, in 1987. Its establishment is traced to a closely knit group of friends and associates, all active in *Al-Falah* mosque which at the time counted as Surabaya's biggest. Most founding members were businessmen, involved in different commercial sectors; there were also a few academics involved, professing mostly secular subjects. Some of the founders were from well-known local Javanese families, while others were descendants of Arab traders from Hadhramout who had arrived in the city relatively recently. What united them all, the narrative of SPU's foundation goes, was their deep-rooted piety and commitment to the wider process of Islamic reformation. Of equal standing was their shared distress about the fate of those less fortunate in their midst, especially as far as their religiosity, family circumstances and educational attainment was concerned. More particularly, SPU was established with a view to turn into a permanent institution what was, up to that point, a temporary arrangement: SPU came to be when it became obvious to several mosque committee members in charge of collecting zakat during the last few days of Ramadan that dispensing such funds immediately and without any long-term plan to the poor and the needy found in the vicinity, was not bearing any significant results to their well-being. With their needs addressed provisionally only, the poor would return for more aid, year-in and year-out. A more systematic, more enduring approach was required so as to maximise (*optimalkan*) impact and improve (*meningat*) livelihoods. The up-scaling involved the devising of a post-traditional method of managing zakat and other donations through the creation of a specialist, enduring organisation such as SPU, itself first registered as a philanthropic foundation (*yayasan*) and consequently, after the passing of the 1999 zakat administration law, licensed as a national-level LAZ.

One of the unique features of SPU is its springing from a mosque: SPU continues to maintain a loose connection with its origin place, especially in the perception of several donors I met. The latter took the two organisations to be undisguisable, even though nowadays they correspond to entirely separate legal and institutional entities. As I discuss below, the active cultivation of ties with mosques has proven key in SPU's strategy for growth and the establishment of branches in other cities. Rather than coming up with new, innovative and imaginative organisational solution to old problems in the way PIM has done, SPU has been more concerned to adopt and adapt customary practices to fit a set of changing and increasingly challenging circumstances. Its approach to socio-economic justice has a down-to-earth attitude associated with tried and tested methods, often presented with disarming honesty and decency. In the words of Ahmad Yassin, the marketing manager who has been employed in the organisation for twenty-four years, SPU 'aspires to mediate (*mediasi*) between the haves and the have-nots, the rich and the poor' with full knowledge that this '*mediasi* is not going to change the world nor to eradicate poverty from the face of the earth; rather more modestly, it is just going to diminish (*mengurangi*) the troubles the poor face.'

SPU implements its mediation in a way that attends not only to dire conditions of the poor. Equally important to the organisation are the life circumstances of the better-off, primarily its donors. True to stressing the line that connects SPU with more a traditional rationale supporting the performance of good deeds (*amal*), Ahmad Yassin laid equal emphasis on the services to donors the organisation performs, assisting them in generating merit (*pahala*) and ultimately qualifying for salvation in the hereafter (see Chap. 4). In his words,

> SPU's work in the field of philanthropy (*filantropi*) is the product of collaboration with donors. Such collaboration is presented to Allah as worship (*ibadah*). The monetary value of funds collected is not of primary importance; what is primary is their optimal use. All the programs developed by SPU have as their purpose the optimisation (*optimalisasi*) of funds. The aim of such optimisation is to confer upon donors and SPU staff the title of *soleh* or pious person. Everybody should be careful with regards to good deeds (*amal*) to preserve the purity of their intention (*ikhlas*). What must be avoided at any cost is for donors and staff to do what they do for the purpose of *pamér* (Javanese, showing off). The right intention (*niat*) should be the acquisition of Allah's favour (*ridho*). SPU was created for optimizing (*optimalkan*) *zakat*, *infak*, *sedekah*. In Islam, we have the notion of *amal jariyah*: it denotes a good deed which effects are capable of multiplication (*amal yang memiliki multiplier efek*). Even though the person who performed the good deed might be dead, the deed itself still creates merit (*pahala*) for the donor. For example, those who helped in the establishment of a mosque will receive merit for as long as the mosque is of benefit to others. For example, those who train teachers: for as long as the teachers one has trained are

> involved in teaching, the trainer himself/herself will receive merit. Take the case of scholarships. This is also a case of *amal jariyah*. The person who has been schooled with a scholarship might go to become a successful person and create new knowledge that will, in turn, be passed on to future generations. *Jariyah* is all about multiplication, optimisation.

SPU has successfully converted the traditional conception of *amal jariah* or *jariyah* into the shape of a modern, specialist institution; its establishment is a monument to the power of *amal jariah* to insure the enduring presence of good deeds, making sure that a future is bound to arrive in the shape of an advanced, better version of the present. *Amal jariah* is, in other words, envisioned as effecting a slow but incremental improvement in current conditions, opening up a pathway for prosperity to usher in. Its practice is synonymous with enhancing the lives and afterlives of donors and recipients alike (see Anderson 2018). With the intermediation performed by SPU, a win-win situation for everyone involved is outlined.

In 2011, SPU was running a total of six separate programmes for the benefit of the poor and the needy. All six programmes conformed to the paradigm of *amal jariah*, with sustainable interventions in education, Islamic propagation (*dakwah*), mosque construction and maintenance, orphan support and humanitarian assistance geared towards improving the long-term material and spiritual situation of recipients, in this life and the afterlife, generating enduring benefits. The emphasis for SPU officers was, once again, on empowering (*memberdayakan*) the poor in such a way that in the not-so-distant future they would proclaim themselves *mandiri*, meaning independent, autonomous and free from aid. In the context of education, the programmes include scholarships for pupils in need of assistance with meeting the indirect costs involved in attending school, such as purchasing uniforms, pens, bags and so on. Donors are paired to specific pupils and are encouraged to continue supporting their development, considering themselves as 'foster parents,' receiving school reports, etc. SPU also offers aid to schools with regards to purchasing equipment necessary for their smooth functioning such as desks, chairs, computers and so on, helping at the same time with teacher training expenses when required. In the field of Islamic propagation, it is active in sending religious instructors (*da'i*) in remote villages to assist locals with improvements in religiosity. The field of operation of *da'i* is limited mostly to East Java, a province that along with Central Java was once the stronghold of *abangan*, a Javanese religious complex that Muslims modernists from the later nineteenth century onwards considered heterodox and sought to reform (see Hefner 1987; Ricklefs 2012). The process has been marked with considerable success; nowadays one hardly encounters anyone calling himself *abangan* in East Java, only rarely becoming witness to its ritual practices, except for out-of-the-way hamlets, far from main roads and the reach of young, committed preachers (see Beatty 2009). SPU also runs programmes centring on orphans: the latter include financial assistance for improving the state of orphanages, the provision of scholarships for orphaned children and business capital for their lone parent to set up an enterprise. In 2002, SPU initiated its humanitarian assistance programme, involving support to victims of natural disasters, inclusive of health services and the provision of clean water and food, and took part in relief efforts in Aceh after the catastrophic tsunami in 2004. In 2010, the humanitarian aid programme was expanded with the addition of a foray into empowerment: this was SPU taking its first, tentative steps in the field of Islamic micro-finance, and involving the disbursing of capital to entrepreneurially minded recipients in the form of either *hibah*, the Islamic quintessential gift inter vivos, or *qordul hasan*, an interest-free loan.

The growth of SPU programmes, their diversification and multiplication, is supported by a considerable rate of expansion both in terms of the monetary value of funds collected and the numbers of people counted as donors. As Table 3.2 makes aptly clear, the funds SPU has collected in the city of Surabaya have increased significantly over the past twenty years, with the rate of growth exceeding 220%. Most funds collected belong to the category of *infak*, corresponding thus to voluntary donations which unlike zakat, are unrelated to the donor's degree of affluence and level of income. Such has been the dominance of charitable donations (*infak*) that in the first few years of its operation, SPU's finance department did not record zakat funds into a separate category for their monetary value was

Table 3.2 *Surabaya Peduli Ummat*, breakdown of funds collected between and 1990 and 2010 in Indonesian rupiah

Year	*Zakat*	*Infak*	*Other*	*Total*[a]
1990				128,546,055
1995				702,792,525
2000	188,432,384	1,984,999,340	600,733,328	2,774,165,052
2005	2,659,963,427	13,993,177,569	178,208,057	16,831,349,053
2010	4,242,618,974	23,679,872,868	385,278,807	28,307,770,649

[a]Before 2000, zakat represented a negligible amount of all funds collected and was not recorded into a separate category by the organisation's finance department

Table 3.3 *Surabaya Peduli Ummat*, breakdown of donor numbers between 1990 and 2010

Year	*Donors*
1990	8095
1995	29,595
2000	39,184
2005	78,140
2010	87,464

too minute to make a difference. The overwhelming preponderance of *infak* over zakat is, to a large degree, a consequence of the socio-economic profile of the majority of SPU's donors. While the overall number of SPU donors has risen steadily, from 8095 in 1990 to a remarkable 87,464 in 2010 (see Table 3.3), the situation remains that SPU donors continue to come from the lower socio-economic strata of the city's population, to be found amongst the thousands of salaried office and backroom staff, factory supervisors and workers, shop assistants and other service personnel, as well as artisans, technicians and small-size entrepreneurs that make up the commercial backbone of this vibrant provincial powerhouse. While neither the organisation itself nor myself have undertaken any survey that could provide the necessary statistical data to back such assertion, it is the unvaried impression of several SPU staff I interviewed as well as the outcome of my own fieldwork in the city, that the majority of SPU donors are drawn from a strata located between those living in apparent security and comfort, on the one hand, and those in obvious need and perpetually at risk, on the other. Such people are devoid of ownership of agricultural land and of any savings to matter to qualify for paying zakat; most likely, they also lack the steady income level required for the obligation to conduct *zakat penghasilan* (zakat on salary). Nevertheless, they are making enough money to support their families and even though their financial position might be subject to fluctuations and changes, they do maintain an interest in the lives of those less fortunate who, after all, surround them.

SPU is incredibly meticulous in its cultivation of a network of donors spanning the city, offering them many free-of-charge services. In contrast with PIM whose contact with donors is rather minimal, SPU runs several services for the benefit of donors, including family training sessions where husbands learn how to behave as *qowwamah* (leaders) and wives as *solehah* (pious), so that their family is *sakinah mawaddah wa rahmah* (peaceful and full of love). In addition, parenting workshops impart skills for better communicating with one's children, motivating them to study hard. In parallel, there is training on offer for the children of donors, normally taking place on school holidays, relating effective methods of study such as quantum learning and speed reading. In collaboration with the mosque it sprang from, SPU is offering a free consultation service in Islamic law, with special reference to family law. The mosque runs a *Biro Konsultasi Keluarga Sakinah* (consultation office for peaceful family) SPU donors can access free of charge. At the same time, SPU donors have access to *kajian* (religious study) sessions held at the mosque. The sessions involve the chance to engage in dialogue with a national religious figure visiting the city, deepen one's knowledge of the faith through explications of *hadith* literature (reports regarding the deeds and words of the Prophet Mohammad) and the opportunity to improve one's skill in reciting the Al-Quran, usually by undertaking tuition on a group basis.

Over the years SPU which claims to have a presence in 25 provinces in Indonesia, has established a system of offices (*kantor kas*) dedicated exclusively to fundraising, alongside a network of semi-autonomous branches. The latter are additionally charged with implementing interventions of their own making and design to their immediate locale. The network is at its densest in Java where SPU maintains three branches in the cities of Malang, Jember and Jakarta. In 2012 SPU's offices in Banyuwangi and Kediri, both in East Java, were expected to convert themselves into semi-autonomous branches. SPU's method of branching out involves a repetition of its origin: it usually begins with SPU looking to establish a partnership with a mosque found in another city. Such mosque is expected to be politically neutral and independent of association with a religious mass organisation such as *Nahdlatul Ulama* and *Muhammadiyah*. From the moment such partnership is struck to the point when the new institution is in position to go independent, SPU expects ten years or so to have lapsed. I was told that for a local office to be upgraded to a semi-autonomous branch two things are required: first, 70% of the staff is expected to be from the locality, with the remaining 30% coming from Surabaya, sent over by headquarters. Second, meetings are to be held twice annually between the headquarters and the branch so that activities are coordinated and solutions in common are sought. At all times, a key criterion for turning a local office into an independent branch is its ability to pay for all its administration costs from funds raised locally and for these administrative costs to correspond to less than 15% of the total funds raised. It is in this that SPU is multiplying and optimising the trust it has been rewarded with: planting the seed of justice in the shape of *amal jariah*, the goodness that endures into the future, is supplemented by strengthening the sense of ownership of the new institution by the local community.

Contesting the Future

On August 16, 2012, *Pondok Infak Mulia*, *Surabaya Peduli Ummat*'s branch in Malang, along with another 18 persons and *Lembaga Amil Zakat*, including *Dana Keadilan Indonesia* (see Chap. 4), submitted a formal request to the Constitutional Court (*Mahkama Konstitusi Republik Indonesia*) to conduct a review into the constitutionality of Zakat Administration Law No. 23, 2011. The law which had been approved at the end of 2011 sanctioned a new framework concerning zakat administration in the country, putting in place a new architecture that, significantly, pivoted in favour of state institutions (*Badan Amil Zakat* or BAZ). While the previous law (Zakat Administration Law No. 38/1999) had provided for a symmetry of BAZ and LAZ with their roles and functions mirroring each other, several LAZ found the 2011 legal framework to be completely unjust (*tidak adil*): it was perceived to be utterly partial to the state, distinctly unfair to them and possibly contravening the Indonesian constitution. Contesting the law publicly was a risky business but sentiments of indignation were equally strong. Not only did the new framework ignore the leading roles civil society–based zakat management institutions had played over the past decade in improving zakat management through institution building and the promotion of modern standards of professionalism, transparency and accountability, but the law was felt to have been designed with the explicit aim of seriously harming LAZ, undermining their operations to the extent of directly threatening their very existence.

The move to request a judicial review brought the sense of justice animating the hearts and minds of those involved in zakat affairs to the centre of attention: at stake was not only inadequate recognition of past achievements, but primarily a contest over the future and its direction. Was zakat as a financial asset and instrument of socio-economic empowerment to become a matter to be entrusted to state actors or a matter of trust in the powers of civil society to deliver prosperity for all? The ability of state law to prescribe both the essence of justice and the contents of the forthcoming was put to the test: by means of an appeal internal to the law process itself, that is the filling of a review request made to the Constitutional Court, a body counted amongst the judicial institutions of the government of Indonesia, the dispute over the future of zakat was to be settled. In these circumstances however, a significant yet subtle inversion was being accomplished: from the very ground which a sense of justice in Islam is understood to arise from and to be revealed, zakat was being converted to an issue adjudicated by reference to standards and norms set by a wholly different set of principles, that is those embedded in the Indonesian constitution. In other words, a significant shift in the practice of zakat had irrevocably occurred in the process of opting for a judicial review: the conception of zakat as the foundation of justice in Islam, one of the most important ideas advocated by intellectuals in the 1980s and 1990s in Indonesia (see Chap. 2), was being side-lined by the inexorable rise of a situation whereby zakat was subject to the statute-making processes of the nation-state, becoming entirely engulfed as an object amongst other objects by the application of national law, concerns over legality and conventional judicial procedures.

Ironically it was leading LAZ that since 2002 had been pushing for changes and amendments to be made to the 1999 law through their professional body, Forum Zakat. Amongst the changes proposed in the period leading up to 2011 was the idea of establishing a Ministry of Zakat and Wakaf to deal with both assets exclusively and on a separate basis from the Ministry of Religion which was widely conceived to be untrustworthy, if not corrupt. Other suggestions included for zakat to be managed according to Islamic law (*syariah*) rather than the Indonesian constitution, and for it to become mandatory with penalties imposed on well-off Muslims who failed to meet their obligation (Salim 2008: 57). In 2009, the Ministry of Religion prepared a draft law that proposed sanctions against non-complying *muzakki* and made provisions for the introduction of further tax concessions for zakat payment. However, the ministry's draft also sought to wrest total control of zakat by centralising its management within BAZ or government-run institutions, abolishing the existence of LAZ from the statute book and requiring those LAZ operating in the country to merge with BAZ (Fauzia 2013: 251). Though such abolition clauses did not make it to the final text of the Zakat Administration Law No. 23/2011 as approved by the People's Representative Council, the new law did nevertheless reassign LAZ as 'assistants' to government zakat institutions, using the designation *pembantu* itself carrying the meaning of helper and servant, especially in the sense of domestic staff. This was a designation LAZ found deeply offensive, troubling and discriminatory, especially under a constitution that guarantees equality before the law to all legal persons. At the heart of their concerns was the suspicion that the Ministry of Religion and BAZNAS might capitalise on such designation to force LAZ to transfer all zakat funds collected each year to BAZNAS and for BAZNAS to release some or all assets back to original collectors on condition of receiving a formal request from them, itself accompanied with a detailed budget and specific plans regarding programme implementation. Such an arrangement, it was feared, would most certainly put out of business most, if not all, LAZ as it would deny them of autonomy and flexibility. A series of conditions stipulated in the new law such as the requirement placed on LAZ to form Islamic mass organisations (*organisasi masyarakat Islam*) and the acquisition of a favourable recommendation by BAZNAS, were seen in the same, mistrustful and apprehensive light. In addition, the penalty the 2011 law imposed on traditional *amil* operating in the guise of temporary committees out of local mosques, small prayer houses and Islamic boarding schools, in the form of one-year jail term or a hefty monetary fine, equivalent to 50 million rupiah or US $5500 when acting without the necessary state authorisation, was widely interpreted by LAZ as part of a resolute campaign by the state and its organs to impose a virtual monopoly on zakat collection. The threat of initiating criminal proceedings against unsuspected *amil* was perceived to have been designed as leverage, compelling traditional zakat collectors into acquiring such licence through collaborating with government zakat bodies, channelling all zakat collected locally into state coffers.[15]

The Constitutional Court's decision, reached in October 2013, backed the overall direction towards greater state centralisation of zakat management in Indonesia: while the decision affirmed the broad architecture the 2011 law put in place, it also offered some respite to LAZ and informal zakat committees so as to reassure their continuous existence within a much-changed regulatory framework and institutional architecture. By declaring Indonesia to be a *religious welfare state,*[16] the panel of presiding judges affirmed the interest and responsibility the Indonesian state has in improving public welfare (*kesejahteran umum*), while counting zakat amongst the many instruments available to it for achieving such purpose. In particular, the court pronounced it to be an obligation of the state to get actively involved in managing zakat so that zakat management in Indonesia becomes *efektif* and *efisien*. It also found that the state which has a duty of providing protection to all its citizens shares with zakat the same broad objectives, namely that of 'advancing general welfare and implementing social justice on behalf of the people of Indonesia' (*memajukan kesejahteran umum dan mewujdkan keadilan sosial bagi seluruh rakyat Indonesia*). By making zakat and the state commensurate to each other in terms of justice, the court's ruling bolstered the new architecture the law put in place. According to the new arrangements, the government, represented by the Ministry of Religion and BAZNAS, would act as the overall regulator and supervisor of zakat affairs as well as coordinator, organiser and operator for the collection, management and distribution of zakat, respectively. All such capacities except that of operator were to be exclusively held by the state and its organs. In general terms, the Constitutional Court's decision was duly aligned, perhaps inadvertently, with those who promoted zakat's greater centralisation on the basis of emulating the time of the Prophet: it is often mentioned in zakat circles in Indonesia and elsewhere that during the life time of the Prophet and his successors (the four rightly guided caliphs), zakat was a tax imposed by the state and wholly managed by the *diwan*, an administrative body of appointed officials. This is so for the court's decision accepted wholesale the rationale witnesses representing the state put forward in the hearings: according to them, the centralisation of activities was essential for enhancing and improving the collection and distribution of zakat as allowing for greater control over a national asset was best guarantee for attaining greater benefits. Behind such rationale were unfounded allegations that LAZ were spending a disproportionate amount of zakat and other Islamic funds for internal purposes, awarding senior management lucrative salary packages and buying fancy cars to drive around. Tighter regulation and oversight, inclusive of re-licensing and regular reporting requirements, were designed to put a stop to such events from occurring.

The court offered however some respite to LAZ and traditional zakat collectors with removing the obligation for LAZ to (re-)constitute themselves as Islamic mass organisations. At the same it rejected the outright criminalisation of unlicensed, temporary *amil* committees as being premature. In the latter case, the court found that the state, particularly BAZNAS, had to work harder to reach deep into each corner of the territory of the nation-state before such extreme measure could become applicable. As a result, the Ministry of Religion through Government Regulation No. 14/2014 subsequently instructed each district throughout Indonesia to establish a local BAZNAS branch to assist with the enactment of 2011 law. The court's ruling did maintain some pressure on traditional *amil* to corroborate with the state, placing them under the explicit legal obligation of having to inform respective authorities of their involvement in managing zakat funds: in case such notice has been served, no criminality inhered. So far, no one has been prosecuted under this proviso, even if local *amil* have continued to do what they always have done, that is collect and distribute zakat on the basis of the trust they have been granted by the local communities they serve. As for LAZ, the requirement of reporting annually to BAZNAS was maintained by the court's decision. In a brief visit to Indonesia in October 2018, senior LAZ managers confirmed that LAZ must submit audited reports regularly to the authorities, along with a breakdown of zakat funds distributed to each category of *mustahik*. However, such legal obligation is considered light, given that their worst fears have been averted and no asset transfers to state institutions have been demanded. On the other hand, the very asymmetry the 2011 zakat law instituted in the relations between government-run bodies and LAZ has left an indelible stain: the CEO of *Dana Keadilan Indonesia* described the current state of affairs as a game of football with his team facing FIFA and FIFA acting as opponent as well as overall regulator and match referee.

Derrida en Indonésie

Critical legal studies can't, even for a moment, take for granted the claims law makes for itself: its rhetoric of acting as the promotor and guarantor of justice can't be accepted as a given under any circumstances, especially late modern ones. And if this anti-foundationalist stance is to be applied at all, it must be applied with consistency; here, in Indonesia, and everywhere. Accordingly, law's performativity has to be interrogated for the paradoxes it contains, its rhetoric questioned, its logic complicated. Derrida's own reading of the law owes much to Montaigne who was first to seek to distinguish law from justice, observing that 'even our [16th century French] law, it is said, has legitimate fictions on which it founds the truth of its justice' (Derrida 1990: 939). But what is a legitimate fiction? Derrida asks, only to immediately answer that it is the fiction necessary to establish the law as the source of justice. Acute observers of social life know only too well is that one obeys the law not because it is just but because it has authority. Such authority has been established on top of a past event of revolutionary proportions that in turn provides the context for current legal principles, standards and procedures. Any observer of social life moreover knows that challenging the authority of the law and contravening its stipulations, carries consequences and incurs punishment for the law has the surplus capability to defend its authority through the imposition of penalties. If law is largely a temporal effect, the outcome of a past event that is performatively repeated in the present through further regulatory utterances and undertakings, the inclusion of the supplementary dimension whereby law enforces itself on the populace under its jurisdiction as essential in its operation, means that law is neither about justice nor about righteousness. Instead the law pivots around the application of force as an absolute necessity both for its establishment in the past, its actualisation in the present and perpetuation in the future. To this violence, both originary and unending, self-referential and self-perpetuating Derrida assigns the role of the ground on which law, any law, erects itself. Such violence is both entirely arbitrary and absolute, acting as the transcendental condition for the standards and values law proposes and promotes. 'Since the origin of authority, the foundation or ground, the position of the law can't by definition rest on anything but themselves, they are themselves a violence without ground' (Derrida 1990: 943).

Justice by distinction exceeds legal reasoning and judicial procedure. Whereas law is prescriptive and calculative, productive of normativity and certainty, justice 'carries life beyond present life,' 'beyond law and beyond the norm' (Derrida 1994: xx). Justice as urgent call and insistent demand placed upon one by an-other measures each and every one of us against an impossible task: it constantly tests our strength to maintain an openness to life, while enduring intense aporias, welcoming the unknown, the strange and unforetold. For Derrida to whom justice is guaranteed by none other than uncontrollable ghostly apparitions that remind one of unaddressed wrongs, evades both the absolute distinction between presence and absence and the dictates of the present. Instead, it arises from the potential contained at the gap separating the two sides of the ontological divide, erupting from the very intervals marking the passing of each present to the next. This is justice in the process of untangling itself from the stranglehold of an absolute law, joining the power of time to bring about the new. Untimely and unexpected are the visitations performed by ghosts: equally inconvenient and unconventional should our responses be to the call for justice. A response is just, Derrida indicates, only on condition it affirms time, splitting it open, participating in *différance*, thus endlessly differing/deferring. 'Beyond right, and still more beyond juridicism, beyond morality, and still more beyond moralism, does not justice as relation to the other suppose on the contrary the irreducible excess of a disjointure [....]

some "out of joint" dislocation in Being and in time itself, [...] that would alone be able to *do justice* or to *render justice* to the other as other?' (Derrida 1994: 32, italics in the original).

Fully cognizant of the struggle justice is involved in to uncouple itself from the asphyxiating embrace of the law, I have concentrated my efforts in this chapter in throwing light on the opposite procedure, charting the manner in which justice in the name of zakat has been entrenched in the statute books of the Indonesian nation-state. In the process, I have also paid close attention to one side of the institutional entities the state in its law-making process has created and deployed in domesticating zakat for the welfare of the nation. In particular, I have looked into two specific LAZ with an eye to comparing and contrasting important differences emerging as to their roots in associational life, organisational shape, scope of interventions and programme aspirations. My overall effort has been to show first, the temporal unfolding of the domestication of zakat conceived as justice in the country: this has been a process that begun with *reformasi* and was marked by an unmatched enthusiasm and creativity related to the political project for the Islamisation of both state and civil society. Unsurprisingly perhaps, by the early 2010s such passion had given way to frustration, anger even: the promulgation of a new Zakat Administration Law in 2011 foregrounded a strong state about to wrest almost total control over the project of zakat as justice, using whatever social energies were left over by *reformasi* for furthering its own interests. I take the decision the Constitutional Court reached to reinforce such a conservative turn of affairs. The courts' decision corresponds to the end point of my research: undoubtedly, things have moved on since then, novel points of resistance have emerged, new openings for justice to escape have been created. However, this is a story for another book to tell.

Second, I have endeavoured to conceptualise law and the entities it has given rise to, in terms of time, focusing the analysis on the consequences that law- and institution-making have been having on the future in terms of seeking to engineer it as a predictable outcome of operations performed in the present. Such operations comprise of legal frameworks, institutional instruments, judicial procedures, technical interventions, expert forms of knowledge, programmes, plans, accounts, audits and so on. My description of the temporal effects legal and institution-building practices has been having, has emphasised the ways in which the passing of time is understood as the outcome of specific legal and organisational interventions, whereby the future is carefully designed and predicted to conform to a political *telos*. The transformation of ***mustahik*** into ***muzakki***, that is, the conversion of zakat claimants, primarily the poor and the needy, into people affluent enough so as to qualify for the payment of zakat, is an objective shared equally by state actors and civil bodies involved in zakat management in Indonesia. Such *telos* anticipates a future full of promise: even though the precise mechanism of bringing about such transformation is yet to be determined, the future is nevertheless, taken as largely known in advance, its basic contours having been already identified and recognised as desirable, valuable and necessary. In the chapters that follow, I go on to discuss in greater ethnographic detail and depth the practices through which such a prosperous and pious future is made to come about, examining both zakat's theological underpinnings in Islamic eschatology and its complex, ambiguous and intricate entanglements with contemporary neoliberal tenets and priorities.

Notes

1. The Department of Religion's 'Technical Guidance Regarding Zakat Administration' No. D291/2000 regulates the rates for calculation of the amounts of *zakat maal* to be paid, standardising in effect what has been up to that point a matter of Islamic jurisprudence, and thus subject to considerable debate and disagreement amongst experts (see Hooker 2008: 32–36). At the same time, the urge to regulate zakat, both *maal* and *fitrah*, has been strengthened by several local governments issuing regional regulations (*peraturan daerah*); except for zakat, *syariah* by-laws usually concern themselves with prohibiting gambling, prostitution and the consumption of alcohol (see Buehler 2008; Salim 2015: 97–99).
2. According to Lindsey (2012: 165), the draft bill included a clause that implied state coercion in the conduct of zakat but the phrasing was subsequently revised, removing the possibility of such interpretation.
3. The drafting of the 2011 bill was both prolonged and extremely complex, involving different teams, several drafts and counter-drafts (see Fauzia 2013: 248–256; Lindsey 2012: 172; Susetyo 2018). It is worth noting that the draft submitted by the Ministry of Religion sought to abolish LAZ, create a monopoly on zakat management by a new body under its auspices and impose penalties for all Muslim citizens who those failed to transfer their zakat to it. Due to strong opposition by LAZ and political parties at the House of People's Representatives, none of these clauses made their way to the final bill.

4. As Derrida puts it, 'one cannot speak *directly* about justice, thematise or objectivize justice, say "this is just" and even less "I am just," without immediately betraying justice, if not law (*droit*)' (1990: 935).
5. For founding and mission of Bank Muamalat, see Hefner 2003. On Indonesian Islamic banking, see Saeed (2004) and Ismal (2013) and on Malaysian Islamic banking, see Rudnyckyj (2019). Choudhury and Malik (1992) and El-Gamal (2006, 2007) discuss the basic principles of Islamic economics and banking, respectively.
6. PIM also accepts donations from non-Islamic, local and international partners, including corporate social responsibility funds, such as Pertamina, the Body Shop Foundation, the Indonesia Stock Exchange and Japan International Cooperation Agency.
7. Along the way PIM started collecting, managing and distributing grants and donations destined for humanitarian relief operations both in Indonesia and abroad, corporate social responsibility funds released from many different companies and corporations it established partnerships with.
8. While preferred *sedekah* beneficiaries are normally one's close associates, such as relatives and neighbours, no one is barred from acting as a potential recipient, including non-Muslims and animals. In addition, while Muslims are encouraged to pass things they love and treasure, *sedekah* is not limited to objects of monetary value for anything of benefit to an-other like a greeting or a smile, counts as such.
9. *Wakaf* is subject to distinct regulation, both in terms of Islamic jurisprudence and in terms of Indonesian state law. Partly because it often involves parcels of land and/or entire buildings, it has been subject of a greater degree of Indonesian state intervention and bureaucratic administration from colonial to present times (see Lindsey 2012: 173–184; Jahar 2006).
10. All data supplied has been kindly provided by the finance department of PIM.
11. Government-sponsored agencies had been established in 1968 with Soeharto's encouragement and were known as BAZIS (*Badan Amil Zakat Infak dan Sedekah*). The majority of the funds collected came from salary deductions of Muslim civil servants who had no real option but to agree to it. With the possible exception of the BAZIS DKI Jakarta, they were overly distrusted by local communities, suspected for funds' mismanagement.
12. This equal standing was undermined however in the subsequent guidelines (*Pedoman Teknis Pengelolaan Zakat No. D-291/2000*) issued by the Ministry of Religion that assigned LAZ the status of collection units (*unit pengumpul zakat*), making them subsidiaries of BAZ. The relative standing of LAZ to BAZ became one of the main issues of contention with respect to the 2011 Zakat Administration Law, see below.

13. Though the law stipulates certain categories of zakatable wealth, it fails to note that such a list could never be exhaustive for any list of zakatable items is itself the subject of scholarly debate and historical variation. In addition, the calculation of the threshold (*nisab*) above which an item becomes subject to zakat, the respective rates to be applied and the time of conducting zakat, are left unelaborated in the statute. Such matters which, again, vary from one school of Islamic jurisprudence to another are discussed in guidebooks published by the Ministry of Religion such as the *Pedoman Teknis Pengelolaan Zakat No. D-291/2000.*
14. This accords with the decision of the Fatwa Commission of the Indonesian Council of Islamic Scholars (*Majelis Ulama Indonesia*) that notes that an *amil* can deduct up to 12.5% of zakat funds collected for operational costs. It moreover stipulates that further funds can be deducted for same purposes from other categories of donations such as *infak/sedekah*, see *Keputusan Komisi Bl Ijtima Ulama Komisi Fatwa se-Indonesia III Masalah Yang Terkait Dengan Zakat* on January 26, 2009.
15. The 2011 law also included heavy penalties—five-year jail term or 500 million rupiah fine—for those found guilty of misuse of zakat and other Islamic donation funds, inclusive of contravening unspecified *syariah* regulations.
16. The term is in English and italics in the original, see p. 92 of *Putusan No. 86/PUU—X/2012 Mahkamah Konstitusi Republik Indonesia.*

Bibliography

Alfitri. 2006. The Law on Zakat Management and Non-Governmental Zakat Collectors in Indonesia. *International Journal of Not-for-Profit Law* 8 (2): 55–64.

Anderson, Paul. 2018. "An Abundance of Meaning": Ramadan as an Enchantment of Society and Economy in Syria. *HAU: Journal of Ethnographic Theory* 8 (3): 610–624.

Bamualim, Chaider. 2009. Islamic Philanthropy in Indonesia: Trends and Challenges towards Social Justice. *Kultur* 4 (1): 75–88.

Beatty, Andrew. 2009. *A Shadow Falls: In the Heart of Java*. London: Faber and Faber.

Bruinessen, Martin van, ed. 2013. *Contemporary Developments in Indonesian Islam and the "Conservative Turn" of the Early Twenty-First Century*. Singapore: Institute of Southeast Asian Studies.

Buehler, Michael. 2008. The Rise of Shari'a by-Laws in Indonesian Districts: An Indication of Changing Patterns of Power Accumulation and Political Corruption. *South East Asia Research* 16 (2): 255–285.

Choudhury, Masudul Alam, and Uzir Abdul Malik. 1992. *The Foundations of Islamic Political Economy*. New York: Palgrave.
Derrida, Jacques. 1990. Force of Law: The "Mystical Foundation of Authority". *Cardozo Law Review* 11 (5–6): 919–1045.
———. 1994. *Specters of Marx: The State of Debt, the Work of Mourning, and the New International*. London: Routledge.
Effendy, Bahtiar. 2003. *Islam and the State in Indonesia*. Singapore: Institute of Southeast Asian Studies.
El-Gamal, Mahmood. 2006. *Islamic Finance: Law, Economics, and Practice*. Cambridge: Cambridge University Press.
Fauzia, Amelia. 2013. *Faith and the State: A History of Islamic Philanthropy in Indonesia*. Leiden: Brill.
Firdaus, Mohammad, et al. 2012. *Economic Estimation and Determinations of Zakat Potential in Indonesia*, IRTI Working Paper Series. Jeddah: Islamic Research and Training Institute.
Halimatusa'diyah, Iim. 2015. Zakat and Social Protection: The Relationship Between Socio-Religious CSOs and the Government of Indonesia. *Journal of Civil Society* 11 (1): 79–99.
Hefner, Robert. 1987. Islamizing Java? Religion and Politics in Rural East Java. *Journal of Asian Studies* 46 (3): 533–554.
———. 2000. *Civil Islam: Muslims and Democratization Indonesia*. Princeton: Princeton University Press.
———. 2003. Islamizing Capitalism: On the Founding of Indonesia's First Islamic Bank. In *Shari'a and Politics in Modern Indonesia*, ed. A. Salim and A. Azra, 148–167. Singapore: Institute of South East Asian Studies.
Hooker, M.B. 2008. *Indonesian Syariah: Defining a National School of Islamic Law*. Singapore: Institute of Southeast Asian Studies.
Ismal, Rifki. 2013. *Islamic Banking in Indonesia: New Perspectives on Monetary and Financial Issues*. New York: Wiley.
Jahar, Asep Saepudin. 2006. The Clash of Muslims and the State: Waqf and Zakat in Post-Independence Indonesia. *Studia Islamika* 13 (3): 353–395.
Latief, Hilman. 2013. Islamic Philanthropy and the Private Sector in Indonesia. *Indonesian Journal of Islam and Muslim Studies* 3 (2): 175–201.
Lindsey, Tim. 2012. Islam, Law and the State in Southeast Asia. In *Volume 1: Indonesia*. London: Tauris.
Rahardjo, Dawan. 2003. Filantropi Islam dan Keadilan Sosial: Mengurai Kebingungan Epistemologis. In *Berderma Untuk Semua*, ed. Idris Thaha, xxxiii–xxxxxv. Jakarta: CLC.
Ricklefs, Merle. 2012. *Islamisation and Its Opponents in Java: A Political, Social, Cultural and Religious History, c. 1930 to Present*. Singapore: National University of Singapore Press.

Rudnyckyj, Daromir. 2019. *Beyond Debt: Islamic Experiments in Global Finance*. Chicago: University of Chicago Press.

Saeed, Abdullah. 2004. Islamic Banking and Finance: In Search of a Pragmatic Model. In *Islamic Perspectives on the New Millennium*, ed. Virginia Hooker and Amin Saikal, 113–132. Singapore: ISEAS.

Salim, Arskal. 2008. *The Shift in Zakat Practice in Indonesia: From Piety to an Islamic Socio-Political- Economic System*. Chiang Mai: Silkworm Books.

Salim, Delmus Puneri. 2015. *The Transnational and the Local in the Politics of Islam: The Case of West Sumatra, Indonesia*. Dordrecht: Springer.

Susetyo, Heru. 2018. *Zakat Laws in Indonesia*. Depok: Faculty of Law, University of Indonesia.

Weir, T.H., and A. Zysow. 2012. Sadaka. In *Encyclopaedia of Islam, Second Edition*, ed. P. Bearman, Th. Bianquis, C.E. Bosworth, E. van Donzel and W.P. Heinrichs. Consulted online on 10 November 2018. https://doi.org/10.1163/1573-3912_islam_COM_0956

CHAPTER 4

Anticipating Life

For Arief—a man in his late 20s and father of two kids—working for one of Indonesia's leading *zakat* management organisations was the first step towards a much-coveted goal: becoming a successful entrepreneur and renowned philanthropist. As a child, Arief looked up to his grandfather, a decorated veteran of the national revolution, and planned to join the Indonesian navy. However, his exam performance sent him back to the drawing board. After achieving a degree in agribusiness, he took up several odd jobs till, at a friend's instigation, he found employment at *Dana Keadilan Indonesia* (DKI), a prominent zakat management body. There, he ran empowerment programmes involving *syariah*-approved modes of micro-financing, the aim being to turn the country's multitude of poor into skilled and pious entrepreneurs through interventions in education, health and capital provision. Entrepreneurship was very much part of the future Arief saw for himself as well. His dream was to set up his own business venture and become rich enough to afford to send his kids to respectable schools, buy his wife a big house and a luxury 4×4 and treat his extended family to nice clothes and the *hajj* pilgrimage to Saudi Arabia. He further envisioned to use part of his wealth-to-come to establish a charitable foundation for aiding orphans and widows and to disseminate business know-how to the poor. His approach to his current job was as a kind of training (*latihan*): employment in a respected organisation with a 'strong corporate culture' and 'clear and effective systems and procedures', and an ethic that wedded work to piety was an essential preparation, he

K. Retsikas, *A Synthesis of Time*,
https://doi.org/10.1007/978-3-030-34933-2_4

said, for his future success as a businessman. All that was required to achieve his dream was two things: first, he had to work harder than ever before, and second, he had to intensify his worship of Allah.

The attainment of religiously informed and socially responsible wealth is a desire widespread in the metropolises of Java, especially amongst the middle-class people I encountered in the early 2010s. It was as if the air circulating in urban highways, along with pollution particles and the smell of spicy food, also carried an intense drive: in Osella and Osella's apt phrase, the atmosphere was filled by the desire for 'making good and doing good' (2009). Everyone seemed caught up in it: starting from schoolchildren to grandmothers and from street vendors to civil servants, the craving for success with a social conscience had been spreading fast, animating daily struggles, giving life a distinct temporal direction and purpose. The present chapter aims at understanding the emergence and effects of the early twenty-first-century craving for pious entrepreneurial success by focusing on the practices people consistently and regularly undertake in order to actualise such future prosperity, making it come about. The desire for overcoming the present, especially its restrictions and limitations, both financial and those related to the implementation of the faith, infused the work routines of employees of zakat management bodies such as Arief and others at DKI. It also pervaded the set of relationships between LAZ employees and recipients of zakat and other Islamic funds, especially as far as the dispensation of advice and the training of offer was concerned. As this is neither a psychological nor a psychoanalytic study of desire but an anthropological analysis of temporality, I am concerned with the social conditions of such desire's emergence, looking in particular at the effects desire has been having on the texturing of time, the contours of the social and the fabrication of subjectivities. In other words, what is at stake in the ensuing discussion is a conjoined elaboration on the cuts in time and the kinds of persons introduced, instituted and sustained by a particular body of practices as carried out by LAZ in Indonesia in the process of managing zakat and other charitable donations.

Such a set of practices hardly exists in a historical-cultural vacuum. A significant body of literature on Southeast Asia approaches contemporary forms of capitalist accumulation through their intersection with Islamic ethics, stressing the consequences of such a juncture for the active cultivation of new forms of subjectivity. Research by Sloane (1999, 2011), Sloane-White (2017), Njoto-Feillard (2004, 2012) and Rudnyckyj (2011, 2019) shows that Muslim reformers' stress on self-vigilance, self-discipline and personal accountability both inform and are informed by global corporate cultures and neoliberal values. The latter extend outwards from the marketplace, seeking to envelop every arena of social life.[1] To the extent that neoliberal tenets are congruent with the demands of post-Fordist production and supportive of requirements for labour flexibility, capital mobility, transparency and technological innovation, the cultivation of corresponding sets of dispositions and sensibilities amongst the population is a matter of utmost political significance. Due to its close articulation with religion, such a political project is in many contemporary Muslim societies infused with an aura of sacredness: economy's strict compliance with *syariah* is deemed by many of its proponents as evidence of Islam's capacity to domesticate and/or ameliorate the negative sides of neoliberalism, combating the latter's excessive freedoms and the promotion of secularism and materialism (see Atia 2013; Tuğal 2017; Ismail 2013; Hendrick 2013).

The present chapter pays explicit and consistent attention to the ever-present salvific undertones of Islam's contemporary articulation with the forces of neoliberalism, thus departing from current understandings of the processes at play in significant ways. Central to this departure is the claim that the religiously informed desire for entrepreneurial success as realised in contemporary Indonesia is permeated by a mode of temporality that privileges the future at the expense of the past and the present. This temporal orientation has important consequences for subject-making for it forces the subjectivities fabricated to take a distinctively asymptotic form. In other words, the practices necessary for the attainment of *syariah*-inspired wealth result in the production of self-differing subjects, that is, subjects whose past, present and future actualisations lack coincidence and complete convergence. In the immediate context of zakat management practices, a subject's temporal unfolding is explicitly understood to consist of a chain of actualisations which despite many veritable connections, differ markedly from each other. In other words, the subjects emerging from such process correspond to temporary instances and impermanent manifestations of a much wider process of becoming; as such, they are characterised by inconstancy, instability and variability, attributes which are very much the contrary of those highlighted in the literature.[2]

The conceptual attention the present work pays to gaps and discontinuities abounding in social life is coupled with the stress it puts on questions regarding the manner in which such gaps and discontinuities are instituted and sustained. It is my contention that the variability that characterises the chain of a subject's ongoing actualisations is directly related to temporal intervals and that such intervals are inaugurated by and founded on the undertaking of practical exercises. Corresponding to events, that is, both unique and unrepeatable occurrences, practical exercises of the sort described in this chapter and the next ones insert cuts in the flow of time, making time pass and stretch discontinuously into the future. The subjectivities that emerge out of such events are meant to be improved, enhanced and upgraded versions of past ones. With desire guiding the process of subject production towards specific ends, such carefully designed subjectivities correspond to approximations of a future people, that is, a people who are yet-to-come. The making of future people is a rigorous process: the attainment of desired forms of subjectivity is itself subject to incessant demands for its products to display a greater degree of perfection and higher levels of sophistication. In the Indonesian context I am addressing here, the people-to-come are commonly conceived of as richer and happier, healthier and more pious than those of past and present generations. They are also understood as having a greater chance of achieving salvation in the hereafter than past and present peoples do.

My concern with the temporality of social practices and their combined effect on subjectivity owes much to Michael Foucault's genealogical studies (2007, 2008) and his concept of 'governmentality.' Foucault employs this term as a guide for the historical reconstruction of the co-emergence of modern forms of power, scientific modes of rationality and the conception of the individual as an autonomous agent. His studies show how, in the course of more than two millennia, the classical Greek concept of *oikonomia* that originally concerned the proper regulation of the household, came to acquire the meanings we currently attribute to it, via early Christian conceptions of pastoral care. Foucault argues that the modern idea of the economy as a well-defined field of practice endowed with evident borders and distinctive norms owes its emergence as much to the liberal art of government as originally formulated by the philosophers of the Scottish Enlightenment (see also Kahn 2004), as to more recent transformations of political economy thinking by the German and the American schools of neoliberalism. While Scottish Enlightenment writers set up the market as a field of human practice that best works when kept apart from state intervention, neoliberal political economists of the post-World War Two era conceived it not as naturally existing domain but a constituted object that requires constant intervention and support by a complex array of institutional actors, inclusive of the state, for its existence and operation.

In this regard, Foucault deployed the concept of governmentality (2007: 363–366) as a guideline for the analysis of the historically varied ways in which each epoch conceived of the economy and sought to manage and control it. At the same time, he expanded the problem of government to include not only concerns pertaining to 'the governing of others,' but also those arising from 'the governing of the self,' thus adumbrating the close link between the exercise of power, the economy as an object of knowledge and intervention and processes of subject-making.

For Foucault, the understanding of the subject in terms of human capital is a key component of neoliberal forms of governmentality: human creative powers are understood in terms of actual and potential skills, knowledge and dispositions, which are, in turn, the result of past and future investments in nutrition, education, training, love, friendship and so on (2008: 219–233). This articulation is a significant departure from eighteenth- and nineteenth-century understandings of persons as citizens endowed with a bundle of inalienable rights: in their place, neoliberalism places a premium on persons assuming full responsibility for their own investments in all aspects of life. Through equipping them with techniques such as a cost-benefit analysis and by means of placing them in competition with one another for scarce resources, it demands of subjects to learn to orient themselves to themselves, and to others, as entrepreneurs in search of optimising the capital they command. As Lemke puts it, 'neoliberalism no longer locates the rational principle for regulating and limiting the action of the government in a natural freedom that we should all respect, but instead it posits an artificially arranged liberty' (2001: 200). Self-determination is cultivated through making subjects responsible for bearing the consequences of their own decisions while insisting that decisions must be taken on the basis of a rational assessment of alternative courses of action, including of likely risks and probable gains and losses.

Foucault's genealogical study of economic rationality is important for my purposes for two reasons: first, by highlighting the intimate connection between the welfare of the population and the objectives of governmentality, he opens up the possibility of considering practices of care for others as fundamentally related to the exercise of power. Governmentality, argues Foucault, 'has the population as its target, political economy as its major form of knowledge, and apparatuses of security as its essential technical instrument' (2007: 108). As such, it strives 'to improve the condition of the population, to increase of its wealth, its longevity, health' (2007: 105), and relies on the science of political economy to furnish it with all the necessary knowledge regarding its principal object. By disentangling the analysis of power from the study of the state, Foucault conceived domination as diffused throughout the space of the social, to be produced and reproduced through practices of subjectivation. In this regard, he postulated neoliberal governmentality as hinging on two inseparable elements: the production of subjectivities in the manner of *homo economicus* and the earmarking of civil society as an expansive domain of application. In an ideal situation, he writes,

> Civil society is [...] the correlate of a technology of government the rational measure of which must be juridically pegged to an economy understood as process of production and exchange. [...] *Homo economicus* is, if you like, the abstract, ideal, purely economic point that inhabits this dense, full and complex reality of civil society. Or alternatively, civil society is the concrete ensemble within which these ideals points, economic men, must be placed so that they can be appropriately managed. So, *homo economicus* and civil society belong to the same ensemble of the technology of liberal governmentality. (Foucault 2008: 296)

Taking its cue from this insight, the current chapter complements and advances further the analysis of zakat's intimate involvement with power as set out in the previous one: whereas Chap. 3 laid out the conceptual and ethnographic basis for a consideration of national zakat legislation as foregrounding a mode of violence perpetrated by the state, the current chapter considers the domain of civil society, itself pertaining to faith-based non-governmental organisations and their activities in managing poor, as equally problematic. The pairing of the mass creation of entrepreneurial subjectivities and the promotion of associational life under the aegis of the concept of 'civil society' as currently played out in Indonesia must, therefore, be interrogated rather than uncritically accepted for the effects it produces on time, life and subjects. As several influential writings on the processes under way for reforming 'philanthropic' practices according to the dictates of universal democratic marketisation make aptly clear (Green and Bishop 2008; Nickel and Eikenberry 2009; Muehlebach 2013; Atia 2013; Tuğal 2017), civil society can no longer be taken as either an innocuous counter-balance to the state or entirely separate from the market, free from considerations of profit and returns on investment.

Second, implicit in Foucault's account is the argument that neoliberal subjectivities' orientation to time privileges the future: as entrepreneurs, neoliberal subjects are forward-looking, expectant and cautiously optimistic (Gireudeau 2012). The valuation of everyday behaviour in terms of investment decisions means that value is conceived of as accruing from returns that are yet-to-come (Monaghan and O'Flynn 2012; Appadurai 2015; LiPuma 2017). This is mainly because profits are forecast on the basis of risk calculations, themselves made possible through the deployment of actuarial tables. Contrary to popular conceptions, neoliberal practice does not involve an affirmation of chance. While it is true that rates of return increase in proportion to risks taken, it is control over and leverage against adverse future outcomes that is sought through the development and application of a variety of techniques such as the algorithms provided by probability theory, on which contemporary investment banking is based on (Maurer 2002; Zaloom 2009). The question arising is, therefore, the following: if neoliberalism entails an appreciation of the yet-to-come, how does it actually make time pass and the future arrive? What are, in other words, the mechanisms it deploys for marking and synthesising time? To the extent that all aspects of social life are to be treated as investments, time is of the essence. Since it is taken as axiomatic that value derives from the future, the instituting of temporal breaks is a primary concern to all and every project towards life's financialisation: without breaks and intervals, there would be neither return nor value, surplus or otherwise. In contrast to the liberals of times past, who took time's passing as a natural occurrence that nevertheless required careful studying and measuring, the same can't be said for contemporary neoliberalism. From the plotting of time in business plans regarding turnover projections to the invention of machines that allow money to be transferred from one bank to another in 'real time' (Riles 2004), and from personal insurance spreadsheets that prepare us for avoidable accidents and the unavoidability of death to the provision of credit, the calculation of instalments and the operation of secondary markets in derivatives (Miyazaki 2007; Ortiz 2014), it is obvious that time is no longer assumed as either set or given (see also Retsikas 2018).

The present chapter supplements Foucault's genealogical readings of times past through an inquiry into the temporality our epoch fosters and propagates. Where Foucault encountered differences in history—he was always on the lookout for 'the different concepts that enable us to conceive of discontinuity (threshold, rupture, break, mutation, transformation)' (2002: 5)—the current study encounters the other in the very present that organises and governs (self-) presence. In this regard, it is of some interest to note that the Greek term *oikonomia* is a composite word, consisting of *oikos* (house/household) and *nomos*, usually translated as regulation and law in general. Indeed, Foucault's concept of governmentality is a philosophical elaboration of *oikonomia*'s close connection to the regulation of conduct, one's own and that of others. Etymologically speaking, however, *nomos* is derivative of the ancient Greek verb *nemo* (*νέμω*), itself connoting the activity of apportioning, allocating and dividing, and conveys the exercise of a force impelling to such action. Consequently, the current study is an attempt to place acts of partition and division (of time and subjects) at the centre of scholarly attention, while attesting to the forces and influences exercised in their incidence.

Ekonomi Islam

As a response to the devastating economic crisis of 1997 and the political turmoil following Suharto's resignation in 1998, Indonesians have been desperately seeking for new and effective ways of overcoming the crisis, carving out a path towards prosperity and justice. After having experimented for half-a-century with socialist policies under Sukarno (1949–1965), followed by state-led development under Suharto's authoritarian rule (1966–1998), Indonesia took a new turn when in the wake of the Asian crisis, it underwent a series of neoliberal democratic reforms. The reforms implemented ranged from the decentralisation of power away from Jakarta, the holding of 'free and fair' elections featuring a bewildering array of new political parties and the promotion of 'free' press and civil society associations as key players in the game of politics. At the same time, they involved the gradual removal of state subsidies, the advancement of competition and market rule[3] and the creation of a vibrant service sector based on the new consumption habits of the rising numbers of those self-styled as middle class. In the early 2010s, Indonesia came to be considered by many as a regional economic powerhouse: growth accelerated to around 6%, foreign investors flocked back to the country and government bonds regained their investment-grade rating. The impression that the good times were back was strengthened by a significant boom in the construction and retail sectors, with property prices rising high and luxurious shopping malls appearing in many cities.

These developments have been accompanied by major challenges, the most important of which is perhaps what Robinson and Hadiz (2013) describe as the emergence and consolidation of oligarchic rule. Such rule is 'defined by an increasing fusion of wealth and politico-bureaucratic power, articulated in the relationships and interminglings between the leading families of business and those of politics and the bureaucracy as they became enmeshed directly in the ownership and control of capital' (Robinson and Hadiz 2013: 34). As a result, corruption continues to be perceived by many as rampant, and socio-economic inequalities are experienced as persisting, if not actually growing. To ameliorate this situation, the government, international funding bodies and non-governmental organisations have been seeking to sustain growth, improve employment and effect a more equitable distribution of wealth through, among other things, the cultivation of a new generation of future entrepreneurs. In 2011, the then President Susilo Bambang Yudhoyono argued that the way to national prosperity required for *rakyat* (the people) to create new products and new business ventures by becoming entrepreneurs. To this, the then Cooperatives and Small and Medium Enterprises Minister added that the number of entrepreneurs had to be raised: it has historically been very low, accounting for 0.24% of the population, and well below the optimum of 2%.[4] A year later, Dr Gusti Muhammad Hatta, Minister for Research and Technology, in an interview with Forbes, noted that Indonesia has one of the lowest rates of new business creation in Asia, a fact he attributed to difficulties with accessing capital and inadequate training.[5]

The politics of development of a class of indigenous entrepreneurs, particularly through generous support to small and medium enterprises, has long been a project of a loose group of urban Muslim intellectuals arguing for the revival of the faith. Starting from the late Suharto period onward, such religious cum political actors have sought to put Islam into everyday practice by proposing, amongst other things, the creation of a *syariah*-based economy whose main purpose is to serve the people (*ekonomi Islam/ekonomi rakyat*). In broad terms, *ekonomi rakyat* was conceived as relating to the conduct of livelihood activities in a manner compatible to 'Islamic law' (*syariah*), indexing a system of just economic practice that would benefit the masses of poor and disadvantaged Muslims inhabiting the rural hinterlands and urban slums. Such Islamic economy was originally meant as an alternative to the top-down, undemocratic policies of the New Order and its system of *rentier* capitalism, especially with regards to the advantages accrued to a restricted class of businessmen, usually of Chinese background and their associates in the bureaucracy and the army (Lubis 2004; Saeed 2004; Njoto-Feillard 2012; Choiruzzad 2013). Since the early 1990s and despite many serious internal disagreements over its 'architecture,'[6] the demand for *ekonomi Islam* has witnessed key advances such as the operation of several *syariah*-compliant financial institutions, inclusive of three Islamic commercial banks, more than a hundred *Syariah* People's Credit Banks and thousands of Islamic micro-finance institutions. At the same time, the discipline of Islamic economics has come to be taught at several leading universities and other institutes of higher learning, featuring specialist departments with expert programmes of study, regular conferences and the publication of specialist journals. In addition, the movement has been instrumental in the successful operation of several zakat management bodies engaged in disaster relief, poverty alleviation and advocacy, both on a national and an international level.

To many *ekonomi Islam* advocates, the 2008 credit crunch and the ensuing turmoil in Euro-America provided ample evidence of the weaknesses of neoliberal capitalism, underlying the future advantages of a fully Islamised economy. In place of capitalism's excessive reliance on finance products and markets, the adherents of *ekonomi Islam* I met in Jakarta and Surabaya in 2011–2012 emphasised the indissoluble connection of Islamic banking and finance with the 'real' economy whereby the former aids the production of 'actual' goods and services. Similarly, they castigated neoliberalism for the promotion of unwarranted risks and unhinged speculation and critiqued its dependence on the creation of 'virtual' wealth. In contrast to a situation whereby money has no fixed value due to having been decoupled from any objective standard, *ekonomi Islam*, some argued, will be based on gold bullion (Amin 2007). Most importantly, neoliberal capitalism was deemed as cruel, putting short-term profit before public welfare, jeopardising the livelihoods of millions of people for the pleasure of a minority. In contrast, advocates of *ekonomi Islam* stressed that the economy is meant to serve the overall purpose of *syariah,* which is the achievement of justice (*keadilan*). As the convenor of a workshop on the 2012 Islamic Economy Outlook put it, for justice to take hold, *ekonomi Islam* would have to be an *ekonomi rakyat*, a people's economy, destined to empower the poor and destitute.

For many advocates of a *syariah*-based approach to livelihood in Indonesia, the key to a viable and sustainable Islamic economy does not solely depend on the success of big Islamic financial institutions. Instead, it involves the cultivation on a massive scale of scores of Muslim entrepreneurs whose attitude to work and wealth is permeated by the desire to please Allah and receive due reward in this life and the hereafter. According to them, it is not enough for the project to involve the better-off and the educated: at the same time that a new generation of Islamic economics graduates is produced, efforts are currently underway for the poor to be engaged with and brought into the fold. In this regard, *ekonomi Islam* seeks to empower (*memberdayakan*) the millions of Indonesians active in the informal sector, principally, the petty traders and street vendors, as well as the unemployed, in such a way that it is possible for them to achieve self-reliance (*kemandirian*). On the whole, the strategy adopted for *ekonomi Islam* future's blooming necessitates sustained interventions for poverty alleviation. Such interventions are geared towards the cultivation of particular sets of dispositions and sensibilities amongst the urban and rural poor considered as much conducive to entrepreneurial success as to salvation in the hereafter. In this respect, strengthening the faith of the poor through the conduct of *dakwah* (Islamic propagation) activities goes hand in hand with the dissemination of entrepreneurial values: the spread of holy words is supplemented with the provision of capital and training necessary for the poor to set up profitable businesses.

As several scholars have noted for other places in the world (Atia 2013; Tuğal 2017; Rudnyckyj 2019), despite its robust criticism of capitalism, in Indonesia too, the movement for the Islamisation of the economy provides strong intellectual and political support for the creative, yet incomplete and unstable, combination of market rule with the *syariah*. In this regard, the everyday application of the faith is wedded to the expansion of capital (human, monetary and symbolic) the faithful command, with the intensification of worship deemed as integral for a rise in future profits. However such cohabitation is constantly haunted by the ever-present possibility of coming apart, principally because of the market overtaking the faith and the faithful giving in to immoral, selfish desires for wealth accumulation without caring either for God or for human others. If this was to become true, market forces would have gained the upper hand, having succeeded in enveloping religion, making it subservient to the promotion of their own ends and purposes. Of course, the very reverse to market supremacy can also happen. In this regard, the faithful are constantly exhorted to make sure that it is the priorities of Islam and its teachings that take precedence over and above those of the market. Failure to demonstrate this precedence in everyday life means that one might be destined for an afterlife in hell, rather than a place in paradise. As I go on to elaborate below, widespread and intense concerns over death and one's afterlife chances have important consequences for the insecure and ongoing articulation of neoliberalism and Islam, as they reveal that the outer limits of the process of commodification coincide with the rising powers of religion to promise life eternal. Death and what follows its happening present capitalism with an inescapable event it can admittedly do very little about. At best, it can postpone its coming for a short-while and/or make death less painful and perhaps more comfortable. In contrast, Islam, along with other religions, has seized upon the inescapability of death, turning it into an exclusive domain: death is the very terrain on which religions advance their distinct imaginings as to what life, prosperity and happiness are ultimately about. In this regard, the future Islam envisions extends far beyond the most distant horizons capitalism is capable of foreseeing: while capitalism can see nothing beyond the end of this life, the Muslim faithful anticipate a life beginning after this life is over, with death ensuring the passage from the one form to the other. The significance of death and life eternal for the temporality at play in Islamic interventions to raise the poor out of misfortune is discussed further below, after the entanglements of Islamic zakat management bodies with entrepreneurship have been considered in some depth.

Lifelong Schooling

Dana Keadilan Indonesia is an Islamic welfare organisation actively involved in poverty alleviation efforts through *syariah*-inspired interventions in health, education and employment. DKI was established in Bandung, West Java, in 1998. It is widely considered to be an offshoot of the *tarbiyah* movement and is closely related to the Prosperous Justice Party (*Partai Keadilan Sejahtera*) founded in the same year. The *tarbiyah* movement emerged in the 1970s out of the Salman mosque of the Bandung Institute of Technology, its activism quickly spread around campuses all over the country. The movement placed emphasis on *dakwah* activities, and facilitated an increase in students' observing Islamic tenets in their everyday life such as wearing the headscarf and studying the Quran. It drew inspiration from Egypt's Muslim Brothers and endeavoured to apply Islam to all spheres of social, political and economic life. Accordingly, both DKI and PKS emphasise moral reform and the education of the public through *dakwah* (Islamic propagation) while advocating for democratic politics and the creation of a vibrant civil society (Hasan 2009; Permata 2008): at the heart of their policies and programmes is the conviction that the moral principles and universal values of Islam provide a solution to the

Table 4.1 *Dana Keadilan Indonesia*, funds in billion rupiah

Year	*Total funds collected*
1999	0.8
2000	2.10
2001	2.19
2002	4.19
2003	6.46
2004	8.92
2005	45.26
2006	29.52
2007	50.16
2008	71.40
2009	107.3
2010	135.1
2011	145.9

Table 4.2 *Dana Keadilan Indonesia*, number of donors

Year	*Total*
2007	28,300
2008	47,427
2009	68,399
2010	84,369
2011	99,238

persistence of corruption and the widespread occurrence of poverty and inequality plaguing the nation. They draw the majority of their support from a core constituency related to wider *tarbiyah* networks and increasingly from the rising number of middle-class professionals living in major urban centres.

Since its inception, DKI has witnessed remarkable growth. In 2011, it had a total of 44 offices in 18 provinces, employed 620 people and collected more than $16 million in donations—including zakat and corporate social responsibility funds—from almost 100,000 donors, both corporate and individual (Tables 4.1 and 4.2).

Within a relatively short period, DKI has managed to establish a well-integrated network of schools, clinics and community centres across the nation-state. Its rapid expansion has partly to do with the distinctive approach DKI brought to matters philanthropic in Indonesia, especially the deployment of corporate governance models and managerial know-how to guide its operations. In line with modern standards, DKI comprises three boards: the board of trustees, the board of *syariah* supervisors and the board of directors. It has a Chief Executive Officer presiding over section directors and programme managers, all of whom aim to create value for donors and beneficiaries alike through the deployment of managerial competencies. As I was repeatedly told by DKI senior managers, such competencies are identical to the ones deployed in commercial establishments, including the ability to take decisions, make plans and lead subordinates, the capacity to develop ideas and implement strategies and the skill to set achievable goals, communicate proficiently and meet targets. In the case of DKI, such competencies extend to the skilful recitation of the Quran and advanced understanding of and implementation of Islamic precepts in everyday life. All DKI employees have developed the required competencies through previous schooling: however, promotions are conditional on the undertaking of additional training and require obtaining relevant certification for both religious and managerial/technical subjects.

The strong corporate ethos is further evinced by the fact that the organisation is part of a business consortium that includes several commercial ventures DKI's original founder established subsequently. These for-profit ventures include an Islamic finance company, an Islamic insurance firm, an information technology company, several agribusiness and *halal* meat-processing ventures and a human resources consultancy. Often times, senior staff move from one company to another, bringing along and disseminating new forms of technical know-how. Collaboration across the consortium takes many forms: the consortium's for-profit ventures normally transfer zakat levied on their profits, along with corporate social responsibility funds, to DKI to manage and distribute, the Islamic insurance firm provides sickness and pension cover to all employees of the consortium while DKI staff often participate in training and motivation sessions offered by the consortium's human resources consultancy firm.[7]

DKI recruits mainly from amongst the youth: recent university graduates, male and female, are its preferred employees. Candidates must also be able to demonstrate a strong commitment to Islam, usually involving active membership in a Muslim student organisation such as KAMMI (*Kesatuan Aksi Mahasiswa Muslim Indonesia*, The Indonesian Muslim Student Action Union).[8] According to senior staff, the initial focus was on recruiting pious Muslims with a good grasp of Islam and an interest in its social mission. However, the policy was revised soon after it became apparent that many recruits lacked the competencies essential to the successful implementation of poverty alleviation programmes. Today, recruitment priorities favour university graduates with a degree in secular subjects such as law, English language, accounting, economics and IT. However, candidates are still expected to have a strong religious outlook and a proven track record in organisational and leadership skills, having acted as heads or deputies in student or local associations. Most of the staff I came to know in the 12 months I spent with the organisation were in their mid-20s; medium-level managers were slightly older, usually in their early 30s, while the CEO was in his mid-30s. It is also worth noting that several staff were married to colleagues, often working in different sections of the organisation.

DKI prides itself for caring intensely for its staff, providing many training opportunities for it to improve and expand its skills and capacities. As a senior manager put it, 'DKI is a school for us; we learn everyday.' Working for DKI was widely conceived as accruing more than a salary to live on: in addition to mediocre monetary returns, staff was actively encouraged to count on the religious merit (*pahala, sawāb* in Arabic) engagement in the propagation of the faith and the promotion of the public good generates. Such merit the faithful rely on for the Day of Judgment as counterweight to sins committed. Though the overall value of *pahala* accumulated was held to be unknown (see below), the production of merit was explicitly talked about amongst staff as an ongoing investment, that is, a practice destined to bear significant yields when the end-of-time arrives. Along with merit, the desire to learn new skills was highly emphasised as a sign of professional virtue and religious piety. The aim of such learning is the making of the world anew in the near future. As the same manager put it, 'DKI's task is to build a civilisation which will come to fruition in ten or twenty years' time. This civilisation will be based on persons able to feel for others because they will be motivated by the teachings of the Quran and humanitarian values. In our times, lots of people care only about themselves. DKI desires to instil feelings of care for others to everyone, including its staff.'

For the ideal Muslim personnel to take shape and for the required affects to develop, the organisation is running a training regime for staff to undertake at regular and irregular intervals. While training may vary according to individual circumstances and the needs of specific branches, regularity is a feature of daily and weekly work schedules. Such schedules are implemented with a great degree of uniformity across the organisation's branches. Along with emphasising discipline, homogeneity and consistency, the training in question underscores the desirability of bringing about improvement to self and society, aiming at cultivating the required self-confidence in one's ability and commitment to effect progress.

Daily training amounts to an intensive and repetitive event that shapes not only the subjectivities of those involved but informs time itself, making time pass and marking its passage. Within the overall utopian orientation of the *ekonomi Islam* movement, the training involved is a very important time-synthesising technique deployed for hastening the advent of the future. This hastening requires deep cuts to be made in the flow of time so that an opening comes about through which the very future civilisation DKI intends on building, appears in the distance. The anticipation of a future life improved requires the instituting of regular events that interrupt and unhinge the present. In this respect, the regularity with which training is undertaken should not be taken to imply mere repetition and the return of the same. Quite the opposite is true: such regularity indexes an intense commitment to bringing about an Islamic alternative future conceived of as attainable by means of organising orderly and uniform events that have the power to affect time as much as the people enveloped in it.

For DKI staff, the working day starts at 8 o'clock sharp, if not slightly earlier, as fines are incurred to latecomers. The first item in the agenda is a motivation session, called *inspirasi pagi* (morning inspiration), aiming to create the required enthusiasm for a successful working day. The motivation session lasts thirty minutes: it begins with Quranic recitation, followed by *hadith*—collections of the sayings and deeds of the Prophet—and the recital of Allah's ninety-nine names under the guidance of soft Arabic music (*dhikir*). While the Quranic recitation and the *hadith* narration are performed with staff taking turns, *dhikir* engages staff in collective worship. Sometimes, seating arrangements index mosque practices, with female staff donning the headscarf seated at the back of the room, away from men occupying the centre. Often, the *hadith* chosen have immediate significance. An often narrated *hadith* is the following: the Prophet said 'if you help your brother, Allah is going to reward you both in this world and the afterlife'; the Prophet said 'if you cover the shame of your brother, Allah is going to cover your shame'; the Prophet said 'Allah is going to help you as long as you come to the aid of your brothers.' Even though its message is clear enough, the session's leader is keen to remind everyone that good deeds (*amal*) are God-pleasing, mandatory and rewarding.

In the first part of *inspirasi pagi*, staff displays circumspection, concentration and contemplation: they speak softly with eyes downcast and hands tied together. This reverential atmosphere is soon broken with everybody rising from their seats for the (re-)taking of an oath to occur. The oath which upholds faith in the desirability of social transformation affirms the future. It also reasserts a commitment to managerial values proclaimed with much boisterousness. The session is delivered by a senior staff reading from a script, which includes the oath's content, contains notes as to its oral delivery—encouraging participants to declare 'in spirited manner,' 'full of intent,' and 'resoundingly'—along with images of body movements that should accompany each and every utterance. In a carefully choreographed manner, the body of DKI staff is prompted to assume as much the mode of presence of a boxer who delivers blows to invisible enemies while promoting Allah's cause, as to exemplify the assuredness and confidence of professional men and women intent on building partnerships for social justice.

The second half of *inspirasi pagi* starts with the session leader declaring 'Greet the great transformation!' to which all and sundry respond with the cry 'leave behind the ordinary.' The response is punctuated with the right hand, situated at the level of the waist, moving forward, fist clenched. Immediately after, everybody shouts out aloud 'achieve the extraordinary,' moving the left arm forward, fist clenched. Then, the right hand comes back into play, with all yelling '[I/We] can (*bisa*), [I/we] can, [I/we] can.' Each time '*bisa*' is uttered, the right hand is driven forward at the level of the chest with great intensity and purpose. This assertion of self-belief is succeeded by the admission of obligation: next everyone declares '[I/We] ought to,' with the left hand moving outwards, punching the air. Finally, God is brought into the fold: all shouting 'Allah is great' with great excitement, with the right hand extending above the level of the head, stretching the body towards the sky.

While remaining standing up, staff proceed to a raucous recitation of DKI's mission and vision statement while taking turns. The statement is known by heart and is delivered with much steadfastness and resolve. These qualities are entrenched in the sound waves that voices generate: their reverberation around the room creates a specific oral and auditory environment that affects all present. Such affective performance is supported by staff assuming body postures, such as standing to attention while facing each other and exchanging sharp, meaningful looks. The mission statement which is treated with near sacral respect is as follows:

> *VISION*
> *To become a first-rate and trusted international zakat management organisation.*
> *MISSION*
> *1. To develop people's potential for self-reliance through empowerment programmes.*
> *2. To improve the quality of service through excellence in human resources.*
> *BRAND VALUE*
> *Trusted: To conduct business in a professional, transparent and trusted manner.*
> *Progressive: To be brave in innovating and educating for the purpose of greater benefit.*
> *Humanitarian: To facilitate humanitarian efforts with sincerity and inclusivity.*

The oath entails pledging one's allegiance to a broad spectrum of neoliberal values the organisation strives to implement internally and disseminate across Indonesian society. Beyond procedural matters and regulatory frameworks, the implementation of values such as transparency, innovation and continuous improvement requires the acquisition of everyday habits. Such habits are partly instilled and cultivated by the faithful execution of training routines such as *inspirasi pagi*. *Inspirasi pagi* turns abstract values into concrete plans for action through daily, steadfast repetition: commitment is cultivated through the demonstration of oral strength and verbal clarity; team-work and synergy are enhanced through the sequential arrangement of delivery; sincerity and honesty are encouraged by means of staff facing each other.

Before a prayer marks the end of the session, staff undergoes a further exercise, reciting yet another text. The exercise is titled 'greet the culture of work' (*salam budaya kerja*) and celebrates work as a virtue while enlisting the preferred manner for its conduct. It too relies on a combination of verbal and kinaesthetic techniques to shape subjects accordingly and make time pass. *Salam budaya kerja* is explicitly oriented towards the future both in terms of creating a people appropriate to it, envisaging its coming as a time of pious prosperity. The text guiding the performance notes that it should be 'led by the leader with zest of movement, voice and unified intent.' The exercise involves six distinct movements and begins with staff extending their right hand sideways, with the palm wide open, shouting out aloud 'trust' (*amanat*). Then, they close their palm to form a fist while crying out 'professional' (*profesional*). The third movement requires the right hand displaying an open palm at a forward position, with everyone declaring 'facilitation' (*kemudahan*). Next, both hands are brought to the level of the chest, forming an X, and everybody shouts 'synergy' (*sinergi*). The fifth movement brings the right hand back to a forward position. This time the open palm faces downwards, and everyone screams 'targeted distribution' (*ketepatan penyaluran*). Finally, the right-hand indexes the taking of an oath and everyone pronounces 'clarity of reporting' (*kejelasan laporan*). By means of these six distinct movements, personnel become somatically cognizant and corporeally aware of the key activities DKI routinely undertakes. These are the solicitation of donations (trust), the management of funds (professional), the implementation of empowerment programmes (facilitation), the building of partnerships (synergy), the running of poverty alleviation programmes (targeted distribution), accompanied by transparent, accountable reporting (clarity of reporting). Such activities are considered essential for engineering a better future-to-come.

The session concludes with a request for Allah's intercession, with the prayer inflecting the occasion as a ritual event. In conjunction with the Quranic recitation that opens the session, the concluding prayer acts to enclose the iteration of managerial values and business practices within an Islamic frame, itself capable of domesticating their secular and foreign connotations. In addition, it strives to re-orient the purpose of work from profit generation to ultimate redemption. In this regard, the temporality *inspirasi pagi* sets in train references the metaphysics of salvation as set out in Islamic scriptures. The quest for redemption is of paramount importance for understanding the temporal horizon staff training and poverty alleviation interventions are situated in, with salvation involving both deliverance from poverty and misery in this life and escape from punishment and suffering in the afterlife.

Encountering the Future

The DKI training regime aims to disseminate *ekonomi Islam*'s potent mix of entrepreneurial and religious priorities and values to staff as well as the country's poor through targeted interventions in the fields of education, health and micro-finance. *Syariah*-compliant community development programmes run by the organisation deploy a variety of techniques and knowledge sets for bringing about improvements in the life circumstances of the poor by means of increasing the capital they command. DKI staff talk explicitly about the different kinds of capital (monetary, human, social, etc.) the poor should have access to and has designed its own programmes for addressing their deficiencies. Key in its approach is the identification of districts (*kecamatan*) in urban and rural areas marked by persistent poverty, despite their inhabitants having some sort of capital available to them. Though the conduct of surveys, DKI classifies poor populations as either *miskin*, broadly referring to the working poor and those with unstable and unreliable sources of income, or *rentan*—the susceptible ones—designating all those insecurely and tangentially located above the poverty line, yet constantly facing the risk of falling back into it. To simplify things somewhat, DKI offers free education and health services to *miskin* with the long-term view of transforming them, and their children, into *rentan*. The *rentan* it primarily supports through offers of monetary capital and business training, assisting them with setting up and running sustainable micro-businesses, essentially turning them into Indonesia's future Muslim entrepreneurs.

In 2011–2012, I observed closely DKI micro-finance programmes in Surabaya, East Java and Ciputat, just south of Jakarta. These programmes were supported either by *sedekah/infak* (voluntary alms) or by corporate social responsibility funds that national and global conglomerates transferred to DKI to manage (see Chap. 7). Despite significant differences in micro-credit distribution (CSR funds were distributed on a free-gift basis, while *sedekah/infak* funds were circulated as interest-free loans), in all other respects, staff charged with the task of preparing Indonesia's next generation of Muslim entrepreneurs placed outmost importance on empowering the poor. In this context, staff was actively encouraged to think of themselves as 'guides' (*pendamping*) capable of delivering the poor out of their suffering with their main roles understood to be (a) providers and surveyors of empowerment (*pemberdaya* and *surveyor pemberdayaan*, respectively), (b) motivators (*penggerak lingkungan*) and (c) people's advocates (*advokat masyarakat*). According to DKI, making monetary capital available to the poor was not sufficient in and of itself for empowerment to take hold. Instead, the poor had to be carefully 'guided' so that their 'mind-set' was transformed in such a way that new expectations of economic success, novel aspirations of upward social mobility and higher standards concerning piety and business practice were promoted and sustained. Indeed, one of the main risks DKI staff identified with unsupervised capital provision was for the poor to 'misuse' the money for immediate consumption purposes such as paying school fees or utility bills, instead of taking a more long-term view and investing it either by setting up a small business or improving an already existing one, thus slowly working their way out of poverty.

The poor who consented to be 'guided' into future prosperity were, in their vast majority, married women with several children of various ages: they were collectively referred to as *binaan*—'assisted/targeted members/protégés'—and *ibu-ibu*—'mothers.' Despite the acknowledgement of fathers and husbands as the main breadwinner and household authority, local gender ideologies encourage mothers to assume roles exceeding the purely domestic ones, undertaking whatever action is necessary in order to protect and serve their dependants who they strive to provide for with a determination and selflessness that men are supposed to be lacking. The 'mothers' DKI sought to empower were economically active either in the formal economy as factory workers or shop assistants or in the informal sector working as street vendors, food-stall operators and local bazaar sellers of a vast array of goods, ranging from clothing, household utensils and medicine to food and drinks. It is primarily amongst the ranks of these self-employed, small-scale tradeswomen striving to make a meagre living to supplement their husband's own that DKI focuses its effort. The fact that these women have commercial experience, are in dire need of credit and other forms of support and have a basic only understanding of Islam, often of the 'traditionalist' variety, makes them ideal in the eyes of DKI for purposes of business training and, to a lesser extent, indirect religious instruction.

Along with dispensing micro-credit, DKI staff held weekly or biweekly consultancy sessions with female protégés to discuss and assess the challenges the latter faced in running their businesses, whereby either party could draw attention to issues, pose questions and make suggestions and requests. The sessions provided ample opportunity for DKI staff to investigate a variety of commercial issues such as the sourcing of materials, the pricing and marketing of products, the rate of profit and the potential for expansion. Visits to homes and market-stalls were accompanied by training the protégés in unfamiliar techniques such as accurate and thorough book-keeping. DKI staff was well-aware that the products the *binaan* sold had to conform to state regulations. To this end, they held events to disseminate information about banned additives used extensively to enhance the taste and appearance of foodstuffs. At times, DKI staff approached specific *binaan* with ideas about developing innovative products: handing out recipes for foods from other parts of Indonesia, supplying new designs for T-shirts and developing organic, health drinks were measures taken to cultivate true entrepreneurial spirit amongst the poor. Such occasions were also prime opportunities for staff to deliver motivational messages that would enhance the *binaan*'s eagerness for economic success and heighten their commitment to Islamic pietism. However, religious devotion was mainly promoted in an indirect manner and revolved around facilitating Quranic study groups: such groups met weekly or biweekly, often under the tutoring of DKI volunteers who were university students well-versed in the Islamic sciences.

Welfare interventions geared towards improving the lives of the poor amount to events that insert cuts in the flow of time, breaking time up into intervals. The latter provides the space needed for pursuing higher returns in terms of wealth and personal piety. This 'spacing' of time around planned and regular events allows for reflection to take place so that new ways are found for achieving empowerment and progress. For example, the repayment schedule of interest-free loans provided by DKI has an undeniable periodicity with instalments arranged in monthly intervals. This periodicity is replicated in the visits staff pays to women's homes and stalls for the provision of training and general guidance as well as in Quranic study group meetings. DKI empowerment programmes are structured around the holding of events for the benefit of the poor, with such events assuming a recurring, persistent and intensive character. For the duration of such programmes, DKI staff and *binaan*'s interactions focus on assessing the present while making plans and preparations for a better future. In seeking to steer the future in a specific direction, that is, towards a *syariah*-inspired mode of entrepreneurship, DKI concentrates on holding events, which, in turn, insert breaks and gaps in the routines, habits and temporal sequences permeating the lives of the poor. Such breaks are of major value for they supply the reference points required for measuring progress in terms of profits and advancements in business success and personal piety. As such, welfare interventions perform a major governmental function through the effects they have on the organisation of time: by means of opening time up, they introduce intervals that aim to nurture the emergence of a future people, that is, a people who are much improved and enhanced versions of past and present peoples. The focus *ekonomi Islam* places on people becoming more pious Muslims and more successful traders means that the subjects it fosters acquire consistency through the endless pursuit of self-perfection. Such pursuit is measured on a scale containing countless intervals whereby yet-to-come actualisations are conceived as superior, enriched versions of present ones.

One of the most telling cases of the timework involved relates to the invitation DKI secured for the most promising of its *binaan* to a promotional event held in December 2011 in Surabaya. The event was jointly organised by the branch of a conventional, high-street bank and a relatively obscure manufacturer of motorised vehicles and took place in an upmarket restaurant opposite the five-star Shangri-La Surabaya hotel. The event, featuring speeches by the city administration and local chamber of commerce officials about the vital importance of small and medium enterprises for the health of the economy, also included a crush-course in business management by one of Surabaya's most popular motivational speakers, a young man of mixed Chinese-Javanese ancestry. When asked the reason why DKI took its *binaan* to the event, Arief, the man in charge, replied that '*insyallah*, it will inspire them to get ahead in business by revisiting their practices, and come up with new ideas and innovative products.'

In a nutshell, the event which opened with live pop music and closed with a sumptuous buffet lunch was about the promotion of a new vehicle, a motorised three-wheeler, featuring a flexible rear end of adequate carrying capacity to function as a vendor's mobile shop. In his PowerPoint presentation, the company vice-director stressed the advantages of three-wheel motorised mobility set against the relative stillness of stands most small-scale traders operate from and the prohibitive cost involved in four-wheel ownership and maintenance. In a series of well-drawn images, he sought to demonstrate the versatility of the vehicle's rear end: it could be customised for many purposes, ranging from carrying fuel or water to selling ice-cream and clothes to an open-air restaurant equipped with its own kitchen. As for covering the costs of its acquisition, one should not worry, he insisted, for help was at hand from the event's other sponsor, Bank Danamon. Taking his turn, the bank's manager laid out the full gamut of services available, inclusive of current and savings accounts and credit facilities for small and medium entrepreneurs, paying attention to the criteria they must fulfil for their loan application to be successful. After the event was over, Arief admitted that the bank's interest-bearing loans ruled out any collaboration with DKI's protégés: listening however to what the bank manager and company director had to offer was valuable for broadening their horizons, embracing a future full of potentiality.

For the *binaan* to go ahead and actualise such potentiality, more than business equipment and credit facilities are required; indeed, entrepreneurial know-how and high levels of motivation are essential. Once again, such assistance was on offer, courtesy of the appropriately named Bani

Firdaus (Son of Paradise), 'Surabaya's No1 business coach.' Bani begun his session with wordplay and the making of a promise: 'I promise you that although you came here today as *Usaha Kecil Menengah* (UKM, micro-entrepreneurs), I will make sure you become *Usaha Kecil Miliaran* (UKM, micro-billionaires).' Quite fittingly his formula for success involved three disciplines, the most important relating to time. The first discipline involved money and was about accurate accounting: knowing exactly how much it costs to make or trade a product is as vital as knowing the rate of profit necessary to keep a business sustainable, he said. The second was related to staff discipline, making sure one's employees meet productivity targets. Bani was in favour of taking a hard line, arguing that 'if staff is not hardworking, then he/she should be laid off; if staff is not on time, then he/she should be laid off.' The third, time discipline, was the most crucial for it marked the difference between employees and entrepreneurs. Employees work for a specific amount of time, normally between 9 am and 5 pm, he said. Entrepreneurs, by contrast, use all the time at their disposal to conduct and improve business: an entrepreneur is the one who works constantly, always looking for ways to increase her profit margin. According to Bani, the problem is that a lot of micro-entrepreneurs in Indonesia work in a disjointed fashion, that is, some days they work a lot, some others they work only a little: his advice was that they should break such habit, and by means of developing a consistent work routine, they should work almost without a pause, as perpetually and incessantly as humanly possible.

The Ultimate Promise

Bani Firdaus' promise and the more general promise DKI and other LAZ or zakat management bodies make to the poor in terms of delivering them from persistent poverty through regular infusions of capital and the dispensing of info-training is situated within a broader framework. The importance of such a framework is that it exceeds the economy understood in a narrow, restricted sense. The promise of future prosperity LAZ advance is embedded within a wider horizon of profound salvific connotations. Such a horizon conceives of life and well-being in an expansive sense. By both echoing and repeating a much more capacious promise on the basis of which all living takes its significance from, LAZ re-affirm Islam as a distinct basis of operation. The promise made by Islamic welfare organisations references the overarching promise Allah Himself made to mankind: on condition of strict conformity with His commandments, Allah has promised that He will deliver mankind to a life eternal, that is, a life full of joy, free from pains and agony.

In the Quran, Allah asserts that he created the earth and the seven heavens for all his creatures and that he appointed man as His viceroy on earth. For humans, life on earth constitutes a set of trials and tests based on which their destiny will be decided (Khouj 1992; Oualaalou 2018). The heavens, which are perceived by Muslims worldwide to be spatio-temporal regions separate from earth, are the abode of paradise and hell; as such, they are the destination of mankind following upon death. After death, Allah has promised to resurrect the deceased, re-uniting their soul with their body, so that every single human that has ever existed can be present on the Day of Judgement. The purpose of the judgement is for Allah to exercise His dominion: for humans, it involves finding out whether one's resting place will be in paradise, including the Firdaus (the highest part of paradise) or will be thrown in hell (Mufti 2015). Muslim imagery describes paradise as an eternal garden with rivers of wine, milk and honey flowing uninterrupted. At the other end, hell is portrayed as a place of torture where offenders receive punishments commensurate to the sins committed and the debits incurred while on earth. The conviction that death is not the end of life, but a passage to an afterlife which could be free from necessity and toil, full of everlasting happiness, corresponds to a fundamental presupposition that no Muslim I know of has ever expressed doubts or misgivings about. The same is true for the notion that a Muslim's life on earth, his/her deeds, actions and interactions with others are anything but the groundwork of and preparation for a life in the hereafter.

The overriding importance of the promise of salvation as pronounced in Islam can't be stressed enough. For people of faith, concerns with salvation exceed in magnitude and urgency all other worries, with assurances over attaining redemption superseding other pledges and declarations. At precisely this point, neoliberal capitalism faces severe limits as to what it can promise to do and deliver with the faith acquiring surplus strength. Let me explain. While the commodification of life has been unrelenting over the last two centuries, in Indonesia as much as everywhere else, with new articles fabricated and marketed with every new turn of technological innovation and specialist intervention in fields as diverse as fertility, knowledge and the environment, the mortal character of existence remains a drama the market has yet to devise adequate solutions for. While life itself can be inaugurated, improved and prolonged with the deployment of instruments and techniques made available by means of capitalism's ongoing search for new vistas for profit generation, death itself, as a destiny facing all living creatures, inclusive of humans, remains unaffected by capitalism's triumphant march. True, the processes surrounding death and death's implications for the living have been duly arrested by commodity exchange. The means of such capture include pensions for old age, the provision of medical care and insurance, funeral processions, wills, legacies and inheritance rights. Nevertheless, the desire for life eternal has no recourse of becoming fulfilled, in the foreseeable future at least, by the possibilities afforded by commodification. Death and its corollary, the desire for life unlimited, occupies the very limit contemporary forms of governmentality can neither fully satisfy nor completely arrest. At the same time, the market can neither evade nor surpass the inescapability of death. It is precisely at this point that neoliberalism, as described by Foucault (2007, 2008), reaches an impasse and the economy as commonly conceived assumes secondary importance, becoming subject to a force promising to deliver what the market can't do. This promissory force conventionally labelled as religion—in this case, Islam—involves the making possible of life eternal.

For Muslims, death is not the *telos* of life but a break, a caesura, marking the beginning of an altogether different life. In addition, for faiths such as Islam whereby salvation is not sought on the basis of doctrines of predestination such was the case for sixteenth-century Protestants as described by Weber (1985), between this life and the next life, a thread is presumed to persist. This is so for the activities undertaken during one's lifetime carry unmistakable consequences regarding the possibilities opened by death. In Islam, the thread connecting this life with the next places great emphasis for the attainment of salvation on good deeds (*amal*): along with Allah's mercy, the latter are attributed the capacity of directly affecting and openly influencing one's posthumous destiny. Reiterating a common saying, this is how Nasim Setiawan, the communication and resources director of *Pondok Infak Mulia*, put it to me in an interview: 'this life is a farmland for the afterlife (*dunia ini ladang bagi akherat*); so we have to plant lots of virtues and do lots of good deeds so that we can have a plentiful harvest and when we die we are happy'. Clarifying further the stakes involved, Ahmad Yassin, the marketing manager of *Surabaya Peduli Ummat*, on another occasion, explained that 'on judgement day, everyone will receive a book enlisting all their good deeds while alive (*buku amal*);

those who are to go to paradise will receive it with their right hand; those who receive it with their left hand or with their backs facing the Creator, will go to hell.'

Conducting zakat worship, making voluntary donations (*sedekah*) and endowing one's assets for public welfare purposes (*wakaf*) count as good deeds (*amal*). So too are a wide set of activities ranging from specific ones, such as praying five times a day, fasting during Ramadan and reciting the Quran, to general ones such as spreading the faith (*dakwah*), observing closely the *syariah* and putting Islam to practice in every facet of life. In this regard, activities such as collecting, managing and distributing Islamic funds for the benefit of others count as *amal*, incurring *pahala* or salvific credits. The same goes for the acceptance of whatever assistance is on offer from the side of the poor, especially when it does not involve begging, which is widely frowned upon and discouraged. Moreover, when such assistance is put into good use, such as for the betterment of the life conditions of the recipients' children, as the *binaan* indisputably do, it too counts as an act of selfless sacrifice, qualifying as *amal*. The *amal* poor recipients perform is compounded by the intensification of worship they engage in as a result of their engagement with Islamic welfare organisations. *Amal* include acts of kindness the poor routinely perform, however trivial in monetary terms these might be (Osella and Widger 2018). Finally, to the extent that life on earth is considered to be a trial and test of faith, an attitude of acceptance is also marked as meritorious: accepting one's lot inclusive of poverty without grievance towards the Creator and without envy and resentment against those faring better in status and wealth is yet another act of piety presumed to make the poor honourable in the eyes of Allah.

When situated within salvific contexts, the value of conducting, managing and receiving zakat and other Islamic funds is no longer attached to furthering the purposes of governmentality: it no longer derives from the services it performs to the management of the population. Instead, the value of Islamic welfare interventions is intimately related to the contribution it makes towards securing future salvation for those involved: *amal* performed in this life are rewarded in salvific credits (*pahala*, *sawāb* in Arabic) as well as in sustenance (*rezeki*, *rizk* in Arabic) (Joll 2012; Mittermaier 2013, 2014; Anderson 2018; Kochuyt 2009). While *rezeki* is received in this life, in the form of good health, longevity, a loyal and pious spouse, a great number of descendants, monetary wealth and so on, *pahala* comes into effect after death, with the specific amount awarded revealed on Judgment Day. In general, *pahala* allows for the conversion of monetary wealth generated and accumulated through market transactions in this life into posthumous well-being. This is the case whereby rich benefactors dedicate part of their wealth to the building of mosques and orphanages with a view to securing a place in paradise. Still, this does not mean that a place in paradise is a commodity that can be bought or sold on account of capital expended: the direction of encompassment is actually the reverse as salvation has no price, it is itself priceless. Strict conditions are placed to ensure this to be the case with Islam stressing the importance of intention when undertaking such activity. In Islam, for pious activity to generate *pahala*, the right *niyat* (intent) is paramount: it should come straight from the heart and sincerely meant for Allah's glorification. Such is the paradox of salvation that if value is transferred or managed with the expectation of self-aggrandisement and self-promotion, *amal* is without effect in generating merit.

Pahala comes into force immediately upon death: it expresses the value accumulated for the good deeds performed in this life while making possible for the atonement of sins. In this regard, *pahala* denotes a unit for measuring and storing value, furnishing the means for accounting for the credit and debts the faithful have amassed during their lifetime. Islam relies for the delivery of judgement on a God, the creator of the universe, acting as sovereign: non-submission to divine Will amounts to an insult that requires the meeting out of punishment; conversely, sincere compliance earns His favour. The faithful are expected to account for their actions immediately after death when two angels—Munkar and Nakir—put a series of questions to the deceased, passing provisional judgement. The second, and most important ruling, is deferred till the Day of Judgement, when Allah is to make His final decision as to who will enter paradise and who will be sentenced to hell. In addition to merit being a medium of value that conjoins a person's life on earth to his/her afterlife, it functions as an object of exchange, becoming itself an article of transfer between persons, primarily the living and the dead. Muslims insist that each person is individually accountable for his/her actions. Yet, despite the fact that actions have single authors and sins are not subject to sharing, the merit the undertaking of virtuous deeds generates can be dedicated to the benefit of others, influencing their prospects for salvation. In Muslim Indonesia, rites of commemoration include efforts towards influencing the posthumous condition of ancestors through making merit: instead of claiming ownership, those attending reassign it to the dead (Bowen 1993;

Telle 2000; Retsikas 2007). Though there are sharp disagreements between traditionalist and modernist Muslims regarding who can generate merit for whom, there is wide acknowledgement of the maxim that salvation is an open-ended process that is not restricted to one's own actions but others can contribute to it as well on account of (self-) sacrifice.

Friends in Indonesia repeatedly stress that Muslims hold two different accounts: one in the bank, the other with Allah. In the former, value is expressed in rupiah, in the latter, in *pahala*. While it is certainly the case that rupiah are not exchangeable for a place in paradise, monetary wealth can be dedicated to the promotion of good, and the elimination of evil, as defined in *syariah*, activities which earn posthumous credits. The crux of the matter is that unlike the bank balance, nobody knows how much one has in store in merit: the amount of *pahala* accumulated by each and every faithful is a mystery to all but Allah, with the balance awaiting inspection on Judgement Day (Mittermaier 2013). Notwithstanding some notable exceptions (see Retsikas 2018), the element of uncertainty in salvation is fundamental: while worldly currency is varied and its amount is known for it is computable, the currency of merit is universal, yet corresponds to a puzzle for it bypasses human enumeration and defers computation. Because Allah's wisdom is greater than human reason, advance counting of *pahala* is basically pointless. In this regard, Katz's comment that the significance of divine rewards in the history of Sunni Islam 'lies in the wondrous and beneficent incommensurability of meagre human actions and bounteous divine reward, rather than in any numerical equivalency' (2007: 211) is particularly apt. Additionally, because the overall salvific economy is grounded on human impermanence, the theme of uncertainty pervading posthumous credit is particularly pronounced. In this regard, the futility and sheer hopelessness of counting *pahala* duplicate the unpredictability and inescapability associated with death's coming. Seen in this light, the overall importance of Islamic welfare interventions inclusive of giving, managing and receiving zakat and other forms of assistance exceeds concerns over value narrowly defined. The Islamic metaphysics of death and the openings death presumably creates in terms of potential afterlives foreground an alternative, *non-economistic conception of the economy*. The alternative economy of salvation Islam has put in place by means of speculative efforts as to distinct ways of securing well-being in life unending makes death and its aftermath central to ascertaining the significance of living economically.

A Life Synthesis

Despite apparent similarities relating to treating all action in the present as an investment bearing future returns, while foregrounding the figure of the entrepreneur as the most appropriate agent for carrying such responsibility forward, the case in favour of Islamic religiosity in contemporary Indonesia being subject to a rapid, deep and irreversible process of neoliberalisation (Rudnyckyj 2011; Hoesterey 2015) is neither straightforward nor simple to assert. In this respect, I concur with Mittermaier who writing about a different part of the world, argues that Islam in today's Egypt 'is not only affected by but also exceeds and speaks back to capitalist imaginaries' (2013: 276). My argument has been that key in causing such excess and disputation to arise is a *non-economistic concept of the economy* that Islam, along with other religions, such as Christianity, Buddhism and Judaism, advance, each in their own way, calling upon the faithful to cherish and put it into practice with dedication and commitment at every moment and turn. I have shown that the foundation of a non-economistic concept of the economy is the primacy, the faithful accord to the promise Allah made to mankind of attaining salvation in a life eternal, that redemption can be sought in a life extending beyond death. As the twelfth-century Muslim thinker al-Ghazali noted, the Quranic verses and prophetic reports suggest that 'the meaning of death is only a change of state (*taghayyur hal*, Arabic). And indeed the soul survives after its separation from the body: either in a state of suffering or comfort' (quoted in Moosa 1999: 13).

For the faithful, death denotes not life's cessation, but a temporary break in the unfolding of a life eternal, a momentary yet momentous caesurae in life everlasting. As such, death foregrounds an alternate economy, itself unrestricted by secular assumptions regarding the generation of value and human welfare. In a move that intends to supplement Foucault's genealogical readings of the emergence over the *longue durée* of the economy as a distinct domain of human rationality in Western Europe, I have argued that in the case of contemporary Muslims in Indonesia, the activity of dividing, cutting and apportioning that the concept of *oikonomia* itself entails as necessary for the generation of well-being, refers to a synthesis of life performed across the ontological divide instantiated by death. In the scheme of things economic, as proposed and implemented by *ekonomi Islam*, actions in this life have consequences for the afterlife with good deeds incurring credits and bad deeds accruing debits. The separation that death brings about between a person's present and future selves is accompanied by a fostering of connections that allow for balances to be carried forward and for full accountability to be deferred till the Day of Judgement. Rather than instituting the economy as a separate domain with a *sui generis* body of norms and expectations, *ekonomi Islam* subjects and subordinates each cut performed in the production and distribution of value to the ultimate cut, that is, the break ushered by death and the promise for divine retribution/reward that follows upon it. Because it has never sought to dis-embed economic transactions from the wider redemptive processes and salvific objectives, *ekonomi Islam* counts on death as a prerequisite for life eternal to furnish the means through which a final reckoning of value is to be conducted.

And yet, the contemporary moment means that *ekonomi Islam* is fully entrenched within a powerful diffusion of concepts, standards and practices that the term neoliberalism sums up with a unique vigour. Centring on the assumption of market efficiencies and the propagation of the figure of the entrepreneur as a new kind of economic agent who uses money accessed in the present in order to make more money return in the future, neoliberalism promises to ameliorate conditions in this life—conceived within a more proximate and immediate horizon—through the very financial intermediation of each and every aspect of it. The proliferation of Islamic welfare organisations both in Indonesia and elsewhere, part of the rationalisation of their objectives, along with the modernisation of their modes of operation and intervention can't be divorced from the playing out of neoliberal forces on a global scale. However, this does not mean that an Islamic conception of welfare has been engulfed by the powers of a market emanating from without. While it is certainly true that many are claiming that the most efficient and effective mode of delivering Islamic welfare to the poor is through NGO-style organisations that are themselves structured according to corporate criteria and operate in accordance with managerial standards so as to promote and cultivate amongst the destitute and their own employees the norms and expectations of entrepreneurship, it is still the case that we are not dealing here with blind imitation. As Tuğal puts it for the case of Egypt and Turkey, Islamic welfare organisations are a 'participant in the marking of a variegated, contested modernity,' neither a passive 'victim of global convergence nor an isolated alternative' (2017: 225). As the project of neoliberalism met serious obstacles with the onset of the financial crisis in 2008 and the spread of its effects in the populations of the US and Europe, proponents of *ekonomi Islam* in Indonesia argued with new vigour that working out *syariah*-compliant alternatives to capitalist value production is the right path to pursue. Righteousness, in this instance, originates from seeking to earn Allah's favour and endeavouring to achieve a greater degree of redistribution, furthering socio-economic justice.

As well as making themselves strategic actors of an alternative process of value generation, zakat management bodies seek to address the failings of the nation-state to provide welfare to the local population and the dead-ends previous generations of Islamic radicalism bequeathed to contemporary movements for the revitalisation of the faith. In contrast to previous generations of Islamist movements in Indonesia, which placed a premium on staging a revolution so as to create, sooner rather than later, an Islamic state as a key instrument in the implementation of 'divine rule' on earth (see Formici 2012), DKI and other organisations have deferred all talk about the urgency of an Islamic revolution, concentrating their efforts instead in making small, incremental steps towards advancing what they perceive to be the interests of Islam and Muslims (see Bayat 2013). In this context, the *ekonomi Islam* movement with its emphasis on *syariah*-compliant solutions has spearheaded the establishment of Islamic financial institutions, inclusive of welfare organisations, with an eye towards reforming the conduct of the economy, improving the skills of human subjects and influencing the curve of time. In this regard, the poverty alleviation interventions undertaken by zakat management bodies involve much more than the provision of free services in the fields of education, health and micro-finance. Poverty interventions are mainly geared towards making time pass through opening a route to a future anticipated as an improved and enhanced version of the present. The effort expended towards making such a future arrive is directly correlated with systematically cultivating a people proper to it, a future people of pious entrepreneurs to duly populate an upcoming prosperous and pious earth. In place of pursuing a politics of upheaval involving the outpouring of public violence and revolutionary fervour, DKI and other Islamic welfare organisations in contemporary Indonesia have privileged a reserved and quieted yet assertive and insistent mode of drawing a prosperous and pietistic future near by means of attempting to administer time anew. Key in this ministry has been the propagation of a non-economistic concept of the economy, an embracing of death and the insertion of specific, yet inconclusive, cuts in the flow of time. In the next chapter, I turn to a more detailed exploration of the intervals fashioned in Islamic micro-finance initiatives and the effects they have on the synthesis of time. To aid this objective, I will conduct a more systematic discussion of the concept of promise, looking in more depth and detail into its philosophical and ethical underpinnings by means of an excursion into the work of Gilles Deleuze.

Notes

1. The literature on neoliberalism is vast and growing; in addition to Foucault's (2007, 2008) genealogical account, Harvey's (2005) work concentrates on the rise of global inequalities while Wacquant's (2012) focuses on the continuing importance of the state and its penal regimes.
2. Much of the literature on Islamist forms of subjectivity places undue emphasis on the achievement of piety as a teleological rather than an open-ended process (see Mahmood 2005), whereby unqualified criteria of evaluation apply with absolutist force (see Kloos 2017). As Marsden (2005), Schielke (2009) and Simon (2009) have noted there is little room left in such studies for the exploration of inconsistencies, uncertainties and contingencies.
3. For an overview of developments instituted by the World Bank, see Li (2006). Kusno (2012) charts major changes in the provision of housing in urban Indonesia.
4. http://www.thejakartapost.com/news/2011/02/02/sby-says-indonesia-needs-more-entrepreneurs.html
5. http://www.forbes.com/sites/donaldfrazier/2012/05/14/indonesian-minister-we-need-four-million-entrepreneurs/
6. Hefner (1997) notes the acute differences over *ekonomi Islam* between populists and technocrats, and 'traditionalists' and 'modernists.'
7. Such partnerships extend to PKS: during the 2012 Jakarta gubernatorial election, DKI staff was encouraged to assist PKS-backed candidates with their campaigning and election monitoring.
8. KAMMI is closely affiliated with the *tarbiyah* movement.

Bibliography

Amin, Riawan. 2007. *Satanic Finance*. Jakarta: Celestial Publications.

Anderson, Paul. 2018. "An Abundance of Meaning": Ramadan as an Enchantment of Society and Economy in Syria. *HAU: Journal of Ethnographic Theory* 8 (3): 610–624.

Appadurai, Arjun. 2015. *Banking on Words: The Failure of Language in the Age of Derivative Finance*. Chicago: University of Chicago Press.

Atia, Mona. 2013. *Building a House in Heaven: Pious Neoliberalism and Islamic Charity in Egypt*. Minneapolis: University of Minnesota Press.

Bayat, Asef, ed. 2013. *Post-Islamism: The Changing Faces of Political Islam*. Oxford: Oxford University Press.

Bowen, John. 1993. *Muslims through Discourse*. Princeton: Princeton University Press.
Choiruzzad, Shofwan Al Banna. 2013. More Gain, More Pain: The Development of Indonesia' Islamic Economy Movement (1980s–2012). *Indonesia* 95 (1): 125–172.
Formici, Chiara. 2012. Islam and the Making of the Nation. In *Kartosuwiryo and Political Islam in 20th Century Indonesia*. Manoa: University of Hawaii.
Foucault, Michel. 2002. *The Order of Things*. Oxon: Routledge.
———. 2007. *Security, Territory, Population*. Hampshire: Palgrave Macmillan.
———. 2008. *The Birth of Biopolitics*. Hampshire: Palgrave Macmillan.
Gireudeau, Martin. 2012. Remembering the Future: Entrepreneurship Guidebooks in the US, from Meditation to Method (1945–1975). *Foucault Studies* 13: 40–26.
Green, Micheal, and Matthew Bishop. 2008. *Philanthrocapitalism*. London: Bloomsbury Press.
Harvey, David. 2005. *A Brief History of Neoliberalism*. Oxford: Oxford University Press.
Hasan, Noorhaidi. 2009. *Islamist Party, Electoral Politics, and Da'wa Mobilisation Among Youth*. Singapore: RSIS Working Paper.
Hefner, Robert. 1997. Markets and Justice for Muslim Indonesians. In *Market Cultures: Society and Morality in the New Asian Capitalisms*, ed. R. Hefner. Boulder: Westview Press.
Hendrick, Joshua. 2013. *Gülen: The Ambiguous Politics of Market Islam in Turkey and the World*. New York: New York University Press.
Hoesterey, James. 2015. *Rebranding Islam: Piety, Prosperity, and a Self-Help Guru*. Stanford: Stanford University Press.
Ismail, Salwa. 2013. Piety, Profit and the Market in Cairo: A Political Economy of Islamisation. *Contemporary Islam* 7 (1): 107–128.
Joll, Christopher. 2012. *Muslim Merit-Making in Thailand's Far-South*. Dordrecht: Springer.
Kahn, Victoria. 2004. *Wayward Contracts: The Crisis of Political Obligation in England, 1640–1674*. Princeton: Princeton University Press.
Katz, Marion. 2007. *The Birth of the Prophet Muhammad*. London: Routledge.
Khouj, Abdullah Muhammad. 1992. *The End of the Journey: An Islamic Perspective on Death and the Afterlife*. Washington, DC: Islamic Centre.
Kloos, David. 2017. *Becoming Better Muslims: Religious Authority and Ethical Improvement in Aceh, Indonesia*. Princeton: Princeton University Press.
Kochuyt, Thierry. 2009. God, Gifts and Poor People: On Charity in Islam. *Social Compass* 56 (1): 98–116.
Kusno, Abidin. 2012. Housing the Margin: Perumahan Rakyat and the Future Urban Form of Jakarta. *Indonesia* 94: 23–56.
Lemke, Thomas. 2001. 'The Birth of Biopolitics': Michel Foucault's Lecture at the Collège de France on Neo-Liberal Governmentality. *Economy and Society* 30 (2): 190–207.

Li, Tania Murray. 2006. *Neo-liberal Strategies of Government through Community: The Social Development Program of the World Bank in Indonesia*. International Law and Justice Working Papers No. 2.

LiPuma, Edward. 2017. *The Social Life of Financial Derivatives*. Durham: Duke University Press.

Lubis, Nur. 2004. Financial Activism Among Indonesian Muslims. In *Islamic Perspectives on the New Millennium*, ed. Virginia Hooker and Amin Saikal, 91–112. Singapore: ISEAS.

Mahmood, Saba. 2005. *Politics of Piety. The Islamic Revival and the Feminist Subject*. Princeton: Princeton University Press.

Marsden, Magnus. 2005. *Living Islam*. Cambridge: Cambridge University Press.

Maurer, Bill. 2002. Repressed Futures: Financial Derivatives' Theological Unconscious. *Economy and Society* 31 (1): 15–36.

Mittermaier, Amira. 2013. Trading with God: Islam, Calculation, Excess. In *A Companion to the Anthropology of Religion*, ed. Janice Boddy and Micheal Lambek, 274–293. Somerset: Wiley.

———. 2014. Beyond Compassion: Islamic Voluntarism in Egypt. *American Ethnologist* 41 (3): 518–531.

Miyazaki, Hirokazu. 2007. Between Arbitrage and Speculation: An Economic of Belief and Doubt. *Economy and Society* 36 (3): 396–415.

Monaghan, Lee, and Michael O' Flynn. 2012. The Madoffization of Society: A Corrosive Process in an Age of Fictitious Capital. *Critical Sociology* 39 (6): 869–887.

Moosa, Ebrahim. 1999. Languages of Change in Islamic Law: Re-Defining Death in Modernity. In *Perspectives on Islamic Law, Justice and Society*, ed. R.S. Khare, 161–197. Boulder: Rowman & Littlefield.

Muehlebach, Andrea. 2013. The Catholicization of Neoliberalism: On Love and Welfare in Lombardy, Italy. *American Anthropologist* 115 (3): 452–465.

Mufti, Imam Kamil. 2015. Belief in Life After Death. https://www.islamreligion.com/articles/38/belief-in-life-after-death/. Accessed 5 Apr 2019.

Nickel, Patricia, and Angela Eikenberry. 2009. A Critique of the Discourse of Marketized Philanthropy in Fast Capitalism. *The American Behavioral Scientist* 52 (7): 974–989.

Njoto-Feillard, Gwenaël. 2004. Insuffler l'Esprit du Capitalisme à l'Umma: La Formation d'une 'Éthique Islamique du Travail en Indonesie. *Critique Internationale* 25: 93–116.

———. 2012. *L'Islam et la Réinvention du Capitalisme en Indonésie*. Paris: Karthala.

Ortiz, Horacio. 2014. The Limits of Financial Imagination: Free Investors, Efficient Markets, and Crisis. *American Anthropologist* 116 (1): 38–50.

Osella, Filippo, and Caroline Osella. 2009. Muslim Entrepreneurs in Public Life between India and the Gulf: Making Good and Doing Good. *Journal of the Royal Anthropological Institute* 15 (S1): S202–S221.

Osella, Filippo, and Tom Widger. 2018. 'You Can Give Even If You Have Only Ten Rupees': Muslim Charity in a Colombo Housing Scheme. *Modern Asian Studies* 52 (1): 297–324.

Oualaalou, David. 2018. The Afterlife and Death: An Islamic Perspective. In *The Routledge Handbook of Death and the Afterlife*, ed. Cadi K. Cann, 356–365. London: Routledge.

Permata, Ahmad. 2008. *Islamist Party and Democratic Participation*. PhD Thesis, Westfälischen Wilhelms-Universität, Munster.

Retsikas, Konstantinos. 2007. Being and Place: Movement, Ancestors, and Personhood in East Java, Indonesia. *Journal of the Royal Anthropological Institute* 13 (4): 969–986.

———. 2018. Multiplication through Division: Value, Time, and Prosperity in Indonesia. *HAU: Journal of Ethnographic Theory* 8 (3): 656–671.

Riles, Annalise. 2004. Real Time: Unwinding Technocratic and Anthropological Knowledge. *American Ethnologist* 31 (3): 392–405.

Robinson, Richard, and Hadiz Vedi. 2013. The Political Economy of Oligarchy and the Reorganisation of Power in Indonesia. *Indonesia* 96: 33–56.

Rudnyckyj, Daromir. 2011. *Spiritual Economies: Islam, Globalisation and the Afterlife of Development*. Ithaca: Cornell University Press.

———. 2019. *Beyond Debt: Islamic Experiments in Global Finance*. Chicago: University of Chicago Press.

Saeed, Abdullah. 2004. Islamic Banking and Finance: In Search of a Pragmatic Model. In *Islamic Perspectives on the New Millennium*, ed. Virginia Hooker and Amin Saikal, 113–132. Singapore: ISEAS.

Schielke, Samuli. 2009. Being Good in Ramadan: Ambivalence, Fragmentation, and the Moral Self in the Lives of Young Egyptians. *Journal of the Royal Anthropological Institute (N.S.)* 15 (S1): S24–S40.

Simon, Gregory. 2009. The Soul Freed of Cares? Islamic Prayer, Subjectivity, and the Contradictions of Moral Selfhood in Minangkabau, Indonesia. *American Ethnologist* 36 (2): 258–275.

Sloane, Patricia. 1999. *Islam, Modernity and Entrepreneurship Among the Malays*. New York: St Martin's Press.

———. 2011. Working in the Islamic Economy: Sharia-ization and the Malaysian Workplace. *Sojourn* 26 (2): 304–334.

———. 2017. *Corporate Islam: Sharia and the Modern Workplace*. Cambridge: Cambridge University Press.

Telle, Kari. 2000. Feeding the Dead: Reformulating Sasak Mortuary Practices. *Bijdragen tot de Taal-, Land-, en Volkenkunde* 156 (4): 771–785.

Tuğal, Cihan. 2017. *Caring for the Poor: Islamic and Christian Benevolence in a Liberal World*. New York: Routledge.

Wacquant, Louis. 2012. Three Steps to a Historical Anthropology of Actually Existing Neoliberalism. *Social Anthropology* 20 (1): 66–79.

Weber, Max. 1985. *The Protestant Ethic and the Spirit of Capitalism*. London: Unwin.

Zaloom, Caitlin. 2009. How to Read the Future: The Yield Curve, Affect, and Financial Prediction. *Public Culture* 21 (2): 245–268.

CHAPTER 5

Promising Deliverance

In a poor and overcrowded neighbourhood in Surabaya, Indonesia, amid narrow and twisting backstreets, clogged by speeding motorcycles, boisterous school children and passing-by vendors and filled with an assortment of tiny houses, themselves scantly equipped with modern facilities, yet sheltering from the heat and the rain a multitude of poor families, lives ibu Nurhayati. Nurhayati is a forty-something migrant to the city, wife of an on-and-off construction worker and mother to five children. By her own admission, she has become a more pious Muslim recently. At the request of an Islamic welfare organisation, she got involved with a couple of years ago, she began praying five times a day, accompanying her prayers with the recitation of an oath. The oath Nurhayati, along with many other women in the vicinity benefiting from the delivery of financial and other services by the said organisation, repeat is as follows:

> In the name of Allah, the most merciful, the most beneficent, it has already become my obligation to worship Allah, do my very best to earn my livelihood, improve my business, school my children, follow the rules of the cooperative. Allah is my witness in everything I say and do.

The oath is an appeal to Allah to witness one's determination to keep true to one's promise. Such a promise involves an intensification of worship alongside an amplification of efforts made towards improving one's socioeconomic standing. The oath is also a promise itself, a pledge strengthened by such appeal. Attached to *sholat*, the compulsory five-a-times

K. Retsikas, *A Synthesis of Time*,
https://doi.org/10.1007/978-3-030-34933-2_5

prayer, it forms an integral part of an oral ritual facilitating human-divine communication. As such, it partakes of the nature of the prayer, which, according to Mauss (2003), revolves around the glorification of the creator, including the capacity of causing Him to act in the desired manner.

By means of making Allah the witness as well as the addressee, the oath the beneficiaries recite expressly renews the covenant binding believer and Allah together. This covenant is intrinsically related to the promise God in Islam has made to (wo)man of granting rewards in this world and guaranteeing resurrection and eternal life in the *akherat*, the world-to-come (Riesebrodt 2010). This promise has been made in exchange for (wo) man's everyday remembrance of God in worship and for sticking closely to His 'law,' the *syariah*. In this regard, the Maussian capacity of prayer of 'causing God to act' (2003: 53) should be re-calibrated to take into account the aspect of constant renewal. Seen in this light, praying is primarily aimed at enticing the divine to *act anew* in response to (wo)man's (re-)action. The oath ibu Nurhayati and the other women perform is, therefore, dedicated to the reiteration of promises once exchanged, reaffirming the pledges each side has made to the other, instantiating the recommencement of their relation.

The theme of renewal and repetition is vital for two reasons: first, because it highlights the intermediation of time in the unfolding of relations, bringing into focus the existence of a gap, an interval or a fracture (*diastema*) in the enactment of the social, most particularly in human-divine relations. It is precisely because of the occurrence of this break in time, of this temporal interruption having taken place that a renewal of promises is constantly required so that communication across the divide can be re-established. Second, because the temporality of human-divine relations as currently played out in Indonesia as well as elsewhere in the Islamic world, is not a mere repetition of past patterns of religiosity. The practice of Islam is increasingly inflected and interpolated by new modes of scriptural interpretation, broadly referred to as Islamic modernism, as well as a new series of interventions to go with it.[1] In this regard, it is important to note that not only do such inflections correspond to deep cuts in the historical trajectory of the faith, but the related sets of interventions seek to shape its future in particular ways, making it follow specific trajectories and move towards specific ends.

In a narrow sense, the present chapter is preoccupied with charting the multifaceted intervention of a specific Islamic charitable organisation that, in 2010, chose this specific neighbourhood of Surabaya for the conduct of *dakwah* (religious propagation). Such intervention involved the carrying out of an experiment in the powers of Islamic micro-finance for bringing about change and prosperity to the poor. More broadly, it is concerned with the effects of this experiment on time. In particular, by means of Deleuze's (2008) tripartite division of time and the concepts of promise and the cut advanced here, it looks into the temporal properties of such interventions and their consequences, political, economic and so on, for times-yet-to-come.

It was back in 2010 when Mariam, an unmarried and highly educated young woman donning the veil visited for the first time this part of town. Mariam was employed by *Indonesia Mandiri* and the purpose of her visit was to scope the potential for the successful implementation of Islamic community development. The plan involved the creation of a viable, sustainable, *syariah*-compliant financial institution charged with dispensing micro-credit to the poor and entailed a particular promise. The promise Mariam made to locals was that through the application of a particular set of Islamic financial instruments and know-how, as well as by means of their own hard work and amplified piety, the local poor (*miskin*) would eventually achieve *mandiri*. *Mandiri* is a difficult term to translate, for it is ubiquitous in the discourse of community development in Indonesia, but is roughly equivalent to autonomy, independence, self-reliance, sovereignty even, in the sense that one is able to stand on one's own feet, that one has become one's own master.[2]

The empowerment programme, which was wholly funded by *zakat* to the tune of 100 million rupiah or roughly $11,000 pledged to convert the neighbourhood's poor from *mustahiq* (zakat recipients) into *muzakki* (zakat payers) in the near future. Undeniably attracted by the promise of prosperity and autonomy, as well as by financial capital made instantly available, more than 200 women and two men enlisted themselves to the programme. From then on, they had to keep up with a regimen of house visits and weekly meetings required for the purposes of loan advancing, as well as develop new skills related to deferred payments making, record keeping and monitoring. The enlistees also had to participate in motivational sessions. Led by Mariam herself, such sessions freely mixed the religious and the entrepreneurial and involved her dispensing advice on issues relating to everyday conduct as regulated by Islamic law and revealing the secrets of the success of businessmen of national and international renown.

The highly paradoxical governmental process of making others self-reliant was planned to last for two to three years. I observed this process during its final and most crucial period, that is, just before *Indonesia Mandiri* was to formally withdraw from running the Islamic micro-financial institution it helped create by transferring the responsibility for its management to Nurhayati and two other women. In what follows, I reflect on the experiment the organisation and the residents of this poor neighbourhood conducted, focusing primarily on its effects on time. I am particularly interested in exploring the mode of time synthesis performed in Islamic micro-finance interventions involving the religious supply of credit and the social creation of debt. I approach this experiment through drawing on Deleuze (2008) and the concept of promise I develop here. I argue that the analytical promise the concept of promise holds is partly related to its ability to describe a field of practice that is at once theological and economic. As such, the analytical significance of promise is intrinsically related to its capacity to bring attention to the efforts and the stakes involved in achieving future redemption both in the shape of prosperity and abundance in this world and in the form of salvation and deliverance in the next.

Time and Experiments

Perhaps the year 1991 can be taken as the starting point for the conduct of a most significant experiment in Indonesia. The experiment called for the radical reconfiguration of what the 'modern constitution' (Latour 1993) has incessantly sought to separate through the institutionalisation of a sphere of religion as distinct from the domain (and logic) of the economic. And while Indonesia can be rightly considered a latecomer in the field of Islamic banking and finance—the country's first Islamic bank was founded relatively late, in 1991—the country's Muslims soon took the challenge up most enthusiastically. In years that followed, urban middle-class Indonesian Muslims went to establish two additional Islamic banks, tens of Islamic banking units belonging to conventional banks, more than a hundred *Syariah* People's Credit Banks and thousands of Islamic micro-finance institutions. At the same time, several Islamic welfare organisations active in the fields of disaster relief, education, health and micro-credit also came into being. And while social scientists have done well to document large Islamic banks (see Hefner 2003; Rifki 2013; Saeed 2004) and commercial Islamic micro-finance providers (see Seibel 2012, Sakai 2008, 2010; Antonio 2008) operating in the country, relatively little is known about their smaller and more *sosial* counterparts, the *Lembaga Amil Zakat* or zakat management bodies and the innovations they have introduced in the economic life of the nation. Commercial orientations aside, what all such institutions share is the fact that they adhere to Islamic modernism, a movement that seeks to revitalise the faith by making it fit for the contemporary world. In this regard, all these organisations correspond to the institutional form the efforts of modernist Muslim intellectuals worldwide have taken with respect to elaborating an Islamic alternative to capitalism (Tripp 2006; Choiruzzad 2013). Starting from the publication of *First Principles of Islamic Economics* (2011) by Maulana Maududi in 1969, this alternative is founded on the prohibition of *riba*, commonly conceived as equivalent to interest,[3] and the promotion of zakat as the key financial instrument for the generation of wealth, the alleviation of poverty and the promotion of social justice.

Given Islamic economics' roots in worship, it should come as no surprise that the discipline and its offshoots—banking and finance—readily acknowledge, as it were, the validity of Callon's (2007) famous argument that the economy requires 'performation.' Callon's thesis is primarily conceived as a critique of classical economics' position that the institution of the market and competition are natural and given. As counterweight, his approach focuses on the myriad of processes, relationships and activities that are necessary to take place for the market economy to come into being, that is, to be produced and maintained in its historically and culturally specific form. The economy, as envisaged both by Callon and leading Islamic economists such as Siddiqi (1983) and Warde (2010), encompasses both human and non-human 'actants' and involves a multitude of material and immaterial processes and resources. In this regard, concepts, values, algorithms and texts are as important as labour, skills, commodities and the stock exchange for the realisation and perpetuation of the economic. Most importantly, as Callon himself has put it, 'the notion of performation leads to that of experimentation' (2007: 345). As an unstable, uncertain and incomplete accomplishment, the economic field is proximate to a laboratory in which a plurality of activities and programmes are conceived of and tested in order to find out what works and what doesn't. In the case of an Islamic economy, such laboratory procedures also answer to additional demands related to the jurisprudential discovery and application of divine decrees. Seen in this light, Callon's thesis should be expanded to include the fact that in an Islamic economy, Allah in the shape of His voice in the Quran and the Prophet in the form of collections of his deeds and words (*hadith*) are immanent presences in and integral parts of a field of practice which only reductively can be described as 'economic' for it is at the same 'religious,' and 'political,' and 'social' as well.

If the last two decades correspond to the time of the conduct of an experiment in Indonesia concerning the viability of an Islamic economy, then one may well ask, what is the time its clock strikes? What is, in other words, the epoch the practices and procedures of an Islamic economy aim to inaugurate? Once the issue is conceived in this manner, further questions become available for posing. For example, how does an Islamic economy make time pass? What does the future that Islamic economic actors are after ultimately look like? What sorts of cuts do the instruments of an Islamic economy carve in the flow of time? What kinds of temporal trajectories do the tools deployed make individual Muslims trace? Finally, how do the enacted principles of an Islamic economy make prosperity, justice and salvation arrive?

In his insightful and engaging book on alternatives to capitalism, Maurer makes the point that 'Islamic banking and Ithaca HOURS[4] are self-conscious retrogressions that place the "alternative" behind in time rather than ahead in the future,' moving thus essentially backward in time, for they place 'the past ahead of the now' (2005: 77; see also 2006). According to Maurer, the very past such projects intend to make return is not a creative variation of what has already happened; rather the 'past ahead' amounts to the coming back of the long gone and is a repetition of the known. This view is echoed in other writings, most notably in the highly critical accounts of Kuran (2004) that charges Islamic economists with attempting to turn things back to sixth century Arabia, that is, the time of the Revelation. At first sight, this stance might seem to carry some analytical weight. This becomes apparent in the case of *Indonesia Mandiri*'s 'mother' organisation, *Pondok Infak Mulia* (PIM). As I discussed in Chap. 3, PIM is a non-governmental Islamic welfare foundation established in the early 1990s. From its inception till the late 2000s, the foundation had its staff take weekend leave on Fridays and Saturdays, paid their wages in *dinar*[5] and had its accounts conform to *hijra*, the Islamic calendar. And yet, characterising such practices as 'retrogressive' prejudges the experiments involved, reducing their complexity, implicitly labelling them as 'Islamist' or 'fundamentalist.' To back up claims to the opposite, one could readily refer to counter-examples. For instance, both *Indonesia Mandiri* and *Pondok Infak Mulia* are well known in Indonesia for their 'liberal' or 'moderate' understanding of the faith as well as for actively promoting 'civil society' and 'democracy,' the latter conceived in light of broad, universal values. However such counter-examples will hardly suffice to persuade sceptics; in addition, such characterisations are mostly irrelevant for my purposes. Rather, what is required is engaging head-on with a question more fundamental and pressing. This is the question of time, the conceptualisation of its passing, the organisation of its synthesis and the evaluation of its effects. In order to do precisely that, I am turning my attention to Gilles Deleuze's unsurpassable study, *Difference and Repetition* (2008). However, I do not intend this excursion to be an 'application' of Deleuze's philosophy on Indonesian material but to involve the staging of an encounter in the process of which both sides—'Deleuze' and 'Indonesia'—are productively transformed.

The Deleuzian Time Synthesis

Deleuze's starting point is broadly the same as Nietzsche's (2003): the re-evaluation of all values through breaking Western metaphysics open for the radical task of immanent critique to begin again. Such critique is carried out within a conceptual horizon that involves refraining from searching for origins, evoking universal laws and postulating ultimate causes. This is so for Deleuze's intellectual and political agenda privileges the undetermined and the open, gestures to the aporetic and affirms the novel and the other (see Deleuze 2008; Deleuze and Guattari 2004). In a nutshell, Deleuze's labours are set upon reactivating in thought and life a pure, unadulterated potential, usually referred to as the virtual.[6] His take on time, a concern that permeates his work from his early study on Nietzsche (Deleuze 2012) through his 'mature' years and into his later studies on cinema (1992, 1997) must be understood with this in mind. For the pure potential to be reactivated, and for the given and the known to make space for the undetermined, time must be rethought. To this end, Deleuze subjects to critique three prevailing paradigms of the temporal in Western philosophy: Hume's habitual time, Bergson's memorial time and Nietzsche's eternal return. According to Deleuze, only a reworking of the third synthesis is adequate to the task of affirming the future and unleashing the potential contained therein from everything that attempts to hold it down and separate it from what it can be. As he puts it,

> the eternal return affirms difference, it affirms dissemblance and disparateness, chance, multiplicity and becoming. […] The eternal return eliminates precisely all those instances which strangle difference and prevent its

> transport by subjecting it to the quadruple yoke of representation. Difference is recovered, liberated, only at the limits of its power—in other words, by repetition in the eternal return. (2008: 373)

Deleuze grants Hume with being the first philosopher to have explicitly tackled the problem of time from the perspective of difference: this was mainly down to Hume's attention to mind's capacity for contemplating sequences of repetitive events (Deleuze 2008: 90–101). Such sequences organise or synthesise time in terms of habits whereby habits correspond to expectations regarding the occurrence of a reproducible pattern of incidences themselves stretching out to infinity on both directions of time's arrow, that is, towards both the future and the past. For Hume, habit brings time into being through repetition that, in turn, involves the unending return of the present. As Deleuze notes, Hume's philosophical attitude amounts to a passive synthesis of time that constitutes 'the present in time' and 'time as a living present' (2008: 97). More particularly, the Humean synthesis accomplishes to conceive of time by means of organising sequences of events with such sequences inserting cuts in the otherwise unmarked flow of time. These cuts allow habit to organise time first, by separating time out into discrete units, that is, instants or moments, and second by contracting one instant to another in a succession or series, themselves forming a chain of anticipated events. Each time the instants in question return, they constitute present time. 'It is in this present that time is deployed. To it belong both the past and the future: the past in so far as the preceding instants are retained in the contraction; the future because its expectation is anticipated in the same contraction. The past and the future do not designate instants distinct from a supposed present instant, but rather the dimension of the present itself' (Deleuze 2008: 91).

Deleuze both admires Hume's synthesis and finds fault with it. He comments Hume for being able to 'draw something new from repetition, to draw difference from it' (however small or trivial it might be), showing the ways in which 'difference inhabits repetition' precisely because 'difference lies between two repetitions' (2008: 97). However, Deleuze identifies major problems with Hume. These problems have to do with the fact that Hume's synthesis holds hostage the alterity of the past and the unexpectedness of the future to the identity of a present that forever returns, albeit with minor modifications. Consequently, Hume has no way of dealing conceptually with the fact that time unfolds in a discontinuous, irregular, interruptive manner. 'By insisting upon the finitude of contraction, we have shown the effect: we have by no means shown why the present passes, or what prevents it from being coextensive with time' (Deleuze 2008: 101). In order to find out precisely what causes time to pass, Deleuze turns to Bergson, whom he credits with being the first to provide the conceptual means that allow for time's passing to be thought philosophically.

For Deleuze, the Bergsonian synthesis centres on memory, with the latter revealing the transcendental form of time, that is, the splitting of time in two directions. If the Humean synthesis amounts to time's 'foundation' for it constitutes the almost self-same present, the Bergsonian synthesis corresponds to time's 'ground.' Here, memory constitutes time in terms of 'a pure, a priori past.' Bergson's thought rightly credits such past with being both independent from the present and absolutely primary to it in the sense of corresponding to its presupposition. Compared with the first synthesis, the second synthesis of time contains, therefore, a supplementary dimension and is, for this reason, superior to the first. The supplementary dimension relates to memory 'obliging' time to split open and divide itself up, articulating an internal rapture that is incessantly repeated through its workings. According to Deleuze's reading of Bergson, memory forces any given present moment to bifurcate into two series: one series builds upon reminiscence and entails the reproduction of a former present while a second series grows out of reflection and involves the present becoming aware of itself. In-between the two series, a gap emerges, allowing difference and discontinuity to erupt out into the open as a kind of displacement by which the past is repeated only in terms of a present that is different from that which it has been. In this regard, Deleuze argues,

> '[Hume's] passive synthesis of habit constituted time as a *contraction* of instants with respect to a present, but the active synthesis of memory constitutes it as the *embedding* of presents themselves. The whole problem is: with respect to what? It is with respect to the pure element of the past, understood as the past in general, as an a priori past that a given former present is reproducible and the present present is able to reflect itself' (2008: 102–3; italics in the original).

Recognition of memory's effects on time involves an understanding of time in relation to three inescapable paradoxes. With the past operating as an orchestrating force imposing its pattern on the temporal,[7] the paradoxes animating the Bergsonian synthesis are the following: the contemporaneity of the past with the present it was, the co-existence of the past and the present in reminiscence and the pre-existence of a past that was never present. The first paradox gives us the reason why the present comes to pass: 'every present passes in favour of a new present, because the past is contemporaneous with itself as present' (Deleuze 2008: 103). The second paradox provides the means for memory to accomplish its synthesis: it effectively transforms the present (and the future) into dimensions of the past. The third paradox grounds time into an absolute horizon located beyond recovery, providing the synthesis with the transcendental element appropriate to it (Deleuze 2008: 104).

According to Deleuze, the major advantage of Bergson's time synthesis was to 'include' difference: difference is 'included' in the form of memory splitting time into two directions as indicated in the first and second paradoxes. It is also 'included' with respect to the third paradox, that is, to 'a pure, a priori past' that remains alien to the present and thus pregnant with un-actualised potential. The second synthesis entails, however, a serious disadvantage, itself stemming from 'the Platonic tone in Bergson' (Deleuze 1991: 44) and the overall effects of the privileging of memory in a Platonic search for truth, itself motivated by a return to the original as an extra-temporal guarantor of all values. As Williams' perceptive commentary on Deleuze's *Difference and Repetition* makes clear (2011: 84–86), Deleuze is at pains to draw a line separating his work and that of Plato, who posited that the purposeful return to the Idea from which all phenomena decline in an order of diminishing resemblance as the philosophical task par excellence, crediting reminiscence with the priority to lead this process towards a recuperation of origins. It is precisely because Deleuze wants thought to break free from a tradition that is in the habit of anchoring value to the past, devaluing thus both the present and the future, and which moreover arranges truth in terms of layers of resemblances, culminating in the 'in itself' of an ideal or an essence, that Platonism, any form of it, must be overturned and the metaphysics of memory overcome (see also Ansell-Pearson 2010). This is how Deleuze puts the necessity for demoting memory and the recessive synthesis it accomplishes in favour of a third, forward-looking one: 'The question is whether repetition may be understood as operating from one present to another in the real series, from a present to a former present. In this case, the former present would play the role of [...] an ultimate or original term which would remain in place [...] [and which] would be the one which provides the *thing* that is to be repeated. As a consequence, repetition would in principle conform to the model of a material, bare and brutal repetition, understood as the repetition of the same' (2008: 127–128; italics in the original).

What is the way out of habit and reminisce? If the same and the original manage to ultimately domesticate the potential the caesuras regularity and mnemosyne briefly introduce to time, what is the best way of going about unburdening time from their determinations? This is as much a conceptual as a political question, and Deleuze points to Nietzsche for an answer, at once repeating and reworking the latter's philosophy. Deleuze's argument is that the only way to make difference and potentiality objects of affirmation is to centre our conceptualisation and practice of time on times-yet-to-come, future times (see also Voss 2013). The primary technique that accomplishes such forward-looking synthesis is Nietzsche's eternal return: it 'constitutes a future which affirms at once both the unconditioned character of the product in relation to the conditions of its production, and the independence of the work in relation to its author or actor' (Deleuze 2008: 117). The eternal return splits time differently: in place of the past and the present, it privileges the indeterminacy and chance of the future. The eternal return amounts to a 'machine' that produces surplus outflows the multi-directionality and metamorphic capacities of which indicate that the cuts it inserts in the flow of time are sufficiently sharp and deep to allow for the dislodging of the effects of habit and memory to take place. If the first synthesis constitutes time's foundation while the second amounts to time's ground, the eternal return effectively 'un-grounds' time, opening it up for all that is to come.

Deleuze likens the eternal return to a 'decentred circle' (2008: 141) that foregrounds a new mode of repetition whereby what is repeated is neither the almost self-same present nor the ideal image of the past. Instead, what is relentlessly reiterated is the cut, the caesura, the incision. The future is welcomed and the potential contained therein is unleashed because the intervals the eternal return institutes acquire consistency through their unlimited replication and their infinite multiplication. 'Repetition no longer bears (hypothetically) upon a first time which escapes it, and in any case remains external to it: repetition bears upon repetitions. [...] It is repetition itself that is repeated' (Deleuze 2008: 367). The eternal return performs time as forward split, in favour of a future itself conceived as radically other and always already in the process of arriving. If it subordinates both the past and the present to their ultimate passing, it does so precisely because it pledges time to the new and the upcoming. The eternal return's close association with death (2008:

138–139) gives it the power of annihilation over the known and the habitual. The destruction it unleashes is directly related to the intensive quality of the incisions it performs: as Reynolds puts it, the eternal return is principally designed so as to 'intensify our experiences of each moment' (2004: 9), renewing our conceptual and political commitment to life and thought unknown for and unanticipated.[8]

Deleuze grants Nietzsche with having not only conceived time anew but also with having invented a new way of inhabiting it for the eternal return is also a test to which all values and concepts are to be subjected in order for their life augmenting, potential enhancing properties to be evaluated. For Deleuze,

> Nietzsche's secret is that *the eternal return is selective.* [...] The eternal return is not only selective thinking but also selective Being. Only affirmation comes back. [...] The eternal return should be compared to a wheel whose movement is endowed with a centrifugal force that drives out everything negative. (2005: 89; see also 2008: 370)

To the extent that the eternal return hastens the time of the yet-to-come, opening up new paths for the future to come about, it also stands guard to the passageways it itself carves out. Its guard could perhaps be imagined as involving the casting of a most beautiful, elaborate and strong net, wide and fine enough to allow only for certain 'elements' to go through while blocking the remaining out. According to Deleuze, what the eternal return allows to pass is all that escapes the determinations effected by the first and the second synthesis: both past forms and present quantities are blocked, both the set of conditions pertaining to an action and the agents who carry it out are obstructed from returning. What comes to pass is only the 'formless' (2008: 269), the 'unconditioned in the product' (2008: 370), the undetermined; it is only becoming that goes through (see also Zourabichvili 2012; Retsikas 2012).

The current chapter explores promising as a time synthesising device, first by relating it to the eternal return and then subjecting it to the test the latter administers. I consider the reciprocal making of promises described in the previous and the current chapters in light of the eternal return, and endeavour to assess the effects it has on the future. What I want to find out is how the practice of promising involved in the dispensation of financial and other aid by zakat management bodies in contemporary Indonesia orients itself to difference. What I want to establish is the extent to which such an exchange of promises regarding deliverance from poverty and future prosperity unlocks and unravels the potential contained in the very breaks it itself introduces to time, with a view of passing an interested judgement on its very practice. My point of departure is that promising partakes of the character of the eternal return in the sense that it is forward-looking, explicitly embracing the yet-to-come. In promising, value derives from drawing the future near. At first glance, both promising and the eternal return involve a commitment to departing from the way things are and work for bringing about an imminent transformation. Seen from the perspective of an exchange of pledges, the future appears as decisively new, for time is made to embark on a different trajectory through the caesuras reciprocal promising inserts in its flow. Despite the apparent similarity, a question remains: is promising equally selective of what comes to pass as the eternal return demands of it? Are the cuts and caesuras it inserts in favour of the propagation of life and thought unexpected as required by the test of the eternal return? This concern is very significant, for upon closer inspection, promising seems to be permeated by ambiguity and to be haunted by an internal split. Such split involves two irreconcilable forces fighting one another for supremacy over the potential promising unlocks.

To the same extent I mean this exercise to be a reading of Islamic micro-finance inspired by Deleuze, I also add to Deleuze studies an ethnographically grounded theoretical route that is yet to be travelled. What this study of Islamic economic life from Indonesia offers is a timely reminder that the outright privileging of the future in the Deleuzian/Nietzschean time synthesis is not adequate in and of itself for relativising the effects of habit and memory on thought and politics. This is primarily because promising has a dual, 'schizoid' and distressed constitution: it is animated as much by the affirmation of alterity as by its negation. While affirmation embraces all that the future has to offer, negation works hard to tame the forthcoming, capturing and deploying particular aspects of it for the benefit of the return of the present improved. In the place of the open and the undetermined, the negative cultivates unresponsiveness to chance and apathy to otherness. At the same, it seeks to draw a certain difference from the yet-to-come in the sense of accomplishing certain advances and bringing about particular forms of increase. This negative side of the future time synthesis is supplementary to its Deleuzian/Nietzschean dimension and is permeated by what I call, borrowing a term from Li's (2007) critical ethnography of development processes in

Indonesia, 'the will to improve.' 'The will to improve' corresponds to a variant of the negative and its most dangerous manifestation.

In his early study of Nietzsche, Deleuze writes that 'the eternal return is the synthesis which has as its principle the will to power' (2012: 46). The latter is an 'essentially *plastic* principle' (2012: 46) that corresponds to the 'genetic' element that foregrounds Life's relational character, especially with regards to the entanglements of forces in endlessly unfolding and forever changing relations of control and submission (2012: 46–48). As well as comprising the 'given' in Life and the *raison d'être* of Life's relational constitution, the will to power refers to an 'a-subjective' principle in terms of which Nietzsche and Deleuze recast the problem of agency in philosophy: in that respect, Deleuze writes that '[f]orce is what can, will to power is what wills' (2012: 47). The will to power is, therefore, a transcendentally deduced yet empirically manifest principle that is immanent in living: as such, it 'is no wider than what it conditions, that changes itself with the conditioned and determines itself in each case along with what it determines' (Deleuze 2012: 46). Such qualities bespeak of it being coterminous with Life, situated neither above nor beyond Life, and indicate its plasticity whereby its irrepressible inclination for changeability underscores a resilience of endless repeats. Will to power's plasticity is amply demonstrated in the variable shades it assumes in the course of living, with the affirmative and the negative being the most crucial and critical. In this respect, Deleuze brings due attention to Nietzsche's analytics that relies on a double distinction; as well as differentiating forces into active and reactive ones so as to designate their disposition to creativity, Nietzsche draws a most important distinction between the affirmative, life-enhancing, life-embracing qualities of the will to power and the life-denying, life-depreciating, nihilistic qualities of its twin sister, the will to nothingness (2012: 50, 163). For Nietzsche, determining the quality of the will permeating the phenomena under consideration is paramount for ascertaining their value and judging their significance, with Deleuze arguing that Nietzsche insists that '[t]he value of a value consists in the quality of the will to power expressed in the corresponding thing: is the will to power affirmative or negative and of what nuance?' (2012: 51).

I claim that the will to improve presents a shade of the will to nothingness: it belongs to the latter for it too depreciates Life on the basis of a fiction. However, it differs from the will to nothingness in significant ways, for the fictions involved are discrete and separate. How so, one may ask? Another name for the will to nothingness is nihilism. Nihilism negates this world for it invents 'the idea of another world, of a supersensible world in all its forms (God, essence, the good, truth)' (Deleuze 2012: 139). In this regard, nihilism subjects Life to such an allegedly superior plane that, in turn, cultivates reactive forces. Reactive forces block active forces from doing what they can do through promoting standards and measures that nurture guilt, resentment and bad conscience. In contrast, the will to improve cultivates active forces, for it encourages desire and rewards self-belief. The reason for this is that the fiction the will to improve presupposes involves a longing for life improved: it is, in other words, based on the imagining of the present world in an upgraded, enhanced and progressive state that is yet to be achieved. Instead of ascribing to this world the value of nil, the will to improve distributes value across decimal points that measure the distance that remains to be traversed towards Life finding completion and perfection in the future. However, this 'optimism' is contained within a specific set of parameters. The will to improve sanctions only particular types of activity and seeks to channel creativity down specific tracks. Because not all possibilities opening up are welcome, some active forces are blocked and neutralised in a manner similar to nihilism. However, because action and motion remain crucial for bringing about desired outcomes, other active forces are admitted to, appropriated and nurtured by the will to improve, becoming subject to intensive training regimes that aim to shape them into adequate instruments and appropriate tools for achieving prescribed ends and measurable targets.

In general terms, the will to improve encourages the making of plans for achieving progress, inspiring exhaustive searches for the optimum and most efficient means available for attaining development. Because desire has already been given an object to invest itself, the future the will to improve aims to instal has been conceived in an anticipatory manner. Furthermore, its arrival has already been plotted through mathematical calculations, and it has been represented in diagrams and maps. It is with regards to anticipation that the will to improve differs most profoundly from the will to power. Because it is free both from objects and from subjects of desire, the will to power opens up onto and leads into a future that is impossible to predict. In effectively locating the future beyond forecasting, the will to power embraces time in all its purity and emptiness. No prognosis can foretell such future's contours; no divination or prophecy can predict its shape. The future the will to power therefore embraces is a future fully given to questions and aporias. In contrast, the will to improve actively seeks to bring about a future that is both recognisable and expected. Though it departs in some respects from the present, such departure is a matter of degree and quantity rather than of kind and quality. As such, the future the will to improve privileges remains closely connected to present dictates; this is a future given to knowledge and to the same returning, albeit with minor alterations, cast as improvements.

Another way of conceptualising the split constitution of promising relates to its orientation towards the potential encapsulated in the yet-to-come, something which is accessible only through the making of temporal incisions and the organisation of associated intervals. If/when promising is permeated by the will to power, it works so as to amplify potentiality. The incisions it inserts in time aim to uncover and free all the potential involved therein. At the same time, it gives itself fully to the future, affirming all that the latter might have to offer. Promising of this sort exemplifies Nietzsche's *amor fati:* it entails intense upheavals and demands the complete overcoming of the present and self-presence now! In contrast, the will to improve approaches potentiality as a resource to be captured and used. Part of the way it operates rests on arresting those potentialities offering the best chance for bringing about an improvement of present states while exhausting and wearing down everything that resists domestication and opposes the faithful reproduction of the present. To put it yet another way, the two faces of promising relate to each other in a disjunctive manner: the future anticipated by the will to improve is a figure effected by the forceful capture of potentiality and its yoking to effecting progress. In contrast, the future unanticipated is the quickening of potentials still contained yet remaining largely un-actualised in every presence and every present and their decoupling from the usages to which they have been put.

For Muslims, death is a cut and an opening to another life. This other life is to arrive with the Day of Judgment and it is commonplace for the faithful to associate this fateful day with the destruction of the cosmos as we know it and its subsequent making anew (Smith and Haddad 2002; Rustomji 2009). It is usually said that on such occasion, the heavens will be redrawn by the creator and the earth will be equally revamped; humans will be resurrected and judged with the pious set to enjoy an eternal life in the Garden, free from strife, toil, decay and death. This is Allah's promise to the faithful. Despite many speculative attempts undertaken mainly in pre-modern times at envisioning in greater detail the contours of the hereafter, most Muslims in Indonesia today adopt an aporetic stance, emphasising their bewilderment, awe and wonder about what Allah has in store for them. This promise I take as indicative of the will to power for it is affirmative of difference and the potential the future involves. I also see it as immanent in the field of Islamic micro-financial interventions: it is renewed and reactivated by the oath the zakat recipients dutifully perform five times a day. What I wish to concentrate on here, however, is the other side of promising and explore in greater detail its architecture, operation and effects. In order to do precisely that, I am returning to the ethnography of a specific Islamic micro-finance experiment in Indonesia.

Financialising Worship

As I have noted, the experiment *Indonesia Mandiri* was running involved making available financial capital. This capital had been collected by *Pondok Infak Mulia* in the form of zakat from the Jakarta metropolitan area. It was subsequently passed to *Indonesia Mandiri* for the purpose of running *syariah*-compliant community development. The categorisation of funds as zakat is of utmost importance.

Zakat is the third pillar of the faith and a central component of ritual life, constituting an act of worship decreed by Allah as His due. As outlined in Chap. 2, the ritual involves a wealth transfer that is both an obligatory payment by the better-off of a determinate portion of their lawful, hoarded property for the benefit of certain categories of people, the most important being the poor and the needy, and the right (*hak*) of those persons who belong to one of the eight categories of lawful claimants as enumerated in the Quran. Zakat comprises both a ritual duty to Allah and a property right of others. With the exception of the first few centuries when zakat was collected and distributed by the state, for most of Islam's history, zakat has been transferred directly or person-to-person by individual Muslims whose duty it is to hand it over to those individuals entitled to it (Fauzia 2013). Despite the fact that that zakat transfers usually involve the intermediation of mosque committees, the transfers have usually been accomplished with almost-immediate and near-instantaneous effect, especially since such committees do not endure for very long. However, over the past couple of decades and as a result of a rising interest in zakat as an economic instrument, the 'traditional' manner of dispensing zakat has come under intense criticism by proponents of Islamic modernism both in Indonesia and across the Islamic world (see Kahf 1989; Sarif and Kamri 2009). The debate is over whether zakat is to be transferred to the poor and the needy with immediate or delayed effect and relates to the permissibility of imposing certain conditions to the way it is to be used subsequently by the *mustahiq* (the zakat claimants, literally the ones entitled to zakat). In other words, the debate concerns the way the right of *mustahiq* is to be advanced and exercised for zakat is promised, sooner or later, to be theirs to own and dispense. One of the consequences of this debate has been a noticeable shift in the conceptualisation of zakat, with its conduct becoming less of a recognisable ritual and more about the effective deployment of a financial asset. Along the way, zakat has come to be increasingly understood as endowed not only with the efficacy of assisting wo(man) to commune with the divine but also of improving his/her socio-economic position in this world.

In Indonesia, *Pondok Infak Mulia* and *Indonesia Mandiri* are amongst the first Islamic organisations to transform zakat collection and distribution through the deployment of modern management techniques and a professional and bureaucratic structure. Both emphasise the mediation of experts for the conduct of Islamic welfare. For the experiment to be successful, the two organisations deploy particular sets of knowledge, principally those related to community development, after having dutifully distilled them through the application of the principles of Islamic economics. Islamic economics' singular aim is the development of *syariah*-compliant models and processes for modern Muslims to abide with in the pursuit of livelihood activities. As I came to learn through attending a 10-week course in one of the country's best Islamic economics departments, for zakat to reach its full potential, it has to be treated as financial capital dedicated to improving the human resources of the poor and the needy. This improvement is partly accomplished through encouraging the poor and the needy to defer immediate pleasure and engage in entrepreneurial activity. The first part of the experiment takes place in the classrooms of Islamic economics departments where zakat is being taught as an instrument for poverty alleviation. From there, it travels to the field of charitable interventions, involving the application of this knowledge to the everyday life of poor recipients. To discuss the first part of the experiment, I revert briefly to an edited section of my field-notes of the said course.

> Today's meeting was all about zakat as an instrument of poverty alleviation with the lecturer saying that if Indonesia is to become prosperous, zakat has to be deployed as *investasi positif. Positif* is the opposite of *konsumtif*, indicating an investment capable of having lasting effects. To demonstrate his

argument the lecturer gave the following example: family A is poor (*miskin*) for it can't meet its needs—its income is enough to buy 10 kilos of rice per month while its needs are equivalent to 20 kilos. Family A is the neighbour of Family B. Family B is well-off (*mampu*) and because its income exceeds a certain threshold (*nisab*), it has to pay zakat. Let's say that the zakat due is 100,000 rupiah per month and that the monetary value of one kilo of rice is 10,000 rupiah. Family B transfers its zakat to family A. The important thing is that there are two ways to go about this transfer. One way is to give Family A 100,000 rupiah every month to buy rice, helping it meet its consumption needs. There is no denying that this is good both for the family in question and the overall economy for it brings about an increase in demand which in turn helps increase overall supply which then goes to stimulate growth. However, the second way is preferable for it corresponds to *investasi positif*. It involves passing the zakat due to a professional zakat management body which runs an empowerment program and encouraging Family A to participate in it. This way Family A will acquire both new skills and the capital required to start a micro-business such as selling vegetables in the market. The aim is to make Family A self-reliant (*mandiri*) so that it does not have to rely on zakat anymore. *Zakat produktif* is about empowerment and the development of human capital (*sumber daya manusia*). Prophetic traditions (*hadith*), the lecturer continued, duly attest to zakat pertaining to production rather than consumption. According to reliable reports, a man once asked the Prophet for charity. The Prophet asked the man whether he owned anything of value. When the man replied that he owned some clothing and a cap for drinking water, the Prophet auctioned the items and he passed the proceeds to the man in question, advising him to buy food for his family with half of the money and use the other half to buy an axe to chop wood in the forest to sell subsequently in the market. When the Prophet met the man again a couple of weeks later, the man said he had made ten times more than what he had started with. The Prophet congratulated him, saying that 'asking' (*minta*) is appropriate only for those who are too old, too young, or too infirm to work or for those who are in immediate need of food and shelter.

The casting of zakat as financial capital is supported by several *fatawa* (edicts) issued by the Indonesian Council of Islamic Scholars (*Majelis Ulama Indonesia*)[9] that several people in the country recognise as Indonesia's supreme authority in matters of the faith. It also supported by zakat management laws No. 38/1999 and No. 23/2011 (see Chap. 3) which state that once the immediate needs of the poor have been satisfied, it is lawful for the rest of funds to be used for productive purposes, that is, as capital dispensed in the form of credit for the establishment of micro-enterprises. This assemblage of Islamic jurisprudential knowledge and state power is, however, seriously contested by other scholars mostly associated with *Nahdlatul Ulama* who are used to arguing from a more traditional point of view. Their opinions in this matter raise a series of very significant concerns. Chief among these is the worry that when zakat is not disbursed immediately to *mustahiq*, it puts obstacles to the exercise of a God-given property right (see also Mahmud and Shah 2009; Sarif and Kamri 2009). Coupled with this is the concern that the disbursement of zakat in the form of interest-free loans by empowerment bodies turns, effectively, the *mustahiq* into debtors and the *amil* (the zakat management agencies) into creditors. In addition, some traditionalist scholars point out that it is not permissible for zakat to be accompanied by the imposition of conditions relating to usage; otherwise, zakat is no longer a right but is effectively repositioned as a gift (*hibah*), which, in turn, is an altogether different category and subject to different regulations.[10] Because zakat is not *hibah*, the argument continues, it should be up to *mustahiq* to decide what to do with it. To more traditional scholars then, the 'micro-finance revolution' in zakat management introduces disapproved and unlawful innovations in what is taken to be an immutable area of the faith.

Such a traditionalist view enjoys wider currency in Indonesian society. Despite the fact that *Surabaya Peduli Ummat* (SPU), the Surabaya-based LAZ discussed in Chap. 3, is far from subscribing to *Nahdlatul Ulama*'s traditionalist version of the faith, representing instead a moderate version of Islamic modernism and thus closely associated with *Muhammadiyah*, Indonesia's second-largest Islamic organisation, when it comes to zakat SPU's position matches closely some of the traditionalist arguments outlined above. This unexpected alignment is manifested in SPU choosing to separate carefully and consistently between its welfare programmes funded by zakat and its microfinance programmes, which have been running since 2010 and funded by *sedekah*[11] donations. Key in SPU's decision to studiously refrain from deploying zakat in microfinance programmes have been acute concerns regarding the juridical requirement for zakat to reach the poor and the needy as directly and immediately as possible, meaning that any intervention in its disbursement involving third parties, such as SPU and temporal gaps, should be kept to a minimum. In this regard, SPU's microfinance programmes involve the disbursement of credit in the form of either free gifts (*hibah*) or interest-free loans (*qardhul hasan*): while the former are transferred without any return stipulated but sometimes with conditions attached, the latter necessitate the return of capital lend within an agreed period. As the SPU manager in charge of empowerment programmes put it to me, because zakat does away with requiring returns of any kind, corresponding instead to wealth rightly owned by the poor and the needy, it is distinct both to loans and to gifts. In her view, and the view of SPU's *syariah* board, the very distinctiveness of zakat makes it an ill-fitting instrument for delivering *syariah*-compliant microfinance.

The reservations and objections to the deployment of zakat as credit/debt for productive purposes are counter-acted not only with reference to the Prophetic example cited above that lends its authority to modern 'adaptations' but also by fresh jurisprudential reasoning. The latter sanctions the deferred transfer of zakat to claimants. In particular, a *fatwa* issued by MUI and entitled *Using Zakat for Investment* (no. 4/2003) opines that 'although the original rule is to give zakat immediately (*fauriyah*), the distribution of *zakat maal* from *amil* to *mustahiq* can be delayed (*dita'khirkan*) when there is no *mustahiq* or for the sake of greater public good (*maslaha*).' The edict is significant not only for opening up further the path towards the greater financialisation of worship but also for instituting a break and introducing an interval in the overall temporality organising the transfer of zakat. Whereas in the past, the immediate transfer of wealth due to others worked so as to minimise, and even negate, the existence of such interval, a set of new jurisprudential understandings, working in tandem with the discipline of Islamic economics and new forms of civil society institutions, seek to bring about such a synthesis of time that widens already existing temporal gaps and heightens the significance attributed to chronological breaks. Key in such attempts is the redeployment of the concept of *ta'khir*, meaning delay and postponement, and the jurisprudential creation of an analogy (*qiyas*) between the ritual of prayer (*sholat*) where deferral is usually allowed when certain conditions, such as travel or ill health, prevail[12] and the ritual of zakat. According to MUI's guidance, the delayed transfer of zakat ownership rights applies only to *mustahiq*; those under the obligation to pay zakat are encouraged to meet their obligation immediately, that is, before a full calendar year has passed. The delay in zakat reaching the *mustahiq* is justified on account of the greater benefit (*maslaha*)[13] that is assumed to accrue both to the poor and the needy and to society as a whole, in the course of the instituted interval and as a direct result of the intervention of professional zakat management bodies. In other words, such an approach to zakat gives time a specific value; this is the value of achieving greater *maslaha* or public benefit. The value of public benefit and its achievement are of an anticipatory and promissory nature; they are expected to occur at a future time, pointing towards an epoch of plenty that is yet-to-come.

The conceptual and institutional artifice erected around the temporal interval (*ta'khir*) means that a poor person's right over the zakat due is not violated. The exercise of this right is, however, suspended. For those who subscribe to the artifice, it is the promise of future prosperity that requires and justifies such suspension. For the duration of the interval, the claimants are expected to be willingly subjected to empowerment training programmes that include the acquisition of entrepreneurial skills and the deployment of micro-credit. Both tools are generally thought of as necessary, yet not sufficient, conditions for achieving prosperity. Seen from this perspective, the debt obligation the disbursement of zakat in the form of micro-credit creates is conceived of as a technical rather than a legal issue. This is for *ta'khir,* in a manner reminiscent of Agamben's (2005) work on law and the state in Europe, institutes the interval as a lawful state of exception. The suspension of rights and the active creation of debt that take place during the time of the break are, therefore, conceived of as entirely provisional. Any unwelcome complexities involved are thought of as destined to find resolution at such point in the near future when the ownership of zakat will be eventually passed to *mustahiq* who, in the meantime, will have been duly reformed by the training on offer.[14]

The Return

I have already shown how the cut in time has been conceived and sanctioned in contemporary Islamic welfare interventions in Indonesia. Now, I turn my attention to its effects. At stake is the organisation of the time of the interval in terms of its 'architecture' and the way it orients itself to the future. To repeat, the question guiding my analysis is whether the interval's architecture makes the present return as an improved version of the self-same existent or it opens time up for good, welcoming the arrival of the radically other and affirming the difference of the yet-to-come. It is of considerable value to note that the architecture *Indonesia Mandiri* deploys in its empowerment programmes is based around *syariah*-approved contracts; the latter provide the overall framework within which time is punctuated and the return is actively pursued. Versions of well-known Islamic forms of financing such as those of *murabaha*, *musharaka* and *mudaraba* outline, in some detail, the contributions and responsibilities of the two parties involved: the trainees who are also the zakat recipients, on the one hand, and the trainers/the zakat management body on the other. Such contracts set up a specific horizon for relations to be actualised; this horizon pertains to an exchange of promises. The promises, as instantiated in the contracts in question, tie the honouring of obligations to future redemption and apprehend it as referring at once to prosperity and affluence in this life and to salvation and deliverance in the next.

Indonesia Mandiri is a non-profit organisation aiming to empower marginalised communities in both rural and urban settings. Empowerment is conceived of as self-reliance that is attainable through the implementation of a specific 'architecture' the organisation's team of experts has devised. This 'architecture' involves a number of things: first, the formation in the area of intervention of small groups, consisting usually of women; second, the provision of training, supervision and monitoring by an IM employee; and third, the cultivation of local cadres who, at the end of the programme, will take charge of the micro-financial institution IM has established with the use of zakat funds. The architecture of the experiment is both spatially and temporally delimited. It involves a territorially defined unit of intervention, the district (*kecamatan*), and rests on an evolutionary grid, itself marked with phases and dates, with the whole process planned to last for two to three years. In addition to its *sosial* mission, the experiment is also an exercise in *dakwah* or Islamic propagation, constituting a meritorious activity for all those who participate in it, thereby generating salvific credits (*pahala*). Because the *syariah*-compliant model of financing puts the tenets of Islamic faith into practice at the level of everyday life, it amounts to an act of piety that enthusiastically promotes the good and the recommended while putting a halt to the perpetuation of forbidden and/or disapproved of activities. Seen from this perspective, the contemporary impulse towards the financialisation of worship is supplemented by an equally important force, as *dakwah* activities seek to encompass all kinds of activities within the realm of ritual.

Syariah-compliant contracts are explicitly conceptualised as Islam's alternative to conventional, interest-based financing, which the majority of Islamic scholars judge as sinful (see Siddiqi 1983; Warde 2010). At the site of IM's intervention in Surabaya, the Islamic micro-financing of the livelihoods of poor households involved the deployment of three separate *syariah*-compliant contracts, with the first being a sales-based instrument and the other two belonging to equity-based, profit-and-loss financing.

This set of obligations exercised a disciplinary force on the shape of the social, moulding its contours in a highly specific manner; they also textured the time of the interval. This texture revolved around ensuring that investments in labour, piety and money yielded ever bigger returns, making local incomes progressively larger and lives perpetually better. The means through which these improvements were sought relied on the continuous advancement of credit and the ongoing creation of debt as well as on the careful management of monetary obligations through deferred payments and the initiation of lifelong partnerships. My argument is that Islamic micro-finance acted in a pre-emptory manner, anticipating and foretelling the future as a better version of the self-same present, making the present return time and again as almost identical to itself, with the difference each repetition involved having been largely arrested and domesticated by the imperative for uninterrupted progress.

As I mentioned, the 100 million rupiah IM invested in Surabaya came from zakat. This zakat had been initially collected by *Pondok Infak Mulia* in the Jakarta metropolitan area and was subsequently passed to IM. At the latter's hands, it underwent a certain 'purification,' becoming a financial asset. It is precisely in this form that the moneys reached the poor in Surabaya. I should make amply clear that Surabaya's poor recipients were totally unaware of the funds providence, that is, they did not know the money was zakat. As a result, they treated the cash advanced as the property of the organisations involved and held themselves in their debt, both metaphorically and literally. However, PIM's and IM's personnel approached the question in a markedly different fashion, insisting that the organisations held such funds in trusteeship. According to the PIM's and IM's employees I spoke to, the rightful owner of the funds involved was the micro-finance institution IM helped establish as part of its intervention, and by association, the institution's local members, that is, those urban poor who were its affiliates. One of the most important consequences arising from the delay in the transfer of zakat is that the poor can access their share only in their capacity as members of the micro-finance institution in question. Moreover, till the running of this institution, commonly referred to as *Ikhtiar Swadaya Mitra*, is passed to its membership, the management of funds remains at the discretion of *Indonesia Mandiri*.

Indonesia Mandiri initially dispensed funds in the form of credit through the utilisation of *murabaha* contracts. In Islamic banking, *murabaha* is a sale-based instrument and a short-term financing mechanism. In general, it involves the finance institution purchasing a good on behalf of a client and the subsequent selling of the same good to him/her at cost plus a declared margin, with the payment being deferred for a specified time period. In Surabaya, the written contracts that organised such relations identified IM and a named individual as the parties involved, included the value of the good(s)[15] purchased—usually ranging from 500,000 to 1 million rupiah-, specified the number of instalments due and stated the mark-up's price—usually 50,000–100,000 rupiah. However, I should clarify that the mark-up does not amount to profit in this case, as it is used to enhance the capacities of the programme at the local level. This, however, should not detract attention from the fact that such contracts involve, in no uncertain terms, the incurring of debts, stipulating a specific time period for their repayment, normally amounting to a year. The social creation of debt is underlined by issuing each member with an instalment book.[16] This book is a record of the deferred payments due and is routinely inspected once a month by the IM employee in charge of the intervention, during the meetings s/he holds with the groups involved.

Taken together, *murabaha* contracts and instalment books correspond to specific devices for synthesising the time of the interval. In addition to the five-times-a-day prayer and the Islamic calendar, with its rites and celebrations, a new temporal process is initiated through the exchange of promises and the social production of monetary obligations. Time's unfolding is punctuated by monthly intervals and annual cycles. Between the deferred payments, the time the poor have at their disposal acquires significance through the pursuit of monetary value. Such time should not be wasted but instead invested. Accordingly, the money the poor should aim to produce for the duration of time intervals should be of equal value at least to the value of credit advanced and exceed it by a margin. This is so for the amount the poor owe is supplemented by a well-defined surplus, presented as a mark-up. According to IM's plan, the endpoint of this temporal process corresponds to the very point of deliverance. The deliverance in question is conceived as the return of the same enhanced with the payment of the mark-up acting as a sign of the progress achieved. However, such redemption is momentary only: a new cycle of credit/debt is set to begin immediately after, with the initiation of a new round of *murabaha* agreements between the organisation and the poor.

The female recipients of credit/debt I met admitted that the instalments scheme placed new demands on their management of household budgets, requiring a new kind of vigilance to be exercised so that household expenses, which tend to fluctuate wildly due to unstable sources of income, did not compromise their capacity to honour their obligations to IM. Were this to happen repeatedly, it could place their continued participation in the programme under question. Moreover, they said, they stood to lose face to other members and neighbours, with the disgraceful news always making quick rounds. These women I spoke to were eager to stress the capacities of financial discipline and future planning they acquired through the programme, adding that IM was keen to show empathy when a member was unable to make the monthly payment due to circumstances beyond their control.

IM conceives *murabaha* arrangements as inexhaustible, extending into infinity. I was told that a key advantage of *murabaha* (micro-)financing contracts is that they are forever renewable. Immediately after a contract has reached its successful conclusion, it is replaced, if so desired, by a new agreement between IM—or the local micro-finance institution that is set to succeed IM at the end of the empowerment process—and a named, poor individual. This wondrous capacity for constant renewal comes with the expectation and the assurance that the credit to be advanced next time round will be of superior value to the previous one. The infinite, unrestricted character of credit/debt relations is perhaps best communicated by the Indonesian term applied: *pinjaman modal bergulir tanpa bunga*, meaning 'rolling interest-free capital loan,' is the colloquial equivalent of *murabaha*, an Arabic and perhaps more difficult term to inhabit. The characterisation of such loans as rolling (*bergulir*) is of immediate significance: the style of movement indicated denotes the unfolding of a curvature for which the point of arrival differs ever so slightly from the point of departure so that a full, perfect circle is impossible to maintain. Precisely because of the repeated lack of coincidence of beginnings and endings, there is always a gap itself corresponding to some sort of assumed advancement taking place before a new rotation is about to begin.

The capacity to honour obligations is itself held as capable of extending obligations into infinity: the chance of acquiring a higher value loan in each new round of credit/debt circulation is deemed as absolutely necessary for creating enough 'lift' to elevate the poor out of their misery and deliver them onto prosperity. Nevertheless, achieving such incremental 'lift' requires the unending return of value as credit/debt. This is the highly paradoxical effect of the rolling nature of micro-finance contracts employed when extended over time: because the mark-up required in each *murabaha* rotation is geared to enter circulation in the next round as an increase in the amount of credit made available, what has effectively been produced as a supplement during a previous round is actively being recast as an obligation due in the following. In this scheme, the ambiguity of money—it is at once credit and debt (see Graeber 2011) —is underwritten by a specific temporality in which present surpluses quickly turn into future liabilities.

Murabaha or sale-based contracts are not the only ones deployed in the laboratory *Indonesia Mandiri* set up in Surabaya. There are also contracts of the profit-and-loss sharing variety, commonly known in Indonesia as *bagi hasil*, indicating the sharing of the outcome of a venture partnership. Contracts of the profit-and-loss sharing variety apply to the shop the Islamic micro-finance institution owns and operates in the locality; they too have a most profound effect on time, especially with respect to its intersection with labour and consumption. It should be noted that the micro-financial institution IM has established is not only limited to providing credit to the poor but also aims to generate profits through running a commercial enterprise.[17] Part of the zakat funds IM has invested locally were spent on renting a property, training the shop workforce and buying up stock. The shop in question sells a range of basic goods, such as rice, noodles and cooking oil, at prices slightly below market prevailing ones to a clientele that includes the institution's members as well as non-members.

At the end of each commercial day, ibu Nurhayati, the shop's manager, dutifully performs certain mathematical calculations, dividing the daily turnover into two shares. The first share is spent on stock replenishing and amounts to 90% of takings. The rest is subdivided into two further shares. The first share, equalling 40%, belongs to ibu Nurhayati: it is the monetary return for her input into the running of the shop, expressing the value of the time she spends in labour. The forty-sixty split of the modest percentage of 10% earmarked as profit means that ibu Nurhayati and the micro-finance institution that owns the shop have entered into a *mudaraba* partnership. Such partnerships sit at the heart of the promise Islamic welfare organisations makes to the faithful. In Islamic finance, partnerships of this sort typically involve one party providing the finance for a business venture and another party carrying the venture out on the basis of a pre-agreed division of profits (and losses) (see El-Gamal 2006: 155–171; Warde 2010: 145–149). In the case of ibu Nurhayati, however, these promises seem to have borne little fruit as, by her own admission, her monthly income has remained both meagre and largely stagnant at around 700,000 rupiah. As this mother of five put it, a return as small as this is hardly adequate to feed her family and is also well below the 2012 regional minimum salary of 1.25 million rupiah per month.

After having been in this partnership for ten months and having seen no major improvement on her returns, ibu Nurhayati admitted to making alternative plans: she told me she intended to resign from the position of shop manager at the earliest opportunity possible and set up a new business of her own, sewing and selling linen in nearby markets. She had already applied for a loan to the local government to buy a sewing machine and was awaiting the result. In her estimation, the two years she had spent working closely with *Indonesia Mandiri* had been very important: she had managed to get out of the trouble she had run into with local moneylenders and was certain that she was not to go into too much debt again. Her financial recovery had made her optimistic of the future: the time had come to look for new sources of income, as her children were growing up fast and their needs were multiplying, she said.

The remaining 60% of the 10% representing daily takings is further divided in the following way: 30% goes towards the rent for the shop's premises, 20% for operational costs and 10% is put aside in a separate account. This account is broken open once a year, at the end of the fasting month of Ramadan and before the major festivities of *Idul Fitri* begin. This is the moment when the kitty's money is divided (*bagi hasil*) amongst the group of people *Indonesia Mandiri* has selected to act as the shop's business partners (*mitra*). The people so designated come from the pool of the poor who are already in a *murabaha* relation with the micro-finance institution, keep their meagre savings with it and have committed themselves to purchasing regularly from its shop. In 2012, out of more than 200 *murabaha* clients, only twenty were invited to join the venture as partners (*mitra*), supplanting the zakat funds IM had made available for running the shop with their own meagre savings and low purchasing power. Their selection was carried out by IM personnel on the basis of due diligence in the performance of religious duties, consistent servicing of debt and an enhanced capacity for being a good parent as well as an upstanding, law-abiding citizen. On the basis of such criteria, only twenty people were chosen to enter into a *musharaka*-like agreement amongst themselves. In general, *musharaka* contracts represent medium-term, equity-like arrangements in which the parties involved form a partnership for purposes of a joint investment, with the sharing of profits (and risks) being determined on the basis of proportionality (see El-Gamal 2006: 21, 40; Warde 2010: 145–149). In the case of the shop in Surabaya, the principle of proportionality means the greater the value of goods a partner purchases from the shop during a year, the more s/he stands to gain in terms of the share s/he is to be allotted when, at the end of Ramadan, this most sacred time of the Muslim calendar, the kitty is broken open.

The *musharaka* contract forms a step up in the temporal unfolding of the hierarchy of worth *Indonesia Mandiri* has put in place. The offer of the chance to join such a partnership effectively 'upgrades' some amongst the local poor, effectively transforming this minority from the status of a people urgently needed to be taught how to become productive into dependable partners and regular and reliable consumers. This transformation is marked by a change in the instruments deployed, with the incurring of debts giving its place to the apparatus of partnership. On the basis of one having proven his/her capacity to honour debts, one is encouraged and assisted to develop patterns of consumption that are at once consistent and speculative. *Indonesia Mandiri* has implicitly stipulated two major conditions for admittance into the category of partners (*mitra*): as a future partner, a poor woman's shopping has to acquire regularity; as a fellow investor, one's behaviour has to be consistently oriented to a recurring point in the future, itself marked by the anticipated division of spoils. In this regard, the principle of proportionality gives the future a specific value: such value is effectively tied to the present through the spending incurred on everyday household necessities. Overall, the return of the present improved is accomplished through the influence of present consumption exercises on the calculation of rewards-to-come. The predictability and foreseeability of the future is directly related not only to the unending return of value as credit/debt that *murabaha* contracts effect but also to the joining up of future possibilities with present conditions through *musharaka* instruments. As a result, virtually all the potential that has been momentarily freed by the cut has come to be duly arrested, with the future having been turned into a resource for the perpetuation of the present improved.

Counter-Revolution Today

For Deleuze, '[d]ifference inhabits repetition' (2008: 97). This habitation Deleuze links to Nietzsche's eternal return. The significance of the eternal return lies in its capacity to perform a time synthesis that unleashes all that the future entails. Because it is pervaded by the desire for the new and the other, the eternal return works incessantly to make sure that with every move of the clock's dials, as it were, it 'is not the same but the different, not the similar but the dissimilar, not the one but the many' (2008: 126) that are bound to arrive. In counter-distinction to habit and memory, which rely on the present and the past, respectively, so as to synthesise time, the eternal return dares us to think of time as deriving from difference and as coming from the future. For Deleuze, time is nothing more and nothing less than pure potential: an unadulterated, unformed and nebulous *chaosmos*, consisting of a multiplicity of events, all of which exist in a virtual, that is, amorphous and embryonic, state. They are to-come. What the passage of time does, and what the temporal process involves, is the imposition of selection: only certain lines of potential will be allowed to materialise; only certain events will be assisted in becoming actual. Everything else will be excluded and supressed, contained therein as mere latency. The three time-syntheses Deleuze talks about perform this selection differently: operating cyclically, habit repeats the present; working linearly, memory echoes a past which has never been present; proceeding anarchically, the eternal return cuts into a future unknown. By freeing up lines of potential and forms of matter previously excluded, the eternal return effectively redraws the map and reinvents the limits of possibility for thought and politics.

Having restated Deleuze's position ever so briefly, it now time to return to a question I posed earlier in the chapter: if the practice of Islamic micro-finance is not geared towards the repetition of the past, as several scholars have argued, but involves the hastening of a future time, how does the promises it makes relate to the Deleuzian eternal return and its affirmation of difference? Like the eternal return, the promises Islamic micro-finance makes are orientated towards the future. Such a future is envisaged as a radical departure from Western secular modernity and contemporary neo-liberal capitalism. It is also envisaged as free from the poverty and the hardships permeating ordinary lives in Indonesia and many Islamic societies in the twenty-first century. Intrinsic to such promises is the installing of Allah and the Prophet as immanent figures in the pursuit of livelihood activities. The decisiveness of this move should not be underestimated: by opening up livelihood activities to worship, Islamic micro-finance practices effectively link everyday life in the present to salvation in the future, underscoring the radical otherness to come by means of death and the Day of Judgement. In insisting on the importance of the faithful relating to their present selves as future dead, Islamic micro-finance splits human subjects open, constituting them as self-differing and forever becoming. This, I repeat, is no mean feat.

What this study of Islamic micro-finance offers to the philosophy of Deleuze is a critical supplement highlighting that the privileging of future time is not sufficient in and of itself for arresting the negative consequences habit and memory have on time and our habitation of it. This is so because promising is permeated by two counter-opposing, equally immanent, currents: it is as much motivated by the affirmation entailed in the 'will to power' as by the negation involved in the 'will to improve.' In the field of Islamic micro-finance, the 'will to improve' manifests itself in a series of promises that take the form of *syariah*-compliant contracts. Promises of its kind work to anticipate and forecast the future, reducing it to a value-added version of the self-same present. The instruments involved in the unending return of the present as effected by Islamic micro-finance are multiple: first comes the jurisprudential innovation regarding the deferred transfer of zakat. Such innovation allows and sanctions zakat's transformation into a financial asset whereby its transfer to the poor and the needy is made coterminous with the dispensation of credit. Second is zakat's domestication, its participation in the social creation of debt and the proliferation of debt relations amongst marginalised populations of recipients. Third, the advancing of monetary assets in the guise of obligations that require servicing means that the lives of the poor are wedded to recurring cycles of ever-increased amounts of credit/debt being advanced. In this scheme, the pursuit of money is unrelenting, with money becoming elevated to a near-absolute measure of value, at least as far as this life is concerned. The instruments deployed by Islamic micro-finance annihilate everything creative that can't be easily turned into something productive and suppress everything dynamic that can't be simply made into something advantageous and profitable. These obliterations and exclusions are the horrors that recur every time a promise of improvement is made, and a new round of obligation is *ex nihilo* created.

Notes

1. Anthropological accounts of Islamic modernism abound; for recent studies, see Deeb (2006), Mahmood (2005) and Hirschkind (2006). For the way Islamic modernism pertains to zakat, see Chap. 2.
2. Critical studies of development processes in Indonesia include Robinson and Bessell (2002) and Li (2006, 2007).

3. In place of interest, Islamic banking deploys distinct modes of financing themselves developed through innovative engagements with contractual forms already approved by classical Islamic jurisprudence. General studies of Islamic banking include El-Gamal (2006), Kuran (2004) and Warde (2010). Anthropological accounts of Islamic finance include Maurer (2005, 2006) and Rudnyckyj (2019). Some of the contracts currently in circulation in Islamic banking have been transposed to Islamic micro-finance and are considered in this chapter as well as the next.
4. Ithaca HOURS is a currency alternative to the US dollar.
5. The dinar, consisting of 4.4 grams of 24 K gold, was introduced in Indonesia in 2000. Post-2008, the global rise in the price of gold put severe stresses on the organisation's finances, forcing it to stop paying salaries in dinar. Similar problems were encountered with respect to taking Sundays off, a day most businesses and banks are closed across the country.
6. For Deleuze (2008: 280–327), the given is the outcome of a highly specific morphogenetic process through which particular forms emerge out of a highly differentiated, chaotic matter in constant flux. This process is conceived on the basis of a tripartite scheme that posits three closely interrelated planes: the virtual, the intensive and the extensive. Through the mediation of the intensive, the 'chaosmos' of the virtual, that is, pure potential, is processed and organised in the extensive into the distinctive forms we take for granted. However, as soon as such forms emerge, a reverse process begins, disaggregating and disorganising what is already given; this happens before a new cycle of formation/production takes hold. While the concept of the virtual owes much to the work of Bergson (see Deleuze 1991), the unfolding of the twin processes of what are sometimes referred to as 'territorialisation' and 'deterritorialisation' bears the distinctive marks of Nietzsche's concept of the eternal return.
7. In this regard, Deleuze writes, 'The present exists, but the past alone insists and provides the element in which the present passes and successive presents are telescoped' (2008: 107).
8. Deleuze identifies Nietzsche's figures of the 'last man' and the 'man who want to perish' as key in accomplishing the work of annihilation and for converting the negation involved in destruction into the creation and affirmation of the new, preparing, in this way, the path for the 'Overman' (Deleuze 2012: 139–182).
9. The most important *fatawa* on this topic, especially No. 4/2003, No. 8/2011, and No. 15/2011, are included in the *Himpunan Fatwa Majelis Ulama Indonesia Sejak Tahun 1975* published by Erlangga in 2011.
10. For a definition of *hibah* and the way it features in Islamic jurisprudence and Islamic micro-finance, see Chap. 7.

11. Jurisprudentially speaking, *sedekah* is the voluntary alms Indonesian Muslims are 'strongly recommended' (*sunna mu'akkada*) to give: it is normally conceived in counter-distinction to zakat, the obligatory wealth transfer the affluent are required to perform annually as the third pillar of faith. Despite the fact that in the Quran, *sedekah* entertains a wider meaning than zakat, denoting interchangeably mandatory and voluntary transfers (Weir and Zysow 2012), canonical interpretations have given rise to historical practices in which zakat is fixed by law as to the nature and value of property it applies to and the categories of people designated as its rightful recipients. Because no such legal stipulations apply to *sedekah*, the giver is free to decide who s/he will give what, how much and when. As such, *sedekah* is often couched as excess, with zakat indexing the bare minimum of requirements. While preferred *sedekah* beneficiaries are normally one's close associates, such as relatives and neighbours, no one is barred from acting as a potential recipient, including non-Muslims and animals. In addition, while Muslims are encouraged to pass things they love and treasure, *sedekah* is not limited to objects of monetary value for anything of benefit to an-other like a greeting or a smile counts as such. What differentiates *sedekah* from other kinds of gifts, generally denoted with the term *hibah*, is the intention involved: such intention has to be informed by *keikl-hasan*, meaning sincere, earnest devotion, for the main purpose of *sedekah* is to come close to Allah and please Him in the hope of gaining his favour, mainly in the Hereafter.
12. Not all schools of Islamic law allow for the delayed or advanced combination of prayers to occur; notably, the Hanafis oppose *takhir* vehemently while the Shafi'is, Malikis and Hanbalis allow *takhir* only when significant obstacles are faced by the faithful in timely performance of the five daily prayers.
13. *Maslaha* is one of the principles of Islamic jurisprudence; in classical accounts, it sits rather lowly in the overall hierarchy of sources of law; its prominence is rather recent and due to the influence of Islamic modernism (see Hallaq 1997).
14. A recent volume on Islamic micro-finance (Ali 2011) artfully evades getting into jurisprudential debates; yet, its contributors noticeably disagree as to the permissibility of using zakat for micro-credit purposes (see also Obaidullah and Latiff 2008). More recently, the drive towards the financialisation of zakat in Indonesia has gained momentum, with zakat management bodies using some of the zakat collected for the establishment of commercial companies. The intention is to distribute parts of future profits to the poor and the needy. MUI has sanctioned such an approach—see fatwa no. 15/2011—and *Pondok Infak Mulia* is at the forefront of its application with commercial interests in construction, second-hand goods and travel (see Chap. 3).

15. The goods in question almost always refer to equipment essential for productive activities. Such equipment might be a cart for ease of transport or tables and kitchen utensils to equip a food stall. Alternatively, it can be primary materials, such as oil, flour and eggs, to make foodstuffs to sell in the market.
16. The book also records the savings, if any, the poor are keeping with IM, as well as the voluntary alms (*infak/sedekah*) they might entrust the organisation with; in general, aid recipients are actively encouraged both to save and to give to others, however small the amounts might be.
17. Such profits, however, return to circulation in the guise of credit/debt made available to the poor.

Bibliography

Agamben, Giorgio. 2005. *State of Exception*. Chicago: University of Chicago Press.

Ali, Nazim. 2011. *Shari'a-Compliant Microfinance*. London: Routledge.

Ansell-Pearson, Keith. 2010. Deleuze and the Overcoming of Memory. In *Memory: Histories, Theories, Debates*, ed. Susannah Radstone and Bill Schwartz, 131–174. New York: Fordham University.

Antonio Muhammad, Syafii. 2008. Islamic Microfinance Initiatives to Enhance Small and Medium Enterprises. In *Expressing Islam: Religious Life and Politics in Indonesia*, ed. Greg Fealy and Sally White, 253–266. Singapore: ISEAS.

Callon, Michel. 2007. What Does it Mean to Say that Economics Is Performative. In *Do Economists Make Markets?* ed. D. MacKenzie, F. Muniesa, and L. Siu, 311–357. Princeton: Princeton University Press.

Choiruzzad, Shofwan Al Banna. 2013. More Gain, More Pain: The Development of Indonesia' Islamic Economy Movement (1980s–2012). *Indonesia* 95 (1): 125–172.

Deeb, Lara. 2006. *An Enchanted Modern: Gender and Public Piety in Shi'i Lebanon*. Princeton: Princeton University Press.

Deleuze, Gilles. 1991. *Bergsonism*. Trans. Hugh Tomlinson and Barbara Habberjam. New York: Zone Books.

———. 1992. *Cinema 1. The Movement-Image*. Trans. Hugh Tomlinson and Barbara Habberjam. London: The Athlone Press.

———. 1997. *Cinema 2. The Time-Image*. Trans. Hugh Tomlinson and Robert Galeta. Minneapolis: University of Minnesota Press.

———. 2005. *Pure Immanence: Essays on a Life*. Trans. Anne Boyman. New York: Zone Books.

———. 2008. *Difference and Repetition*. Trans. Paul Patton. London: Continuum Press.

———. 2012. *Nietzsche and Philosophy*. Trans. Hugh Tomlinson. London: Continuum Press.

Deleuze, Gilles, and Félix Guattari. 2004. *A Thousand Plateaus. Capitalism and Schizophrenia Vol. 2*. London: Continuum Press.
El-Gamal, Mahmood. 2006. *Islamic Finance: Law, Economics, and Practice*. Cambridge: Cambridge University Press.
Fauzia, Amelia. 2013. *Faith and the State: A History of Islamic Philanthropy in Indonesia*. Leiden: Brill.
Graeber, David. 2011. *Debt. The First 5,000 Years*. Brooklyn: Melville House.
Hallaq, Wael. 1997. *A History of Islamic Legal Theories: An Introduction to Sunnī uṣūl al-fiqh*. Cambridge: Cambridge University Press.
Hefner, Robert. 2003. Islamizing Capitalism: On the Founding of Indonesia's First Islamic Bank. In *Shari'a and Politics in Modern Indonesia*, ed. A. Salim and A. Azra, 148–167. Singapore: Institute of South East Asian Studies.
Hirschkind, C. 2006. *The Ethical Soundscape: Cassette Sermons and Islamic Counterpublics*. New York: Columbia University Press.
Kahf, Monzer. 1989. Zakat: Unresolved Issues in Contemporary Fiqh. *Journal of Islamic Economics* 2 (1): 1–22.
Kuran, Timur. 2004. *Islam and the Mammon: The Economic Predicaments of Islamism*. Princeton: Princeton University Press.
Latour, B. 1993. *We Have Never Been Modern*. Cambridge, MA: Harvard University Press.
Li, Tania Murray. 2006. *Neo-liberal Strategies of Government through Community: The Social Development Program of the World Bank in Indonesia*. International Law and Justice Working Papers No. 2.
———. 2007. *The Will to Improve: Governmentality, Development, and the Practice of Politics*. Durham: Duke University Press.
Mahmood, Saba. 2005. *Politics of Piety. The Islamic Revival and the Feminist Subject*. Princeton: Princeton University Press.
Mahmud, Mek Wok, and Saued Sikandar Shah. 2009. The Use of Zakat Revenue in Islamic Financing: Jurisprudential Debate and Practical Feasibility. *Studies in Islam and the Middle East* 6 (1): 15–30.
Maurer, Bill. 2005. *Mutual Life, Limited: Islamic Banking, Alternative Currencies, Lateral Reason*. Princeton: Princeton University Press.
———. 2006. *Pious Property: Islamic Mortgages in the United States*. New York: Russell Sage Foundation.
Mauss, Marcel. 2003. *On Prayer*. New York: Durkheim Press.
Nietzsche, Friedrich. 2003. *The Genealogy of Morals*. New York: Dover Publications.
Obaidullah, Mohammed, and Hajah Salma Haji Abdul Latiff. 2008. *Islamic Finance for Micro and Medium Enterprises*. Jedda: Islamic Research and Training Institute, Islamic Development Bank.
Retsikas, Konstantinos. 2012. *Becoming – An Anthropological Approach to Understandings of the Person in Java*. London: Anthem Press.
Reynolds, Jack. 2004. Derrida and Deleuze on Time, the Future, and Politics. *Borderlands* 3 (1).

Riesebrodt, Martin. 2010. *The Promise of Salvation: A Theory of Religion*. Chicago: Chicago University Press.

Rifki, Ismal. 2013. *Islamic Banking in Indonesia*. Singapore: Wiley.

Robinson, Kathryn, and Sharon Bessell. 2002. *Women in Indonesia: Gender, Equity and Development*. Singapore: ISEAS.

Rudnyckyj, Daromir. 2019. *Beyond Debt: Islamic Experiments in Global Finance*. Chicago: University of Chicago Press.

Rustomji, Nerina. 2009. *The Garden and the Fire: Heaven and Hell in Islamic Culture*. New York: Columbia University Press.

Saeed, Abdullah. 2004. Islamic Banking and Finance: In Search of a Pragmatic Model. In *Islamic Perspectives on the New Millennium*, ed. Virginia Hooker and Amin Saikal, 113–132. Singapore: ISEAS.

Sakai, Minako. 2008. Community Development through Islamic Microfinance: Serving the Financial Needs of the Poor in a Visible Way. In *Expressing Islam: Religious Life and Politics in Indonesia*, ed. Greg Fealy and Sally White, 267–285. Singapore: ISEAS.

———. 2010. Growing Together in Partnership: Women's Views of the Business Practices of Islamic Savings and Credit Cooperatives (*Baitul Maal wat Tamwil*) in Central Java, Indonesia. *Women's Studies International Forum* 33 (4): 412–421.

Sarif, Suhaili, and Nor Azzah Kamri. 2009. A Theoretical Discussion of Zakat for Income Generation and Its Fiqh Issues. *Shariah Journal* 17 (3): 457–500.

Seibel, Hans Dieter. 2012. Islamic Microfinance in Indonesia: The Challenge of Institutional Diversity, Regulation and Supervision. In *Shari'a-Compliant Microfinance*, ed. S. Nazim Ali. London: Routledge.

Siddiqi, Muhammad Nejatullah. 1983. *Issues in Islamic Banking*. Leicester: Islamic Foundation.

Smith, Jane Idleman, and Yvonne Yazbeck Haddad. 2002. *The Islamic Understanding of Death and Resurrection*. Oxford: Oxford University Press.

Tripp, Charles. 2006. *Islam and the Moral Economy. The Challenge of Capitalism*. Cambridge: Cambridge University Press.

Voss, Daniela. 2013. Deleuze's Third Synthesis of Time. *Deleuze Studies* 7 (2): 194–216.

Warde, Ibrahim. 2010. *Islamic Finance in the Global Economy*. Edinburgh: Edinburgh University Press.

Weir, T.H., and A. Zysow. 2012. Sadaka. In *Encyclopaedia of Islam, Second Edition*, ed. P. Bearman, Th. Bianquis, C.E. Bosworth, E. van Donzel and W.P. Heinrichs. Consulted online on 10 November 2018. https://doi.org/10.1163/1573-3912_islam_COM_0956

Williams, James. 2011. *Gilles Deleuze's Philosophy of Time*. Edinburgh: Edinburgh University Press.

Zourabichvili, François. 2012. *Deleuze: A Philosophy of the Event Together with the Vocabulary of Deleuze*. Trans. Kieran Aarons. Edinburgh: Edinburgh University Press.

CHAPTER 6

Contracting the Future

Not all Islamic charitable organisations involved in empowering Indonesia's poor (*miskin*) employ *zakat* funds to deliver their programmes. *Indonesia Mandiri*'s architecture, the focus of the previous chapter, is perhaps the most innovative (and controversial) in this respect: not everyone subscribes to the premise that the transfer of zakat to its rightful recipients can be deferred, allowing for the third pillar of faith to be deployed in the interim period as an instrument of credit/debt and an occasion for disciplinary training. The present chapter shifts our focus away from zakat and into alternative means of funding for empowerment programmes, looking into yet another financial experiment that involves its own distinct architecture, both in a legal and a social sense. The shift takes us away from Surabaya's city of industry in East Java and into the periphery of the nation's capital city, Jakarta, where back in 2010, *Dana Keadilan Indonesia* (DKI, see Chap. 4) was actively seeking to set up a series of sustainable home industries with the use of corporate social responsibility funds.

The main concern of this chapter is a multidimensional set of indeterminate relations articulated amongst four different parties: Kegan & Milner, a big multinational company in the process of discharging its corporate social responsibility commitments; *Dana Keadilan Indonesia* (DKI), a highly valued and innovative Islamic charitable organisation keen to implement an Islamic vision for a future national economy; ibu Setiawati, a young pious female entrepreneur and inventor of a herbal beverage of great marketing potential, together with a group of four women selected

K. Retsikas, *A Synthesis of Time*,
https://doi.org/10.1007/978-3-030-34933-2_6

amongst the area's reservoir of poor inhabitants, yet considered skilled and responsive enough to take advantage of external financial, organisational and affective investments. It goes without saying that the presence of a fifth, most powerful party, that is, Allah, bestowing his approval upon the *syariah*-compliant proceedings, was a given for all those involved. This is true as much for the charitable body, and the five women participating in the experiment, and to a certain extent, as I will show below, the multinational company's personnel with oversight over the project.

Such assemblage is thought-provoking for my purposes in terms of the promises each party made to the each other and the effects such promises have had on time and its synthesis: a particular modality of connections fostered among the past, present and future was envisioned and encapsulated in a series of letters, memorandums, contracts, notes and reports circulated, revised and signed by the parties involved. What the documents reveal, I argue, is a distinct temporal orientation that conceives the future as the proximate source of prosperity and salvation: as such, an immense effort was put into ensuring that an affluent future arrived sooner rather than later. In this regard, the deployment of specific sets of contractual obligations (and rights) was instrumental in hastening the future's advent and paramount for the experiment's success. What I am setting out to do here is to show the temporal breaks the contractual arrangements committing the parties to the empowerment project were constantly inserting in the flow of time, allowing for prosperity and salvation to cross over and occasioning the coming of the future as anticipated.

Quite paradoxically, the parties involved did not share either a uniform or an unvarying understanding of the mutuality they were creating. Despite a multiplicity of written records drafted and signed at various stages of the process, which were assumed to cement relations upon a most solid ground, the promises undertaken and exchanged were themselves subject to perspectival divergences and positional variations. In other words, each part of the assemblage in the financial experiment did not the share the same vision of the set of the entanglements entailed, having instead a contingent and situated image of its connections with, obligations to and expectations towards each of the other parts. The fact that such images did not fully coincide, overlap or accord with each other did not rule out the possibility of the parts being able to communicate with one another. Quite the opposite is true. Perspectival variation introduced incommensurability and asymmetry as an indispensable adjunct to the repetition of relations: I am, therefore, disinclined to describe the sets of relations as an undifferentiated whole grounded on consensus. Instead, my analysis pays close to perspectival differences and the hierarchy underscoring them.

Matters of perspective, difference and indeterminacy are at the centre of Deleuze's preoccupations with conceiving time anew while making time the 'groundless' basis of conceiving Life anew. As such, his work is of direct relevance to the ethnography this chapter deals with as well. Deleuze's effort at making time the most important dimension in the exercise of thinking is best undertaken in *Difference and Repetition* (2008), his doctoral thesis I discussed critically in the previous chapter, and in his two-volume study of cinema, especially in the second volume subtitled 'The Time-Image' (1997). According to this study, the cinema that emerged from the ruins of the Second World War brought about a Copernican revolution in cinema's relation to time. Because of this, cinema is of immediate significance to philosophy, and anthropology I must add. Where pre-war cinema, Deleuze's argument runs, gave us an indirect sense of time for it subordinated time to movement as in the overall plot of the movie and the development of the action over the course of the film, the new cinema reversed the polarity. By subordinating movement to time, it proceeded to 'suspend' action, allowing thus temporality, that is, time's essential, internal division as the condition of its inescapable, constant passing, to appear in person as it were, that is, directly and 'immediately' on the silver screen. In the English edition, Deleuze employs Hamlet's formula of a 'time out of joint' to denote this profound change of orientation, writing

> Time is out of joint: Hamlet's words signify that time is no longer subordinated to movement but rather movement to time. It could be said that, in its own sphere, cinema has repeated the same experience, the same reversal [as in philosophy from Kant onward] in more fast-moving circumstances. The movement-image of the so-called classical cinema gave way in the post war period to the time-image. (1997: xi)

The concept of time-image Deleuze borrows from Bergson to convey the new cinematic operations, conventions and techniques in terms of which time is shown to be constituted by a deep split down its very middle. This is the image of time in its pure state: where the chronological conception of time constituted time in terms of a succession of actions/habits as a natural occurrence, the time-image accords to internal divisions and repeated cuts the status of events that 'give' time, in life as much as in thinking. In the words of Bergson, the time-image corresponds to a crystal-like assembly, which 'reveals or makes visible the hidden ground of time, that is, its differentiation into two flows, that of presents which pass and that of pasts which are preserved' (Bergson 1989 in Angelucci 2014: 328). According to Deleuze the movie that first captured this essential differentiation as the transcendental condition of time is Orson Welles' *Citizen Kane*.

> The first occasion on which a direct time-image was seen in the cinema was not in the (even implicit) mode of the present but, on the contrary, in the form of sheets of past with Welles' Citizen Kane. Here time became out of joint and reversed its dependent relation on movement: temporality showed itself as it really was for the first time, but in the form of a co-existence of large regions [of the past] to be explored. The scheme of Citizen Kane may appear simple: Kane being dead, witnesses who offer their recollection-images in a series of subjective flashbacks are questioned. But it is more complex than this. The investigation is focused on 'Rosebud' (what is it? Or what does this word mean?). And the investigator carries out soundings: each of the witnesses questioned will be equivalent to a slice of Kane's life, a circle or a sheet of virtual past, a continuum. And each time the question is: [...] is it in this sheet that lies the thing (the being) called Rosebud? (1997: 105)

In Welles' Citizen Kane, the goal of the journalist's inquiry is the discovery of the meaning of this mysterious word uttered by Kane on this death bed, with Kane's death and the enigma posed by Rosebud embedding the recollections of the witnesses of Kane's life within the horizons of an inaccessible, remote past, lying beyond the witnesses' powers of recuperation. It is no accident then that the enigma of the Rosebud is revealed to the cinematic audience only, when, in the last scene, it is shown that Rosebud is the sign written on a sledge Kane used to play with as a child, before it was thrown into a fire. For Deleuze, the difficulties encountered in the non-solution to the enigma by the journalist for the sake of *his* audience are instructive: they exemplify, in visual form, Bergson's notion of Memory as the being of time (see also Bryant 2008: 102–134). Rather than amounting to past as commonly conceived, that is, that which has been or that which was once present and is now past, Memory as conceived by Deleuze, after Bergson, signifies time as conditioned by an a priori past. Such a priori past has never been present and will always remain *passed*: it is precisely because it has never been actual that this pre-existing past amounts to a pure virtuality, a foreign land and a persistent aporia. In short, the inability of witnesses to recall Rosebud countersigns the points Deleuze wishes to put forward, first that Rosebud as an a priori past can only be transcendentally deduced, and second that because it lacks actuality, in its essence, it is free from knowledge and determination.[1]

The present chapter follows the line of inquiry into the indeterminacy of time as far as its virtual dimension is concerned and the latter's impact on the present as actuality. However, the chapter also means to shift the focus away from an inaccessible past that functions as the condition of time's passing, towards outlining the significance of an equally unfathomable, similarly virtual future that acts to make the present pass by embedding it within the delineations and curves of a redemptive horizon. The sheets of time past are here replaced with the folds of times-to-come; similarly, recollecting is giving way to promising. Somewhere in the far distance of Java's metropolises, a future makes an appearance as other than the present, as another present being possible. Such vision takes hold of people, propelling them to undertake promises as means to an end: making prosperity arrive, hastening the return of value multiplied, ensuring salvation in this life and the next bespeak of a commitment to overcoming present circumstances, making space for the new and the other. Part of the reason for foregrounding a future disclosed in acts of promising has to do with supplementing Deleuze's cinematic dialogues: as Deleuze's later studies of time are primarily preoccupied with Memory and the transcendental status of the past, my ethnographic insistence on the future, its essential indeterminacy and the dual character of promising aim to extend the insights of Deleuze into areas he himself did not anticipate. This is meant as an affirmation of his thought and a springboard for an ethnographic exploration, which disrupts anthropological common places. Primary amongst them are the conceptualisation of zakat, and other forms of Islamic value transfers, as variable instances of an unvarying category going by the name of charity, the problematisation of value transfers within an overarching moral framework that already pre-figures what counts as good, and unproductive denouncements of development interventions as manifestations of an illiberal project of governance. In this regard, my work emphasises the perspectival quality of value transfers as events and reiterates their status as indeterminate, enigmatic occurrences for all those involved, including the ethnographer. Inspired by *Citizen Kane*'s enigma of Rosebud, this chapter also bespeaks the truth of perspectives as integral in understanding time's unfolding and the unfolding of human beings in time. After reading Kane's diaries, the journalist interviews his second wife, the head of the board of governors of Kane's newspaper, his best friend and, finally, his butler. As the point of view of each witness differs, in accordance with the differential aspect of life they shared with Kane in one or the other capacity, Kane, as a subject, loses all its presupposed coherence while gaining in dimensions, slowly attaining the status of a quasi-virtual and essentially open multiplicity. This liberation of time, and subjects, through recollection is a feat I endeavour to repeat in this chapter through an examination of the effects of contractual modes of promising.

As in the case of Indonesia Mandiri's experiment in Surabaya, where the beneficiaries' understanding of the funding available as commercial debt (*hutang*) was at variance with the institution's acknowledgement of it being zakat, and thus, the recipients' rightful share, so too in Jakarta's periphery, the multinational company dispensing CSR funds, *DKI*, the Islamic charitable organisation, ibu Setiawati, the entrepreneur-inventor, and the group of four women acting as a production unit differed markedly in their understanding of the experiment. It is my contention that such perspectival differences corresponded neither to cognitive errors or misrepresentations nor did they accrue from inaccuracies in the drafting of contracts that could be eliminated with greater legal circumspection. Rather, the indeterminacy involved constituted, along with the incommensurability and asymmetry of perspectives, a fundamental characteristic of the architecture of the interval instituted. In this sense, perspectival differences co-existed rather uneasily with the set of contractual obligations, exceeding the written and agreed upon while disrupting any related anticipations of future returns. Matters of perspective were also directly related to the unfinished, incomplete status of the experiment, which was already in the making for almost two years when I first encountered it in the field. As I show below, the experiment in Islamic micro-financing in Jakarta's periphery was subject to constant revisions and amendments, implemented every six months or so from its very inception in 2010 till late 2012 when I exited the field.

The constancy of revisions and renewals were imprinted by the will to improve: finding the most efficient way to deliver the poor to a prosperous future necessitated constant vigilance as to the ratio of success and failure and sensitised the personnel involved as to the requirement for alterations to be made and remade in the experiment's design and implementation. And yet, the extent to which such reforms amounted to an invariant variation, it can be said of the experiment to be permeated by aporia and to work to raise the interval to the power of repetition itself. As we saw in the previous power, such are the undeniable signs of the will to power, the affirmative dimension of promise. 'Repetition, writes Deleuze, no longer bears (hypothetically) upon a first time which escapes it, and in any case remains external to it: repetition bears upon repetitions. ... It is repetition itself which is repeated' (2008: 367). With the experiment incomplete and ongoing, indeterminacy was foregrounded as an intrinsic part of the interval, opening present relations up to a future unanticipated: instead, the aporias generated in the process of change placed new demands on the participants, posed novel challenges and threw things upside down. However, along with such affirmative repetitions, there were obligations too, which kept proliferating, stretching their grasp further into the future, extending relations of credit/debt to infinity. Seen from this point of view, the experiment was pervaded by the will to improve: as far as it was oriented towards achieving redemption as the return of the self-same value, expressed mainly in monetary terms, it strived to banish the new and the unexpected, wishing instead for the same-old version of the present to arrive, yet in enhanced and augmented form.

From Corporate Social Responsibility to Gifts (and Back Again)

According to Pak Priyono, the manager of *DKI*'s operations in Ciputat, South Tangerang, the first time the Islamic welfare organisation became involved in the area went back to March 2009 when a 16-metre-high dam constructed in colonial times failed, draining Situ Gintung lake of its waters, and flooding nearby densely inhabited neighbourhoods: as a result, more than 100 people were killed with several thousand more becoming displaced. Though the initial intervention consisted of natural disaster relief, *DKI* soon followed up with opening up an office for the collection of donations from the better-off sections of the populace.

Situated right on the border with Jakarta proper (*Daerah Khusus Ibu Kota Jakarta*), South Tangerang is a city that forms part of the Greater Jakarta metropolitan area, an urban agglomeration surrounding Indonesia's capital and comprising more than 30 million people, one-and-half million of which live in South Tangerang. Such close proximity to the economic and political centre of the country initially made South Tangerang a magnet for industrial and manufacturing plants that sprawled during the Suharto years of export-orientated industrialisation, attracting many newcomers as workers, foremen, suppliers, traders and so on. Closer to present times, a new generation of middle-class professionals has moved into the area, as many companies have sought to relocate away from Jakarta's central business district, newly built areas with greater amenities and more affordable housing have become available and relatively easy commuting remains a possibility for many despite the heavy traffic. When compared to Tangerang city to its north-west and the sere extravagance of Jakarta's southern districts, South Tangerang falls well short of current standards of affluence, displayed in many satellite cities complete with their own shopping malls, private schools and gated communities. Behind the facades of Jalan Juanda populated with relatively upmarket restaurants, giant supermarkets and prestigious universities, South Tangerang is typical of many other parts of the Greater Jakarta metropolitan area: a profusion of heterogeneity means that relative comfort exists side by side with precariousness, and a dynamism emanating from a living in super-dense residential quarters, encompasses stories of both accumulation and loss, of wealth expansion and contraction. As Abdoumaliq Simone, one of the most acute observers of life in Jakarta, notes

> between the superblock and the slum, the ascendant middle class and the [utter] poor, is a 'majority' of which much less is known, perhaps because there is no essential coherence that characterises it. Still, salaried workers in public and service sectors, traders, artisans, sojourners, petty bourgeois entrepreneurs, industrial labour, racketeers, service workers of various skills, and low level technicians and professionals make up the bulk of the population. (2013: 4)

Such urban districts exhibit an incontestable vitality that is often obviated when they are branded as underprivileged, though there is no denying they are that too. That vitality is displayed in the capacity of their inhabitants to make varied use of the materials accessible to them so as to maximise household access to new opportunities: 'using a little of their resources and efforts at a time, there was a continuous testing of waters, finding new vantage points and circuits to which they might connect their residential history, skills, social networks, and jobs' (Simone 2013: 6). Such capacities are, however, unevenly distributed with the concomitant result that while upward mobility is within the grasp of many, the reverse applies with equal force. There are likewise many who are sensitive to slight changes in their mode of livelihood and the overall economy and can find themselves in dire straits easily and abruptly. This uncertainty characterises mostly the lower levels of the 'majority' and is especially prevalent amongst urban informal and unskilled workers who face precarious housing and work situations and who frequently choose jobs or places to live on the basis of life circumstances. With their employment being unstable, and their incomes fluctuating, their living standards remain vulnerable to economic downturns, sudden layoffs and unforeseen shortages of credit, problems with suppliers and/or new orders, evictions and other threats such as natural disasters. It is precisely the presence of such vulnerabilities situated within easy reach of Jakarta's wealthiest areas as the Situ Gintung flood dramatically highlighted, prompting *DKI* to intervene, offering both immediate relief and longer-term empowerment.

The empowerment programme that ran in Ciputat in the early 2010s involved a partnership between Kegan & Milner, a big multinational corporation, providing the funding as part of its social corporate responsibility (SCR) capital while setting key parameters of the intervention, and *Dana Keadilan Indonesia* as the agent with the required expertise to ensure professional design and delivery. Their partnership was formalised with the signing of a Memorandum of Understanding (MoU) between the two organisations in June 2010 and was subsequently renewed twice over, once in 2011 and again in 2012, with significant changes of focus accompanying each renewal. At the same time, the intervention was subject to the internal evaluation carried out every six months by *DKI* expert staffers dispatched from headquarters: their aim was to measure the project's relative success and failure with regards to indicators already set and instigate changes and reforms in the overall architecture, mode of engagement and personnel. During the two years, I managed to chart the changing contours of the partnership from the vantage point of conducting fieldwork with *DKI*'s empowerment officers in Ciputat, *DKI* also underwent major changes as to its organisational structure and strategic priorities that have had a direct impact on the design and delivery of the programme at the local level. I take each and every change of direction, contractual re-negotiation, framework reform and on-the-ground modification to correspond to a new cut being made and a new synthesis effected: constantly reconfiguring the very grounds on which the experiment ran amounted to an invariance that lent the field of relations instituted each and every time an unmistakable dynamism. As new agreements and frameworks were regularly signed and repeatedly revised, the less the future seemed prearranged and the more the present was made to pass: despite the pervasive presence of contractual certainties set out in black and white, the ground was constantly moving.

As it will become clear below, *DKI*'s penchant for regulating its relations with partners, both institutional and individual, through Memorandums of Understanding (MoU), was deeply related to the promotion of what it perceived to be an international corporate ethos, both in the wider Indonesian philanthropic sector and amongst its personnel. Such promotion was already indicated in its self-perceived transition from a faith-based 'traditional' collector of alms to a fully-fledged professional and inclusive body: in 2010, *DKI* underwent a major make-over that saw it change its original logo from Islamic green to the more internationally recognised shape of a heart in bright orange. This change was accompanied by the organisation becoming more global in its outlook and getting involved in international humanitarian affairs such as the plight of Palestinians and the outbreak of famines in Africa. Along with such sweeping changes was the inception and cultivation of a business culture: organisational structures, styles of leadership, accounting procedures and standards of conduct that now included strict dress codes and other work-related disciples were reshaped to underscore the beginning of a new era. The seeking of a big multinational as a partner in an SCR-funded community development project and the choice of framing such relation in terms of a Memorandums of Understanding are indicative of these wider re-alignments of *DKI* in its effort to articulate an Islamic futurity beyond the modern.

Though a non-legally binding, non-enforceable document, an MoU was understood by *DKI* staff as a serious undertaking in a legal sense: its capacity for setting out in some detail the terms and conditions of a partnership, outlining each parties' requirements and responsibilities, expressed the full commitment of both parties to a common cause and line of action. For the first year running, the MoU stipulated that Kegan & Milner would CSR-fund an early childhood education facility or ***paud*** (***pendidikan anak usia dini***) for a total of 1000 under-five-year-olds, all from the vicinity. Funding also covered a health clinic or ***posyandu*** (***pos pelayanan terpadu***, integrated health centre) providing medical, dietary and other support to pregnant women and babies while provisions were also made for a microfinance scheme involving a small number of participants. *DKI* was responsible for setting up from scratch, staffing and running the said institutions, which it eventually did, after successfully overcoming some initial trouble, first with finding suitable premises to house the *paud* and then with persuading local gatekeepers concerned about the organisations' agenda to welcome its presence in their midst. The element of economic empowerment while accorded a small piece of the action in the first year of intervention became the centrepiece of the second. According to *DKI* staff, the change for the 2011–2012 period was instigated by the greater emphasis the organisation started paying to the economic dimensions of poverty alleviation, in addition to education and health. Despite Kegan & Milner never having been involved before in economic empowerment programmes, it accepted the proposal of stepping up the micro-finance component of the MoU and went to release further funds to the tune of three billion rupiah in total. The second MoU stipulated the broad outlines of the micro-finance intervention as involving the creation of six integrated community development centres, with a total of forty women (*binaan*) engaged in each centre. It also set clear targets: for the intervention to be deemed successful, individual incomes would have to significantly increase to the point of exceeding by at least 15% the *nisab*, the cut-off line beyond which one is obliged to zakat transfer—at that time, *nisab* had a monetary value of around 24 million rupiah a year. All the costs of running the programme, including rents for premises and staff salaries, were covered by the CSR funds released.

As Dolan and Rajak (2016) argue, over the past decade, CSR has become established as an orthodoxy both in development circles and in multinational business practices: it is accompanied with a set of standards, auditors and certifiers that make up a mushrooming ethical industry, itself heralding a new era of 'humane capitalism.' What is important to stress is that in the public welfare model which CSR has sought to reshape and redeploy on a global scale, it is the corporation, more than the state, which becomes the direct custodian and guarantor of the public good. Such a role is assumed in a multiplicity of guises: from claiming a duty of care over employees, to environmental stewardship and assertions of benevolent guardianship over local milieus, CSR is a particularly effective tool for millennial capitalism to domesticate critiques levelled against it while advancing a new basis for human welfare structured around discourses of mutuality and empowerment to be delivered by alliances between businesses and civil society organisations. In Indonesia, popular demands for implementing SCR go back to the early 1990s when major court cases involving companies like Nike and Levi's, over labour issues led to a series of legal reforms in the 2000s.[2] These reforms sought, in turn, to set SCR standards for many companies, national and multinational, operating in the country. While SCR is currently compulsory only for state-owned enterprises, which must allocate 2% of their profit, multinationals such as Kegan & Milner are under no enforceable legal obligation to do so. However, major corporations do realise that even though the legal framework is particularly weak, engaging in community development and environmental protection will create a competitive advantage for them. Such an advantage is intrinsically related to building good relationships with the government, the bureaucracy and political parties, both at the national and the local level. As Welker's (2009) study from Sumbawa, Eastern Indonesia, shows very clearly, community development programmes constitute conduits through which sizeable economic resources are channelled through, and shared amongst a variety of actors, the support of which is instrumental for the acquisition of government support and social consent, and the smooth advancement of business.

In the early 2010s, Kegan & Milner was seeking to expand its operations in Indonesia, adding to its extensive sales network in the country a much-needed manufacturing basis. A big American corporation involved in the production of home and personal care products like laundry detergents, toothpaste, soaps, shampoos and conditioners, it planned on entering the Indonesian oleo-chemical industry with an investment worth at least US$ 100 million towards ensuring a sustainable supply for its global fatty alcohol needs. For this reason, it was conducting negotiations with the government for the identification of appropriate sites, the selection of partners and the instigation of tax breaks. At the same time, Kegan & Milner was kicking off the construction of a manufacturing facility in West Java for the production of its own brand of baby diapers, another staple of the corporation's range of products. This second factory was planned to employ some 400 workers and produce mainly for the local market, which according to the company's own statistics, amounted to 17 million babies aged 48 months and under. The company's focus on baby products explains some of the reasons why its CSR was focused on early childhood education: its longer-running partnership with United Nations Educational, Scientific and Cultural Organization (UNESCO) in another locale in West Java since 2008 was similarly geared towards free education services to babies and health facilities for young mothers. Such a focus was enlarged when, in 2011, it dedicated part of its CSR for micro-finance purposes and with the aid of *DKI*, concentrated on the economic potential of women for improving household budgets.

In counter-distinction to the previous chapter where the source of funds for community development came from zakat, in the specific instance of the micro-finance programme in Ciputat, the funds corresponded to a voluntary deduction made from the annual profits of the local subsidiary of a multinational corporation. The gift of a future improved, the partnership of a company and an Islamic welfare organisation were making to locals in Ciputat have had its origin in the world of commercial transactions, of alienated labour and surplus-value extraction. It was also deeply embedded in post-colonial hierarchies and global business asymmetries: its association with a foreign-owned company utilising national resources added dimensions that were deeply problematic and wholly unwelcome to lots of Indonesians and Islamic associations, especially those involved in creating an Islamic economy for the nation and its 'people' (*rakyat*). It should, therefore, be no surprise that the providence of funds was strictly downplayed: while both *DKI* staff and beneficiaries were well-aware of the source—all the community development centres, including the school and the clinic, displayed the company's logo—they maintained an assured disinterest in the issue, rarely commenting or reflecting on it. For, quite appropriately too, the micro-finance capital on offer had, in the meantime, been 'purified': its re-categorisation as *hibah*, the Islamic quintessential gift inter vivos, in the subsequent transfers of value conducted between *DKI* field operatives and local recipients removed by and large any such negative connotations, effectively re-framing the money, materials, info-training handed over, into a divinely ordained and *syariah*-approved value transfer.

Acting as an intermediary, *DKI* faced in two directions at once: acting as a trustee, it received a share of the corporation's profits; acting as an expert in poverty alleviation in a *syariah*-compliant manner, it disseminated Islamic free gifts with the aim of improving human welfare. Engaged both in receiving and giving, it converted capital that had been previously removed from further commercial circuits of dividend payments and/or onward investments into a specifically recognisable form, that of an Islamic gift, *hibah*. In Islamic jurisprudence, *hibah* amounts to a contract: like a commercial transaction, it requires a speech of offer and acceptance that binds the two parties into a mutual agreement. Such agreement involves a transfer of ownership during the lifetime of a donor, with no consideration of a return by the donee (Linant de Bellefonds 2012; Rosenthal et al.

2012). What is particularly fascinating in the case of Islamic micro-finance is not simply the deployment of terms and categories of Islamic jurisprudence formulated in classical times for purposes of contemporary community development. Of primary interest is the transformation of key legal categories into instruments of life's financialisation: as in the case of zakat in the previous chapter, here too, ***hibah*** is the intermediate form finance capital takes in the path towards its own reproduction. This is so for the transfer of value in the form of ***hibah*** came attached with conditions: as was the case with zakat in the previous chapter, its release was possible if and only if the capital, materials and info-training available are put into productive use, primarily for creating sustainable micro-enterprises and effecting increases in the returns on assets. In this configuration, ***hibah***, the Islamic gift inter vivos, occupies the temporary form that credit/debt momentarily assumes in its effort to multiply and propagate itself. As such, the gift is to be found neither in the origin nor the end of humanity's historical procession, as it is often assumed by Maussian and Marxist thinkers but in the unending return of the present: as commodity's inseparable twin and double image, the gift occupies the middle ground, enabling and facilitating the infinite re-creation of finance capital out of the links it establishes between two moments—a 'before' and an 'after'—that are themselves wholly steeped in commodity transactions.

In this phase of the discussion, I have to pause for a moment as the exposition has brought me to a point that requires further clarification and elaboration. In contrast to Tsing's (2013, 2017) argument that the creation of value in capitalism rests on a series of transformations in which capitalism converts the gifts nature gives into commodities and then back again into objects circulated as prestigious gifts and high-end goods, I claim the opposite to be the case. The study by Tsing takes a close look at the way mushroom supply chains operate across the globe and repeats an assumption that has been central in the making of anthropology as a discipline: starting from Rousseau's (1997) classic treatise of man in the state of nature to Mauss' (2011) study of gift exchanges in so-called 'primitive' societies, the gift is axiomatically taken as originary in the double sense of coming before and being primary in an ethical sense to commodity production. It is no coincidence that Tsing's ethnography starts with matsutake mushroom collection taking place in the mountains of the US Pacific Northwest, uncritically describing such collection as an exercise in freedom while under-theorising the forest as an untouched wilderness and unregulated commons. At the other end of transformations mushrooms undergo, Tsing finds Japanese importers who by means of skilful sorting create luxury commodities, that is, goods destined to be bought only for the purpose of being presented as luxury gifts to important social others. For Tsing, 'matsutake is a capitalist commodity that begins and ends its life as a gift. It spends only a few hours as a fully capitalist commodity' (2013: 37). In Tsing's scheme, value accrues from beginnings and endings, with capitalism effecting the necessary connections, appropriating in the process the surplus value created out of transfers. In contrast, my ethnography highlights that it is finance capitalism that is found as occupying both the beginnings and ends of the process of value creation, with the gift taking the role of the always crucial catalyst that allows for the necessary conversions to take place. The Islamic gift or *hibah*, in other words, constitutes a temporal caesura in the flow of time that financial capitalism itself organises and a conduit that ensures capitalism's reproduction. In the dramas I saw played out in Java, the gift signifies neither a natural origin point nor a political or theological *telos*: it co-exists with commodity transactions and forms a pair with them. The relation between the two members of the pair is exclusively asymmetrical: contrary to received wisdom, it is the gift that is the secondary and derivative member of the pair as it plays an auxiliary and supporting role in the creation of value.

The Question of *Seger*

Located a few hundred metres away from the main road that marks the border between South Tangerang and Jakarta proper, and reached through a labyrinth of back streets navigable only by motorbike, hidden deep into the recesses of a densely inhabited residential area, featuring well-proportioned though modest homes, some with well-maintained front gardens and suffused in a peaceful atmosphere one usually encounters in more rural areas of Java, was a house-turned-into-factory where production of *Seger*, a ginger-based drink, had been taking place almost daily for the past few months. *Seger* was the undeniable jewel in *DKI*'s crown in Ciputat: a home industry making an innovative product of considerable marketing potential, and a unique collaboration (*kerja sama*) between a young, ambitious female scientist-entrepreneur and four local women initially brought together and thereafter closely assisted by *DKI* and its programme of dispensing CSR-funded *hibah*. According to ibu Mustika, one of the local women involved and the head of operations, *Seger* not only 'eliminated the boredom' (*mengisi kekosongan*) she was experiencing in her previous instantiation as a housewife (*ibu rumah tangga*) but allowed her to put into practice her aspirations for a better life for her and her family (*aspirasi kehidupan lebih baik*), building her self-confidence enough to pursue the dream of success (*percaya diri bisa sampai sukses*). A native of Wonosobo, Central Java, she moved to Ciputat in her early 20s, after getting married to her husband, also from Wonosobo, and currently making a living as a delivery driver for a major printing company. Together, they have had two children: a son in his first year of a BA in a prestigious university and a daughter attending senior high school. Though not by any means perceived as poor (*miskin*)—the couple is the owner of an unassuming one-storey, two-bed home and her husband's salary qualifies him for the payment of *zakat maal*, which he regularly pays at the end of each month—ibu Mustika welcomed the new opportunities *DKI* presented her and others with when it first announced its running of a micro-finance programme in the vicinity. The fact that her children had grown up enough to look after themselves meant that now was the right time for her to pursue other activities, she said, especially those that would help with getting both her children through university and into well-paid jobs. For this to be achieved, a promise had to be made publicly and duly recorded.

As in other locales in Indonesia where *DKI* is active, the assumption of micro-finance assistance is based on the beneficiaries assuming the position of *binaan* (supervisee, subject of guidance, follower),[3] an undertaking initiated and guaranteed in writing through their performance of a solemn oath. Islamic welfare organisations routinely survey the locales of their intended interventions for the identification of potential recipients and the data they obtain through detailed questionnaires charting the circumstances, activities and assets of those concerned is triangulated with information gathered through personal visits to their houses and enterprises, along with further interviews undertaken with the heads of small administrative units, known in Indonesia as *rukun warga* and *rukun tetangga*. The RT and/or RW heads are called to testify to the character, habits and piety of those they administer, becoming conduits of state records as much as of informal knowledge and intimate gossip. If it all comes together, and specific needs are identified and a particular programme of alleviation is agreed upon, it is then, and only then, that a 'letter of steadfast promise' (*surat perjanjian komitmen*) is issued by *DKI*, which intended beneficiaries are asked to sign. The letter which begins with the customary Islamic invocation *Bismillah Hirrohman-Nirroheem* (in the name of God, the most Gracious, the most Merciful)[4] outlines a series of obligations the signee is willing to assume *ex nihilo*: it is on condition of such assumption that the benefits of *hibah* will accrue. The letter ibu Mustika along with tens of others signed in Ciputat so as to inaugurate their status as *binaan*, makes Allah a party and a witness in the proceedings: at the same time it enshrines the promises made and the obligations incurred with a sacred aura, embedding them within a salvific horizon that indexes the inescapable accounting for one's actions in the *eschaton* of the Day of Judgment.

The standard letter, a copy of which staff kindly passed to me, reads: 'With the hope of acquiring Allah's blessings, the undersigned expresses her true commitment to abide by the regulations set out by *DKI*, so now I pledge to do the following: a. undertake activities deemed obligatory by *DKI*, b. keep up with a clean and healthy living regimen, c. conduct myself in accordance with the *syariah*, performing the five daily prayers, fasting during Ramadan, etc., d. truly make the effort to improve my current condition through patience, hard work, and consistent worship, e. meet the demands made by *DKI* staff for the betterment and progress of us all together.' The promise is validated by three signatures: one belonging to the micro-finance officer in charge and two witnesses, normally the head of RT/RW and another senior male neighbour. It is essential to add that the 'letter of steadfast promise' is accompanied by another document: entitled *surat pernyataan* or declaration, it requests and testifies to the consent given by the parents/guardians or spouse depending on whether the signee is under-age or married. Since most of the *binaan* are married women—I have come across no cases of under-aged *binaan* and only an extremely limited number of male ones—the declaration is very important for it signifies a part-transfer of authority over the conduct of those making the promise. Since both Islamic and Indonesian state law recognise men as heads of households (Munir 2005; Mudzakir 2005; Robinson 2007), basing their authority over women and younger men over the obligations senior men have for providing for the livelihoods of their dependants, the provision of consent means that male heads agree to share from that point onward their authority with *DKI* in presiding over the conduct of household juniors. To put it in more accurate terms, and taking as little for granted as possible, the declaration, taken together with the enactment of the promise, have certain gendering effects: it legally engenders *DKI* as masculine/superior/leading and re-genders *binaan* as feminine/inferior/led. In this context, the reason why so few men participate in charitable micro-finance programmes becomes apparent: entering such a relation with an institution is un-grammatical for it imposes insurmountable obstacles in practically maintaining and performatively re-asserting the position of authority over household decisions and livelihood strategies that Islamic and state law grants them with.

In an interview, ibu Mustika traced the beginning of the current phase in her life back to December 2010 when she became involved in *DKI*'s empowerment programme and met for the very first time ibu Setiawati, her future partner in *Seger*. The occasion for that auspicious meeting was the short-lived Cake House project *DKI* run for the first year of the CSR-funded intervention. According to micro-finance staff, the Cake House project was intended to engage the mothers of children looked after in the pre-school playgroups, in productive activities: by freeing them from child-care for a couple of hours three times a week and teaching them how to make cakes by baker-entrepreneurs, the plan was to provide inspiration (*inspirasi*), training and expert assistance for the establishment of bakery start-ups, that is, home industries with finance provided in the shape of *hibah* for the purchase of materials and equipment. However, things quickly run aground: because the young mothers did not show interest enough in baking, participation was opened up to other categories of local women. Ibu Mustika quickly jumped at the opportunity, she said, as she always wanted to make cakes like those on offer in luxury supermarkets, for her family. In any case, she added, as a mother of two grown-up children, she had plenty of time to spare. It was in this context that she had the chance encounter with ibu Setiawati, a young chemist-inventor-entrepreneur *DKI* recruited to train the *binaan* into making herbal drinks. Despite it being all but a brief meeting lasting no longer than half a day, ibu Mustika was seriously impressed, she said, with the recipes ibu Setiawati had invented to want to do learn more from her. And when the Cake House project ran into yet more trouble, partly because of fluctuations in group membership, and partly because the majority proved either unwilling or unable to take things further than simply learning to bake, she did not give up. The beginning of the second round of CSR-funded interventions, featuring an enlarged micro-finance component in the summer of 2011, provided ample scope for *DKI* and a selected number of *binaan* to move things onto the next stage.

When I met ibu Mustika along with three other women making *Seger* in the converted rooms of a family home in the district of Pondok Anyar, they had been at it for more than nine months. *Seger* was a home industry born from the ashes of the Cake House project: under the combined guidance of ibu Setiawati and *DKI*, the ginger-based secret recipe had been finalised, and a production line had been established, turning up each week almost 100 bright yellow boxes, containing ten sachets each. Crucial in the process was the intensive training ibu Setiawati provided the four women with over a period of several months till all aspects of the production process were running smoothly. Crucial too was the establishment of a division of labour: while ibu Mustika was in charge of operations, especially with the sourcing of the raw materials and keeping the accounts up-to-date, ibu Nabila was responsible for cooking the mixture: making sure that it constantly stirred for at least two hours over a large gas stove was a most exacting job, she said. Ibu Nabila, a Betawi[5] from the vicinity, was in her mid-40s: she was twice married and a mother to five children, three from her first marriage and two from the previous marriage of her current husband, a tricycle driver. Further down the production line, ibu Ningsih and ibu Indah were tasked with refining the mixture: since several blenders proved unable to perform the task to the required standard, ibu Ningsih opted for a big pestle and ibu Indah for a flat ladle. In her 60s, ibu Ningsih was the eldest of the four: she was from Central Java, having moved to Ciputat in the late 1960s together with her mother, after the death of her father. She had two children, one married and working away in Banten, and the other in her late teens living in the family-owned home, a stone throw's away from the *Seger* factory. By contrast, ibu Indah was the youngest and a Betawi: her husband, a travelling marketing rep, herself and her two small children shared the same house with her parents, though they maintained a separate purse. The production process involved two further stages: Ibu Ningsih oversaw the inserting of the finished product into small plastic pouches, and then into bright yellow sachets. Ibu Indah completed the packaging with placing the sachets into soft cardboard boxes, sealing them with tape, readying them for the market.

With the exception of ibu Ningsih and ibu Nabila who had some previous, albeit limited, experience—the former once ran a small stall selling basic household necessities, such as cooking oil and detergent, the latter used to offer to launder the clothes of neighbours to supplement her husband's meagre earnings—this was mostly a group of beginners as far as employment was concerned. And employment had made a direct impact, they said, in the way their daily and weekly routine was organised. While before it was the goings-on in the family home that mostly structured their time—the children leaving for school, the daily trip to the market to purchase food, the husband arriving from work—now their day was equally focused around starting work at 8:30 and finishing at 4, four times a week: Monday, Tuesday, Wednesday and Friday. On Thursdays and Saturdays, the four women said they were attending religious classes in nearby mosques, each running from 9 in the morning to 12 in the afternoon. Taking religious lessons was prescribed in the letter they had signed with *DKI* in terms of their commitment to increase their overall knowledge of the faith and improve their piety. The Thursday class was all about the basics of Quranic recitation while the Saturday session was an introduction to Quranic exegesis. Both classes were organised by local committees and formed part of *majelis taklim*, regular gatherings for religious learning that have gained much prominence in Indonesia over the past decade, particularly amongst Muslim women across the class spectrum (see Srimulyani 2012; Winn 2012). If one adds the five daily prayers all four women were insistent to perform on a daily basis, the image of a tightly organised schedule emerges, itself characterised by time's division into specific periods, each associated with the undertaking of specific tasks, themselves dedicated to the regular, unvarying pursuit of improvements in economic, pietistic and family welfare.

The systematic cuts in the flow of time such activities inserted broke the infinite into a succession of finite phases, each representing a realisation of the value of progress and expansion. Such enactment of time-cuts was intrinsically related to the undertaking of further divisions, themselves providing the means of measuring the distance covered, expressing the degrees of improvement achieved. *Bagi hasil*, literally the apportioning of an outcome, was the key term the four women used to designate the grounds of *Seger*'s operations. *Bagi hasil* is the Indonesian term covering a variety of profit-and-loss sharing partnerships that extend from sharecropping arrangements in the Javanese agricultural hinterland to more modern and explicitly *syariah*-compliant commercial ventures of the kinds involved in *mudaraba* and *musharaka* contracts (see Chap. 5). *Bagi hasil* is also the mode of mutuality Islamic economists and Islamists promote, for it steers well clear from any association with fees set in advance and the uneven apportioning of risks and rewards other forms of approved contracts are perceived, by some at least, to carry, tainting them with unwelcome resemblances to capitalist schemes, themselves based on interest-based financing (Çizakça 2011; El-Gamal 2006, 2007; Udovitch 1970). In the minds of those promoting an *ekonomi Islam*, *bagi hasil* expresses both the purity and the justice of Islam.

As a matter of justice then, ibu Mustika described the apportioning of *Seger* sales activity as follows: 75% of the turnover was for buying the raw materials required for production to endure with the remaining 25% set aside. The latter portion was further subdivided into three parts: 2.5% was transferred to *DKI* as zakat, as all articles of commerce are subject to zakat, 62.5% was transferred to an account kept by ibu Setiawati while the remaining 35% was divided equally amongst the four members of the production group. Ibu Mustika performed such division on a weekly basis, every Saturday, and even though the sales had been picking up in the past few months, the returns on the women's labour remained low by minimum regional salary standards, hovering around 700,000 to 1 million rupiah per month.[6] This money was nevertheless enough (*cukup*), the women said, for paying school fees and other children's expenses, and for making basic household purchases such as rice, cooking oil and so on. '*Insyallah* (God willing), things are to improve soon,' they added.

Though *bagi hasil* is nominally qualified as a partnership, partners are not perceived as equal to each other. In a manner reminiscent of sharecropping arrangement in other parts of Java, both past and present, where the landowner is attributed higher status, on account of his possession of the land, vis-à-vis the tenant farmers (Alexander and Alexander 1982; Manning 1988), here too, the four women referred to, and addressed, ibu Setiawati as their *bos* (boss). *Seger*, they explained, was ibu Setiawati's idea (*ide*): she was the one who had developed the recipe over several years, subsequently sharing her knowledge with them through training. It was also ibu Setiawati who had paid the rent for the premises, had purchased several items of equipment such as ovens, blenders, boxes and so on and had organised the women into a team of producers. In addition, the four women were almost entirely dependent on ibu Setiawati for marketing *Seger*: each week, she would come to collect everything produced thus far, paying 12,000 rupiah for each box, which she would subsequently sell for 18,000 to her clients, mainly shop keepers and market sellers. Though the women were encouraged both by ibu Setiawati and *DKI* staff to market *Seger* themselves on a similar basis, they complained they did not have the time to do so for they were too preoccupied with its production. Speaking to them on several occasions, and being present in several occasions when ibu Setiawati was visiting the factory, it was apparent that the women held themselves to be in her debt: the rather formal way of speaking to ibu Setiawati, the soft and slow manner of engaging her, with their heads slightly bending over forwards, eyes cast mostly downwards or away, indicated a deeper kind of debt that exceeded that of money. A debt of gratitude (*bersyukur*) was what, they said, they felt. The reasons for feeling ***bersyukur*** were many: Ibu Setiawati was a young, educated, determined and more than capable woman who selected them to be her partners, opening an avenue for them to gain income while being patient with the slow progress of the business. Such debt of gratitude was also the case with respect to *DKI*: even though the micro-finance staff they had been dealing with were all male gendered, the women entertained a more casual, informal relation with them than with ibu Setiawati. And yet, a sense of gratitude was pervasive: for running the Cake House project, introducing them to ibu Setiawati, spending time with them and sharing their religious and other knowledge. Everything *DKI* had done for *Seger*, including the provision of working capital—for example, for the purchase of the raw materials expended in training—and of capital for the purchasing of equipment—such as an oven, a stove and a grinder—was offered on the basis of *hibah*, the Islamic free gift requiring no tangible, concrete return, except for an abstract, yet ubiquitous feeling of indebtedness.

Advisers and Partners

It is perhaps surprising to observe that the understanding of *Seger* as a commercial venture was not shared by the four women's significant others: both *DKI* staff and ibu Setiawati described the partnership involved, and the part they themselves played in *Seger*, in a fashion that diverged both markedly and distinctly both from the four women's version and from each other's. If *Seger* was an event, then any question regarding its very nature can only be answered partially and contingently: its event-ness can only be understood in relation to the perspectives immanently occasioned in its happening. The question I am posing in this chapter, namely, 'What is Seger?' can't be approached, let alone 'solved,' without foregrounding *Seger*'s indeterminacy: each time an answer is formulated, it very much arises from a specific standpoint. As such, the perspectives it depends on act as prior in existence and primary in importance. The viewpoints involved in any descriptions of the event as such are not given: rather, they emerge 'organically' from the relations pertaining between the parts brought together, forming the foundations of the undertaking destined to play itself out. Both primary to the actors and immanent to the milieu they emerge from, perspectives should be acknowledged as fundamental in conditioning any given situation: the posing of ethnographic problems, such as 'who speaks?' and 'who/what is this?,' elicit responses which are themselves temporary and provisional: because they are conditioned by perspectives which are more than one and which differ from each other, events perpetuate aporias by being both intrinsically open and unfinished.

For *DKI*, *Seger* was a home industry wholly and exclusively owned by the four women labouring day-in, day-out in producing the ginger-based drink. As far as the organisation was concerned, ibu Setiawati was a charitable enabler: a pious, entrepreneurial woman, she was committed to empower less fortunate women as a testament of her religious faith and expert know-how. For ibu Setiawati, a thirty-year-old mother of three kids, the stakes involved in empowering others did not preclude the concurrent pursuit of commercial profit. Rather than dissociating physics from metaphysics, and moral from economic value, she endeavoured to dispense with such distinctions. According to her understanding, *Seger* was a home industry on its way to becoming a company (*perusahaan*): in this journey, ibu Setiawati was entangled with four other women as an equal partner (*mitra*), assuming an identical share of the profits (and losses) as them taken as a unit. Moreover, to the extent that partnerships of this sort were divinely sanctioned, they were held to procure economic and religious value.

According to Pak Priyono, *DKI*'s head of operations in Ciputat, ibu Setiawati had disavowed any ownership claims she might have had on *Seger* in a Memorandum of Understanding the organisation drafted for the occasion. The MoU had been signed in July 2011, after the second round of CSR—derived funds had become available. The MoU in question marked the end of women's training in the Cake House project and the beginning of *Seger* as a venture: as such, it inserted a cut in time, distinguishing a before from an after, re-commencing a relation on new grounds. Pak Priyono who witnessed the event of the MoU's singing, described ibu Setiawati's role in *Seger* as limited to acting as trainer (*pelatih*) and adviser (*pembina*). Although the document recognised ibu Setiawati as the holder of the recipe's copyright—the formal patent of which she had already secured from the relevant authorities—it committed her to forfeiting of any advantages accruing from its further commercial development. Pak Priyono explained that the intention behind the MoU was to convey the message to everyone involved that even though ibu Setiawati had helped to establish *Seger*, she was not to be identified as its owner (*bukan pemilik*).

This right was exclusive to the four *binaan*, each having an equal share of 25% in the business.

Pak Priyono also stressed that the signing of the MoU between *DKI* and ibu Setiawati in the summer of 2011 was supplemented by yet another contract: another Memorandum of Understanding had been almost synchronously signed between ibu Setiawati and the four *binaan*. According to Pak Priyono, *DKI* was not a signatory in the second MoU. However, the organisation oversaw the document's drafting, which stipulated that the relation between the two parties was to be one of advisor/overseer (*pembina*) and advisees (*binaan*). The second MoU was crucial for it also laid out the basis of *Seger*'s operation: it established the commitment of the *binaan* to produce the drink on a regular basis, working four days a week, ensuring a minimum monthly output while setting the wholesale price of the product upon exiting the factory. It delimited their obligation vis-à-vis ibu Setiawati as they acceded to heeding her recommendations and suggestions for expanding the scope of the home industry. In this regard, the second MoU gave ibu Setiawati a leading role in guiding the venture to sustained growth while also recognising her right to place bulk orders and purchase *Seger* at wholesale price.

The reconfiguration of the relations, rights and obligations between the three parties the two MoUs occasioned, meant that *DKI* was taking a step back from acting as the empowerment agent. Such capacity was being transferred to ibu Setiawati: as Pak Priyono himself acknowledged, *DKI*'s capacities in terms of capital assistance, entrepreneurial expertise and time available for consultation were limited. The demands of taking *Seger* to the next stage of its development required greater financial resources, technical and marketing know-how than the organisation's staff currently had at their disposal. It, therefore, seemed only practical to entrust *Seger*, the loyalty and welfare of the four women to an entrepreneur with a long-term personal stake in the success of the operation. This was especially so for, as he put it, ibu Setiawati was a businesswoman blessed with the 'soul of an empower-er' (*jiwa pemberdaya*).

Over the months following the signing of the MoUs, *DKI* continued to support *Seger* in multiple ways. Though consultation visits had become less regular, staff did assist with marketing the product, placing occasional bulk orders on behalf of personal friends and other branches. The difference between the wholesale and retail prices, amounting to 6000 rupiah per box, made this a worthwhile pursuit for staff while also contributed to increasing output and improving the take-home pay of the producers.

Perhaps more importantly, *DKI* was instrumental in facilitating *Seger* to acquire a PIRT (*Pangan Industri Rumah Tangga*) certificate that guaranteed that it was safe for public consumption. It also began the process of issuing the product's *halal* certification, assisting with the submission of an application to that effect. More decisively, *DKI* introduced *Seger* to the then external relations director of Kegan & Milner, Pak Murtopo, who so astounded he was with the quality of the product and the sincere desire of its producers that he decided to devote his entire *zakat maal* of that year, some 10 million rupiah, to improving the business. Pak Priyono, who was instrumental in introducing Pak Murtopo to the four women, said that the agreement was for a minor part of zakat funds to be spent on finalising the *halal* certificate, with the majority being earmarked for ensuring a reliable supply of ginger. To this effect, *DKI* and ibu Setiawati were in discussions regarding the leasing of appropriate land and the purchase of seeds and fertiliser so as *Seger* to be no longer subject to fluctuations in the price and quality of a key raw material.

For her part, ibu Setiawati described *Seger*, together with her continuing involvement in it, in a fashion that diverged decidedly from Pak Priyono's account of the distribution of rights and obligations. A bespectacled woman in her early 30s, always modestly dressed and softly spoken, ibu Setiawati confirmed that the summer of 2011 was a significant reference point in the setting up of the home industry. However, she described *Seger* as an ongoing partnership (*kerjasama*) that she participated in as an investor (*investor*): such role entitled her to a share equal to that of her partners, the four women taken as a single unit. Such arrangement she said was clearly laid out in the Memorandum of Understanding signed between the two parties when they agreed to come together to form *Seger* in July 2011. According to ibu Setiawati, the MoU's had been drafted by herself and her husband, Pak Rizki, with the precise arrangement having been inspired by *syariah* principles of commercial partnership as laid out in *musharaka* and *mudaraba* contracts.[7] Indeed, the distribution of rights and obligations in the MoU, as described by ibu Setiawati, displayed a creative take on these classic instruments of Islamic financing. Because she was not a mere advisor in *Seger* but an investor who had committed financial capital in the venture and had assumed additional directorial responsibilities,[8] the MoU, she said, entitled her to receive 35% of the monthly revenue. The four women responsible for daily production were authorised to receive an equal amount to hers, that is, 35% of the monthly turnover as compensation for their investments of labour. Their share was to be further subdivided on an equal basis, giving each member a cut equivalent to 8.75% of the total. The remaining 10% was earmarked for the renewal of production, corresponding to the rough estimate of the cost for the purchase of raw materials.[9] As far as ibu Setiawati was concerned, this mode of division foregrounded the parity characterising her relation to the producers. In this vein, she stressed that the four ***binaan*** were not her employees (***bukan karyawan***) but her partners (***mitra***) and fellow entrepreneurs (*pengusaha*). Even though she was the one with the prime responsibility of devising new ways for ensuring the home industry's expansion not only through marketing the product to new clientele but also through innovations in its production and changes in the supply chain, she insisted that decision-making was a collective exercise in which her labouring partners had a significant role to play. And the more experience in business they gained, the more time went on, the more she expected them to assume a pro-active role, especially with respect to marketing where lots of progress was needed to be made for the product to take off.

In contrast to Pak Priyono and *DKI*'s version of mutuality, which featured two MoUs, the first of which disqualified ibu Setiawati from extracting commercial profit from *Seger*, ibu Setiawati's version mentioned only one MoU, which readily acknowledged her right to a share of the value generated. According to the entrepreneur, the MoU duly recognised *DKI*'s contribution to the endeavour by naming the organisation as the sole endpoint of the zakat the trading of the commodity created (2.5% of the proceeds of sale). The transfer of zakat to the organisation was, however, to be deferred for the foreseeable future: as long as the four ***binaan***'s income was low, certainly below the required threshold for them to start paying ***zakat maal***, ibu Setiawati preferred to transfer the zakat from trading *Seger* to the ***binaan*** and their families instead to boost their income. The transfer was scheduled to happen once a year, at the end of the current Islamic calendar, and in the form of a delivery of rice, she added.

From her perspective, ibu Setiawati had been involved in what come-to-be *Seger* the longest, with her efforts at producing a ginger-based drink going back several years, when she was still at college, well before her marriage to Pak Rizki and her becoming a mother with three kids. As a chemistry student, she and her fellow classmates would often use the college lab to make shampoo, body lotions, perfumes and herbal drinks for purposes of making money. The clientele for such products was usually other students looking for a cheap substitute for supermarket available brands. As a student, ibu Setiawati was keen to develop a formula for a ginger-based drink that would be easy to produce, relatively cheap, tasty and commercially viable, she said. When a few years after graduating, *DKI* presented her with the possibility to train other women in making drinks as part of an empowerment programme, she jumped at the opportunity to experiment further with the formulas she had already developed. She was very keen, she said, to continue to try all kinds of different combinations of materials, till she came across the right one, and she credited the training sessions running both during the Cake House project and subsequently with having provided a most creative and intensive setting that had brought the experimental phase of the project to a successful conclusion. Part of the reason why it had taken her a long time to find the right formula, she explained, had to do with the fact that it was very time consuming to experiment with raw materials on her own, especially as her young family was growing fast. It was also because she did not want to use chemicals of any kind—she was a strong believer in healthy eating and though the materials used in *Seger* are not organic, they are almost 100% natural, except that is for a small percentage of preservatives one can't make without.

Ibu Setiawati stressed that *Seger* was not simply a business project (*bukan proyek bisnis saja*) to her but primarily a *proyek pemberdayaan*, an empowerment project. However, this should not be taken to mean that commerce and the generation of monetary profit had no role to play in it, being antithetical to benevolence and the spread of assistance either in principle or in effect. For qualifying a venture as *proyek pemberdayaan* signified the presence of an excess and the attainment of value that is surplus to commercial purposes. Such supplementary value accrues mainly to the faithful from divine rewards they have been promised to receive: as discussed in Chap. 4, the generation of merit (*pahala*; *thawāb* in Arabic) and sustenance (*rezeki*; *rizk* in Arabic) through the performance of compulsory and recommended acts of piety are of central importance in achieving redemption. In the eyes of ibu Setiawati, such rewards, intangible and of immediate bearing for the Day of Judgement, were precisely what qualified *Seger* as an exercise in piety. To the extent that *Seger* was about assisting the underprivileged in attaining some form of economic independence and worked to propagate the faith both by encouraging them to take religious classes and by spreading a divinely ordained manner of conducting one's economic affairs, it was instrumental in multiplying one's amount of merit and sustenance both in this life and the next.

It is important in this regard to add that ibu Setiawati was not alone in pursuing endeavours that creatively combined the commercial with the pietistic. Her husband, Pak Rizki, was also involved in setting up an empowerment project in the nearby city of Tangerang. An information technology graduate in his early 30s, currently making his living as a wholesale trader of frozen beef and fresh fish to restaurants in Jakarta, Pak Rizki explained that he was working closely with Tangerang's division of agriculture to train poor farmers in cultivating ginger! His plan was that once this project was up and running, it would be able to supply *Seger* with the best quality of ginger, adding that this was a win-win situation: *Seger* would cut its costs by bypassing the ginger trader it currently depended on for its supply, and the farmers would have a reliable customer to sell their produce. Pak Rizki admitted that the inspiration for such ventures came from his older brother who had set up his own empowerment programme called *Punk Muslim*. The programme was about street kids (*anak jalanan*) in Jakarta interested in music: it aims to take them away from criminal activities, as he put it, and into the music business by training them to use studio equipment for the recording of religious songs.

An End, and New Beginnings

In early July 2012, the empowerment programme *DKI* ran in Ciputat with the help of Kegan & Milner's corporate social responsibility funds came to an end as the multinational decided to renew the health and schooling aspects of the intervention only, dropping economic empowerment for good after two years. This was bad news both for the majority of staff employed at the DKI local branch who had to look for new jobs and for the tens of groups of *binaan* which production activities would no longer be supported by *hibah* inputs, financial and otherwise. According to *DKI* senior staff, the multinational's priorities lay well within the Millennium Development Goals[10] for which it was easier to demonstrate success. Economic empowerment programmes take years of sustained effort, they explained, to achieve their goals in terms of improving the beneficiaries' income while education and health programmes are easier to evaluate as statistics concerning child mortality rates and maternal health are easy to gather and schooling is based around exams and graduations. Despite its disappointment over such development, the Islamic welfare organisation was readily putting in place alternative arrangements to support some of the *binaan* groups with own funds. As far as *Seger* was concerned, all the parties involved expressed qualified optimism about its future. As if it was an umbilical cord severed for a new life to achieve independence, *Seger*'s female producers were preparing to move premises to a new site located nearby as they found rent to be significantly cheaper there. They were also looking forward to recruiting a sales assistant to help with marketing: Ibu Setiawati had arranged for *Seger* to be allocated a spot free of charge at a market owned by the municipality on a long-term basis. And at the same time, courtesy of *DKI*'s extensive network of friends and supporters, *Seger* was to feature in a television programme focusing on success stories of empowerment interventions, and the four women were eagerly waiting for the film crew to visit.

Whatever the future trajectories *Seger* was to follow, these were foregrounded by a set of legal instruments and professional practices centring on an exchange of promises. The deployment of contracts recognisable both as to their Islamic variety—*hibah* and *musharaka/mudaraba*—and of secular-in-inspiration standards of good corporate governance—corporate social responsibility and memorandums of understanding—was of central importance in the effort of making value out of dividing time up and synthesising its passing. Key in the extraction of value was the collective orchestration of an interval as of utmost significance for the success of the endeavour: it is in terms of such interval that the exchange of promises attempted to render the future an object of anticipation, planning, calculation and measurement. The interval instituted by the memorandum of understanding between the corporation and the Islamic charitable organisation was given further depth, greater detail and additional substance by subsequent contracts themselves involving several other parties, most importantly an entrepreneur/inventor and four labouring women drawn from amongst a pool of worthy recipients. Such contracts foretold the contours of a future endlessly coming: located in a far-off horizon, the future conjured was predicted to be a prosperous one, filled with value, monetary and otherwise, for enjoyment in this life and the next. Contracts were repeated time and again, with every new repetition attempting to draw this future ever so nearer, enticing it to disclose its riches. Constantly proliferating relations with other parties enacted in new agreements inserted ever new cuts in the flow of time, manifesting the operations of the will to improve in full swing. To the extent that the return of value had already been prefigured in the shape of money and merit (*pahala*), the future envisioned held no real surprises: it was simply full of more-of-the-same. It was precisely this return of value as more-of-the-same that the deployment of contracts was meant to ensure: blocking everything else that could not be expressed as either money or merit from returning, contracts of both the Islamic and the secular variety hindered the erupting of a future unanticipated from taking place.

And yet, what the will to improve and the contracting of the future failed to fully domesticate was *Seger* itself, which remained an unresolved enigma and a persistent aporia for all concerned, including this anthropologist's study. Very much like the sign Rosebud in Orson Welles' *Citizen Kane*, the more talk about it there was and the greater the effort expended in defining what it was, the opaquer and the more impenetrable the enterprise was turning. With every new contract being signed, and with every new agreement being renewed, *Seger*'s shape was becoming less and less determined: *Seger* was constantly defying the gravity generated by the setting out of rights and obligations in precise and exact terms, slipping smoothly out of the framings created to host it. At the heart of its indeterminacy laid perspectival differentials and positional divergences. As Deleuze's analysis of Welles' film makes apparent (1997: 98–104, 126–136), such differentials amount as much to uncrossable distances that connect things by separating them out as to insurmountable gaps that sever things always already linked. Perspectival differentials connote the necessary affirmation of a transcendental fissure as the condition of possibility of relations as unfolded in time.

To Kegan & Milner, *Seger* was a demonstration of its commitment to global standards of good corporate governance. Such standards are held to ensure the welfare of the whole of the global community through the inclusion of the poor and the underprivileged in the warmth embrace generated by the neoliberal sharing of excess-value production. A testament to capitalism's abiding by the ethics of sacrifice in a means-ends relationship, Kegan & Miller's offer of a share of its profits in the guise of corporate social responsibility enabled the setting up of *Seger* as an empowerment exercise and a commercial enterprise dedicated to aiding four individual women in their pursuit of economic independence and profitability. To *Dana Keadilan Indonesia*, *Seger* was a demonstration of the productivity of making Islam work in the modern, corporate world and of its dedication to the cause of creating an Islamic economy in Indonesia. By means of converting the profits of a multinational company into *hibah*, the Islamic gift inter vivos, it sought to transform scores of what it saw as economically unproductive housewives into pious entrepreneurial subjects. In this endeavour, the generation and proliferation of relations of symbolic debt were as instrumental as the instituting of hierarchical relations: between the organisation and the *binaan*, a clear and unambiguous delineation of the positions of leader/creditor and followers/debtors was put in place, according to which the former acted as a benevolent provider of the main ingredients of the latter's future progression to and eventual success in achieving self-reliance. To ibu Setiawati, *Seger* was both a personal exercise in piety and a commercial undertaking, itself enabled as much by a third-party corporate gift that required no return as by her own technical know-how and experimentation. Conceiving of her relationship to the four women working in *Seger* as one of parity and partnership allowed her to maintain that the assistance she was offering did not violate the latter's dignity and self-respect, a move that paradoxically guaranteed her own distinction: as far as it was she who granted them parity, such attribution also underscored her own elevated distinctiveness. To the four female staffers, *Seger* was a daily habit acquired in the past couple of years as part of their struggle for ensuring their and their families' survival in a tough city environment like that of Jakarta, marked by extreme disparities of wealth and a rising Islamic consciousness. Not wanting to downplay the significance that any future profits and salvific rewards might have had for the four *binaan*, my sense is that their perspective was imbued by considerations at once more earnest and pressing: getting involved in *Seger* was their way of assisting their families, primarily their children, with getting ahead in life. Getting them through compulsory education, helping them get a university degree, purchasing much-coveted domestic appliances, such as fridges and washing machines while sharing their husbands' pressures as far as meeting household financial obligations were concerned, were the immediate objectives *Seger* was to serve. To these women then, *Seger* was first and foremost a medium for improving family life: everything else, inclusive of piety, was refracted through the lens of kinship, with motherhood foregrounding the paramount sense of fulfilment and obligation these and other subjects of Islamic micro-finance in Indonesia were endowed with.

Notes

1. Deleuze writes in this respect that 'memory is not in us; it is us who move in a Being-memory, a world memory. In short, the past appears as the most general form of an already-there, a pre-existence in general, which our recollections presuppose' (1997: 96).
2. The relevant legislation relates to the State-Owned Enterprises Law (Law No. 19/2003), the Investment Law (Law No. 25/2007), and the Limited

Liability Company Law (Law No. 40/2007). Article 74 of the latter imposes an obligation to engage in environmental social responsibility on companies active in the natural resources sector and/or in a related sector (see Rosser and Edwin 2010). More than ten years on, the government has yet to issue an implementing regulation, making the article unenforceable. Most importantly, should companies fail to implement CSR, the legislation lacks specific sanctions, making CSR a voluntary undertaking.

3. *Pembinaan* (guidance, supervision) is, along with *golongan ekonomi lemah* (weak economic groups), the key concepts through which past and present Indonesian governments have deployed in their efforts to prop up small and medium enterprises in the country (Berry et al. 2001: 377). The support historically offered to such groups comprises of interventions Islamic welfare organisations have imitated: credit availability, training in technical skills and entrepreneurship, marketing assistance, access to equipment and facilities, inclusive of banking, are deeply embedded within a paternalistic ethos according to which those who rule and know best are conceived to have a definitive obligation to guide and uplift those inferior and in need.
4. The phrase is used extensively in everyday life, opening each and every action undertaken to the acquisition of Allah's blessing. It is also the standard opening for commercial contracts offered by Islamic banks in Indonesia (see Lindsey 2012: 123).
5. The Betawi, Jakarta's 'original' inhabitants, are considered a separate ethnic group. They are the descendants of people who gathered in Batavia (Jakarta's colonial name) from the seventeenth century onwards, coming from many different parts of the Malay world, including other parts of Java. Their Malay-based language is distinct both from Sudanese, which is primarily spoken in West Java, and Javanese, spoken in most parts of Java, and consists of many loan words from Hokkien Chinese, Dutch and Arabic.
6. In 2012, the South Tangerang minimum salary, as determined by the Governor of Banten, was a bit over 1.5 million rupiah (see *Keputusan Gubernur Banten 561/Kep. 1/2012*).
7. *Mudaraba* is a partnership contract in which one party contributes capital and the other labour and business expertise with a view to sharing profits according to a predetermined ratio. In essence, *mudaraba* is a specific case of *musharaka*, a joint venture contract of wider application, which in Arabic means 'sharing.' In *musharaka*, two or more parties may contribute some, not necessarily equal, percentage of the three factors of economic production (financial capital, labour and entrepreneurial know-how). Here too, the proportion of profit (and loss) to be distributed amongst the partners must be determined and agreed upon in advance, at the time of the contract.
8. Her investment, involved amongst other things, rental costs for the premises for a whole year, the costs of designing *Seger*'s logo and boxes, and

money for the purchase of production equipment such as ovens, grinders and so on. DKI readily acknowledged that the monetary value of such investment far exceeded the contributions it itself had made in the form of CSR-funded *hibah*.

9. This mode of division departs significantly from the joint venture contracts of Islamic financing for it proceeds on the basis of monthly revenue, not profit. My guess is that this is because small- and medium-scale traders and entrepreneurs in Java are used to work on the basis of *omset* (turnover), encountering difficulties in calculating and accounting for the costs of inputs and outputs in a detailed manner. *Omset* is calculated on a daily or monthly basis and forms the primary referent for judging whether a venture is sustainable and profitable or not, against the background of a rough estimate of production costs. It is significant to add that the costs of production do not normally include the labour expended, especially as all or most of labour in SMEs is provided by family members, both junior and senior.
10. The Millennium Development Goals (MDGs) are eight international goals that all 193 UN member states agreed to achieve by 2015, amongst which are the eradication of extreme poverty and hunger, the reduction of child mortality rates, improving maternal health and ensuring environmental sustainability.

Bibliography

Alexander, Jennifer, and Paul Alexander. 1982. Shared Poverty as Ideology: Agrarian Relationships in Colonial Java. *Man (N.S.)* 17 (4): 597–619.

Angelucci, Daniela. 2014. Time. *Deleuze Studies* 8 (3): 324–333.

Berry, Albert, Edgard Rodriguez, and Henry Sandee. 2001. Small and Medium Enterprise Dynamics in Indonesia. *Bulletin of Indonesian Economic Studies* 37 (3): 363–384.

Bryant, Levi. 2008. *Difference and Givenness. Deleuze's Transcendental Empiricism and the Ontology of Immanence*. Evanston: Northwestern University Press.

Çizakça, Murat. 2011. *Islamic Capitalism and Finance: Origins, Evolution and the Future*. Cheltenham: Edward Elgar.

Deleuze, Gilles. 1997. *Cinema 2. The Time-Image*. Trans. Hugh Tomlinson and Robert Galeta. Minneapolis: University of Minnesota Press.

———. 2008. *Difference and Repetition*. Trans. Paul Patton. London: Continuum Press.

Dolan, Catherine, and Dinah Rajak. 2016. Introduction. Toward the Anthropology of Corporate Social Responsibility. In *The Anthropology of Corporate Social Responsibility*, ed. C. Dolan and D. Rajak, 1–28. New York: Berghahn.

El-Gamal, Mahmood. 2006. *Islamic Finance: Law, Economics, and Practice*. Cambridge: Cambridge University Press.

———. 2007. Mutuality as an Antidote to Rent-Seeking Shariah Leverage in Islamic Finance. *Thunderbird International Business Review* 49 (2): 187–202.

Linant de Bellefonds, Yvon. 2012. Hiba. In *Encyclopaedia of Islam, Second Edition*, ed. P. Bearman, Th. Bianquis, C.E. Bosworth, E. van Donzel and W.P. Heinrichs. Consulted online on 13 June 2018. https://doi.org/10.1163/1573-3912_islam_COM_0283

Lindsey, Tim. 2012. Between Piety and Prudence: State Syariah and the Regulation of Islamic Banking in Indonesia. *Sydney Law Review* 34: 106–127.

Manning, Chris. 1988. *The Green Revolution, Employment, and Social Change in Rural Java*. Singapore: Institute of Southeast Asian Studies.

Mauss, Marcel. 2011. *The Gift: Forms and Functions of Exchange in Archaic Societies*. Trans. Ian Cunnison. Mansfield Centre: Martino Publishing.

Mudzakir, Ro'fah. 2005. The Indonesian Women's Movement and the Issue of Polygamy. In *Approaches to the Qur'an in Contemporary Indonesia*, ed. Abdullah Saeed. Oxford: Oxford University Press.

Munir, Lily Zakiyah. 2005. Islam and Gender: Reading Equality and Patriarchy. In *Islam in Southeast Asia: political, social and strategic challenges for the 21st century*, ed. K.S. Nathan and Mohammad Hashim Kamali. Singapore: Institute of Southeast Asian Studies.

Robinson, Kathryn. 2007. Islamic Influences on Indonesian Feminism. In *Identifying with Freedom: Indonesia after Suharto*, ed. Tony Day. New York: Berghahn Books.

Rosenthal, F., C.E. Bosworth, J. Wansbrough, G.S. Colin, H. Busse, and B. Spuler. 2012. Hiba. In *Encyclopaedia of Islam, Second Edition*, ed. P. Bearman, Th. Bianquis, C.E. Bosworth, E. van Donzel and W.P. Heinrichs. Consulted online on 13 June 2018. https://doi.org/10.1163/1573-3912_islam_COM_0282

Rosser, Andrew, and Donni Edwin. 2010. The Politics of Corporate Social Responsibility in Indonesia. *The Pacific Review* 23 (1): 1–22.

Rousseau, Jean Jacque. 1997. *The Social Contract and Other Later Political Writings*. Ed. and Trans. Victor Gourevitch. Cambridge: Cambridge University Press.

Simone, Abdoumaliq. 2013. Cities of Uncertainty: Jakarta, the Urban Majority, and Inventive Political Technologies. *Theory, Culture & Society* 30 (7/8): 243–263.

Srimulyani, Eka. 2012. *Women from Traditional Educational Backgrounds in Indonesia: Negotiating Public Spaces*. Amsterdam: Amsterdam University Press.

Tsing, Anna. 2013. Sorting Out Commodities: How Capitalist Value Is Made Through Gifts. *HAU: Journal of Ethnographic Theory* 3 (1): 21–43.

———. 2017. *The Mushroom at the End of the World. On the Possibility of Life at Capitalist Ruins*. Princeton: Princeton University Press.

Udovitch, Abraham. 1970. *Partnership and Profit in Medieval Islam*. Princeton: Princeton University Press.

Welker, Marina. 2009. "Corporate Security Begins in the Community": Mining, the Corporate Social Responsibility Industry, and Environmental Advocacy in Indonesia. *Cultural Anthropology* 24 (1): 142–179.

Winn, Philip. 2012. Women's Majelis Taklim and Gendered Religious Practice in Northern Ambon. *Intersections: Gender and Sexuality in Asia and the Pacific* 30: 1–15.

CHAPTER 7

Soliciting Time

Of the dramas played out during Ramadan in Java, the excitations the sight of 'beggars' evokes among the good people of the middle class are unmistakable. For every year it is the unfailing concern of the media—as well as many an overheard conversation in buses, offices and shopping malls—that the major cities of the island, and Jakarta especially, are repeatedly 'swamped' by tens of thousands of allegedly 'professional beggars' (*pengemis profesional*). The concerns expressed are multiple. Most often, though, they have to do with the 'beggars' being out-of-towners, basically peasants from the surrounding countryside, who, having made a habit of pretending to be 'destitute and poor' (*fakir miskin*) are managing to make more than a decent living from the proceeds of good people's generosity. Not only are such people lazy and indolent, knowing nothing of the value of work, the allegations go, but they are essentially cunning and deceitful—defrauding honest people, and depriving them not only of their money but also of the prospect of doing good in a meaningful way, that is in a way that makes a difference to worthy recipients. Given the level of public anxiety, the good people of urban centres are evidently protected by the authorities in many a city, where 'begging' has been turned into a crime. In addition, they are repeatedly warned to avoid giving, that is *giving in* to the fake pleas for help and mercy of street-roaming strangers.

The elicitation of goodness during Ramadan takes other forms as well, some of which have come under the scrutiny of the authorities, both state and religious ones. An incident which marked public perceptions

K. Retsikas, *A Synthesis of Time*,
https://doi.org/10.1007/978-3-030-34933-2_7

inexorably took place in 2008 in the coastal city of Pasuruan, in East Java, where during the Ramadan month of that year several people, all of whom were women, died in a stampede. Their deaths were linked to the public distribution of *zakat* carried out by Haji Syaichon Fikri, a wealthy trader of bird nests, leather products and cars. In provincial Java it is customary for large crowds of destitute people from the immediate locality and its environs to form outside the residences of wealthy individuals, normally upon receiving notice that zakat distribution is to be carried out on specific dates. Fatefully, in September 2008, the 'mass' (*massa*) that had gathered outside Fikri's house made a mad dash for the money, resulting in 21 women dying in the ensuing pandemonium, having been trampled by an out-of-control crowd. According to press reports, the 'mass' had grown impatient after having waited for hours on end for the distribution of money to begin. At the same time, the lack of adequate supervision by the family—which had not notified the police—was also emphasised as having played a role in the deaths. In the aftermath of this *tragedi*, the Indonesian Council of Islamic Scholars (*Majelis Ulama Indonesia*) issued a *fatwa*, an edict that declared this method of zakat distribution unlawful (*haram*) and called for zakat transfers to proceed in an orderly, well-supervised and controlled manner so as to avoid further loss of human life (Fig. 7.1).

Fig. 7.1 Zakat claimants queuing (Image available online, downloaded on 1-12-2015)

In the preceding two chapters I have focused on two particular case studies in order to discuss in detail and at length the new methods and innovative instruments Indonesian zakat management bodies or LAZ, along with other Islamic institutions such as *Majelis Ulama Indonesia*, have devised for enacting the Quranic injunction of transferring zakat and assisting the poor. In particular, I have showed that in Indonesia in the past decade or so, zakat has been effectively reconceived as a financial asset and redeployed as a debt-based instrument for purposes of community development projects that are also *syariah* compliant. In the previous chapter, I discussed the manner in which other financial resources earmarked for community development such as corporate social responsibility, are similarly deployed by LAZ with the purpose of transforming the lower classes of Jakarta's periphery into pious future entrepreneurs. Such people-to-come are dedicated to reproducing commodity production and committed to the deepening of the faith. In both case studies, value transfers framed as Islamic philanthropy (*filantropi*, see Chap. 1) features as the single-most important element that allegedly empowers the poor, while propelling economic and religious welfare to eternal repetition, allowing them to spread onwards and outwards into the distant future. Crucial in the capturing of the potential the future entails are the instituting and the proliferation of obligations, especially those embedded in commercial and symbolic debt relations. The conduct of value transfers works to ensure the passing of time with the obligations created extracting from the yet-to-come the return of value as the self-same version of a present improved. The ethnography I have offered in the previous chapters has also made aptly clear that such value transfers entail a giving as well as a receiving with both activities conducted in a socially approved and politically sanctioned manner. As such, givers and recipients are duly trained in the acquisition of appropriate sets of conducts and have their performances evaluated according to specific standards of behaviour. It is the effective embodiment and habitual display of such conducts that ultimately differentiates the successful Islamic entrepreneurs of the future that LAZ assist in developing, as much from the reviled beggars who hopelessly roam the capital's streets as from the countryside poor who either wait too passively or are way too eager to receive zakat, creating chaos and destruction in the process. From the perspective of LAZ, indolent begging, passive waiting and restless craving amount to conducts that should be eclipsed, only to be substituted by the cultivation of new sets of habits: as far as LAZ are concerned, pious entrepreneurship instantiates an aspiration and an approved mode of desiring future redemption. The extent to which this is true and good pertains to forces explicating the will to improve: this is the image of a prosperous life yet-to-be-achieved as conceived by the will to improve, itself giving birth to a future anticipated and prescribed.

The turning of such an image into reality is however interrupted by other forces operating in the same field of social relations. It is the purpose of the present chapter to make such forces ethnographically manifest and theorise their importance. Explicating the will to power, the forces in question are of immense conceptual, ethical and political significance: they strive to unburden the future from what it ought to be, freeing the potential inhering in times-to-come, affirming chance and the radical alterity of the unknown. In order to welcome the other returning, it is essential that these forces succeed in blocking the establishment and upsurge of obligations and debt relations that Islamic philanthropic activities create and foster. It is precisely because such forces proceed by means of *soliciting* that value is transferred without the expectation of or duty for a return outstanding. Unlike both gifting and commodity exchange where returns are conceived as inescapably owed and due to arrive sooner or later, soliciting opens the present up to a future unanticipated. The eradication of any expectations of future returns on present investments is grounded on soliciting's intimate relation with the other understood both in temporal terms—other-times—and ontological ones—the Other. As I show in this chapter, soliciting works to release the future from anything that attempts to separate it from what it can be because it is primarily the affair of the other: rather than extending the present and self-presence to the outside, soliciting comes from the direction of the future, arriving by way of the other. Its conduct re-inscribes the other and the future as always already primary and predominant, rendering the present and self-presence as derived and secondary, and yet immensely crucial. The passing present and the ever-contingent self-presence are crucial for the affirmative role they are called to play; the eternal return of the different is accomplished on condition the present and self-presence are affirming of soliciting, of other-times as much as the time of the other.

Soliciting amounts to the making of a promise that is outright paradoxical: the promise of no returns functions as the necessary condition of the return of the new and the unexpected. Everything depends on the kind of promise made: pledging oneself to absolute contingency in an absolute manner works in such a way so as to the welcome and raise becoming to the highest degree possible. This raising requires affirmation:

the challenge soliciting's promise of no returns poses demands an affirmative reply: 'yes, yes to "no returns"' it shouts from the bottom of its heart. It is on condition of this challenge and this affirmation that time splits open, the gift-commodity pair are blocked from returning and the new and the unknown usher in. In this chapter, I endeavour to show that soliciting as an activity, together with the affirmation it demands in reply, pass the test of the eternal return as set out by Nietzsche (2006) and Deleuze (2008). Let's remind ourselves of what Deleuze says of the selections the eternal return is capable of performing:

> Eternal return, in its esoteric truth, concerns—and can concern—only the third time of the series. Only there is it determined. That is why it is properly called a belief of the future, a belief in the future. Eternal return affects only the new, what is produced under the condition of default and by the intermediary of metamorphosis. However, it causes neither the *condition* nor the *agent* to return: on the contrary, it repudiates these and expels them with all its centrifugal force. It constitutes the autonomy of the product, the independence of the work. It is repetition by excess which leaves nothing intact [....]. It is itself new, complete novelty. It is by itself the third time in the series, the future as such. (Deleuze 2008: 113, italics in the original)

In renouncing both the conditions and the agent of an action from returning, what the eternal return repeats for all eternity is the undetermined and the formless. Blocked is both the past that furnishes the grounds on the basis of which a course of action is thinkable, possible and desirable, and the present in the guise of an agent, equally precast and moulded so that it has the capacity to carry out the necessary action, seeing it through to the end. What is allowed to pass is the unconditioned as pure becoming; what is allowed to re-appear is difference in itself; all that returns is an open future.

> As Klossowski says, [the eternal return] is the secret coherence which establishes itself only by excluding my own coherence, my own identity, the identity of the self, the world and God. It allows only the plebeian to return, the man without a name. (Deleuze 2008: 113)

'The (wo)man without a name' amounts to the unconventional figure of the subject the eternal return and soliciting foreground. Such a figure is empty of identity and resistant to description. This is not the result of an insurmountable lack akin to a pathological condition. It is rather the outcome of its having succeeded in avoiding capture by the apparatus of power/knowledge and the latter's forceful arrest of becoming. It has therefore escaped subsequent categorisation into natures, classes and types, each with its specific sets of capacities, affordances and abilities. As the empty and pure form of the subject, it persists and endures, forever becoming; it is destined to the future, pre-figuring a people-to-come. But when it is called out, it oftentimes adopts the designation *οὔτις* (nobody, no one), simulating the Homeric hero Odysseus, who choose this name to trick the Cyclops Polyphemus, before proceeding to blind the monster's single eye.

Having no specific, exclusive name means that such figure does not belong to the present, neither does it have a resolute self-presence. As an uncommon subject, it is situated well beyond the identitarian projects of late modernity with their politics aiming at eliciting state recognition in terms of rights, protections and benefits. In desiring anonymity and obscurity over and above sovereign protection, it manifests the positive side of concealment that not having a name affords. It is within the space of concealment that its affirmative politics are founded. The positivity of 'no one' is deeply related to the cuts solicitors perform on time: like ghosts, their arrival marks the re-appearance of an un-tamed residue that keeps on coming suddenly, in a most untimely[1] and inconvenient manner. Being unanticipated and unforeseen, unexpected and uncontrolled are essential characteristics of the time synthesis solicitors perform: the kind of promises they make and incessantly repeat depend on unpredictability, volatility and randomness. As well as the content of their promises being unalike since they offer no returns, their conduct of promising occurs in a most startling manner. As the ethnographic example below demonstrates, coming out of nowhere, and receding back into the shadows, is the most fitting conduct for those that persist without a name!

Vanishings I

During my stay in Surabaya in the same rainy season of 2011–2012 that forms the focus of Chap. 5, I was struck by a couple of occurrences that did not easily fit into the normal schedule of giving and receiving. These occurrences involved the transfer of value conducted by means other than contracts, the generation of obligations and the expectations of returns. Rather the transfer was accomplished on the basis of a resourceful extraction of value: wealth was forcefully removed in such a way that it disappeared from view with little or no trace left behind of those who performed the deed. In this chapter I relate these occurrences and draw out their implications for an anthropology of time synthesis.

According to ibu Nurhayati, the forty-something mother of five young children and newly appointed manager of the Islamic micro-finance institution I discussed in Chap. 5, there were a few cases in which people were able to claim the zakat funds on offer without subjecting themselves to related disciplinary procedures, which would have put them in a position of indebtedness—at once symbolic and material. The two cases of which ibu Nurhayati was aware took place in the initial stages of the programme, involving people who had since left the city of Surabaya, having disappeared from the face of the earth—thereby remaining anonymous and unidentified to the authorities. Equally, in our discussions, ibu Nurhayati refrained from naming them. The claims such people put forward to zakat implicated the powers of drawing wealth out, soliciting its value: their conduct in seeing that the value transfer was carried out depended on the deployment of craftiness, shrewdness and disguise. What they did was the following. In order to qualify for financial assistance, the two agents in question simulated their involvement in micro-enterprise by constructing a set of impromptu food stalls using equipment borrowed on the spur of the moment from friends and relatives. They thus used chairs, tables and cooking pots to give the appearance of running their own enterprise that, in turn, could make much use of the assistance offered by the Islamic micro-finance institution. The simulation took full advantage of the unsuspecting representative of *Indonesia Mandiri*, the institution in charge of empowerment, who had given them advance warning of a visit to validate their activities. As a result, they had the time needed to conceive an ingenious plan, the successful execution of which meant that as much as 1 million rupiah changed hands. After such transfer the solicitors made a quick exit, never to be seen again, their names and faces now forgotten.

Ibu Nurhayati, as well as many others involved in the practice of Islamic micro-finance, found such simulation rather reprehensible, as there was guile and cunning involved. Yet, they also stressed that the people concerned were not guilty of misappropriation, theft or anything of the sort. Moreover, they had no case to answer for to authorities.[2] In their capacity as poor, theirs was, and remained, a valid claim to zakat. In this regard, the validity of zakat entitlement renders all other concerns as secondary and contingent. The same applied to other zakat beneficiaries who, as micro-finance recipients, found themselves unable to repay the loan advanced when, for a variety of reasons, their business ran into trouble, they fell ill or were otherwise unable to work. According to representatives of the same Islamic micro-finance institution in Surabaya, they too were exempt from the typical obligations surrounding loan repayment, for their zakat right overrode any responsibilities ensuing from the credit contract that they had signed. The overall significance of such a mode of transferring value was confirmed when, in an interview with Prof. Muhammad Amin Suma, Dean of the Faculty of *Syariah* and Law at the esteemed *Universitas Islam Negeri Syarif Hidayatullah Jakarta*, he too posited the primacy of zakat as right, over and above any attempt to turn it into a credit/debt instrument, observing that

> It is ok to give *zakat* to the poor as capital. In the process of empowerment, some *mustahiq*'s business is successful, and then there are those who are not. The latter might find themselves in difficulty when trying to return the money lent. In the past, there were many cases of wiping the record clean, when the issue of debt was not pursued further. But this presented us with new problems, as many people thought that it was okay to take [*ambil*] the funds without any obligation to return them. Because of such problems, this method [of dispensing *zakat*] should no longer be used. The poor should be given *zakat* as capital, but there should no longer be any requirement regarding its return.

In what follows I explore as fully as possible the implications this manner of conducting zakat worship has: I am particularly interested in the cuts soliciting inserts in the flow of time, especially as far as the ways in which it unburdens the future from onward obligations of forthcoming returns are concerned. As I show, soliciting is bound with struggles against the assumption of the subject position of aid recipient: it rejects the discipline the acceptance of beneficence incurs, especially in the shape of required entrepreneurial endeavour, loan repayment schedules and a new cycle of credit/debt advancement. As such, soliciting is intimately related with the effort to turn the gift upside-down and inside-out: the reconfiguration of zakat from a philanthropic gift that passes from a superior to an inferior into an accomplishment that primarily depends on the manifest agency of an unnamed other is its major objective. I argue that it is on the basis of soliciting's reconfiguration of value transfers that time is synthesised anew: no longer a case of the passing of the present into a future improved, soliciting inserts such a cut in the flow of time that makes the present pass without returning. The liberation of value from the obligation of reciprocating with an equivalent or greater return is crucial for the performance of the third synthesis of time whereby soliciting operates as the sign of the will to power, opening the present to a future unknown.

In order to appreciate the time synthesis soliciting performs, I start with a critical evaluation of the anthropological and philosophical literature on the gift. It is the conducting of the conduct of anthropological description I focus on, to argue that our quandaries and difficulties with the gift as an analytical category could be examined anew and repositioned with a change of perspective which is also a change in knowing. Such a change I claim is afforded by moving anthropological emphasis away from the gift, and in favour of soliciting. To this end, I engage in a deconstructive reading of Mauss' foundational text (2011) on the subject, together with a few subsequent and significant re-assessments of the gift as performed in key anthropological texts. The purpose of the exercise is to elicit some of the elements, or dimensions, relating to value transfers that Mauss' study and subsequent analyses have excluded and actively suppressed from their considerations. My discussion includes taking a closer look at Derrida's (1992) own critical engagement with Mauss' study: the purpose is not so much the repetition of Derrida, but the discovery of a profound and unrealised potential in Derrida's own critique that is in turn necessary for recalibrating and renewing the political and analytical potential of soliciting for our understanding and habitation of time.

The Gift and the Given

It is perhaps Marcel Mauss' study of *The Gift* (2011), more than any other book, that has furnished social anthropology with a foundation in the double sense of formulating a distinctive object of study, conveyed by concepts such as the primitive and the non-Western other, and equipping the discipline with a characteristic purpose, itself closely connected to the value of conducting a critique of modern living and its attendant processes of commodification. Since its publication in 1925, *The Gift* has exercised a profound influence in anthropological imagination, shaping it in a homologised series of binaries which—in structuralist fashion, and extended over time—can be summarised as follows: Western:primitive:: culture:nature:: commodity:gift:: alienation:reciprocity:: equality:hierarchy:: the individual:the dividual. The impression Mauss' essay has made in anthropology is massive, and deservedly so, for no other text has unearthed more archaeological treasures, so to speak, with every new excavation that has taken place. And even if Lévi-Strauss' (1987) reading of the gift as reciprocity, together with Sahlins' (1974) elaborations on it, have exercised an enduring influence in the discipline, subsequent critical engagements by Bourdieu (1977), Parry (1986), Strathern (1988), Raheja (1988), Weiner (1992), Godelier (1999) and Laidlaw (2000) have carried our lasting fascination with *The Gift* to new heights. This is despite the fact that there is now a mounting disagreement amongst commentators about what Mauss truly said, meant to say and actually wrote. Such excitement is partly related to the way Mauss' short study is organised, discussing complex ethnographic and historical materials in a distinctly cursory and preliminary manner, while speculating on an evolutionary path covering thousands of years. At the same time, anthropological debates around *The Gift* have also been linked to the book's political objectives insofar as Mauss offered the gift as a point of contrast to commodity production, conceiving it as essential to a socialist time-to-come (Mauss 2011: 63–81). It is perhaps because of such qualities that anthropological fervour over the study's significance endures, and the potential for novel readings remains undiminished.

Having re-read *The Gift*, I must admit that there is no doubt that reciprocity, with its attendant obligations of acceptance and return, is firmly and explicitly rooted in the basic contours of the text (2011: 37–41). In this regard, Mauss writes that the obligation to give is 'the essence of [North West American] potlatch. A chief must give a potlatch for himself, his son, his son-in-law or daughter and for the dead' (2011: 37). Equally, the obligation to receive is 'no less constraining. One does not have the right to refuse a gift. To do so would show fear of having to repay, and of being based in default' (2011: 39). Finally, the obligation to repay is 'the essence of potlatch. [...] [It] must be returned with interest like all other gifts' (2011: 40). The entire project of *The Gift* is conceptually founded on the Maori concept of ***hau***, the 'spirit of things': assuming quasi-universal validity, it is the ***hau*** of the gift that according to Mauss ensures and guarantees with an invisible, irresistible force that a return is always due for every passing present; otherwise, misfortune strikes (2011: 8–10). Leaving aside the unquestionable romanticism that attributes the gift to the primitive other, it is of the essence to note that the all-important distinction Mauss operates with, that between gifts and commodities,[3] is compelling only on condition that we set aside the fact that they are both instances of exchange and thus, require legal sanction to be operable. In other words, rather than forming binary opposites, gifts and commodities are instances of value transfer that share a common ground: both presuppose the organisation of the social in terms of contractual obligations that, in turn, necessitate the invention and application of law.[4] Despite their assumed critical bend as far as furnishing a critique of commodity production, it is an undeniable that Mauss (2011), and before him Marx (2010) took for granted a contractarian model of the social that is at least as old as Hobbes' and Rousseau's treatises on the subject: whether in the form of a counter-gift or wages paid for labour time expended, the premise of reciprocity pertains to a key presupposition. In both accounts, the postulate of a commensurate return amounts to an uncritically adopted theoretical *and* moral foundation: the honouring of contracts and the honour of being contracted is of outmost importance both ethically and conceptually. This is true of Mauss who conceives the gift in terms of three key obligations: to give, to receive and to reciprocate are the conditions of possibility of so-called primitive exchange. In this regard, concerns over the commensurability or equivalence between gifts and counter-gifts are highlighted as crucial for the sequencing of actions, and the reproduction of bonds renewed at every point of exchange. As for Marx (2010), the norm for equivalence in giving and receiving was deployed as a meta-value in terms of which he conducts his evaluation of capitalism as exploitative. It is only to the extent that the wage-labourers produce more value than they receive in compensation that capitalism is critiqued for the alienation it enables, with surplus-value functioning as the source of profit. But while Marx strived to describe commodity production from the perspective of the exploited proletariat, it is a different story with Mauss. Mauss' perspective inadvertently and consistently privileges the act of giving, and the side of the giver, even as this position is duly acknowledged as reversible and interchangeable. Specifically, the three obligations he identifies as essential are arranged in an exact temporal sequence that begins with giving, followed by receiving, and culminating in repaying (2011: 37–41). Here giving supersedes in importance both receiving and returning; the main function of the latter two is to supplement giving in such a way that the circle is closed, and the contract honoured. Furthermore, the analytical primacy accorded to giving is attributed with moral valence by Mauss, who treats giving as synonymous with upright conduct, prescribing the Maori proverb 'give as much as you receive, and all is for the best' to his contemporaries as a guide for realising true socialist ethics (2011: 69).

These issues notwithstanding, Mauss is also making a series of crucial observations about the Melanesian *kula* (the ceremonial exchange system conducted in Papua New Guinea). It is my contention that these observations correspond to what is virtually hidden and suppressed as much in the overall visibility organising *The Gift* as in subsequent anthropological debates concerning reciprocity. A critical reading of this literature should begin from precisely this point. In Mauss' text, the observations in question are mostly ethnographic and have to do with the spells the would-be gift-receiver performs in advance of his/her encounter with the would-be gift-giver. Some of the theoretical issues the spells speak to, have been taken up by Beidelman (1989), Weiner (1992) and Graeber (2001), who in their own particular ways highlight the agonistic and competitive nature of gift exchanges, and the dilemmas, deception, cunning and even coercion that pervade the conduct of such games when status distinctions and social hierarchies become increasingly entangled with them. Taking my cue from such studies, I too proceed to recast the so-called gift-receiver from a *passive* into an *active* figure; however, I also venture further afield by explicitly considering the gift from the vantage of soliciting, itself an activity which almost amounts to stealing, and yet manages successfully to sidestep the law and morality, and their negative consequences.[5] The account I offer here stems in the first instance from a fuller recognition of the actor, who by a variety of means draws out, elicits or solicits a gift. The importance of soliciting is that it anticipates a partnership, and thereby creates the position of the donor, as well as pre-figuring the act of giving itself. In affirming the other side of the gift, and the work accomplished by the soliciting agent, I endeavour to describe a mode of violence that precedes the moral, the legal and the contractual. Such a force I argue amounts to the indispensable ground on which the social is constituted.

Let us return to Mauss' observations, briefly. Drawing on Malinowski's (1922) equally classic study of the Trobrianders, Mauss talks about a magic formula called the 'spell of the conch-shell' (2011: 23–24). Such a formula is extensively used for invoking *kula* valuables and is meant to charm and attract—towards the would-be donor—the very 'objects' the person who casts the spell intends to ask and receive from him. At the same time, the spell is also conceived of as having the supplementary efficacy of bringing such a state of excitement to the mind of the donor-to-be, causing him to be extremely open-handed and generous. Otherwise, it might occur to him to keep the 'objects' gathered for himself. The end of the spell is especially revealing for the tone of *kula* relationships: 'I shall *kula*, I shall rob my *kula* [partner]; I shall steal my *kula* [partner]; I shall pilfer my *kula*. … My fame is like thunder, my steps are like earthquake'

(2011: 95). A series of similar spells, Mauss continues, express the same idea, casting the would-be donor as a crocodile and a bird of prey working for the benefit of his partner—that is the would-be receiver—by collecting and bringing him the very things the latter desires so strongly.

The solicitation of the gift, particularly of the violent or extractive type, is not limited to Melanesia; and Mauss makes no secret that the potlatch of the North West American coast is especially animated by rivalry and antagonism as well as by excess, theatricality and the destruction, rather than the preservation, of value. Thus, amongst the Tlingit and the Haida of Alaska, he argues, 'the only way to demonstrate one's fortune is by expending it to the humiliation of others, by putting them in the shadow of one's name' (2011: 37–38). In the same vein, Mauss continues noting that to take part in a potlatch is to accept a challenge, for failure to make a return is 'enslavement for debt,' as in these societies, 'face is lost for ever if a worthy return is not made or if equivalent value is not destroyed' (2011: 41). With ethnographic observations such as these, one is left wondering why Mauss so readily associates the gift with morality and goodness, espousing so eagerly a purportedly alternative economy of values that is based on 'the joy of giving in public, the delight in artistic expenditure, the pleasure of hospitality in the public or private feast' (2011: 67), and why he recommends with such excitation social insurance, mutual funds and the cooperative movement as the future return of the ancient institutions of the gift? In succumbing to these temptations Mauss is surely not alone; an expansive body of anthropological work on the gift, reciprocity and charity is similarly pervaded by moral concerns and quests.[6] And yet one cannot escape wondering what the anthropology of the gift would be like if it had not been written from the perspective of a morally charged giving, but rather from the perspective of an amoral soliciting? What if, in other words, the gift was no longer to be conceived as an adjunct to giving but as the accomplishment of soliciting? What if we were to apprehend giving as a secondary operation, and, instead of seeing it as productive of the gift, described it as the by-product of taking?

I must be precise here; soliciting creates value by means of drawing out wealth. As such it involves a taking as its appendage. However, the taking involved is not the same as stealing; it is also entirely independent from borrowing and totally alien to accepting, especially insofar as the latter entails gratitude, indebtedness and self-effacement. There is simply a *taking* that follows *soliciting*—coming after it—in the place of stealing, borrowing or receiving. This chapter which is inspired as much as by

Melanesian 'spell of the conch-shell' as by case of the vanishing micro-finance moneys in Surabaya, is an attempt is to think about the conditions of possibility of soliciting, itself referring to activities that can be described ethnographically and inscribed with theoretical potential. An anthropology of soliciting aims to deal ethnographically with the ways in which transfers of value are accomplished through means other than those involving contractual obligations stipulating future returns. As such, it calls for an ethnography sensitive enough to avoid succumbing to the logic of the state and evade capture by the apparatus of morality. As a theoretical stance, it calls for due recognition of the application of force necessary in conducting value transfers, affirming rather than negating the violence involved. This affirmation is directly contingent on the violence coming from outside the law and morality, located beyond the space of the state and on the far shores of the self-styled righteous. As the very force that puts time on a different course, this violence promises to make the present pass: by overcoming the normative, disrupting the expected, overthrowing the habitual, it performs the purest of caesuras and accomplishes the most unadulterated of openings to becoming. The violence involved is neither assumed nor achieved; it is neither legitimate nor illegitimate; moreover, it is neither moral nor immoral. Because it is wholly coterminous with *vios* (life) and play; it simply is.[7] To better apprehend the violence at hand, an excursion into Derrida's critique of the Maussian gift is required.

One More Time!

To a certain extent soliciting is closely related to the concept of elicitation Strathern (1988) deployed in her ground-breaking work on Melanesia. Undeniably inspired by Mauss, Strathern advances her own aesthetics of social relations in the region and proposes that they are based on specific modalities of making things known through exchanging valuables and engaging in displays. Strathern takes gift exchange to correspond to 'moments of bursting forth' whereby a specific aspect of a thing or a person is temporarily revealed by means of elicitation. Such revelations, her argument continues, require 'an external audience or partner who, having elicited it, is also the coercive cause of the act' (1988: 297). This partner is of course none other than the donee(s), who, displaying his/her agency, proceeds to draw out the gift, making it part of him- or herself. Elsewhere I have myself taken advantage of Strathern's approach to portray neighbourhood exchanges in Java (Retsikas 2012). More recently, I have however grown wary of elicitation, and this is so for a number of reasons. For one thing, the concept carries echoes of the Socratic Method, the famous *maieutics* deployed in the search for the true and the good—things often taken as identical—through engagements in public debate. Elicitation might thus not be strong enough to break with this tradition. Furthermore, it shies away from coming to full terms with the violence inhabiting its organisation and deployment, and in its close association with performances and displays, it is too enmeshed with public acts. The emphasis on display comes at the expense of more covert, secret and stealthy ways of acting, and of their particular aesthetic and effect.

I have therefore come to prefer, and now wish to propose, the concept of soliciting. Soliciting comes from the vocabulary of Derrida (1978), who deploys it as a synonym for deconstruction. It denotes the shaking of a totality; linguistically, it is composed from *sollus*, which in Latin denotes 'the whole,' and from *citare*, meaning 'to put in motion.' For Derrida, solicitation is threatening to any philosophy or morality, for it entails the possibility of illuminating not only its basic supports and overall architecture, but also that very secret place which any philosophy or morality must hide so as to remain a philosophy or morality. As such it bears the potential of allowing us to see that very part or quality which must be suppressed and excluded in order to constitute truth and the good. Deconstruction is therefore both a philosophical method and a political exercise, for it strives to unhinge our values and draw a line of flight for us to follow, overcoming the present, becoming-other. In this precisely at this point that Derrida's project meets that of Nietzsche; Nietzsche's (2003) credo of the trans-valuation of all values, inclusive of the will to truth, the will to knowledge and the will to good, forms a most significant counterpoint to the contractarian model in the sense of providing a critique of exchange. As I show below, this is the call Derrida responds to, and following him, I do too. In this context, soliciting signifies counter-values as much as the bursting out of suppressed and the un-tamed.

This is how Derrida's translator, Alan Bass, defines solicitation in his introduction to the English edition of *Writing and Difference* (1978):

> Every totality, [Derrida] shows, can be *totally shaken*, that is can be shown to be founded on that which it excludes, that which would be in *excess* for a reductive analysis of any kind. [...] This etymological metaphor covering a philosophical-political violence is also implied in the notion of *archia* [...].

> *Archia* derives from the Greek *archē*, which combines the senses of a founding, original principle and of government by one controlling principle [...]. Philosophy is founded on the principle of the *archia*, on regulation by true, original principles; the deconstruction of philosophy reveals the differential excess which makes the *archia* possible. (1978: xviii)

Derrida's aim is to open things up once again so that we can experience them anew. Part of his strategy is to induce such an intense feeling of aporia and wonder to his readers that a new beginning in philosophy is launched. For this to happen, Derrida dwells on impasses in thought, and ponders over logical impossibilities. By forcibly shaking Western metaphysics, he strives to arrive at a place where the formal rules of logic no longer apply, showing all the while how the 'traditional' conception of phenomena in exclusive terms—that is, as either this or that—is reductionist and founded on exclusions. In place of a metaphysics, then, which approaches truth as contingent on a priori essences and fixed origins, Derrida favours difference, defining phenomena 'inclusively'—that is, as *both* this *and* that—and as always unfolding, shifting, becoming. These tactics permit Derrida to unbound and release the excess that traditional metaphysics has captured and repressed, thus allowing thinking to begin anew.

As is well known, Derrida (1992) has himself solicited Mauss' study and found the repressed element to correspond to what is normally construed as the 'free,' 'pure,' 'selfless' or 'disinterested' gift.[8] According to Derrida, the 'pure' gift remains an impossibility in Mauss' study, for the gift is always conceived as being caught up in the circle of reciprocity. By following a regular movement in time and space as set out in the three obligations, the gift as a spontaneous, 'pre-objective' and un-reflexive gesture towards the other is negated, for it is duly domesticated by the dictates of return. 'If the gift is annulled in the economic odyssey of the circle as soon as it appears *as* gift or as soon as it signifies *itself as* gift, there is no longer any "logic of the gift," and one may safely say that a consistent discourse on the gift becomes impossible: It misses its object and always speaks, finally, of something else' (1992: 24)—that is reciprocity, exchange, contract, debt, sacrifice, the economy and so on.

Reacting to the negation of the gift, Derrida formulates two essential conditions for it to be rethought: (a) that giving must be conceived independently of involving, demanding or anticipating a return; and (b) that for (a) to be possible, both the donee and the donor must not recognise themselves as such. For, the moment such recognition occurs, the gift and the relation to the other it privileges—a relation unburdened by contract, obligation, debt and hierarchy—ceases to exist. On the positive side, Derrida invites one to reconceptualise the gift as contingent on forgetting—the forgetting of the passing of the gift, and the forgetting of that forgetting—arguing that what this double forgetting evinces is something other than a sociological category, a theological name or a philosophical identity. The French philosopher wisely refrains from specifying what this 'something other' might be; instead he employs most general and cryptic terms, writing that it has to do with 'a set of traits defining a given situation in which something, or "that" ["*ça*"] is established (as in expressions "the human condition," "the social condition," and so forth)' (1992: 17).

There is no question that what Derrida is after here is the elaboration of an ethics for living and analysing. Such an ethics he strives to ground on the aporias generated by the gift, for a genuine gift is actually possible only when it is not understood as such. For Derrida, thinking of the gift in these terms is extremely important. It indicates an opening towards realising an immediate relation to the Other that affirms rather than negates his/her alterity. The French philosopher poses this relation as contingent on the 'pure' gift and its double forgetting. What this forgetting ensures is the Other's ontological primacy and political autonomy. In other words, forgetting acts to mitigate the violence that the passing of the gift effects on the other in terms of the ever-present possibility of construing him/her, even momentarily, as a recipient in need and/or beneficiary of one's largesse. The problem Derrida identifies with reciprocity is principally that it places the other into (temporary) debt, making him/her politically inferior and ontologically secondary to, even derivative of, the self. It is precisely this degradation, arising in the unfolding of the social, that Derrida cautions against. So much is apparent in the way Derrida reads 'Counterfeit Money,' where he implicitly counter-poses Baudelaire's story to Mauss' study, and in the way he has elsewhere talked about hospitality (2000) and the ethics of sacrifice (2008).

Derrida's critique of Mauss is worth repeating, for the paradigm *The Gift* has set for anthropology is no easy matter to circumvent. Derrida's argument against reciprocity springs from the recognition of the violence the passing of the gift exacts on the other who, by implication and necessity, is reduced to a beneficiary and aid recipient. Writing some twenty years later, Didier Fassin repeats this very point with further clarity and eloquence in his critique of modern humanitarian governmentality, writing that contemporary global practices of giving dedicated to redeeming the other from poverty, natural disaster and so on, 'institute a radically unequal order that is the mark of the humanitarian relationship—a structural fact regardless of the motivations of the actors. This inequality is unavoidable' (2012: 253). For Fassin, humanitarian reason is permeated by the very paradox Derrida's double forgetting sought to overcome: the very gesture that appears to grant the others recognition as fellow human beings, that is the donor's motion of manifest care, acts at the same time to 'reduce them to what they are not—***and often refuse to be***—by reifying their condition of victimhood while ignoring their history and mutating their words. Humanitarian reason pays more attention to biological life of the destitute and unfortunate, the life in the name of which they are given aid, than to their biographical life, the life through which they could, independently, given meaning to their own existence' (2012: 254, my emphasis).

A series of questions inescapably arise: has Derrida gone far enough in soliciting the hidden presuppositions, and in freeing the potential of the element(s) otherwise suppressed? Is double forgetting potent enough to dispel humanitarian reason? Has Derrida provided us with an alternative way to conceiving the other and the 'social condition'? I would argue that there is still more that needs to be done in our rethinking of the gift, and in our affirmation of the other. The problem is mainly this: the ethics Derrida espouses still pertain to the perspective of the donor, as it is the donor whom Derrida sees as ultimately responsible for the forgetting to take effect. The more successful the donor is in his struggle against the work of memory, the more the violence he/she exercises on the other stands to be allayed and inhibited from breaking out. Derrida therefore evokes a self-disciplining and self-effacing subject, who values the aesthetics of humility and modesty, and is in total control of bodily and mental functions. It is precisely because of such evocations that Derrida's analytics fall back into the trap of reproducing the very asymmetries they endeavour to banish. In other words, the distinction is still on the side of the donor. For it is still the donor who, in instantaneously forgetting the gift, displays an undeniable superiority, itself stemming from his/her intention to save the donee from indebtedness and obligation. The theological–philosophical metaphysics Derrida so thoroughly derides somehow manages to sneak back in.[9] The quest therefore must begin anew: Is there another way for personal responsibility to be conceived? Is there a different manner for the other to become manifest and for an alternative mode of violence to come into play? I would like to think so and will suggest that the answer to these questions hinges on describing the event of time's passing from the perspective of soliciting. The soliciting in question involves secrecy and stealth, and it welcomes the exercise of a force with this secrecy, with this invitation acting as the main channel for affirming the primacy of the Other. A return to ethnography and Java will show us precisely how, despite the problems already identified, we can critically reassert deconstruction, and creatively redeploy and renew Derrida's analytical emphases and political priorities.

Vanishings II

When a relatively new and expensive laptop computer disappeared from the house of Haji Kamil in a well-off neighbourhood in central Surabaya, the haji suspected foul play. Although he was not 100% sure, he put the blame on his security staff, and in particular on a young man he had dismissed the previous week for being lazy and absent-minded. The young man who had barely been at the job for three months had contacts in the city's underworld, the haji asserted, a claim few people in Indonesia would find implausible. However, the haji refrained from contacting the police about the theft. This could have been either because of fear of reprisals from the alleged thief's friends in the criminal underworld, or because of perceptions of the police as reluctant to intervene where there are no additional incentives on offer. And so, the matter of the laptop's disappearance was quickly forgotten, never mentioned again either by the haji or by his family.

A couple of months after the incident, a quite different version of events came to my attention. According to this version, the disappearance of the laptop was not down to theft. The bearer of news was a street food vendor who owned a stall selling chicken soup outside a mosque located a few hundred metres from the haji's house. He too had heard of the disappearance (*hilang*) of the laptop, but he put it down to zakat, the Islamic wealth transfer. According to the vendor, the haji was notorious all over Surabaya for his extravagant lifestyle, numerous and luxurious houses and his taste for sports cars. Additionally, he was known to have recently taken as a second wife a very beautiful and relatively young *dangdut* (a popular music genre) singer. Though the haji owned a large transport company sending off goods to distant ports in Eastern Indonesia, as well as abroad, the vendor claimed that he had gained most of his wealth from lending money on interest. This is a most contentious practice the majority of Muslim jurists classify as unlawful (*haram*), and of which many Javanese strongly disapprove, due its predatory and exploitative connotations, especially when it involves lending to the poor and marginalised. Perhaps to reinforce his point, the vendor portrayed the haji as a mean and stingy person who was moreover indifferent to the goings-on of the neighbourhood, adding that he was known to be negligent in his observance of zakat.[10] He further noted that, in addition to being the duty of well-off believers, which is owed to God, zakat was also the right of the destitute and the poor (*hak fakir miskin*).

The street vendor's comment about zakat being a right is particularly significant as far as soliciting is concerned. For one thing, the vendor's comment echoes normative jurisprudential conceptualisations of zakat as an entitlement (*hak*) pertaining to eight categories of persons, all of which are listed in the Quran.[11] Amongst them, the most important are the destitute and the poor (*fakir miskin).* Furthermore, the vendor's remarks also resonate with another set of views that conceive of wealth, its proliferation and/or disappearance as intimately connected with zakat via the intervention of Allah. Somewhat simplified, such views run as follows: if a well-off Muslim pays zakat as required, one's wealth, affluence, well-being, business and so on will be protected and multiplied by Allah; for Allah rewards handsomely, those who follow His commandments (see Retsikas 2018). However, if a duty-bound Muslim fails to perform zakat worship, his possessions will be destroyed, vanish and/or go missing; for Allah duly punishes those who disobey him. A case in point as to the truth of the latter is related by Brenner in her monograph on the demise of the once affluent *batik* trading families of Solo, Central Java. According to locals of Solo, the non-transfer of zakat by wealthy individuals was causally related to the latter's experience of ill fortune. In particular, Brenner writes that

> There was broad speculation as to what had caused the downfall of this [Atmosusilo] family. A former *juragan* [entrepreneur] of the Kauman suggested this was God's retribution for Atmosusilo's greediness and his failure to give the alms [sic] (*zakat*) required of all Muslims who can afford it. In fact, it was not uncommon to hear devout Muslims from outside the community, Arabs as well as Javanese, remark that the downfall of Laweyan [Brenner's field locality, and Solo's *batik* industry centre] as a whole had been brought about by its residents' unwillingness to give the obligatory alms despite their abundant wealth. (1998: 212)

In this regard, the implications of the vendor's comment—that is that the disappearance of the laptop was related to zakat—could not have been clearer. There was no theft involved at all; the disappearance of the laptop was the result of the exercise of a right (*hak*); the laptop's rightful owner was not the haji, but the person entitled to the haji's zakat. A person probably belonging to the category of the 'destitute and poor' had taken the laptop in place of the zakat that the haji had failed to observe—that is, as his outstanding zakat. Somewhat differently put and allowing for the divine to come into the picture more fully, the vendor's comments could be taken to highlight the following: the laptop had been removed by Allah as retribution for the haji's laxity in performing zakat. Such removal was a stark reminder that he should correct his ways if he did not wish to see his fortunes reversed. Subsequently, the laptop had been allocated to another person; such a person probably belonged to the poor and destitute category. For, according to scripture, the latter count amongst the rightful owners of zakat.

Concerns over wealth, its mode of acquisition and the enforcement of one's rightful share are central to this episode of urban life; so too are imperatives for justice and the requirement for stealth and secrecy in its attainment. In exploring such issues, it is appropriate to remind ourselves that the discourse on zakat as currently promoted in Indonesia and elsewhere, both by activists and Islamic scholars, construes zakat primarily as an obligation and debt to Allah; it is thus conceived as equivalent to a tax levied once a year on certain types of property and at certain rates (al-Qardawi 2000; Mas'udi 2005; see also Benthall 1999). Alternatively, zakat may be construed as alms; in this case it is made equivalent to a hand-out, amounting to a philanthropic activity performed by the affluent for the benefit of the disadvantaged (Bamualim et al. 2006; Latief 2014; Salim 2008; Singer 2008). These two conceptualisations are intimately connected, for the carrying out of zakat as a duty involves the subsequent transfer of the wealth involved to the poor and the needy in the manner of a gift. However, as I showed in Chap. 2, the alternative position of zakat as an entitlement pertaining to specific categories of persons signifies a 'minor' position in the literature, remaining largely unelaborated and inadequately attended to. This 'minor' position is nevertheless acknowledged in many key writings on the subject and is recognised by all the Islamic welfare organisations I worked with in Indonesia. In particular, such 'minor' reading of zakat is admitted in the writings of such luminaries as Sayyid Qutb, the famous intellectual and leading member of the

Muslim Brotherhood in Egypt in the 1950s and 1960s, who notes in passing that zakat 'is as much the right of those who receive it as it is the duty of those who pay it' (2000: 164). For Qutb, zakat is instrumental in the achievement of economic justice as envisioned in Islam, for it corresponds to a mechanism of redistribution. In addition, it effects the 'purification of property itself, because it means paying what is due on the property, after which its possession is legal' (2000: 162). Similarly, Yusuf al-Qardawi, one of the most widely recognised amongst contemporary authorities on zakat jurisprudence, concurs that zakat is indeed a right. This is in spite of the expert jurist advocating that zakat collection should be performed, and enforced, by the state apparatus in all Muslim majority countries, a move that turns zakat into official fiscal instrument and state revenue stream. However, while reflecting on the wisdom found in several Quranic verses dating from the Meccan period, al-Qardawi briefly and casually observes that their aim is to make 'sincere believers realize [that] their wealth is not only for their use. They realize that part of it belongs in fact to the needy not as a charitable gift given with condescendence but as a clear-cut right without humbleness on the part of the receiver or pride on the part of the payer' (2000: 9). This is stance is confirmed by Maulana Wahiduddin Khan, a much respected Indian Islamic scholar, famous for his translation of the Quran to contemporary English, who writes that 'the Qur'an uses the term "*haq*," the right of the poor; so what the wealthy man is asked to give is not charity but that which should come back to the poor, as a matter of right' (2004: 95).

This 'minor' or 'counter-hegemonic' understanding of zakat is affirmed in Java, both by referring to zakat claimants as *mustahiq*, a jurisprudential term literally designating in Arabic those entitled to zakat, and in everyday life every time something goes missing. Three of the most common responses to vanished wealth are that a robbery (*maling*) has taken place; a *tuyul*—a spirit in the shape of a human child—has been at play, acting on behalf of his human master; or that the property in question corresponded to unpaid zakat—that is, zakat due to others. While the first two responses acknowledge an illegal removal, and recognise an illegitimately exercised violence, the third response puts the blame squarely on the person who has yet to transfer the zakat due. Such a person is normally denounced for committing *kurang amal*, that is for having done less than his/her fair share of good deeds, having failed to meet his/her obligations to others.[12] In this context, the non-transfer of zakat is equivalent to theft due to the misappropriation of wealth that is not one's own to retain, but rather another's to dispose and enjoy. The violence recognised by the third response is therefore seen as emanating from the unlawful retention of value and the inappropriate withholding of wealth that belongs to others. In this context the forceful and stealthy soliciting of zakat is on the other side of the illegal and the illegitimate, corresponding to a requirement for the realisation of justice.

Zakat has serious implications for our understanding of property rights in Islam, and Muslim countries in general. Such rights are conceived of and practiced on grounds other than those recognised in liberal political economies that prioritise the human person, and the claims the latter, understood as an individual separate from all other like entities, has to the product of its labour, or to equivalent recompense. As MacPherson (1962) has distinctly shown, exclusive, alienable rights over individually held property emerged in Europe in the seventeenth century as a concomitant of the process that resulted in the historical transition from feudalism to capitalism. MacPherson argues that it was John Locke who articulated most clearly the emerging theory of 'possessive individualism,' according to which each and every individual is endowed with a 'property in his own person,' forming thus a person who legally owns, first of all, his or her own body and all the labour that proceeds from it. While 'possessive individualism' construed land and capital as unequally distributed amongst men, labour as a new kind of property each man was conceived to have, was underscored as universal condition, functioning as the common denominator for an inclusive definition of humanity. In this context, zakat's great conceptual importance is that it severs the connection European Enlightenment and capitalism postulate as natural between the person, his/her labour and the automatic ownership of its products. Zakat is due because the value one generates through one's labour is not one's own to keep (or offer as a gift) as it properly belongs to others. Adjusting our language requires that we speak of wealth transferred (or handed over) rather than given, donated or the like: a *mustahiq* is not a recipient, much less a beneficiary, but a person entitled to a portion of the wealth created. Recognition of the rights of *mustahiq* requires therefore the payment of zakat—that is, the calculation of the exact portion of wealth due to others and of its prompt transfer. According to this perspective, it is only the remainder one can claim to legitimately possess and dispose of; it is only what remains after a process of calculation, division, partition and transfer of zakat has taken place that is legally one's to take hold of, dispose and enjoy. In other words, the kinds of property rights envisioned are neither absolute nor automatic but rather derivative, consequent and contingent on the performance of zakat. Zakat is the cut that forms the grounds on which the person can claim what is left as his/her own. In this context, rightful claims do not accrue mechanically from the labour process but follow upon zakat's estimation, separation and allocation. Moreover, such claims are better understood within a theological context that fully acknowledges Allah as the creator of everything and of humankind as His steward.

Enforcing the *hak* (right) to zakat in the manner of soliciting rests on taking.[13] Such taking neither succeeds giving nor presupposes presenting. It is neither equivalent to receiving, nor does it assume formal accepting. In most general terms, it amounts to a value transfer accomplished by means of craftiness, shrewdness and concealment. Soliciting recognises the other—the one to whom zakat is due—as capable of acting purposefully, effectively and efficiently with a view to seeing his/her divine-given rights restored and respected. Moreover, it entails that the other conducts his/her affairs in such a way that his/her identity remains elusive and secret. Secrecy is also involved in the way value transfers are conducted. The other the forceful taking of zakat brings forth is unknown and unknowable. As such he/she is free from the violence the bestowal of names and the passing of the gift incur on their recipients, who have their identities given and fixed in the very process of giving. In contrast, due to the importance of stealth and concealment, soliciting exceeds pure giving in safeguarding and maintaining the other's primacy. Indeed, the value of concealment is often expressed in Islam when scholars emphasise that giving in secret is often preferable to giving in public. This is because giving in public potentially compromises both *muzakki* (zakat payer) and *mustahiq* (zakat claimant). It allows the *muzakki* to feel important in the presence of an audience, and to gain in status what they 'lose' in wealth; while at the same time it imposes upon the claimants an inferior position, for they are made to look like recipients of aid. In this regard, several Islamic scholars emphasise that transferring zakat with the wrong set of intentions, such as those of pride and self-righteousness, risks invalidating the ritual, possibly transforming it into sin. In surpassing both giving in secret and giving in public, soliciting is always on the side of the other, to whom zakat is due, for it affords him/her unrecognisability and anonymity. By effectively locating the other beyond the grasp of identification, soliciting construes him/her as a known unknown—an ever-present mystery and persistent aporia.

Soliciting is not limited to considerations regarding the gift, but extends to the bazaar economy where encounters between buyers and sellers involve elaborate performances of deference, sweetness, contestation, trickery and force. This much should be apparent to anyone who has spent time in a Javanese or, for that matter, any Southeast Asian market, where intense, lively and often fiercely competitive bargaining takes place between, usually female, sellers and buyers over the price of the goods on offer. In their research on markets in Java, Jennifer and Paul Alexander (1987) have described with great insight the basic contours this alternate soliciting involves, with sellers trying to achieve as high a price as possible through attracting the attention of passers-by, engaging in rapid-fire patter, language level manipulation, regular complimenting, occasional anger and even ridicule (see also Brenner 1998). For their part, buyers' craftiness in acquiring goods for as low a price as possible involves avoiding giving in to seller's bids through interchanging items, walking off, feigning sudden disinterest or requesting extras. Undeniably this is a battle of wills where the rapid valuation of goods is interjected with temporary valuations of the persons involved in terms of their social worth.

Perhaps a most memorable case that exemplifies soliciting in the bazaar relates to Boehari, a primary-level educated food-stall owner, selling fried rice to travellers at the busy Probolinggo—Jember highway in East Java in the late 1990s. Amidst the strong currents of politico-economic change sweeping Indonesia at the time, Boehari's participation in the call for the *reformasi* of the polity combined an everyday implementation of justice with his struggle for making a living. Boehari was charging his customers, most of which were out-of-town travellers, myself included, different prices for the same portion of food depending on his carefully calibrated impression of their relative level of affluence/poverty. An acute sense of self-sufficiency and contentment with one's life was Boehari highly subjective yet admirably consistent approach to pricing. As a response, Boehari's clients would subsequently engage with him in a game of haggling that extended from soft tactics such as feigning surprise at how high the price was, to exasperation and public annoyance, sometimes moving away from his

(*continued*)

(continued)
stall overtly upset at his insistence! To the extent that soliciting is about agonistic value transfers, uncertain values and a valued practice itself, it is of direct relevance to the way the bazaar economy operates, given the latter's embedded-ness in the asymmetric flows making up the social in Java. However, the soliciting I speak of in relation to zakat goes one important step further than that practiced in the market, for it works to ensure the anonymity of the other. In resisting the impulse of objectification, it maintains that the other's identity remains hidden from view. Moreover, the soliciting I highlight here welcomes the force coming from the side of the other, seeking to affirm rather than domesticate or subdue the violence the other brings to the relation, raising it to the nth degree.

Soliciting bypasses considerations of crime, effectively 'bracketing' human law within the demands of justice which, crucially, is of divine inspiration. Enforcing zakat through soliciting is located on the outside of human law, on a vast 'territory' making up a frontier and constituted by a limit. The significance of the limit is to demarcate an exterior and infinite space permeated by otherness: the otherness of the divine, inclusive of the alterity of divine authority. The purpose of the frontier is to guard against a collapse, or breakdown, in the difference between the divine and the human—which for Islam would amount to unbelief, a major sin. When viewed in these terms, it is impossible to equate the removal of wealth through claiming zakat to a crime, for it is simply an act favourable in the eyes of God.[14] As I have already stressed, ***muzakki*** who duly observe their obligations are expected to see their wealth multiplied; in contrast, those reluctant to part with what is due to others will see their wealth reduced. This reduction is not due to criminal activity; rather it is precisely what is necessary for justice to be achieved. The justice in question exceeds any sense of fairness that human beings might conceive or implement; to the faithful, it is the most perfect form of justice, with its unrivalled perfection guaranteed by its emanation from the divine other.

Enforcing this higher sense of justice requires the deployment of stealth and covertness.[15] Concealing the identities of those involved is paramount to its realisation; managing not to exercise violence against the other requires that the identity of *mustahiq* remains hidden and indeterminate. This indeterminacy is accompanied by two further, equally crucial features. First, justice is unavoidable, inevitable and unpreventable; it will be achieved whatever happens. Sooner or later, either in this life or in the next, it will come. To the extent that there is no escape from it, all the future has to offer is to occasion justice, acting as its apposite timing. In this regard, every passing of the present brings justice closer. Second, for this passing to take effect, soliciting has to take place. Soliciting has agency always already located on the side of the other. It is Allah and the *mustahiq* who act. The 'I,' the *muzakki*—that is, the donor—merely re-acts. Both characteristics place soliciting at odds with justice as currently pursued in Indonesia, and elsewhere. In the last decade or so, the enforcement of the right to solicit zakat in the country has been turned into a bitterly fought battle between institutions representing the state and civil society associations (Fauzia 2013; Latief 2013a, b; Salim 2008). The battle revolves around questions over which side is more legitimate in assuming and pursuing zakat's enforcement. On the one hand, advocates for the state eagerly remind the faithful of the example the Prophet set in Medina, where he imposed zakat as state tax. To this, advocates for voluntary associations stress that state officials in Indonesia and elsewhere in the Muslim world are often guilty of dishonest and corrupt usage of public funds. For their part, state advocates worry that the potential for corruption and dishonesty inheres equally in civil society organisations, some of which are alleged to award their managers large salaries and maintain close connections to political parties, especially Islamist ones. In response, zakat activists and relevant civil bodies routinely emphasise the injustices the Indonesian state has perpetrated against its own people, stressing the ways in which state policies are responsible for widespread poverty and mass suffering. Despite their differences, which are both numerous and not insignificant, both sides of the argument purport to act in the name of Allah, to be defenders of *syariah* and natural allies to the destitute and poor. They conceive of zakat justice as realisable and deliverable exclusively through their intermediation, portraying themselves as both central and essential in its dispensation. In this regard, both sides are very similar; by making themselves indispensable in the application of the rights of others, they seek to arrest zakat and its soliciting, domesticate its excess and appropriate its power—including significant financial resources—for own ends. Whether such projects are authoritarian/patrimonial or liberal/neoliberal is not what matters most. What is of utmost concern is that, in constantly referring to *mustahiq* as recipients and beneficiaries—and circulating their images in newspapers, magazines and TV advertisements—both state institutions and civil society bodies perpetrate violence. For, under these circumstances, soliciting is characterised neither by concealment nor secrecy; what is more, the right to zakat is denied as one's own to claim.

Begin the Begin

The issue of zakat and its enforcement must be thought anew, with soliciting pointing a way out of the limits imposed by the state-civil society distinction. By means of artfully carving a space in-between the legal and the illegal, soliciting escapes the sanctions of human law. Indeed, solicitors 'interpret' the law by means of constantly testing its limits, illumining its breaking points and shaking its foundations from within. In addition, they evade succumbing to standards of upright conduct by moving in a lateral, sideways manner, cutting across the hilly terrain of social mores. In the latter respect, recognition of the conceptual and political importance of soliciting requires first and foremost that our conceptualisation on zakat as a gift, and our valorisation of the gift itself, must be constituted anew. For our inquiries have so far been conducted from the perspective of the giver and have uncritically equated giving with morality and civility, the good and the true. This has been the case as much with studies which, following Mauss, equate the gift with reciprocity as with critical re-assessments of the obligation to return such as Derrida's. In counter-distinction, I have highlighted the powers of soliciting and the perspective arising from acts of taking as irreducible and prior to giving. Soliciting comprises the shaking of totalities; as such it violently opens up the space for a new ethics to emerge. This ethics is necessary for both analytical and political purposes. Soliciting demands the radical reconfiguration of the other; it is not enough simply to recast the other from a passive recipient of a generously bestowed gift into an active figure in its presentation. The sweeping move is rather to conceive the other as the cause of, and the occasion for, the self. For the Muslims with whom I am familiar, rights of ownership are established only after the zakat due on the wealth in question has been paid and transferred to those entitled to it. It is on condition of the recognition of other people's rights as prior that one's wealth is bound to subsequently increase. Viewed in this context, the concealment, anonymity and secrecy soliciting affords the *mustahiq* begins to make new sense: for wealth, prosperity, well-being to be achieved, the other must remain inviolate and hidden. For vitality and profusion to come about, the requirement is for the other to endure as the known unknown; this vital excess the other signifies is beyond the goodness of the gift, beyond the honour of the contract, beyond the lights of reason.

Soliciting is beyond our esteemed constants for it is solely preoccupied with the performance of a time synthesis whereby the will to power assumes the predominant role. In this case, the present is made to pass by means of the application of a force that comes from the outside, manifesting itself in an untimely manner, behaving unexpectedly, surprisingly, unforeseeably. The transfer of value soliciting performs amounts to a cut in the flow of time such that it opens the present up to the coming of a future unbound; it is precisely because soliciting differs both from gift-giving and commodity exchange, denoting performances unencumbered by the promise or expectation of a return that it synthesises time differently. In refusing to make reciprocity a key presupposition for the generation of value, soliciting underlines the critical trans-valuation of our values. Reciprocity with its expectation of due returns generates obligations which burden the future with the weight of the present and the past, thus ensuring that the same returns time and again. In this case, the future has been foretold for it has been prefigured to fulfil promises already made. In counter-distinction, soliciting promises no returns; in this way, it acts to sever the conducting of value transfers from the anticipation of an equivalent or greater future yield. It is precisely the promise of no returns that frees the future from the repetition of the present and the past, allowing soliciting to usher in all that is meant to be. Despite its eventful character, soliciting is neither an exceptional nor a rare occasion: in this, it differs from miracles and revolutions. Rather, it corresponds to an ordinary and unmarked occurrence, like a knock on the door or a chance encounter, the full significance of which can only be established a posteriori in terms of the consequences they carry. 'Has the present been left behind, has a new situation arisen, are we in a totally different land?' are the only questions pertinent to soliciting.

If soliciting manages to overcome the present, it is because it comes from the other, signifying other-times and the time of the other. Its openness to whatever the future holds is doubled up by an openness to the agents of the future, the solicitors, the (wo)men without names, the unidentified shakers of the law and morality. What soliciting demands as its analytical due is the recasting of the figure of the donor from a subject who acts in the name of human law, always already on the right side of moral conduct, to a person equipped with the capacity to re-act to untimely events in an affirmative matter. Key in this affirmative attitude is the welcoming of soliciting with its promise of no returns: supporting and encouraging the violent shake-up the other and the future are capable of exercising on what one holds dear is crucial for meeting the challenge each and every unexpected encounter demands of us. To the extent that solicitors provide the occasion for a time synthesis that truly delivers the unending return of the future, one's affirmative stance supplements the operation, completing the move of time's passing. What is at stake here has nothing to do with valorising passivity; far from it. Under the signs of the other and the future, it is the open which is pro-actively affirmed, its powers raised to the highest degree possible. The open inheres and subsists in soliciting for the latter has neither an end nor a beginning. The promise of no returns is repeated time and again; in every turn of its unfolding, soliciting starts anew, beginning afresh.

Notes

1. The term 'untimely' is employed here in conformity with Nietzsche's use of the concept of *unzeitgemässe* in 'Untimely Meditations' (2005). His meditations on his present (mid- to late nineteenth-century Germany) are untimely precisely because of his urgent pre-occupation with the future; as the philosopher of counter-values, Nietzsche sought to ground his critique of the values of his time on a future unburdened by them.
2. The 1989 Religious Judicature Act vests Islamic courts in Indonesia with the substantive jurisdiction and enforcement powers over economic transactions based on Islamic law (Cammack and Feener 2012).
3. One of the most intriguing problems in anthropology is the distinction between gifts and commodities. On the basis of the Maussian paradigm, Gregory for example argued in 1982 for the formalisation of the distinction along the lines of a sharply drawn dualism, writing that 'commodity exchange is an exchange of alienable objects between people who are in a state of reciprocal independence that establishes a quantitative relationship between the exchanged. ... Gift exchange is an exchange of inalienable objects between people who are in a state of reciprocal dependence that establishes a qualitative relationship between the transactors' (1982: 100–1001). However, in 1997, Gregory revised his previous position arguing instead for their contemporaneous existence in most societies. Gregory's redrawing of the distinction was part of a revisionist attitude and the result of the triple realisation that commodity exchange in the West is still embedded within the socius (Granovetter 1985), that gift exchange actually dis-

plays both agonistic and acquisitive tendencies (Weiner 1992), and that, in such circumstances, one and the same article can feature both in commodity and gift exchange (Miller 2001; Addo and Besnier 2008).

4. In this sense, the social cannot be said to derive from gift exchange, for the gift is itself dependent on practices of promising and punishing. This was the thrust of Lévi-Strauss' (1969) argument: in making the incest taboo the starting point of culture, Lévi-Strauss recognised that the law, that is prohibition, provides the necessary ground for exchange to take place, and for the social to come forth. The incest taboo is, in this context, the grounds of a promise: for every woman a man gives up as a partner, another one becomes available by another man.
5. Despite highlighting the tensions and dynamics of agonistic exchange, neither Weiner (1992) nor Beidelman (1989) describe things from the perspective of the would-be gift-receiver. Quite the contrary is true, especially for Weiner, whose keeping-while-giving paradox remains encased within a logic of accumulation that is difficult to disassociate from similar tendencies arising within commodity production. Graeber's (2001, 2011) studies remain closest to Mauss' aims and are similarly motivated by a commitment to socialist ethics or what he calls 'individualistic communism' [sic] (2011: 159). The emphasis is here, once again, on the free and moral individual who gives generously.
6. Such attitude is perhaps nowhere more apparent than in the moral economy approaches of Geertz (1963) and Scott (1976), both working on Southeast Asia, with Java looming large. Such approaches have been rightly critiqued by many for their ideological basis, as they adopt a specific folk model about the ideal shape of social relations, one based on harmony, solidarity and mutual aid, while redeploying it in the guise of sociological account. This selective adoption is conducted on the grounds of a convergence between the analyst's bourgeois ethics of good life and certain peasant models of value. In the end, the treatment of the gift as reciprocity remains wholly subordinate to moral standards uncritically presumed as universal. Here, the moral itself, its conditions of possibility, along with its effects, escape critical scrutiny. Contrary to such approaches, my effort is to highlight soliciting as a practice unburdened by moral questions, precisely because it comes before the gift, amounting to the latter's cause and ground. As such, soliciting serves values other than liberal ones. To achieve this effect I, too, ally myself with certain local perspectives, and use them as the springboard for a more abstract discussion on the stakes involved in making promises, and positioning oneself in time.
7. Agamben (2005), reflecting on Benjamin, reiterates a crucial distinction: mythico-juridical violence is always a means to an end and thus susceptible to legal reasoning; in contrast, 'pure violence' is free from such determinations for it precedes the law and reason, and is as innocent as children's play.

8. For an anthropological critique of Derrida, see Laidlaw (2000). My own position is that Laidlaw has misunderstood Derrida's wider philosophical project and aims. Moreover, Laidlaw's Jain material does not convincingly demonstrate the existence of pure gift in India; because Jain renouncers do bestow their blessing, however inaudible or muffled it is, on those presenting them with food, Laidlaw unwittingly confirms Derrida's position regarding the impossibility of the so-called 'pure' gift.
9. This shortcoming is particularly apparent in 'The Gift of Death' (2008) where Derrida affirms the prophetic figure of Abraham as iconic. For Derrida, Abraham's love of God foregrounds a superior ethics of sacrifice which inaugurates a break away from the ethics of reciprocity permeating everyday human affairs. Abraham's preparedness to give death to his only son is, he writes, 'beyond recompense or retribution, beyond economy, without any hope of remuneration. *In this instant*, God gives him back his son and decides [...] to reinscribe sacrifice within an economy by means of what thence-forth resembles a reward' (2008: 95, emphasis in the original). While 'The Gift of Death' is in continuity with 'Given Time' as far as a critique of reciprocity and an affirmation of the 'pure gift' is concerned, there is no longer in it an emphasis on forgetting, single or double. Indeed, one might argue that Derrida's position has shifted in favour of memory and commemoration as the inscription of the gift relation is represented as irrevocably and irremediably asymmetrical and always on the side of the donor who is this time reconfigured as the Creator and absolute sovereign.
10. As Darmadi (2013) notes for West Java, the figure of the haji is quite often implicated in accusations of social aloofness with rumours linking the attaining of fast wealth with the practise of usury, and of unconstrained desires demonstrated by polygamous lifestyles.
11. These are mentioned *in Surat At-Taubat*, verse 60; they are the destitute, the poor, the zakat collectors, new converts, slaves, debtors, those advancing God's cause and the wayfarers.
12. The flip side of this attitude to wealth is the reward one gets for having performed an unselfish or charitable deed. This reward is commonly denoted by the terms *pahala* and *rezeki* that refer to a gift from God that is also one's due recompense for prior acts of personal sacrifice. While *pahala* refers to credit to be used in the afterlife, *rezeki* is for rewards bestowed in his life. Such rewards include health, longevity, monetary wealth, good fortune in acquiring a spouse and affluence in terms of descendants. Such attitudes have recently been repackaged and propagated anew by Muslim TV evangelist Yusuf Mansur (2008, see Retsikas 2018) and *syariah* entrepreneurship guru Ippho Santosa (2010).
13. Writing with respect to Middle-Eastern societies, Rosen acutely observes that matters of rights are inexorably related to matters of force and its

application. In particular he writes, 'Arabs frequently use the word that is usually translated as 'rights' (*haqq*, pl. *huquq*), but its implications are not the same as the Western idea of a right. [*Haqq*] does not convey the Western sense of an indubitably supportable claim. One only has rights, the Arabs say, to the extent one can enforce them. To be away from your "rights"—that is to be away from your land, the people who support your claim to that land—is to have no right' (2000: 79–80).

14. A verse from the Quran often cited in Islamic circles preoccupied with zakat proclaims: 'Take *sadaqah* (alms) from their wealth in order to purify them and sanctify them with it and invoke Allah for them. Verily! Your invocations are a source of security for them, and Allah is All-Hearer, All-Knower' (At-Taubah 103).
15. Stealth and concealment, which are associated by Nietzsche with a joyful future, are attributes of its prophet, Zarathustra. In Part I, Zarathustra, along with praising the overcoming of the present, is portrayed as joining in stealth: 'Why do you creep about so timidly in the twilight, Zarathustra? And what do you conceal so cautiously beneath your coat? Is it a treasure that was given to you? Or a child that was born to you? Or do you yourself now walk the paths of thieves, you friend of the evil' (Nietzsche 2006: 48).

Bibliography

Addo, Ping-Ann, and Niko Besnier. 2008. When Gifts Become Commodities: Pawnshops, Valuables, and Shame in Tonga and the Tongan Diaspora. *Journal of the Royal Anthropological Institute* 14 (1): 39–59.

Agamben, Giorgio. 2005. *State of Exception*. Chicago: University of Chicago Press.

Al-Qardawi, Yusuf. 2000. *Fiqh Al-Zakat: A Comparative Study of Zakat Regulations and Philosophy in the Light of the Qu'ran and the Sunna*. Vol. 1 & 2. Jeddah: Scientific Publishing Centre King Abdulaziz University.

Alexander, Jennifer, and Paul Alexander. 1987. Striking a Bargain in Javanese Markets. *Man (N.S.)* 22 (1): 42–68.

Bamualim, Chaider, et al., eds. 2006. *Islamic Philanthropy and Social Development in Contemporary Indonesia*. Ciputat: Centre for the Study of Religion and Culture.

Beidelman, Tom. 1989. Agonistic Exchange: Homeric Reciprocity and the Heritage of Simmel and Mauss. *Cultural Anthropology* 4 (3): 227–259.

Benthall, Jonathan. 1999. Financial Worship: The Quranic Injunction to Almsgiving. *Journal of the Royal Anthropological Institute (N.S.)* 5 (1): 27–42.

Bourdieu, Pierre. 1977. *Outline of a Theory of Practice*. Cambridge: Cambridge University Press.

Brenner, Susanne. 1998. *The Domestication of Desire: Women, Wealth, and Modernity in Java*. Princeton: Princeton University Press.

Cammack, Mark, and Michael Feener. 2012. The Islamic Legal System in Indonesia. *Pacific Rim Law & Policy Journal* 21 (1): 13–42.
Darmadi, Dadi. 2013. Mr Hajj, Pak Haji. In *Figures of Southeast Asian Modernity*, ed. J. Barker, E. Harms, and J. Lindquist. Honolulu: University of Hawaii Press.
Deleuze, Gilles. 2008. *Difference and Repetition*. Trans. Paul Patton. London: Continuum Press.
Derrida, Jacques. 1978. *Writing and Difference*. London: Routledge.
———. 1992. *Given Time: I. Counterfeit Money*. Trans. Peggy Kamuf. Chicago: University of Chicago Press.
———. 2000. Hospitality. *Angelaki: Journal of Theoretical Humanities* 5 (3): 3–18.
———. 2008. *The Gift of Death and Literature in Secret*. Trans. David Wills. Chicago: University of Chicago Press.
Fassin, Didier. 2012. *Humanitarian Reason: A Moral Critique of the Present*. Trans. Racheal Gomme. Berkeley: University of California Press.
Fauzia, Amelia. 2013. *Faith and the State: A History of Islamic Philanthropy in Indonesia*. Leiden: Brill.
Geertz, Clifford. 1963. *Agricultural Involution*. Berkeley: University of California Press.
Godelier, Maurice. 1999. *The Enigma of the Gift*. Cambridge: Cambridge University Press.
Graeber, David. 2001. *Toward an Anthropological Theory of Value: The False Coin of Our Own Dreams*. New York: Palgrave.
———. 2011. *Debt. The First 5,000 Years*. Brooklyn: Melville House.
Granovetter, Mark. 1985. Economic Action and Social Structure: The Problem of Embeddedness. *American Journal of Sociology* 91 (3): 481–510.
Gregory, Chris. 1982. *Gifts and Commodities*. London: Academic Press.
Khan, Maulana Wahiduddin. 2004. The Concept of Charity in Islam. *International Journal of Civil Society Law* 2: 93–97.
Laidlaw, James. 2000. A Free Gift Makes No Friends. *Journal of the Royal Anthropological Institute* 6 (4): 617–634.
Latief, Hilman. 2013a. Islam and Humanitarian Affairs: The Middle Class and New Patterns of Islamic Activism. In *Islam in Indonesia: Contrasting Images and Interpretations*, ed. J. Burhanudin and Kees van Dijk. Amsterdam: Amsterdam University Press.
———. 2013b. Islamic Philanthropy and the Private Sector in Indonesia. *Indonesian Journal of Islam and Muslim Studies* 3 (2): 175–201.
———. 2014. Contesting Almsgiving in Post-New Order Indonesia. *American Journal of Islamic Social Sciences* 31 (1): 16–50.
Lévi-Strauss, Claude. 1969. *The Elementary Structures of Kinship*. Boston: Beacon Press.
———. 1987. *Introduction to the Work of Marcel Mauss*. London: Routledge & Kegan Paul.

MacPherson, C.B. 1962. *The Political Theory of Possessive Individualism. Hobbes to Locke*. Oxford: Oxford University Press.
Malinowski, Bronislaw. 1922. *Argonauts of the Western Pacific*. London: Routledge.
Mansur, Yusuf. 2008. *An Introduction to the Miracle of Giving*. Jakarta: Zikul Hakim.
Marx, Karl. 2010. *Capital: A Critique of Political Economy, Vol. 1, Book 1. The Process of the Production of Capital*. Trans. Samuel Moore and Eduard Aveling. London: Electric Book Co.
Mas'udi, Masdar Farid. 2005. *Pajak itu Zakat: Uang Allah untuk Kemaslahatan Rakyat*. Bandung: Mizan.
Mauss, Marcel. 2011. *The Gift: Forms and Functions of Exchange in Archaic Societies*. Trans. Ian Cunnison. Mansfield Centre: Martino Publishing.
Miller, Daniel. 2001. Alienable Gifts and Inalienable Commodities. In *The Empire of Things*, ed. F. Mayers. Santa Fe: School of American Research Press.
Nietzsche, Friedrich. 2003. *The Genealogy of Morals*. New York: Dover Publications.
———. 2005. *Untimely Meditations*. Cambridge: Cambridge University Press.
———. 2006. *Thus Spoke Zarathustra*. Cambridge: Cambridge University Press.
Parry, Jonathan. 1986. The Gift, the Indian Gift and the 'Indian Gift'. *Man (N.S.)* 21 (3): 453–473.
Qutb, Sayyid. 2000. *Social Justice in Islam*. Kuala Lumpur: Islamic Book Trust.
Raheja, Gloria. 1988. *The Poison in the Gift*. Chicago: University of Chicago Press.
Retsikas, Konstantinos. 2012. *Becoming – An Anthropological Approach to Understandings of the Person in Java*. London: Anthem Press.
———. 2018. Multiplication through Division: Value, Time, and Prosperity in Indonesia. *HAU: Journal of Ethnographic Theory* 8 (3): 656–671.
Rosen, Lawrence. 2000. *The Justice of Islam: Comparative Perspectives on Islamic Law and Society*. Oxford: Oxford University Press.
Sahlins, Marshall. 1974. *Stone Age Economics*. London: Tavistock Publications.
Salim, Arskal. 2008. *The Shift in Zakat Practice in Indonesia: From Piety to an Islamic Socio-Political- Economic System*. Chiang Mai: Silkworm Books.
Santosa, Ippho. 2010. *7 Keajaiban Rezeki*. Jakarta: Kompas Gramedia.
Scott, James. 1976. *The Moral Economy of the Peasant: Rebellion and Subsistence in Southeast Asia*. New Haven: Yale University Press.
Singer, Amy. 2008. *Charity in Islamic Societies*. Cambridge: Cambridge University Press.
Strathern, Marilyn. 1988. *The Gender of the Gift*. Berkeley: University of California Press.
Weiner, Anne. 1992. *Inalienable Possessions: The Paradox of Keeping-While-Giving*. Berkeley: University of California Press.

CHAPTER 8

Rewinding the Reel

Throughout the book, I have endeavoured to expound on a metaphysics of time as the never objectifiable depth and unfathomable interval from which objects and subjects, actual and virtual, emerge towards our always already transient and situated apprehension. My guides in this effort have three philosophers and founders of the poststructuralist movement: contrary to the majority of their predecessors, Deleuze, Foucault and Derrida have stubbornly resisted the incorporation of time to thought as an object amongst other objects, refusing to submit temporal succession to a principle, an identity and/or an essence deemed transcendent and a priori. This crucial repositioning of the scholarly task, I have claimed, has yet to be fully appreciated and duly explored in social anthropology, a discipline which has traditionally treated time as derivative of the value of human labour and/or the work of culture representation. Contrary to received disciplinary wisdom, I have reiterated the core poststructuralist position, and have posited time as the irreducible sign of an overflowing excess. Corresponding to the ever-shifting ground of lives unfolding, the ever-mutable earth of lives advancing, time amounts to the constancy of the inconstant in which all life is enveloped. So far, one thing should be apparent: rising the practice of thinking to reflect and reprise the constitution of time, while affirming and releasing its powers, is not a simple or automatic task. It necessitates the recognition of the internal fissuring of time as the very condition of its passing, thus making difference and division, rather than identity and substance, the most appropriate stage for enacting our

K. Retsikas, *A Synthesis of Time*,
https://doi.org/10.1007/978-3-030-34933-2_8

thinking. For this recognition to have any chance to make a difference though, it must be repeated time and again: as a result, the reconfiguration of concepts given, along with the composition of ever new ones amounts to a prerequisite for productively matching the challenge at hand.

In good anthropological fashion, I have relied on first-hand, detailed ethnography to provide the basic materials with which to craft, develop and refine a set of concepts designed in turn, to function as critical supplements to poststructuralist philosophy's own models and theories. Based on a non-secular view of death as an opening to an afterlife as encountered amongst the Muslim faithful in Java at the turn of the twenty-first century, I have proposed *a non-economistic concept of the economy*: complementing Foucault's insistence on conducting genealogical inquiries into the givens of our epoch, I have laid emphasis on the importance of starting from, and staying with, an unrestricted notion of value. In the specific ethnographic case under consideration, such analytical move involved placing economic circulations within the perceived parameters of the cosmos, extending the determination of value well beyond Western liberal concerns over present utility and future exchange, so that it takes full account of the most fundamental uncertainty affecting Muslim believers in the everyday pursuit of livelihood, namely the likelihood of effecting salvation (and avoiding damnation) in the hereafter. What the transfer of value in the name of *zakat* as key aspect of the practice of the faith makes abundantly clear is that salvific concerns are of immediate import, economic *and* otherwise. Such import orients the faithful towards a specific temporal horizon whereby a future-yet-to-be-decided, a future uncertain assumes an unparalleled centrality.

A question arises in this respect: how one is to inhabit time so that the future delivers on its potential? How one is to dwell on time so that the yet-to-come already highlighted as the ultimate source of value hurries the arrival of prosperity, well-being and happiness? If zakat corresponds to a caesura the Muslim faithful insert with great regularity in the flow of time, separating a 'before' from an 'after' while responding to a divine injunction, how are they situating themselves, politically, ethically and ontologically, in the midst of the unfolding of this event so that their proximate and final redemption is a likely occurrence? By means of the deployment of the concept of the synthesis of time I borrowed from Deleuze, I strived to show that each of the agents populating the interval, itself created by the transfer of value as zakat, performs the time synthesis in a distinct and divergent manner. Despite the fact that all the agents involved in the interval, legislating its incidence, managing its manifestation and soliciting its eventfulness, appear to be contemporaries and to exist at the same time, they do nevertheless inhabit time differently and variably. One way to theorise this variance is to say that seeming simultaneity is constantly been undone and overtaken by an *asymmetric heterochrony* occupying its very kernel. As a relation of *relata*, the differential syntheses of time performed by the Indonesian state, the zakat management bodies and the stealthy, anonymous solicitors connect and communicate with one another within the duration marked by the transfer of value. Within such delimited period, the very mode of their evolving connection, that is, the synthesis of the syntheses, is full of asymmetry, incommensurability and disjunction. As a result, their communications know not of a uniform, homogenous time, a time shared and at ease with itself. Instead asymmetric heterochrony generates a time out of joint, a time unhinged, marked by enormous distances and dissenting breaks. It is precisely because each the agents of the interval repeats the caesura under the sign of zakat differently, that their repetitions are related disjunctively: as such, the habitations in question are all true yet their truths are perspectival and positional. The positive lack of a common denominator to act as the ground of a forced commensurability means that the intimate enmity the agents, together with their differential syntheses, maintain with one another replicates time as difference in itself, reinstates time's internal fissure in another register and repeats the interval at the heart of an impossible simultaneity.

Asymmetric heterochrony is set in motion by the zakat conductor (*muzakki*) performing a cut in the wealth s/he possesses, separating the portion that is rightfully his/her to claim from the portion due to others. It is on condition of the performance of this cut that the zakat conductor can envisage a future time when his/her soul will be effectively purified of the adverse debits accumulated, with the remaining wealth becoming blessed for his/her enjoyment to occur. At this precise moment two interventions take place, both of which bear significant time effects. By intervening in the conduct of zakat through appropriate legislative measures, the Indonesian state acts so as to embed zakat and the interval its transfer has generated, in the repetition and perpetuation of the state's own foundation. Arguing that its intervention promotes a zakat-grounded concept of justice to take effect, the state performs a synthesis of time that bounds the future arrival of fairness and prosperity within an enclosure delimited by the monopoly the state enjoys of arbitrating, and enforcing, the line separating the legal from the illegal. The implementation of legal measures in the present amounts to the repetition of a violence enacted in the past:

it is a constant reminder of a deadly force which past unleashing founded the state, acting as the source of its existing powers. Such is the synthesis of time the state performs that the future zakat is destined to bring about, becomes a subordinate dimension to times past, delegated to the role of making the founding violence pass into the yet-to-come, encompassing the upcoming in a tight, asphyxiating embrace.

Zakat management bodies perform a synthesis of time which is entirely distinct when compared to the state's own: theirs is geared towards effecting not the infinite return of a founding violence, but the unending repetition of a present improved. In this regard, their interventions, especially in the field of Islamic micro-finance, are designed so as to open up the door to the yet-to-come envisaged as the source of all that is presently valued, cherished and desired, namely pietistic credit and monetary wealth. By initiating a delay in the dispensation of financial 'aid' and holding fast to the break by implementing training regimes, themselves aiming to create a future generation of Muslim entrepreneurs, Islamic micro-finance performs a cut in time, ***promising*** to deliver the masses of the poor and the underprivileged to a value-added, quantitatively better version of the selfsame present. In the synthesis of time effected, the future rather than being welcomed with everything it has to offer, is instead subjected to a ruthless process of selection: only those components of it that conform and comply to present values and dictates are allowed to pass the strict controls installed at the forward limit of the interval; in contrast, the constituents unsuited to such ends that challenge present standards due to being purveyors of new values, hinge on being actively suppressed and/or outrightly banished. However, the battle for the future as the pure and empty form of time, that is a future undetermined and unburdened by the present and past is yet to be decided. Thanks to the practice of ***soliciting***, a series of anonymous agents work tirelessly to make a difference, acting as the decisive force in catalysing an event, opening up a route towards the unanticipated and the different. By successfully drawing zakat out and productively resisting any assignation of names, remaining unidentified and unidentifiable, solicitors place themselves beyond the reason of the state and outside the purpose of civil society. The practice of soliciting value in unforeseen secrecy conducts a distinctive synthesis of time, avoiding repeating both the violence conserved in law and the morality preserved in the gift. Soliciting amounts to a challenge, equally political, ethical and critical, and an invitation: its methods for transferring value are categorically just, yet also completely involuntary, and even though its happening is untimely and unexpected, soliciting requires no return for its completion to take effect. Its demand for no returns to values already elicited turns the past and the present into subordinate dimensions of a future unknown, amounting to the insertion of a temporal cut that welcomes other times and the time of the others to begin anew.

* * *

It is August 2019 and Joko Widodo, the seventh president of the republic, has just held a press conference in which he announced that East Kalimantan will be the site for the country's new capital. While the relocation of Indonesia's capital to a new site might not be a surprise to many who have followed recent events closely, it nevertheless signifies an important turning point. Jakarta which suffers from severe subsidence, making the coastal city vulnerable to rising sea levels, with its worst-affected neighbourhoods reportedly sinking by 10–20 centimetres per year; Jakarta with its dire problems of air pollution, seasonal flooding and horrendous traffic congestion; Jakarta with its population bursting, presently in excess of 30 million people, sitting on the north-western corner of the most populous island on the planet, sucking energy, money and people from all over the archipelago; Jakarta with its poor urban planning on land that was originally a swamp, the reclaimed, renamed site of Batavia, the capital of the colony of Dutch East Indies, is finally set to make way for another spot situated in another island, away from the majestic Java of old. In his state of the nation speech earlier in the same month, Jokowi reportedly asked all officials and representatives in attendance to support his administration's plan to relocate Indonesia's capital to Kalimantan. 'The [new] capital is not only a symbol of our nation's identity, but also represents our nation's development,' he said at the time, adding that such move 'is for the sake of realizing an equitable and just economy.'[1] The capital's relocation, which is estimated to cost some 30 billion US dollars and is planned to start in 2024 with the transfer of some 1.5 million civil servants to a new administrative centre, promises a new beginning for the relatively young nation. Moving the capital close to the geographic centre of Indonesia's archipelago of 17,000 islands and giving it a technologically smart and environmentally green shape is a political pledge that aims to re-found the nation and the state within a set of future assurances of equality, fairness and opportunity for all its citizens. It is precisely at this instant that another story has begun!

Note

1. https://www.thejakartapost.com/news/2019/08/26/breaking-jokowi-announces-east-kalimantan-as-site-of-new-capital.html?src=mostviewed&pg=/

Bibliography

Abdul-Rauf, Mohammad. 1984. *A Muslim's Reflections on Democratic Capitalism*. Washington, DC: American Enterprise Institute for Public Policy Research.

Abubakar, Irfan, and Chaider S. Bamualim. 2006. *Filantropi Islam and Keadilan Sosial*. Ciputat: Centre for the Study of Religion and Culture.

Addo, Ping-Ann, and Niko Besnier. 2008. When Gifts Become Commodities: Pawnshops, Valuables, and Shame in Tonga and the Tongan Diaspora. *Journal of the Royal Anthropological Institute* 14 (1): 39–59.

Agamben, Giorgio. 2005. *State of Exception*. Chicago: University of Chicago Press.

Al-Ghazali, Abu Hamid Mohammad ibn Mohammad. 1966. *The Mysteries of Almsgiving*. Lahore: Sh. Muhammad Ashraf.

Al-Qardawi, Yusuf. 2000. *Fiqh Al-Zakat: A Comparative Study of Zakat Regulations and Philosophy in the Light of the Qu'ran and the Sunna*. Vol. 1 & 2. Jeddah: Scientific Publishing Centre King Abdulaziz University.

Alexander, Jennifer, and Paul Alexander. 1982. Shared Poverty as Ideology: Agrarian Relationships in Colonial Java. *Man (N.S.)* 17 (4): 597–619.

———. 1987. Striking a Bargain in Javanese Markets. *Man (N.S.)* 22 (1): 42–68.

Alfitri. 2006. The Law on Zakat Management and Non-Governmental Zakat Collectors in Indonesia. *International Journal of Not-for-Profit Law* 8 (2): 55–64.

Ali, Nazim S. 2011. *Shari'a-Compliant Microfinance*. London: Routledge.

Amin, Riawan. 2007. *Satanic Finance*. Jakarta: Celestial Publications.

Anderson, Paul. 2018. "An Abundance of Meaning": Ramadan as an Enchantment of Society and Economy in Syria. *HAU: Journal of Ethnographic Theory* 8 (3): 610–624.

Angelucci, Daniela. 2014. Time. *Deleuze Studies* 8 (3): 324–333.

K. Retsikas, *A Synthesis of Time*,
https://doi.org/10.1007/978-3-030-34933-2

Ansell-Pearson, Keith. 2010. Deleuze and the Overcoming of Memory. In *Memory: Histories, Theories, Debates*, ed. Susannah Radstone and Bill Schwartz, 131–174. New York: Fordham University.

Antonio Muhammad, Syafii. 2008. Islamic Microfinance Initiatives to Enhance Small and Medium Enterprises. In *Expressing Islam: Religious Life and Politics in Indonesia*, ed. Greg Fealy and Sally White, 253–266. Singapore: ISEAS.

Appadurai, Arjun. 2015. *Banking on Words: The Failure of Language in the Age of Derivative Finance*. Chicago: University of Chicago Press.

Asia Foundation. 2013. *Access to Trade and Growth of Women's SMEs in APEC Developing Economies: Evaluating the Business Environment in Indonesia*. Jakarta: Asia Foundation.

Atia, Mona. 2013. *Building a House in Heaven: Pious Neoliberalism and Islamic Charity in Egypt*. Minneapolis: University of Minnesota Press.

Azhar, Rauf. 2010. *Economics of an Islamic Economy*. Leiden: Brill.

Azra, Azyumardi. 2004. Political Islam in Post-Soeharto Indonesia. In *Islamic Perspectives in the New Millennium*, ed. Virginia Hooker and Amin Saikal, 133–149. Singapore: ISEAS.

Bamualim, Chaider. 2009. Islamic Philanthropy in Indonesia: Trends and Challenges towards Social Justice. *Kultur* 4 (1): 75–88.

Bamualim, Chaider, et al., eds. 2006. *Islamic Philanthropy and Social Development in Contemporary Indonesia*. Ciputat: Centre for the Study of Religion and Culture.

Bayat, Asef, ed. 2013. *Post-Islamism: The Changing Faces of Political Islam*. Oxford: Oxford University Press.

Bear, Laura. 2014. Doubt, Conflict, Mediation: The Anthropology of Modern Time. *Journal of the Royal Anthropological Institute* 20 (S1): 3–30.

———. 2016. Time as Technique. *Annual Review of Anthropology* 45: 487–502.

Beatty, Andrew. 2009. *A Shadow Falls: In the Heart of Java*. London: Faber and Faber.

Bedir, Ahmet, and Şahin Aksoy. 2011. Brain Death Revisited: It Is Not 'Complete Death' According to Islamic Sources. *Journal of Medical Ethics* 37: 290–294.

Beidelman, Tom. 1989. Agonistic Exchange: Homeric Reciprocity and the Heritage of Simmel and Mauss. *Cultural Anthropology* 4 (3): 227–259.

Beik, Irfan Syauqi. 2013. *Economic Role of Zakat in Reducing Poverty and Income Inequality. A Case Study in the Province of DKI Jakarta, Indonesia*. Saarbrücken: Lambert Academic Publishing.

Benthall, Jonathan. 1999. Financial Worship: The Quranic Injunction to Almsgiving. *Journal of the Royal Anthropological Institute (N.S.)* 5 (1): 27–42.

Benthall, Jonathan, and J. Bellion-Jourdan. 2003. *The Charitable Crescent: Politics of Aid in the Muslim World*. London: I.B. Tauris.

Berry, Albert, Edgard Rodriguez, and Henry Sandee. 2001. Small and Medium Enterprise Dynamics in Indonesia. *Bulletin of Indonesian Economic Studies* 37 (3): 363–384.

Borsay, Anne, and Peter Shapely, eds. 2007. *Medicine, Charity, and Mutual Aid: The Consumption of Health and Welfare in Britain, c. 1550–1950.* Aldershot: Ashgate.

Bourdieu, Pierre. 1977. *Outline of a Theory of Practice*. Cambridge: Cambridge University Press.

Bowen, John. 1993. *Muslims through Discourse*. Princeton: Princeton University Press.

Brenner, Susanne. 1998. *The Domestication of Desire: Women, Wealth, and Modernity in Java*. Princeton: Princeton University Press.

Bruinessen, Martin van, ed. 2013. *Contemporary Developments in Indonesian Islam and the "Conservative Turn" of the Early Twenty-First Century*. Singapore: Institute of Southeast Asian Studies.

Bryant, Levi. 2008. *Difference and Givenness. Deleuze's Transcendental Empiricism and the Ontology of Immanence*. Evanston: Northwestern University Press.

———. 2019. The Time of the Object: Towards the Ontological Grounds of Withdrawal, online document. https://larvalsubjects.files.wordpress.com/2011/02/timeofobject-10-tex.pdf. Accessed 20 Aug 2019.

Buchori, Abdusshomad. 2011. *Zakat: Sebuah Potensi yang Terlupakan*. Surabaya: BAZ Jatim.

Buehler, Michael. 2008. The Rise of Shari'a by-Laws in Indonesian Districts: An Indication of Changing Patterns of Power Accumulation and Political Corruption. *South East Asia Research* 16 (2): 255–285.

Callon, Michel. 2007. What Does it Mean to Say that Economics Is Performative. In *Do Economists Make Markets?* ed. D. MacKenzie, F. Muniesa, and L. Siu, 311–357. Princeton: Princeton University Press.

Cammack, Mark, and Michael Feener. 2012. The Islamic Legal System in Indonesia. *Pacific Rim Law & Policy Journal* 21 (1): 13–42.

Chapra, Muhammad Umer. 1992. *Islam and the Economic Challenge*. Leicester: The Islamic Foundation.

———. 2014. *Morality and Justice in Islamic Economics and Finance*. Cheltenham: Edward Elgar.

Choiruzzad, Shofwan Al Banna. 2013. More Gain, More Pain: The Development of Indonesia' Islamic Economy Movement (1980s–2012). *Indonesia* 95 (1): 125–172.

Choudhury, Masudul Alam, and Uzir Abdul Malik. 1992. *The Foundations of Islamic Political Economy*. New York: Palgrave.

Çizakça, Murat. 2011. *Islamic Capitalism and Finance: Origins, Evolution and the Future*. Cheltenham: Edward Elgar.

Clark, Janine 2004. Islam, Charity and Activism: Middle-Class Networks and Social Welfare in Egypt, Jordan and Yemen. Bloomington: Indiana University Press.

Constantelos, Demetrios. 1968. *Byzantine Philanthropy and Social Welfare*. Rutgers: Rutgers University Press.

Darmadi, Dadi. 2013. Mr Hajj, Pak Haji. In *Figures of Southeast Asian Modernity*, ed. J. Barker, E. Harms, and J. Lindquist. Honolulu: University of Hawaii Press.
Deeb, Lara. 2006. *An Enchanted Modern: Gender and Public Piety in Shi'i Lebanon*. Princeton: Princeton University Press.
Deleuze, Gilles. 1985. *Kant's Critical Philosophy*. Trans. Hugh Tomlinson and Barbara Habberjam. Minnesota: Minnesota University Press.
———. 1991. *Bergsonism*. Trans. Hugh Tomlinson and Barbara Habberjam. New York: Zone Books.
———. 1992. *Cinema 1. The Movement-Image*. Trans. Hugh Tomlinson and Barbara Habberjam. London: The Athlone Press.
———. 1997. *Cinema 2. The Time-Image*. Trans. Hugh Tomlinson and Robert Galeta. Minneapolis: University of Minnesota Press.
———. 2004. *The Logic of Sense*. Trans. Mark Lester. London: Continuum Press.
———. 2005. *Pure Immanence: Essays on a Life*. Trans. Anne Boyman. New York: Zone Books.
———. 2008. *Difference and Repetition*. Trans. Paul Patton. London: Continuum Press.
———. 2012. *Nietzsche and Philosophy*. Trans. Hugh Tomlinson. London: Continuum Press.
Deleuze, Gilles, and Félix Guattari. 1983. *Anti-Oedipus. Capitalism and Schizophrenia Vol. 1*. Minneapolis: University of Minnesota Press.
———. 2004. *A Thousand Plateaus. Capitalism and Schizophrenia Vol. 2*. London: Continuum Press.
Derrida, Jacques. 1978. *Writing and Difference*. London: Routledge.
———. 1988. *Limited Inc*. Evanston: Northwestern University Press.
———. 1990. Force of Law: The "Mystical Foundation of Authority". *Cardozo Law Review* 11 (5–6): 919–1045.
———. 1992. *Given Time: I. Counterfeit Money*. Trans. Peggy Kamuf. Chicago: University of Chicago Press.
———. 1994. *Specters of Marx: The State of Debt, the Work of Mourning, and the New International*. London: Routledge.
———. 1997. *Of Grammatology*. Trans. Gayatri Chakravorty Spivak. Baltimore: John Hopkins University Press.
———. 2000. Hospitality. *Angelaki: Journal of Theoretical Humanities* 5 (3): 3–18.
———. 2008. *The Gift of Death and Literature in Secret*. Trans. David Wills. Chicago: University of Chicago Press.
———. 2011. *Voice and Phenomenon. Introduction to the Problem of the Sign in Husserl's Phenomenology*. Trans. Leonard Lawlor. Evanston: Northwestern University Press.
Dolan, Catherine, and Dinah Rajak. 2016. Introduction. Toward the Anthropology of Corporate Social Responsibility. In *The Anthropology of Corporate Social Responsibility*, ed. C. Dolan and D. Rajak, 1–28. New York: Berghahn.
Economist. 2011. The Few: A Special Report on Global Leaders. January 22.
Effendy, Bahtiar. 2003. *Islam and the State in Indonesia*. Singapore: Institute of Southeast Asian Studies.

El-Gamal, Mahmood. 2006. *Islamic Finance: Law, Economics, and Practice*. Cambridge: Cambridge University Press.

———. 2007. Mutuality as an Antidote to Rent-Seeking Shariah Leverage in Islamic Finance. *Thunderbird International Business Review* 49 (2): 187–202.

Elyachar, Julia. 2005. *Markets of Dispossession*. Durham: Duke University Press.

Encyclopaedia of Islam. 2012. Second Edition. Brill Online. http://referenceworks.Brillonline.com/entries/encyclopedia-of-islam-2. Accessed 12 Nov 2012.

Fabian, Johannes. 2014. *Time and the Other: How Anthropology Makes Its Object*. New York: University of Columbia Press.

Fassin, Didier. 2012. *Humanitarian Reason: A Moral Critique of the Present*. Trans. Racheal Gomme. Berkeley: University of California Press.

Fauzia, Amelia. 2013. *Faith and the State: A History of Islamic Philanthropy in Indonesia*. Leiden: Brill.

Feener, Michael. 2007. *Muslim Legal Thought in Modern Indonesia*. Cambridge: Cambridge University Press.

Firdaus, Mohammad, et al. 2012. *Economic Estimation and Determinations of Zakat Potential in Indonesia*, IRTI Working Paper Series. Jeddah: Islamic Research and Training Institute.

Formici, Chiara. 2012. Islam and the Making of the Nation. In *Kartosuwiryo and Political Islam in 20th Century Indonesia*. Manoa: University of Hawaii.

Foucault, Michel. 2002a. *The Archaeology of Knowledge*. Oxon: Routledge.

———. 2002b. *The Order of Things*. Oxon: Routledge.

———. 2007. *Security, Territory, Population*. Hampshire: Palgrave Macmillan.

———. 2008. *The Birth of Biopolitics*. Hampshire: Palgrave Macmillan.

Geertz, Clifford. 1963. *Agricultural Involution*. Berkeley: University of California Press.

Gell, Alfred. 1992. *The Anthropology of Time: Cultural Constructions of Temporal Maps and Images*. Oxford: Berg.

Gireudeau, Martin. 2012. Remembering the Future: Entrepreneurship Guidebooks in the US, from Meditation to Method (1945–1975). *Foucault Studies* 13: 40–26.

Godelier, Maurice. 1999. *The Enigma of the Gift*. Cambridge: Cambridge University Press.

Goenka, Aditya, and David Henley. 2010. *Southeast Asia's Credit Revolution: From Moneylenders to Microfinance*. London: Routledge Studies in the Growth Economies of Asia.

Graeber, David. 2001. *Toward an Anthropological Theory of Value: The False Coin of Our Own Dreams*. New York: Palgrave.

———. 2011. *Debt. The First 5,000 Years*. Brooklyn: Melville House.

Granovetter, Mark. 1985. Economic Action and Social Structure: The Problem of Embeddedness. *American Journal of Sociology* 91 (3): 481–510.

Green, Micheal, and Matthew Bishop. 2008. *Philanthrocapitalism*. London: Bloomsbury Press.

Gregory, Chris. 1982. *Gifts and Commodities*. London: Academic Press.

———. 1997. *Savage Money*. Amsterdam: Hardwood Academic Press.

Grell, Ole Peter, and Andrew Cunningham, eds. 1997. *Healthcare and Poor Relief in Protestant Europe: 1500–1600*. London: Routledge.

Guyer, Jane. 2007. Prophecy and the Near Future: Thoughts on Macroeconomic, Evangelical, and Punctuated Time. *American Ethnologist* 34 (3): 409–421.

Hafidhuddin, Didin. 2002. *Zakat dalam Perekonomian Modern*. Jakarta: Gema Insani.

Halimatusa'diyah, Iim. 2015. Zakat and Social Protection: The Relationship Between Socio-Religious CSOs and the Government of Indonesia. *Journal of Civil Society* 11 (1): 79–99.

Hallaq, Wael. 1997. *A History of Islamic Legal Theories: An Introduction to Sunnī uṣūl al-fiqh*. Cambridge: Cambridge University Press.

———. 2001. *Authority, Continuity, and Change in Islamic Law*. Cambridge: Cambridge University Press.

Hamann, Byron. 2016. How to Chronologize with a Hammer, Or, the Myth of Homogenous, Empty Time. *HAU: Journal of Ethnographic Theory* 6 (1): 261–292.

Harper, Malcolm. 2017. What Do the Cases Tell Us? In *Islamic Microfinance: Shari'ah Compliant and Sustainable?* ed. Malcolm Harper and Ajaz Ahmed Khan. London: The Schumacher Centre, Practical Action Publishing.

Harper, Malcolm, and Ajaz Ahmed Khan. 2017. *Islamic Microfinance: Shari'ah Compliant and Sustainable?* London: The Schumacher Centre, Practical Action Publishing.

Harvey, David. 2005. *A Brief History of Neoliberalism*. Oxford: Oxford University Press.

Hasan, Noorhaidi. 2009a. *Islamist Party, Electoral Politics, and Da'wa Mobilisation Among Youth*. Singapore: RSIS Working Paper.

———. 2009b. The Making of Public Islam: Piety, Agency, and Commodification on the Landscape of the Indonesian Public Sphere. *Contemporary Islam* 3: 229–250.

Hefner, Robert. 1987. Islamizing Java? Religion and Politics in Rural East Java. *Journal of Asian Studies* 46 (3): 533–554.

———. 1997. Markets and Justice for Muslim Indonesians. In *Market Cultures: Society and Morality in the New Asian Capitalisms*, ed. R. Hefner. Boulder: Westview Press.

———. 2000. *Civil Islam: Muslims and Democratization Indonesia*. Princeton: Princeton University Press.

———. 2003. Islamizing Capitalism: On the Founding of Indonesia's First Islamic Bank. In *Shari'a and Politics in Modern Indonesia*, ed. A. Salim and A. Azra, 148–167. Singapore: Institute of South East Asian Studies.

———. 2006. Islamic Economics and Global Capitalism. *Society* 44 (1): 16–22.

Hendrick, Joshua. 2013. *Gülen: The Ambiguous Politics of Market Islam in Turkey and the World*. New York: New York University Press.
Henley, David. 2010. Microfinance in Indonesia: Evolution and Revolution, 1900–2000. In *Southeast Asia's Credit Revolution: From Moneylenders to Microfinance*, ed. Aditya Goenka and David Henley. London: Routledge.
Himpunan Fatwa Majelis Ulama Indonesia (Collection of Rulings Issued by the Indonesian Council of Islamic Scholars). 2003. Jakarta: The Ministry of Religion, The Republic of Indonesia.
Hirschkind, C. 2006. *The Ethical Soundscape: Cassette Sermons and Islamic Counterpublics*. New York: Columbia University Press.
Hodge, Joanna. 2007. *Derrida on Time*. Abingdon: Routledge.
Hoesterey, James. 2015. *Rebranding Islam: Piety, Prosperity, and a Self-Help Guru*. Stanford: Stanford University Press.
Hooker, M.B. 2008. *Indonesian Syariah: Defining a National School of Islamic Law*. Singapore: Institute of Southeast Asian Studies.
Hospes, Otto, and Hotze Lont. 2004. *Livelihood and Microfinance: Anthropological and Sociological Perspectives on Savings and Debt*. Chicago: University of Chicago Press.
Ibrahim, Barbara, and Dina Sherif. 2008. *From Charity to Social Change: Trends in Arab Philanthropy*. Cairo: The American University of Cairo Press.
Ismail, Salwa. 2013. Piety, Profit and the Market in Cairo: A Political Economy of Islamisation. *Contemporary Islam* 7 (1): 107–128.
Ismal, Rifki. 2013. *Islamic Banking in Indonesia: New Perspectives on Monetary and Financial Issues*. New York: Wiley.
Jahar, Asep Saepudin. 2006. The Clash of Muslims and the State: Waqf and Zakat in Post-Independence Indonesia. *Studia Islamika* 13 (3): 353–395.
Joll, Christopher. 2012. *Muslim Merit-Making in Thailand's Far-South*. Dordrecht: Springer.
Kahf, Monzer. 1989. Zakat: Unresolved Issues in Contemporary Fiqh. *Journal of Islamic Economics* 2 (1): 1–22.
Kahn, Victoria. 2004. *Wayward Contracts: The Crisis of Political Obligation in England, 1640–1674*. Princeton: Princeton University Press.
Katz, Marion. 2007. *The Birth of the Prophet Muhammad*. London: Routledge.
Khan, Maulana Wahiduddin. 2004. The Concept of Charity in Islam. *International Journal of Civil Society Law* 2: 93–97.
Khan, Ajaz Ahmed. 2008. Islamic Microfinance: Theory. In *Policy and Practice*. Islamic Relief: Birmingham.
Khouj, Abdullah Muhammad. 1992. *The End of the Journey: An Islamic Perspective on Death and the Afterlife*. Washington, DC: Islamic Centre.
Kloos, David. 2017. *Becoming Better Muslims: Religious Authority and Ethical Improvement in Aceh, Indonesia*. Princeton: Princeton University Press.

Kochuyt, Thierry. 2009. God, Gifts and Poor People: On Charity in Islam. *Social Compass* 56 (1): 98–116.

Kuran, Timur. 2004. *Islam and the Mammon: The Economic Predicaments of Islamism*. Princeton: Princeton University Press.

Kurniawati, H., ed. 2005. *Muslim Philanthropy. Potential and Reality of Zakat in Indonesia. Survey Results in Ten Cities*. Depok: PIRAC/Ford Foundation.

Kusno, Abidin. 2012. Housing the Margin: Perumahan Rakyat and the Future Urban Form of Jakarta. *Indonesia* 94: 23–56.

Kustin, Bridget. 2015. *Islamic (Micro)Finance: Culture, Context, Promise, Challenges*. Seattle: Bill & Melinda Gates Foundation.

———. 2017. *Islamic (Micro)Finance and the Possibility of Justice*. PhD Thesis, John Hopkins University.

Laidlaw, James. 2000. A Free Gift Makes No Friends. *Journal of the Royal Anthropological Institute* 6 (4): 617–634.

Latief, Hilman. 2012. *Islamic Charities and Social Activism: Welfare, Dakwah and Politics in Indonesia*. PhD Thesis, Utrecht University.

———. 2013a. Islam and Humanitarian Affairs: The Middle Class and New Patterns of Islamic Activism. In *Islam in Indonesia: Contrasting Images and Interpretations*, ed. J. Burhanudin and Kees van Dijk. Amsterdam: Amsterdam University Press.

———. 2013b. Islamic Philanthropy and the Private Sector in Indonesia. *Indonesian Journal of Islam and Muslim Studies* 3 (2): 175–201.

———. 2014. Contesting Almsgiving in Post-New Order Indonesia. *American Journal of Islamic Social Sciences* 31 (1): 16–50.

Latour, B. 1993. *We Have Never Been Modern*. Cambridge, MA: Harvard University Press.

Leeuwen, van Bas. 2016. The Development of Inequality and Poverty in Indonesia. *Bulletin of Indonesian Economic Studies* 52 (3): 379–402.

Lemke, Thomas. 2001. 'The Birth of Biopolitics': Michel Foucault's Lecture at the Collège de France on Neo-Liberal Governmentality. *Economy and Society* 30 (2): 190–207.

Lévi-Strauss, Claude. 1969. *The Elementary Structures of Kinship*. Boston: Beacon Press.

———. 1987. *Introduction to the Work of Marcel Mauss*. London: Routledge & Kegan Paul.

Li, Tania Murray. 2006. *Neo-liberal Strategies of Government through Community: The Social Development Program of the World Bank in Indonesia*. International Law and Justice Working Papers No. 2.

———. 2007. *The Will to Improve: Governmentality, Development, and the Practice of Politics*. Durham: Duke University Press.

Liddle, William. 1996. The Islamic Turn in Indonesia: A Political Explanation. *Journal of Asian Studies* 55 (3): 613–634.

Linant de Bellefonds, Yvon. 2012. Hiba. In *Encyclopaedia of Islam, Second Edition*, ed. P. Bearman, Th. Bianquis, C.E. Bosworth, E. van Donzel and W.P. Heinrichs. Consulted online on 13 June 2018. https://doi.org/10.1163/1573-3912_islam_COM_0283

Lindsey, Tim. 2012a. Islam, Law and the State in Southeast Asia. In *Volume 1: Indonesia*. London: Tauris.

———. 2012b. Between Piety and Prudence: State Syariah and the Regulation of Islamic Banking in Indonesia. *Sydney Law Review* 34: 106–127.

LiPuma, Edward. 2017. *The Social Life of Financial Derivatives*. Durham: Duke University Press.

Lubis, Nur. 2004. Financial Activism Among Indonesian Muslims. In *Islamic Perspectives on the New Millennium*, ed. Virginia Hooker and Amin Saikal, 91–112. Singapore: ISEAS.

MacPherson, C.B. 1962. *The Political Theory of Possessive Individualism. Hobbes to Locke*. Oxford: Oxford University Press.

Madjid, Nurcholish. 2001. Potential Islamic Doctrinal Resources for the Establishment and Appreciation of the Modern Concept of Civil Society. In *Islam and Civil Society in Southeast Asia*, ed. M. Nakamura, S. Siddique, and B. Omar Farouk. Singapore: Institute of Southeast Asian Studies.

Mahmood, Saba. 2005. *Politics of Piety. The Islamic Revival and the Feminist Subject*. Princeton: Princeton University Press.

Mahmud, Mek Wok, and Saued Sikandar Shah. 2009. The Use of Zakat Revenue in Islamic Financing: Jurisprudential Debate and Practical Feasibility. *Studies in Islam and the Middle East* 6 (1): 15–30.

Malinowski, Bronislaw. 1922. *Argonauts of the Western Pacific*. London: Routledge.

Manning, Chris. 1988. *The Green Revolution, Employment, and Social Change in Rural Java*. Singapore: Institute of Southeast Asian Studies.

Mansur, Yusuf. 2008. *An Introduction to the Miracle of Giving*. Jakarta: Zikul Hakim.

Marsden, Magnus. 2005. *Living Islam*. Cambridge: Cambridge University Press.

Marx, Karl. 2010. *Capital: A Critique of Political Economy, Vol. 1, Book 1. The Process of the Production of Capital*. Trans. Samuel Moore and Eduard Aveling. London: Electric Book Co.

Mas'udi, Masdar Farid. 1991. *Agama Keadilan: Risalah Zakat (Pajak) dalam Islam*. Jakarta: P3M.

———. 2005. *Pajak itu Zakat: Uang Allah untuk Kemaslahatan Rakyat*. Bandung: Mizan.

Maududi, Maulana Sayyid Abul Ala. 2011. *First Principles of Islamic Economics*. Leicester: Islamic Foundation.

Maurer, Bill. 2002. Repressed Futures: Financial Derivatives' Theological Unconscious. *Economy and Society* 31 (1): 15–36.

———. 2005. *Mutual Life, Limited: Islamic Banking, Alternative Currencies, Lateral Reason*. Princeton: Princeton University Press.

———. 2006. *Pious Property: Islamic Mortgages in the United States*. New York: Russell Sage Foundation.

Mauss, Marcel. 2003. *On Prayer*. New York: Durkheim Press.

———. 2011. *The Gift: Forms and Functions of Exchange in Archaic Societies*. Trans. Ian Cunnison. Mansfield Centre: Martino Publishing.

Miller, Daniel. 2001. Alienable Gifts and Inalienable Commodities. In *The Empire of Things*, ed. F. Mayers. Santa Fe: School of American Research Press.

Mills, Paul, and John Presley. 1999. *Islamic Finance: Theory and Practice*. Basingstoke: Macmillan.

Miranti, Riyana. 2017. Understanding the Relationships between Development Factors and Regional Poverty: What Have We Learned from Indonesia. *Journal of Poverty* 21 (6): 483–507.

Mittermaier, Amira. 2013. Trading with God: Islam, Calculation, Excess. In *A Companion to the Anthropology of Religion*, ed. Janice Boddy and Micheal Lambek, 274–293. Somerset: Wiley.

———. 2014. Beyond Compassion: Islamic Voluntarism in Egypt. *American Ethnologist* 41 (3): 518–531.

Miyazaki, Hirokazu. 2007. Between Arbitrage and Speculation: An Economic of Belief and Doubt. *Economy and Society* 36 (3): 396–415.

Monaghan, Lee, and Michael O' Flynn. 2012. The Madoffization of Society: A Corrosive Process in an Age of Fictitious Capital. *Critical Sociology* 39 (6): 869–887.

Moosa, Ebrahim. 1999. Languages of Change in Islamic Law: Re-Defining Death in Modernity. In *Perspectives on Islamic Law, Justice and Society*, ed. R.S. Khare, 161–197. Boulder: Rowman & Littlefield.

Mudzakir, Ro'fah. 2005. The Indonesian Women's Movement and the Issue of Polygamy. In *Approaches to the Qur'an in Contemporary Indonesia*, ed. Abdullah Saeed. Oxford: Oxford University Press.

Muehlebach, Andrea. 2013. The Catholicization of Neoliberalism: On Love and Welfare in Lombardy, Italy. *American Anthropologist* 115 (3): 452–465.

Mufti, Imam Kamil. 2015. Belief in Life After Death. https://www.islamreligion.com/articles/38/belief-in-life-after-death/. Accessed 5 Apr 2019.

Munir, Lily Zakiyah. 2005. Islam and Gender: Reading Equality and Patriarchy. In *Islam in Southeast Asia: political, social and strategic challenges for the 21st century*, ed. K.S. Nathan and Mohammad Hashim Kamali. Singapore: Institute of Southeast Asian Studies.

Munn, Nancy. 1992. The Cultural Anthropology of Time: A Critical Essay. *Annual Review of Anthropology* 21: 93–123.

Nickel, Patricia, and Angela Eikenberry. 2009. A Critique of the Discourse of Marketized Philanthropy in Fast Capitalism. *The American Behavioral Scientist* 52 (7): 974–989.

Nietzsche, Friedrich. 2003. *The Genealogy of Morals*. New York: Dover Publications.

———. 2005. *Untimely Meditations*. Cambridge: Cambridge University Press.

———. 2006. *Thus Spoke Zarathustra*. Cambridge: Cambridge University Press.

Njoto-Feillard, Gwenaël. 2004. Insuffler l'Esprit du Capitalisme à l'Umma: La Formation d'une 'Éthique Islamique du Travail en Indonesie. *Critique Internationale* 25: 93–116.

———. 2012. *L'Islam et la Réinvention du Capitalisme en Indonésie*. Paris: Karthala.

Noble Qur'an, the: English Translation of the Meanings and Commentary. Madinah: King Fahd Complex.

Obaidullah, Mohammed, and Hajah Salma Haji Abdul Latiff. 2008. *Islamic Finance for Micro and Medium Enterprises*. Jedda: Islamic Research and Training Institute, Islamic Development Bank.

Obaidullah, Mohammed, and Tariqullah Khan. 2008. *Islamic Microfinance Development: Challenges and Initiatives*. Jeddah: Islamic Research and Training Institute, The Islamic Development Bank.

Oliver, Bert. 2016. Deleuze's "Crystals of Time", Human Subjectivity and Social History. *Phronimon* 17 (1): 1–32.

Ortiz, Horacio. 2014. The Limits of Financial Imagination: Free Investors, Efficient Markets, and Crisis. *American Anthropologist* 116 (1): 38–50.

Osella, Filippo, and Caroline Osella. 2009. Muslim Entrepreneurs in Public Life between India and the Gulf: Making Good and Doing Good. *Journal of the Royal Anthropological Institute* 15 (S1): S202–S221.

Osella, Filippo, and Tom Widger. 2018. 'You Can Give Even If You Have Only Ten Rupees': Muslim Charity in a Colombo Housing Scheme. *Modern Asian Studies* 52 (1): 297–324.

Oualaalou, David. 2018. The Afterlife and Death: An Islamic Perspective. In *The Routledge Handbook of Death and the Afterlife*, ed. Cadi K. Cann, 356–365. London: Routledge.

Parinduri, Rasyad. 2014. Family Hardship and the Growth of Micro and Small Firms in Indonesia. *Bulletin of Indonesian Economic Studies* 50 (1): 53–73.

Parry, Jonathan. 1986. The Gift, the Indian Gift and the 'Indian Gift'. *Man (N.S.)* 21 (3): 453–473.

Permata, Ahmad. 2008. *Islamist Party and Democratic Participation*. PhD Thesis, Westfälischen Wilhelms-Universität, Munster.

Philipp, Thomas. 1990. The Idea of Islamic Economics. *Die Welt des Islams* XXX: 117–139.

Powell, Russell. 2009. Zakat: Drawing Insights for Legal Theory and Economic Policy from Islamic Jurisprudence. *University of Pittsburgh Tax Review* 7 (43): 43–101.

Qutb, Sayyid. 2000. *Social Justice in Islam*. Kuala Lumpur: Islamic Book Trust.

Rahardjo, Dawan. 2003. Filantropi Islam dan Keadilan Sosial: Mengurai Kebingungan Epistemologis. In *Berderma Untuk Semua*, ed. Idris Thaha, xxxiii–xxxxxv. Jakarta: CLC.

Raheja, Gloria. 1988. *The Poison in the Gift*. Chicago: University of Chicago Press.

Rais, Amien Muhammad. 1987. *Cakrawala Islam antara Cita dan Fakta*. Bandung: Mizan.

———. 1998. *Tauhid Sosial: Formula Menggempur Kesenjangan*. Bandung: Mizan.

Retsikas, Konstantinos. 2007. Being and Place: Movement, Ancestors, and Personhood in East Java, Indonesia. *Journal of the Royal Anthropological Institute* 13 (4): 969–986.

———. 2012. *Becoming – An Anthropological Approach to Understandings of the Person in Java*. London: Anthem Press.

———. 2014. Re-conceptualising Zakat in Indonesia: Worship, Philanthropy, and Rights. *Indonesia and the Malay World* 42 (124): 337–357.

———. 2015. The Promise: Islamic Micro-Finance and the Synthesis of Time. *Deleuze Studies* 9 (4): 475–502.

———. 2018. Multiplication through Division: Value, Time, and Prosperity in Indonesia. *HAU: Journal of Ethnographic Theory* 8 (3): 656–671.

Retsikas, Konstantinos, and Magnus Marsden 2018. Alternate Modes of Prosperity. In *Invisible Hands of Life: Alternate Modes of Prosperity*, ed. K. Retsikas and M. Marsden. HAU: Journal of Ethnographic Theory (Special Section) 8 (3): 596–609.

Reynolds, Jack. 2004. Derrida and Deleuze on Time, the Future, and Politics. *Borderlands* 3 (1). borderlands.net.au/vol3no1_2004/reynolds_time.htm. Accessed 11 Apr 2018.

Ricklefs, Merle. 2012. *Islamisation and Its Opponents in Java: A Political, Social, Cultural and Religious History, c. 1930 to Present*. Singapore: National University of Singapore Press.

Riesebrodt, Martin. 2010. *The Promise of Salvation: A Theory of Religion*. Chicago: Chicago University Press.

Rifki, Ismal. 2013. *Islamic Banking in Indonesia*. Singapore: Wiley.

Riles, Annalise. 2004. Real Time: Unwinding Technocratic and Anthropological Knowledge. *American Ethnologist* 31 (3): 392–405.

Robinson, Kathryn. 2007. Islamic Influences on Indonesian Feminism. In *Identifying with Freedom: Indonesia after Suharto*, ed. Tony Day. New York: Berghahn Books.

Robinson, Kathryn, and Sharon Bessell. 2002. *Women in Indonesia: Gender, Equity and Development*. Singapore: ISEAS.

Robinson, Richard, and Hadiz Vedi. 2013. The Political Economy of Oligarchy and the Reorganisation of Power in Indonesia. *Indonesia* 96: 33–56.

Rosen, Lawrence. 2000. *The Justice of Islam: Comparative Perspectives on Islamic Law and Society*. Oxford: Oxford University Press.

Rosenthal, F., C.E. Bosworth, J. Wansbrough, G.S. Colin, H. Busse, and B. Spuler. 2012. Hiba. In *Encyclopaedia of Islam, Second Edition*, ed. P. Bearman, Th.

Bianquis, C.E. Bosworth, E. van Donzel and W.P. Heinrichs. Consulted online on 13 June 2018. https://doi.org/10.1163/1573-3912_islam_COM_0282

Rosser, Andrew, and Donni Edwin. 2010. The Politics of Corporate Social Responsibility in Indonesia. *The Pacific Review* 23 (1): 1–22.

Rousseau, Jean Jacque. 1997. *The Social Contract and Other Later Political Writings*. Ed. and Trans. Victor Gourevitch. Cambridge: Cambridge University Press.

Rudnyckyj, Daromir. 2011. *Spiritual Economies: Islam, Globalisation and the Afterlife of Development*. Ithaca: Cornell University Press.

———. 2014. Economy in Practice: Islamic Finance and the Problem of Market Reason. *American Ethnologist* 41 (1): 110–127.

———. 2019. *Beyond Debt: Islamic Experiments in Global Finance*. Chicago: University of Chicago Press.

Rustomji, Nerina. 2009. *The Garden and the Fire: Heaven and Hell in Islamic Culture*. New York: Columbia University Press.

Saeed, Abdullah. 2004. Islamic Banking and Finance: In Search of a Pragmatic Model. In *Islamic Perspectives on the New Millennium*, ed. Virginia Hooker and Amin Saikal, 113–132. Singapore: ISEAS.

Sahlins, Marshall. 1974. *Stone Age Economics*. London: Tavistock Publications.

Sakai, Minako. 2008. Community Development through Islamic Microfinance: Serving the Financial Needs of the Poor in a Visible Way. In *Expressing Islam: Religious Life and Politics in Indonesia*, ed. Greg Fealy and Sally White, 267–285. Singapore: ISEAS.

———. 2010. Growing Together in Partnership: Women's Views of the Business Practices of Islamic Savings and Credit Cooperatives (*Baitul Maal wat Tamwil*) in Central Java, Indonesia. *Women's Studies International Forum* 33 (4): 412–421.

———. 2014. Establishing Social Justice Through Financial Inclusivity: Islamic Propagation by Islamic Savings and Credit Cooperatives in Indonesia. *TRaNS: Trans-Regional and -National Studies of Southeast Asia* 2 (2): 201–222.

Sakai, Minako, and Amelia Fauzia. 2016. Performing Muslim Womanhood: Muslim Business Women Moderating Islamic Practices in Contemporary Indonesia. *Islam and Christian-Muslim Relations* 27 (3): 229–249.

Salim, Arskal. 2008. *The Shift in Zakat Practice in Indonesia: From Piety to an Islamic Socio-Political- Economic System*. Chiang Mai: Silkworm Books.

Salim, Delmus Puneri. 2015. *The Transnational and the Local in the Politics of Islam: The Case of West Sumatra, Indonesia*. Dordrecht: Springer.

Sandi, Rio, and Ajaz Ahmed Khan. 2017. Co-Operative Islamic Microfinance: Daarl Qu'ran BMT from Jakarta, Indonesia. In *Islamic Microfinance: Shari'ah Compliant and Sustainable?* ed. M. Harper and A.A. Khan. London: The Schumacher Centre, Political Action Publishing.

Santosa, Ippho. 2010. *7 Keajaiban Rezeki*. Jakarta: Kompas Gramedia.

Sarif, Suhaili, and Nor Azzah Kamri. 2009. A Theoretical Discussion of Zakat for Income Generation and Its Fiqh Issues. *Shariah Journal* 17 (3): 457–500.

Schielke, Samuli. 2009. Being Good in Ramadan: Ambivalence, Fragmentation, and the Moral Self in the Lives of Young Egyptians. *Journal of the Royal Anthropological Institute (N.S.)* 15 (S1): S24–S40.

Scott, James. 1976. *The Moral Economy of the Peasant: Rebellion and Subsistence in Southeast Asia*. New Haven: Yale University Press.

———. 1987. Resistance without Protest and without Organisation: Peasant Opposition to Zakat in Malaysia and the Christian Tithe. *Comparative Studies in Society and History* 29 (3): 417–452.

Seibel, Hans Dieter. 2012. Islamic Microfinance in Indonesia: The Challenge of Institutional Diversity, Regulation and Supervision. In *Shari'a-Compliant Microfinance*, ed. S. Nazim Ali. London: Routledge.

Siddiqi, Muhammad Nejatullah. 1983. *Issues in Islamic Banking*. Leicester: Islamic Foundation.

———. 2006. Islamic Banking and Finance in Theory and Practice: A Survey of State of the Art. *Islamic Economic Studies* 13 (2): 1–48.

Simon, Gregory. 2009. The Soul Freed of Cares? Islamic Prayer, Subjectivity, and the Contradictions of Moral Selfhood in Minangkabau, Indonesia. *American Ethnologist* 36 (2): 258–275.

Simone, Abdoumaliq. 2013. Cities of Uncertainty: Jakarta, the Urban Majority, and Inventive Political Technologies. *Theory, Culture & Society* 30 (7/8): 243–263.

Singer, Amy. 2008. *Charity in Islamic Societies*. Cambridge: Cambridge University Press.

Sloane, Patricia. 1999. *Islam, Modernity and Entrepreneurship Among the Malays*. New York: St Martin's Press.

———. 2011. Working in the Islamic Economy: Sharia-ization and the Malaysian Workplace. *Sojourn* 26 (2): 304–334.

———. 2017. *Corporate Islam: Sharia and the Modern Workplace*. Cambridge: Cambridge University Press.

Smith, Jane Idleman, and Yvonne Yazbeck Haddad. 2002. *The Islamic Understanding of Death and Resurrection*. Oxford: Oxford University Press.

Soemitra, Andri. 2016. Higher Objectives of Islamic Investment Products: Islamizing Indonesian Capital Markets. *Studia Islamika* 23 (2): 237–269.

Srimulyani, Eka. 2012. *Women from Traditional Educational Backgrounds in Indonesia: Negotiating Public Spaces*. Amsterdam: Amsterdam University Press.

Ssorin-Chakov, Nikolai. 2017. *The Lenins: A Brief Anthropology of Time*. Chicago: Hau Books.

Strathern, Marilyn. 1988. *The Gender of the Gift*. Berkeley: University of California Press.

Suryahadi, Asep, Gracia Hadiwidjaja, and Sudarno Sumarto. 2012. Economic Growth and Poverty Reduction in Indonesia Before and After the Asian Financial Crisis. *Bulletin of Indonesian Economic Studies* 48 (2): 209–227.

Susetyo, Heru. 2018. *Zakat Laws in Indonesia*. Depok: Faculty of Law, University of Indonesia.

Telle, Kari. 2000. Feeding the Dead: Reformulating Sasak Mortuary Practices. *Bijdragen tot de Taal-, Land-, en Volkenkunde* 156 (4): 771–785.

Tripp, Charles. 2006. *Islam and the Moral Economy. The Challenge of Capitalism*. Cambridge: Cambridge University Press.

Tsing, Anna. 2013. Sorting Out Commodities: How Capitalist Value Is Made Through Gifts. *HAU: Journal of Ethnographic Theory* 3 (1): 21–43.

———. 2017. *The Mushroom at the End of the World. On the Possibility of Life at Capitalist Ruins*. Princeton: Princeton University Press.

Tuğal, Cihan. 2017. *Caring for the Poor: Islamic and Christian Benevolence in a Liberal World*. New York: Routledge.

Turner, Colin. 2006. Wealth as an Immortality Symbol in the Qur'an: A Reconsideration of the māl/amwāl Verses. *Journal of Quranic Studies* 8 (3): 58–83.

Udovitch, Abraham. 1970. *Partnership and Profit in Medieval Islam*. Princeton: Princeton University Press.

Vial, Virginie. 2011. Micro-Entrepreneurship in a Hostile Environment: Evidence from Indonesia. *Bulletin of Indonesian Economic Studies* 47 (2): 233–262.

Visser, Hans. 2009. *Islamic Finance: Principles and Practice*. Cheltenham: Edward Elgar.

Voss, Daniela. 2013. Deleuze's Third Synthesis of Time. *Deleuze Studies* 7 (2): 194–216.

Wacquant, Louis. 2012. Three Steps to a Historical Anthropology of Actually Existing Neoliberalism. *Social Anthropology* 20 (1): 66–79.

Warde, Ibrahim. 2010. *Islamic Finance in the Global Economy*. Edinburgh: Edinburgh University Press.

Weber, Max. 1985. *The Protestant Ethic and the Spirit of Capitalism*. London: Unwin.

Weiner, Anne. 1992. *Inalienable Possessions: The Paradox of Keeping-While-Giving*. Berkeley: University of California Press.

Weir, T.H., and A. Zysow. 2012. Sadaka. In *Encyclopaedia of Islam, Second Edition*, ed. P. Bearman, Th. Bianquis, C.E. Bosworth, E. van Donzel and W.P. Heinrichs. Consulted online on 10 November 2018. https://doi.org/10.1163/1573-3912_islam_COM_0956

Welker, Marina. 2009. "Corporate Security Begins in the Community": Mining, the Corporate Social Responsibility Industry, and Environmental Advocacy in Indonesia. *Cultural Anthropology* 24 (1): 142–179.

Williams, James. 2011. *Gilles Deleuze's Philosophy of Time*. Edinburgh: Edinburgh University Press.

Winn, Philip. 2012. Women's Majelis Taklim and Gendered Religious Practice in Northern Ambon. *Intersections: Gender and Sexuality in Asia and the Pacific* 30: 1–15.

Zaloom, Caitlin. 2009. How to Read the Future: The Yield Curve, Affect, and Financial Prediction. *Public Culture* 21 (2): 245–268.

Zourabichvili, François. 2012. *Deleuze: A Philosophy of the Event Together with the Vocabulary of Deleuze*. Trans. Kieran Aarons. Edinburgh: Edinburgh University Press.

Zysow, Aaron. 2012. Zakāt. In *Encyclopaedia of Islam, Second Edition*, ed. P. Bearman, Th. Bianquis, C.E. Bosworth, E. van Donzel and W.P. Heinrichs. Consulted online on 10 November 2018. https://doi.org/10.1163/1573-3912_islam_COM_0282

Index[1]

A

Afterlife, 11, 57, 88, 115, 120, 123, 129, 130, 132, 134, 244n12, 250

Anthropology, 7–10, 179, 190, 219, 221, 225, 226, 229, 242n3, 249

Asymmetric heterochrony, 251

B

Banking, 5, 20, 24, 25, 100n5, 111, 114, 144–146, 164, 172n3, 208n3

C

Charity, 53, 55, 56, 159, 181, 225, 234

Contract, 22, 23, 25, 30n10, 62n6, 162–169, 171, 172n3, 178, 182, 189, 196, 200, 201, 205, 206, 208n4, 208n7, 209n9, 218, 220, 223, 228, 229, 241

Corporate social responsibility, 6, 75, 100n6, 100n7, 117, 118, 124, 177, 183–191, 204–206, 215

Credit, 4, 9, 12, 13, 18, 19, 22, 25, 111, 114, 125, 127, 131–134, 144, 149, 160, 161, 163–167, 169, 171, 174n17, 177, 183, 185, 190, 208n3, 220, 244n12, 252

Cut (caesurae), 9, 12, 13, 15, 39, 56, 58, 106, 108, 120, 126, 135, 136, 142, 143, 146, 148, 151, 153, 156, 162, 169, 170, 180, 185, 196, 199, 202, 204, 205, 218, 220, 236, 241, 251–253

D

Death, 8, 11, 12, 14, 73, 111, 115, 116, 129–136, 151, 156, 170, 180, 195, 214, 244n9, 250

[1] Note: Page numbers followed by 'n' refer to notes.

K. Retsikas, *A Synthesis of Time*,
https://doi.org/10.1007/978-3-030-34933-2

Debt, 12, 19, 25, 59, 61, 132, 144, 161, 162, 164–169, 171, 174n17, 177, 182, 183, 190, 197, 198, 206, 215, 216, 220, 225, 228, 229, 233
Deleuze, Gilles, 8–10, 13–15, 27, 29n6, 29n7, 30n8, 137, 143, 144, 147–155, 169–171, 172n6, 172n7, 172n8, 179–181, 183, 206, 207n1, 217, 249, 250
Derrida, Jacques, 9, 16–19, 27, 30n9, 41, 72–74, 96–99, 221, 226–231, 240, 244n8, 244n9, 249

E
Economy, a non-economistic concept of the, 11, 12, 134, 136, 250

F
Fatwa (edict), 30n11, 48, 62n5, 161, 173n14, 214
Foucault, Michel, 8–11, 27, 108–112, 130, 134, 137n1, 249, 250
Future, 5–8, 11–16, 20, 27, 28n2, 29n7, 29n8, 30n10, 39, 47, 61, 69, 73–76, 84–86, 88, 92–99, 105–111, 113–116, 119–128, 130, 131, 134–136, 142–144, 146–148, 150–153, 155–157, 162–164, 166–171, 173n14, 177–207, 215–218, 220, 221, 225, 226, 239, 241, 242, 242n1, 245n15, 250–253

G
Gift, 8, 9, 19, 41, 53, 55, 59–61, 76, 89, 160, 161, 173n11, 183–191, 198, 206, 207, 220–226, 228–230, 233–237, 240, 241, 242–243n3, 243n4, 243n6, 244n8, 244n9, 244n12, 252

H
Hibah, 89, 160, 172n10, 173n11, 189–191, 193, 194, 198, 204–206, 209n8

I
Indonesia, 1, 38, 67, 106, 141, 182, 215
Infak, 3, 76, 81, 89, 90, 124, 174n16
Interest, 5, 22–24, 26, 27, 30n11, 45, 50, 68, 70, 75, 90, 94, 98, 112, 118, 124, 136, 145, 157, 172n3, 173n14, 190, 194, 222, 232
Islam, 4–6, 22, 24, 41–44, 46, 47, 50–52, 54, 56, 61, 62n8, 69, 75, 76, 85, 87, 93, 112–116, 118, 125, 128–134, 136, 142, 157, 163, 196, 206, 234–236, 238
Islamic economics, 7, 22, 23, 100n5, 114, 115, 145, 146, 153, 158, 161
Islamic economy, 5, 23, 113, 114, 145, 146, 189, 206
Islamic finance, 7, 21, 22, 24–26, 118, 167, 172n3
Islamic law (*syariah*), 4, 42, 48, 58, 60, 68, 70, 91, 93, 113, 143, 173n12, 242n2
Islamic micro-finance, 7, 20, 27, 83, 84

J
Jakarta, 1, 42, 51, 52, 75, 79, 91, 100n11, 112, 114, 124, 137n7, 157, 164, 177, 182–185, 191, 204, 207, 208n5, 215, 253
Java, 19, 27, 37, 39, 40, 42, 43, 79, 83, 86, 88, 89, 91, 106, 191, 195, 197, 208n5, 209n9, 213, 214, 227, 231, 234, 237, 238, 243n6, 250, 253
Jurisprudence, 7, 40, 42, 44, 47, 49, 54, 62n4, 84, 99n1, 100n9, 101n13, 172n3, 172n10, 173n13, 189, 190, 234

L

Law, national, 93
Lembaga Amil Zakat (LAZ, Zakat Management Bodies), 4–7, 12, 15, 16, 21, 42, 52, 61, 67, 70–72, 74, 79–81, 85, 86, 92–96, 98, 99n3, 100n12, 106, 114, 116, 128, 136, 144, 152, 160, 161, 173n14, 215, 251, 252

M

Majelis Ulama Indonesia (MUI), 30n11, 48, 101n14, 159, 161, 172n9, 173n14, 214, 215
Memorandum of Understanding (MOU), 185–187, 199–202, 205
Micro-finance, 136, 226
Middle-class, 6, 28n2, 42, 106, 117, 144, 184
Morality, 97, 224–227, 240, 241, 252
Mudaraba, 24, 162, 167, 196, 201, 205, 208n7
Murabaha, 25, 26, 162, 164–169
Musharaka, 24, 162, 168, 169, 196, 201, 205, 208n7

N

Nietzsche, Friedrich, 8, 10, 15, 29n5, 30n8, 41, 147, 151, 152, 154, 156, 169, 172n6, 172n8, 217, 227, 242n1, 245n15

P

Philanthropy, 28n2, 54, 55, 60, 87, 215
Philosophy, 7–10, 13, 14, 17, 27, 30n9, 147, 151, 154, 171, 179, 227, 228, 250
Poverty, 1, 4, 9, 21, 22, 26, 27, 28n1, 46, 47, 52–54, 59, 60, 70, 76, 79, 82, 87, 114–117, 119, 123–125, 128, 131, 136, 145, 158, 170, 187, 189, 209n10, 230, 237, 239
Promise, 4–6, 8, 9, 12, 15, 16, 27, 41, 61, 75, 85, 99, 116, 128–133, 135, 137, 141–144, 152, 153, 156, 157, 162, 163, 165, 167, 170, 171, 178, 181, 183, 192, 193, 205, 216–218, 226, 241, 242, 243n4, 243n6, 253

R

Reformasi, 49, 60, 68, 98, 237
Reward (*pahala*), 38, 39, 43, 53, 76, 114, 120, 133, 135, 142, 155, 196, 203, 207, 232, 244n9, 244n12

S

Sedekah, 3, 43, 52, 76, 81, 87, 100n8, 101n14, 124, 131, 160, 173n11, 174n16
Soliciting, 19, 20, 213–242, 250, 252
State, Indonesian, 60, 68, 69, 71, 94, 100n9, 193, 239, 251
Subjectivity, 106, 108, 137n2
Surabaya, 42, 45, 86, 89, 91, 114, 124, 127, 128, 141, 142, 163–165, 167, 168, 177, 182, 218–220, 226, 231
Synthesis, 13–16, 20, 27, 61, 73, 134–137, 144, 147–157, 178, 185, 218, 219, 221, 241, 242, 250–252

T
Taking, 4, 7, 10, 25, 39, 40, 48, 50, 57, 60, 61, 70, 79, 89, 91, 110, 120, 123, 124, 128, 166, 172n5, 190, 191, 193, 196, 200, 206, 221, 224, 225, 236, 240
Time, 7, 38, 67, 106, 142, 178, 214, 249

V
Violence, 18, 46, 69, 72–74, 97, 110, 136, 224, 226, 227, 229, 230, 234–236, 238, 240, 243n7, 251, 252

W
Will to improve, 29n8, 154–156, 171, 182, 183, 205, 206, 216
Will to power, 29–30n8, 154–157, 171, 183, 216, 221, 241

Z
Zakat, 2, 37, 67, 105, 143, 177, 214, 250

The manufacturer's authorised representative in the EU is Springer
Nature Customer Service Centre GmbH, Europaplatz 3, 69115 Heidelberg,
Germany. If you have any concerns regarding our products, please
contact ProductSafety@springernature.com

Printed and bound by CPI Group (UK) Ltd, Croydon, CR0 4YY
30/09/2026
02225235-0003